OXFORD WORLD'

SELECTED POEM

ROBERT BURNS was born in 1759 in the village of Alloway in the Kyle district of Ayrshire in south-west Scotland. His father was a smallholder and gardener and then, from 1766, a tenant farmer. Robert and his brother Gilbert moved the family to a farm at Mossgiel, near the village of Mauchline, after their father's death in 1784. Burns, who had written love-songs since his teens, began to write poetry following models borrowed from verse in Scots by Allan Ramsay and Robert Fergusson, as well as from English poets such as Gray, Shenstone, and Goldsmith. Embedded in the alternative, secular networks of social club and masonic lodge, Burns was able to publish *Poems, Chiefly in the Scottish Dialect* at Kilmarnock in 1786. Its fame spread beyond Ayrshire: in 1787 Burns travelled to Edinburgh to arrange a second edition, and was feted on his arrival by the literary establishment there. The Edinburgh edition of *Poems* was a huge success. In 1788 Burns settled with his wife Jean Armour on the farm of Ellisland on the river Nith in Dumfriesshire, and was commissioned into a part-time post in the Excise service. In 1791 he abandoned the farm, moved to an apartment in Dumfries, and became a full-time exciseman. In this period Burns wrote one of his greatest poems, 'Tam o' Shanter', but devoted most of his creative energy to writing lyrics for popular songs: such is the extent of his contribution to James Johnson's *Scots Musical Museum* that it deserves to stand alongside the *Poems* as the other book by Burns. From late 1792, with war looming with the new French Republic, Burns's radical political opinions threatened his government job; but he kept his post and even continued to publish songs with obvious democratic sympathies. Long-standing health problems, the physical demands of his job, and a recurrence of depressive illness, all contributed to his death in 1796.

ROBERT P. IRVINE is Senior Lecturer in English Literature at the University of Edinburgh. His publications include *Enlightenment and Romance: Gender and Agency in Smollett and Scott* (2000) and *Jane Austen* (2005).

OXFORD WORLD'S CLASSICS

For over 100 years Oxford World's Classics have brought readers closer to the world's great literature. Now with over 700 titles—from the 4,000-year-old myths of Mesopotamia to the twentieth century's greatest novels—the series makes available lesser-known as well as celebrated writing.

The pocket-sized hardbacks of the early years contained introductions by Virginia Woolf, T. S. Eliot, Graham Greene, and other literary figures which enriched the experience of reading. Today the series is recognized for its fine scholarship and reliability in texts that span world literature, drama and poetry, religion, philosophy, and politics. Each edition includes perceptive commentary and essential background information to meet the changing needs of readers.

OXFORD WORLD'S CLASSICS

ROBERT BURNS

Selected Poems and Songs

Edited with an Introduction and Notes by
ROBERT P. IRVINE

OXFORD
UNIVERSITY PRESS

OXFORD
UNIVERSITY PRESS

Great Clarendon Street, Oxford ox2 6DP
United Kingdom

Oxford University Press is a department of the University of Oxford.
It furthers the University's objective of excellence in research, scholarship,
and education by publishing worldwide. Oxford is a registered trade mark of
Oxford University Press in the UK and in certain other countries

First published 2013

First published as an Oxford World's Classics paperback 2014

Impression: 7

Published in the United States of America by Oxford University Press
198 Madison Avenue, New York, NY 10016, United States of America

British Library Cataloguing in Publication Data

Data available

Library of Congress Control Number: 2013943737

ISBN 978-0-19-968232-4

Printed in Great Britain by
Clays Ltd, Elcograf S.p.A.

ACKNOWLEDGEMENTS

As the notes will make clear, this selection owes an enormous if unsurprising debt to twentieth-century editors of Burns, in particular James Kinsley and also, more recently, Carol McGuirk. Any knowledge that this edition can add to theirs is due entirely to the ease with which eighteenth-century texts can now be found and read, and other sources of information traced, online. From my electronic study, across the centuries, a tip of the hat also to William Scott Douglas, whose editions in the 1870s provided an emboldening precedent for the model followed here.

The Beugo portrait from the Edinburgh edition, and the Alloway engraving from Grose's *Antiquities*, are reproduced by kind permission of the Trustees of the National Library of Scotland; gratitude is due to the staff of the NLS, Edinburgh University Library's Centre for Research Collections, and the Advocates Library for all their assistance. Thanks also to Dr Gerard Carruthers and Professor Nigel Leask of the University of Glasgow for their occasional advice and encouragement.

Particular thanks are due to Bob and Jill Elliott for their help with the music, and to Kirsty Law for her transcription of the scores within exacting and, from a purely musical point of view, perhaps eccentric parameters. Robert Burns, in his travails with Stephen Clarke, could have wished for such a collaborator.

CONTENTS

From *Poems, Chiefly in the Scottish Dialect*
(Edinburgh, 1787)

Songs from *The Scots Musical Museum*

Songs from *A Select Collection of Original Scotish Airs, for the Voice* (1798–9)

Other poems and songs published in Burns's lifetime

Other poems and songs published posthumously

CONTENTS

INTRODUCTION

FEW poets are held in such reverence by so many as Robert Burns, both in his homeland and around the world. The vernacular energy of his verse, the simple beauty of his songs, his anger at injustice and hypocrisy; and, framing these, the story of his life, of a man of humble origins rising to fame in defiance of prejudice and persecution; these have won him a following since his death so consistent that it is sometimes referred to as a 'cult'. What follows is a brief survey of that life. Burns's own account of the early part of it can be found in his 1787 letter to John Moore included in Appendix 1 of this volume. Where relevant, the notes to individual poems also refer to the poet's biography. The purpose of this introduction, however, is not to ask how the life finds expression in the poetry: the poems themselves are sufficiently eloquent in that regard. Instead, it will outline the role of the poetry in the life: how his writing allowed Burns to build a certain kind of career out of the resources available to him. Burns was not a prodigy, spontaneously moved to song by untutored feeling; nor was he the passive victim of social and economic circumstance. His poetry does not only reflect his society, but was also his way of acting within it: building friendships, courting lovers, cultivating patrons, and cheering those who, in the dangerous days of the mid-1790s, dared to hope for a better one.

1. Early life

Robert Burns was born on 25 January 1759 in Alloway, a small village near the river Doon just south of the town of Ayr in south-west Scotland (see Map, p. 280). He was the first child of Agnes Broun, a local girl, and William Burnes, originally from Kincardineshire in north-east Scotland who had moved south to find work as a gardener after the failure of his father's farm there ('Burness' is the north-east version of the name). The two-room cottage in which Robert was born was built by William himself from stone, clay, and thatch, on his own smallholding. Literate and devout, but theologically liberal by the standards of his adopted county, William decided not to send his sons to the parish school, but with a group of neighbouring families to hire a young teacher, John Murdoch. Under Murdoch Burns was introduced to English verse and prose from an anthology that included extracts from Shakespeare, Milton, Thomson, and *The Spectator*, to add to the prose of the King James Bible familiar from home. He was also taught how to write and speak in English, as opposed to the Scots used in everyday life. Later, Murdoch would give the Burns boys a volume of Pope's poetry, and get Robert started in French.

In 1766, at the age of 45, William left his cottage and his gardening work for a rented farm further inland called Mount Oliphant. Robert and his brother Gilbert continued to attend school for another two years, until Murdoch moved to take a job elsewhere. At that point the boys were put to work on the farm, although William continued to teach them in the evenings. The farm supported a large family (two daughters born in Alloway were followed by another three children at Mount Oliphant) but did not generate the cash that could have paid for hired labour to help work it. At the expiry of the lease in 1777 the family moved to a new farm, Lochlie (now Lochlea), further east again in the parish of Tarbolton, and William died here in 1784.

On these farms the Burns family did not suffer terrible poverty by the standard of the times. But the life was characterized by hard, unremitting labour for the ageing William and his teenage boys, and by chronic economic insecurity. The Ayrshire economy had suffered lasting damage from the collapse, in 1772–3, of the Ayr bank of Douglas, Heron and Co., in which a high proportion of the county's property-owning families had invested. The struggle to rebuild their capital base put pressure on tenant farmers like William Burnes. To encourage agricultural improvement (enclosure, drainage, fertilization, the introduction of new crops and breeds of stock), rents were set at a high level, proportionate to the income the land could generate once improved. But improvement took time to produce results, and the risk of borrowing money to carry it out usually fell on the tenant, not the landowner. At both Mount Oliphant and Lochlie, the ground proved very poor; William spent his last years in a protracted legal battle with his landlord and his landlord's creditors, which he won just weeks before he died. Robert and Gilbert then moved the family to a third farm, Mossgiel, near the small town of Mauchline.

A self-consciously modernizing society like eighteenth-century Scotland presented opportunities as well as pitfalls for men from this background. There were economic opportunities, and Burns was on the lookout for career-paths that could take him away from, or at least reduce his dependence on, the toil and anxiety of farming. In 1775 he had spent a happy summer studying surveying in his mother's home village of Kirkoswald, and in 1782 there was an ultimately disastrous foray into the flax industry of Irvine, Ayrshire's largest town, which precipitated the first of the depressive episodes that would recur throughout his life. The search for economic security eventually led to his obtaining, through local contacts, an offer of work as overseer on one of the many Scottish-owned slave-plantations in Jamaica, to which Burns planned to emigrate in 1786. There were also opportunities for personal improvement, for the cultivation of the self, rather than the soil, and Burns grasped most eagerly at these. At Tarbolton in 1780, he and his friends founded a 'Batchelor's Club' which was at once a social organization and a debating society, a means of facilitating mutual social and intellectual self-improvement independently of church or college. The following year Burns joined the local Masonic Lodge, which fulfilled a similar function and extended his range of acquaintance into more privileged classes than his own. And above all there was reading and writing. Burns read widely in modern English prose and verse: John Locke's *Essay concerning Human Understanding*, Adam Smith's *Theory of Moral Sentiments*, and the novels of Richardson, Smollett, Sterne, and Mackenzie, as well as Dryden, Pope, Thomson, Shenstone, Gray, Collins, and Macpherson's 'Works of Ossian'. Crucially, probably in 1783, Burns discovered poetry in Scots by Robert Fergusson. Burns had been writing poems and songs in English, the language of the library and the debating society, since his late teens. He had known Allan Ramsay's work in Scots, but the near-contemporary Fergusson demonstrated how Ramsay's language and verse-forms could be brought to bear on the modern Scottish scene. This sparked the astonishing creativity of the Mossgiel years, as Burns's poetry vivified an informed, Enlightenment sensibility with the language of the community in which he lived.

In the same period Burns was pursuing sexual experience with similar enthusiasm. It worried his father in his final years, and it continued to worry his family at Mossgiel, but his pleasure in sex was unabashed. Eventually, inevitably, one of his girlfriends got pregnant: Elizabeth Paton, who had worked for the family at Lochlie. This brought Burns before the church authorities who were responsible for the enforcement of sexual discipline at the parish level. Burns had to pay a fine, and sit with Elizabeth in the 'stool of repentance' to be publicly admonished by the minister back in Tarbolton parish church. By the time the child was born in May 1785, the relationship had ended, and Burns had become engaged to Jean Armour, the daughter of a Mauchline stonemason. Jean was pregnant by March 1786. Hoping to avoid scandal, her parents hurried her out of the parish to relatives in Paisley, away from the prying eyes of the Kirk Session and, most importantly, away from Burns, with whom she was denied contact. In the eyes of Burns, Jean's apparent acquiescence in her parents' tactics looked like the breaking-off of their engagement. In the eyes of the respectable Armours, Robert Burns had no means of supporting their daughter and her child, with little money and no apparent prospects.

2. The Kilmarnock edition

Yet Burns did have prospects. His poems had been circulating in manuscript among his friends, and among his friends' friends. That he was widely known as a poet through this local network put him in a position to do something he could not otherwise have risked: publish a book. Rather than pay a printer to produce a volume in the hope that it would at least recoup its costs in the marketplace, Burns could invite 'subscriptions' which amounted to promises to buy the book in advance. And so he had a prospectus printed, dated 14 April 1786, and headed,

PROPOSALS,
FOR PUBLISHING BY SUBSCRIPTION,

SCOTCH POEMS,
BY ROBERT BURNS.

The Work to be elegantly Printed in One Volume, Octavo.
Price Stitched *Three Shillings.*

As the Author has not the most distant Mercenary view in Publishing, as soon as so many Subscribers appear as will defray the necessary Expence, the Work will be sent to the Press.

Three shillings, though still more than most people could afford, was relatively cheap for a new book in this format. The records of the printer, John Wilson of Kilmarnock, show that at least 400 copies were ordered in this way, justifying a print-run of 612 in total. Of those subscriptions, 145 were collected by Burns's friend in Ayr, the lawyer Robert Aiken; 72 by Kilmarnock wine merchant Robert Muir; 70 by Burns's brother Gilbert; 41 by Mauchline draper James Smith; and 40 by Mauchline lawyer Gavin Hamilton. *Poems, Chiefly in the Scottish Dialect* was published at Kilmarnock at the end of July, 1786.

Both the prospectus, and the title of the published volume, draw attention to the language in which Burns's poems are written. As the change from simply 'Scotch' to 'Chiefly' Scottish suggests, Burns's language is heterogeneous, shifting from Scots to English not only from one poem to the next but from one stanza or line to the next.

Sometimes, indeed, this shift is invisible on the page: what looks like the same word will require a Scottish vowel in one context, and an English vowel in another, to provide the rhyme. Allan Ramsay, more than anyone responsible for the revival of Scots as a literary language in the years after the Treaty of Union with England in 1707, identified this expanded range as the great advantage of the Scottish poet, in the 'Preface' to his *Poems* of 1721:

[G]ood Poetry may be in any Language. . . . [T]he Pronunciation [of Scots] is liquid and sonorous, and much fuller than the *English*, of which we are Masters, by being taught it in our Schools, and daily reading it; which being added to all our own native Words, of eminent Significancy, makes our Tongue by far the completest. (p. vii)

'Our Tongue', on Ramsay's account, is not one language to be contrasted with English: it is a language which has absorbed English into itself as an additional resource, and this provides a useful way of thinking about the language of Burns's verse. In Burns's case, even more than in Ramsay's, this linguistic range is paralleled by the variety of verse-forms, modes, and literary traditions on which the poetry draws. An effect of this is to put the reader into a succession of different relationships to the poetry's subject matter. For example, one of the verse-forms that Burns inherits from medieval Scotland is the 'Christ's Kirk on the Green' stanza, used for 'brawl' poems celebrating popular festivals and disorder (see headnote to 'The Holy Fair', p. 291). Such poems characteristically invite the reader into the community that is being described by demanding that they suspend their own moral attitudes to appreciate the energies and pleasures of a society in the moment of its recreation. Eighteenth-century examples like 'The Holy Fair' in the Kilmarnock *Poems* make an equivalent demand at the level of language, as the poem is consistently conducted in something like the language of the community it celebrates. The absence of moral distance means that no moral judgement can be drawn to round off the poem, so 'The Holy Fair' just ends with the end of the day that it chronicles. In contrast, 'The Cotter's Saturday night' quite explicitly distinguishes between its intended reader, one from the prosperous 'middling sort' such as its dedicatee Robert Aiken, and the cottar class which is its subject, with the speaker of the poem acting as explicator of the latter to the former. The subject matter is essentially the same as that of 'The Holy Fair': the lives of ordinary people in the Scottish countryside. But this matter is framed in the stanza form of Spenser's *The Faerie Queene*, promising the educated reader that it will be moralized in a way corresponding to the literary authority of this source. The language of the poem modulates according to the poet's task of social mediation: the English of the opening address to Aiken is followed by a specifically Scots vocabulary to describe everyday experience, which ebbs in turn as soon as the father pulls out the (English-language) Bible; the poet ends by turning this family into an example of Scotland's moral 'grandeur' (l. 163) and addressing a prayer to the nation and its God, all in English. To say that either 'The Holy Fair' or 'The Cotter's Saturday night' is more successful than the other is perhaps to miss the point: the joy of the Kilmarnock *Poems* lies in Burns's experimentation with the different voices, different genres, different personae and stances towards his material, opened up to him by his literary inheritance and the particular historical moment in which he was writing.

Burns frames this variety in several ways. For the title page of his book, Burns wrote an epigraph, advertising himself as a 'Simple Bard, unbroke by rules of Art', who, inspired by 'Nature' alone, 'pours the wild effusions of the heart'. The poetry that follows is full of delight in wild creatures and in the woods and rivers of his county. But clearly, Burns did not learn the vocabulary of 'the wild effusions of the heart', of 'Bards' and 'Nature', from nature. He acquired it from a mid-eighteenth-century British literary culture which had given up the previous era's deep investment in classical precedents in search of heightened emotional effects such as the sublime and the sentimental. The latter is a particularly important category for Burns. At just the point in the first 'Epistle to James Lapraik' where Burns claims he needs no learning to write poetry, merely 'ae spark o' Nature's fire', he is quoting from the high-priest of the sentimental, Laurence Sterne. Smith's *Theory of Moral Sentiments* (1759) had located the basis of ethics in our capacity to imagine the feelings and perceptions of others, and to imagine how we in turn must appear in their eyes. Some of the poems of the Kilmarnock volume invite us to share in the feelings of another in this way: 'The auld Farmer's . . . Salutation to his auld Mare', for example, or, most famously, 'To a Mouse'. And consistently in these poems and songs, the spontaneous human affections of 'the heart' are defined in opposition to material selfishness taken as the defining feature of a modern commercial society.

> Nae treasures, nor pleasures
> Could make us happy lang;
> The *heart* ay's the part ay,
> That makes us right or wrang. ('Epistle to Davie', ll. 67–70)

This opposition is particularly characteristic of the sentimental novel *The Man of Feeling* (1771) by Henry Mackenzie: 'a book I prize next to the Bible' wrote Burns to his old tutor in 1783.

Yet Burns does something very interesting with his sentimental model. *The Man of Feeling* imagines the attachments of 'the heart' as under siege, as eventually defeated, by 'the world' of economic reality, a world of greed and lies: emotional bonds between particular individuals cannot be generalized into an alternative to money as the organizing principle of society. The feelings cultivated by reading such fiction must be their own reward: the fiction itself warns that they cannot constitute a way of life. Burns's verse epistles in the Kilmarnock edition set out to prove otherwise. Ten lines before those quoted above from the 'Epistle to Davie', Burns imagines the flowers and birdsong of spring inspiring poetry:

> On braes when we please then,
>   We'll sit and *sowth* a tune;
> Syne *rhyme* till't, we'll time till't,
>   And sing't when we hae done.

The first-person *plural* is important here. In offering us this image of creativity as collaboration rather than individual inspiration, Burns also asserts the productivity, rather than the precariousness, of particular sentimental solidarities. This is more than a promise, for we have the poem in front of us as the first fruit of just this collaboration. It is part of the logic of the verse epistle as a genre that it makes the addressee a condition for the existence of the poem. This is obviously true of an epistle to a patron; but also of the Kilmarnock verse epistles, addressed to equals. Even Gavin Hamilton, whose help in getting the Kilmarnock volume published allows Burns to call him 'patron', is addressed *as* an equal ('A Dedication'). For the friendships of the verse epistles are not only literary constructions, offering, like Mackenzie's, an escape from the wider reality of modern society. Rather, they dramatize part of that reality, an already-existing social practice of mutual assistance in the clubs and lodges of Enlightenment Ayrshire; the social practice that, as we have seen, made it possible to publish *Poems, Chiefly in the Scottish Dialect*.

The sentimental sociability of the verse epistles is not the only mode that Burns appropriates from mid-century literary culture and adapts for his own purposes. The Kilmarnock *Poems* use the word 'Bard' (or the diminutive 'Bardie') no fewer than thirty times in the 235 pages between the title and the close of 'A Bard's Epitaph'. The word comes from the Celtic languages, where it just means 'poet'. In English, it had long been used to name the traditional singer of Scottish, Welsh, and, especially, Irish society, originally a man attached to a tribal chieftain whose virtues and victories he commemorated in song. In the middle of the eighteenth century, as part of the shift away from neo-classical literary values and the discovery or invention of indigenous origins for the 'British' nation, this figure had been revaluated and celebrated in Thomas Gray's Pindaric ode 'The Bard' (1757) and James Macpherson's prose-poems of 'Ossian', beginning with *Fragments of Ancient Poetry* (1760). Gray's Welsh bard is the last of his kind, and curses the invading army of Edward I which has murdered all his fellow-bards. Macpherson's Ossian too is the last of his kind, and laments the destruction of his tribe, his father and son included, in a third-century war. To be a bard in Gray's and Macpherson's sense is to mourn the destruction of the social context that gave your song its meaning. In appropriating the term, Burns puts this definition into reverse. For Burns, 'Bard' evokes the *possibility* that a delimited social context might provide the poet with his vocation, not the inevitability of that context's destruction. As with sentimentalism, Burns takes a contemporary literary category that assumes its own social impotence and uses it to claim a certain kind of social authority for himself.

How exactly Burns's social context might be delimited remained an open question at the publication of the Kilmarnock *Poems* in 1786. As we have seen, that volume's enabling condition was a specifically local network of friends and sponsors. When Burns's muse Coila visits him in 'The Vision', her 'mantle' shimmers with the landmarks of Kyle; but her 'robe' is tartan, and she identifies herself as the local agent of a nationwide system of muses overseeing Scottish life. As we have also seen, Burns's language and verse-forms often advertise their origins in a national (that is, Scottish) literary culture. When Ramsay revived the literary use of Scots in the 1720s he had in effect proposed that language, and the history of poetry written in that language, as the vehicle of a Scottish national identity, in the absence of political sovereignty after the Union, and as an alternative to the Presbyterian church, the most powerful national institution left after 1707. To write in the verse forms and modes bequeathed by Ramsay was already to accept a national role. Burns accordingly refers to himself as a 'Scotch Bard', as well as an Ayrshire one, in the Kilmarnock volume, and addresses Scottish MPs, for example, as spokesman for the Scottish people ('The Author's earnest cry and prayer'). What happened after the Kilmarnock edition confirmed Burns, not just as a 'Scotch Bard', but as *the* 'Scotch Bard', a position he occupies to this day.

3. The Edinburgh edition

The Kilmarnock edition of *Poems, Chiefly in the Scottish Dialect* prob-
ably made Burns the substantial sum of around £50. His genius in
verse, and publication by subscription, had allowed him to turn the
cultural capital of his education and the social capital of his friendships
into actual money. In the summer of 1786 Burns still intended to leave
this money for the support of his illegitimate children on his emigra-
tion to Jamaica. But the possibility of publishing a second, expanded
edition also presented itself. Wilson, his Kilmarnock printer, wanted
Burns to advance the cost of the paper for such a volume; Burns, unwill-
ing to do this, planned a trip to Edinburgh, to see if he could make a
better deal there. In the meantime, his local fame was beginning to be
replicated at a national level. Not all his local contacts, after all, were
only local people. Some were wealthy landowners who spent part or
most of the year in their townhouses in the capital. Catrine, a few miles
from Mauchline, was the summer home of Dugald Stewart, Professor
of Moral Philosophy at Edinburgh University. He introduced Burns's
work to the Edinburgh poet Thomas Blacklock, who got hold of the
Kilmarnock book and immediately recommended that a second, larger
edition should be arranged. James Cunningham, Earl of Glencairn,
who had estates in Ayrshire, acquired a copy through his factor there
and was impressed; another local landowner, James Dalrymple of
Orangefield, who knew Burns through the Masons, was related to
Glencairn by marriage. So when Burns set off for Edinburgh in late
November 1786 he carried a letter of introduction from Dalrymple to
this influential Scottish nobleman. A review of the Kilmarnock *Poems*
had already appeared in the *Edinburgh Magazine* for the previous
month (see Appendix 2 of the present volume).

On his arrival, Burns was lionized by literary Edinburgh. Some of
the adulation was superficial and condescending. Scottish Enlight-
enment 'conjectural history' had proposed that poetry, rather than
being the achievement of advanced civilizations like that of Rome or
modern Europe, was rooted in the spontaneous expression of feeling,
equated with a timeless 'human nature'. Not only, therefore, could it
be found in the earliest, most 'primitive' or 'barbarous' states of human
society, it was found there in a purer state, uncorrupted by the con-
straints imposed by later, more complex, social forms. Thus had Hugh
Blair, Professor of Rhetoric and Belles Lettres at the University of
Edinburgh, argued in his *Critical Dissertation on the Poems of Ossian*
(1763). In claiming direct inspiration by Nature, and in adopting the

name of Bard, Burns had invited categorization in this way by his gen-
teel readers, with his difference in social class guaranteeing his close-
ness to nature as Ossian's distance in historical time had guaranteed
his. The re-socialization of these ideas by the poems themselves was
not what won their author access to Edinburgh 'society'.

Still, Burns enjoyed much of what Edinburgh had to offer. He made
many lasting friends in the city. He seized the opportunity for sexual
adventures, both consummated (with lower-class women) and uncon-
summated (with the middle-class Mrs McLehose, separated from her
husband, with whom Burns entered into a protracted epistolary flirta-
tion, writing to 'Clarinda' and signing himself 'Sylvander'). Most
importantly, there was the new edition of his poems, slightly expanded
to include some of the work that Burns had held back from the
Kilmarnock volume or written subsequently. Glencairn introduced
Burns to William Creech, probably the most important 'bookseller'
(that is, publisher) of the Scottish Enlightenment. The Edinburgh edi-
tion was published, like its predecessor, by subscription, but on a new,
national scale: Glencairn's influence helped secure commitments to
2,876 copies at five shillings a copy. Of those among the 1,521 names in
the volume's subscription list that have been identified, around 20 per
cent come from the (relatively easy to identify) land-owning classes,
and the rest from the 'middling sort' of professionals, merchants, and
manufacturers. Burns covered the costs of producing the book (to
rather higher standards than were possible at Kilmarnock) from the
money generated. Three thousand copies were printed and ready for
distribution by 17 April 1787. Five hundred of the subscriptions were
from Creech himself, who sold them from his shop for six shillings.
But Creech's real profit would come from the copyright, which he
bought from Burns for 100 guineas, and which secured him a share of
the takings from the London reprint of 1,500 copies later in 1787, and
from subsequent editions. Burns's profits came to him more slowly
than he would have liked, and it was not until February 1789 that his
accounts were finally settled with Creech for the Edinburgh edition,
but he eventually made about £450 in total.

The plan of slave-driving in Jamaica was finally abandoned after this
spectacular success, and Burns took advantage of his immediate free-
dom by enjoying a series of tours around Scotland, to the Highlands
and his father's ancestral north-east, and to the Borders: getting to
know the country of which he was now acclaimed the national poet.
But Burns does not seem to have considered the possibility of pursuing
writing as a career, for example under the permanent patronage of

Glencairn or another nobleman. Instead, he used the access to influential people that his fame had granted him to secure a government job as an exciseman, checking that manufacturers, importers, and retailers of taxable goods were cheating neither the government nor the public. On his Highland tour he met Robert Graham of Fintry, recently appointed a Commissioner to the Scottish Board of Excise: Burns wrote to him asking for his help. In eighteenth-century Britain, securing the influence or 'interest' of a friend in a high place was how you got a job in government service, and how you got promotion once you had the job. As Glencairn's patronage had made the Edinburgh edition possible, so Fintry's patronage got Burns his place in the Excise. Another contact among the gentry, Patrick Miller of Dalswinton, had earlier offered Burns the lease of a farm on his estate in Nithsdale, in Dumfriesshire. Burns inspected the farm, Ellisland, during his Border tour in the summer of 1787. Returning to Edinburgh via Mauchline, he slept with Jean: the Armours had been reconciled to their son-in-law by his new prosperity. Jean again became pregnant, and in February 1788 produced twins (she had one child surviving from the twins she bore in her previous pregnancy). Burns was commissioned into the Excise in July, and moved to Ellisland, to establish a dairy farm, work part-time in his customs job, and build a modern farmhouse to receive his wife and growing family.

4. The later career

With the publication of the Edinburgh edition, and his subsequent settling with Jean in Dumfriesshire, the second act of Burns's career comes to an end. It is this period that has given us the popular image of Burns: the ploughman-poet, the sociable man's man, the reckless lover. And yet his subsequent career is just as interesting. At this point, Burns seems to have lost all interest in making money from his poetry. He certainly continued to write and publish poems. He sent 18 new poems to Creech for inclusion in a third edition of his *Poems* in two volumes (1793), which also added the already-published 'Tam o' Shanter'. But as Creech held the copyright on this volume, the poet only received twenty complimentary copies in return. He also published poems in newspapers and magazines, and circulated his work among friends and patrons in manuscript form as he always had done, sometimes assembling collections of his work for this purpose. This type of production could be as substantial as the 'Glenriddell Manuscripts': two bound volumes into which Burns transcribed a wide selection of his poems and letters for the library of his friend and neighbour at Ellisland, Captain Robert Riddell. Poetry once again played a role in cultivating local relationships, as it had in Ayrshire, even while Burns remained a famous poet at a national level.

But this period also sees Burns devoting himself to a 'national' project quite different from his self-construction as 'Scotia's bard' in the *Poems*. Among the men he met in Edinburgh was a music publisher called James Johnson, who had begun a collection of Scottish songs in a series of volumes with 100 songs per volume. Burns jumped at the chance to contribute. The songs included in the *Poems* demonstrated his skill with song-lyric, and music was as central to the cultural life of Ayrshire as he found it was to Edinburgh's: both Jean and his mother were skilled and knowledgeable singers. There was time for Burns to add three songs to the first volume of *The Scots Musical Museum* in 1787. For the second volume he sent 41, and over half the total number of songs in Volumes III–V are by Burns. The six-volume collection, finished only in 1803, includes 223 songs from Burns's pen, and such was his influence with Johnson that he became in effect its editor as well. At the same time, Burns began working with another publisher, George Thomson, on his *Select Collection of Original Scotish Airs*. Johnson's *Museum* was produced as cheaply as possible: Stephen Clarke, an Edinburgh organist, added simple bass lines to the score for the voice; pages were printed from pewter plates onto cheap paper in a modest format. Thomson's *Collection* was an altogether more up-market production, providing a full and complex keyboard score as well as the vocal melody printed from copper plates in a large-format volume, and hiring composers as distinguished as Haydn and Beethoven to provide instrumental introductions. In both cases, Burns's work for these collections was collaborative in a more material sense than the *Poems* had been. It was also (more or less, during his lifetime) anonymous; and done without payment.

As to any remuneration, you may think my Songs either *above*, or *below* price; for they shall be the one or the other.—In the honest enthusiasm with which I embark in your undertaking, to talk of money, wages, fee, hire, &c. would be downright Sodomy of Soul! (Letter to Thomson, 16 Sept. 1792)

In the Kilmarnock and Edinburgh editions, Burns's desire to address a national audience, and his pursuit of economic security, had gone hand-in-hand. Now he kept these aspirations apart.

While Johnson gave Burns a free hand, the poet often disagreed with Thomson about the matching of tunes to lyrics and the propriety of

using Scots in the latter. Their disagreements had the benefit of gener-
ating a copious correspondence from which we learn a great deal about
Burns's attitude to song. We can therefore be quite clear about what
Burns was *not* doing in his collaborations with the two men. He was not
composing tunes, but writing new words, or amending existing words,
for tunes that were, in the vast majority of cases, already published in
other collections, of which Burns assembled a comprehensive library.
By the same token, neither was he engaged in the antiquarian or anthro-
pological pursuit of 'folklore'. Unlike, for example, Walter Scott in his
Minstrelsy of the Scottish Border (1802–3), Burns did not understand
himself to be recovering ancient artefacts preserved in a purely oral
tradition, soon to be extinguished by the spread of literacy. Instead, he
was collecting the productions of, and contributing to, a thriving con-
temporary musical culture in which the same songs might be circulat-
ing from singer to singer in a country district, and at the same time
published in Edinburgh or London. (That Johnson calls his collection
a 'Museum' should not mislead us: he is using this word in its original
sense to mean a building dedicated to the Muses, not one in which the
remnants of extinct societies are exhibited.) In the first 'Epistle to
J. Lapraik', Burns describes hearing a song in an Ayrshire cottage at a
'rockin', a winter-evening's work-party at which stories are told and
songs sung to accompany spinning and darning and other domestic
tasks: a folkloric context, to be sure. But the song he hears has adapted
for a tune, possibly of Irish origin, a poem in English from an Edinburgh
magazine (see note to l. 13 of the 'Epistle', p. 319). Burns then took this
song, re-wrote the lyric once again, this time into Scots, and published
it in *The Scots Musical Museum* with a score for its accompaniment on
a piano or a cello. Instances such as this demonstrate that for Burns and
his collaborators, what made these songs 'Scottish' was not their pres-
ervation of a national 'tradition' dating from a pre-modern (and pre-
Union) past; was not, indeed, a question of their origins at all. What
gave them their national status was rather their ubiquity across the
social hierarchy in the present day. They were sung at the keyboard in
Edinburgh parlours and at the fireside in rural cottages alike; a ubi-
quity facilitated, rather than threatened, by popular literacy and the
modern technology of print.

  Of course, Burns was under no illusion that harmonies shared by
rich and poor corresponded to harmony between them. A recurring
feature of the poetry published in the Kilmarnock and Edinburgh vol-
umes is their anger at the callous indifference of the wealthy towards
the suffering of the labouring classes below them. In the context of the

1780s, this could be read as moral criticism of the individuals who occupied the upper ranks of the social hierarchy, rather than a political criticism of the hierarchy itself. In Ayrshire, after all, the politics which most directly affected Burns were church politics, and here Burns found himself in sympathy with the common-sense morality of the 'moderate' party, a party in tune with the priorities of educated gentlemen, and which defended the right of landowners to impose ministers on congregations on their estates; and in conflict with the orthodox theology and strict sexual discipline of the 'popular party', which drew its strongest support from Burns's own class of tenant farmers and self-employed artisans. But Burns's identification with the gentlemen's party in the church, and critique of gentlemanly attitudes to the poor, are both expressions of Burns's commitment to an Enlightenment ideology of 'improvement'. The loss of America had left the British elite divided and defensive, and made reform of a corrupt political system look both possible and necessary. But just as the American Revolution had been led by landed gentlemen in the name of rights and liberties supposedly embodied in the British constitution, so social conditions in Britain might be ameliorated if only landed gentlemen could be shamed into demonstrating the sort of moral leadership exhibited by Washington and Jefferson. The *Poems* can thus be read as advocating solidarity across the social ranks rather than their levelling; a solidarity Burns might imagine in terms of the apolitical 'brotherhood' of the Masonic Lodge and other institutions of enlightened sociability. In this respect, Burns was in tune with the movement, supported by many of his friends among the gentry, both in Ayrshire and Dumfriesshire, for political reform within the framework of the existing British constitution.

Such a reforming agenda seemed at first to receive a boost when constitutional reform got under way in France in the summer of 1789. In fact the effect of the French Revolution, driven forward as it was by the street-level actions of ordinary people, was to close down the reform movement in Britain for a generation. Its advocates found their moderate demands associated with the increasing violence of events in France, and themselves subject to surveillance and persecution from an increasingly paranoid British state. At just the period when Burns launched himself into the collaboration with Thomson, in the second half of 1792, the overthrow of the French monarchy by the people of Paris, and the unexpected triumph of the new republic over its enemies on the battlefield, were celebrated in the streets of many Scottish towns and cities with demands for 'liberty' in Britain as well (see headnote to 'The Tree of Liberty', p. 402). Burns, who had by this time given up the farm at Ellisland to work full-time for the Excise from a new home in Dumfries, had been openly enthusiastic about events in France. But he was a government employee, dependent on the income from his Excise duties to support his wife and children. The 'Year of Liberty' culminated for Burns in an accusation made to his superiors that he had been involved in a disturbance at the theatre in Dumfries at which 'God Save the King' had been booed, and the French Revolutionary anthem, 'Ça ira', called for in its place. The letters written by Burns in his (successful) attempt to avert dismissal are reproduced in Appendix 1 of this volume. And yet Burns continued to produce work whose rhetoric, while perfectly consistent with that of the *Poems* of the 1780s, was rendered unambiguously democratic by the transformed political context of the last decade of the eighteenth century. To demand respect for those who owned no property was now to take a political position, not merely a moral one; and a political position that could lose you your job, or worse. Some of these poems and songs were published anonymously in magazines and newspapers; some were not published until after his death. In the event, it was his increasingly precarious health, and not his political opinions, which came to threaten the Burns household with penury. An exciseman who could not perform his duties was not paid. Burns was laid low with a recurrence of depression in the winter of 1795–6, after the death of a daughter; a long-standing medical problem, combining rheumatic fever and a heart condition, wore him away in the new year, and he died on 12 July 1796.

5. Burns in the public sphere

There is a fourth act to the poetic career of Robert Burns. In the decades following his death, the poems that he had chosen not to publish were collected and printed for the first time. Most of this work had long circulated in manuscript among friends and patrons. The type of publication in which these poems first appeared, and the form they took there, is as much a part of the story of Burns's poetry as the history of the Kilmarnock and Edinburgh editions. It is too diverse a narrative to include in this introduction, and details can be found for each text in its headnote. At the same time, new collections of his work incorporated the poems of the Edinburgh edition, the previously anonymous songs, and the posthumously published material. In his 'People's Edition' of that year, Robert Chambers estimated that over 100 editions of the poems of Burns had been published by 1838, and this level of reproduction continued throughout the nineteenth century. The profound and sustained popularity across the English-speaking world that this indicates was partly a result of a widespread and often prosperous Scottish diaspora across the Empire and in the United States for whom the poems and songs of Burns represented a cherished memory of the old country. Part of Burns's continued popularity must also be connected to the increasing education and organization of working people, their demand for political representation where it was denied them, and their sense that in Burns they found the prophet of their democratic destiny. As his work was translated into other languages, this Burns became celebrated first across the continent of Europe, and then across the world.

> For a' that, and a' that,
> It's coming yet, for a' that;
> And man, and man, the world o'er,
> Shall brothers be, for a' that.

In this song from 1795, 'A man's a man for a' that', the local solidarity of Batchelor's Club and Masonic Lodge in the Ayrshire villages of Burns's young manhood swells into an aspiration to global fraternity. Just as the Kilmarnock edition claimed for its author a national role that he had not yet achieved, so this song dreams of an international solidarity whose promise, more than two centuries later, we have yet to fulfil. The continuing world-wide appeal of Burns's poetry, however it is read, and whatever values are attached to it, perhaps offers some hope that its fulfilment remains at least imaginable.

From the beginning, however, the story of Burns's poetry was often subsumed into the story of Burns the man. The first major edition of the complete works of Robert Burns was Dr James Currie's in 1800, and most of this text is taken up with a biography of the poet, in which the poems are introduced in the context of their composition. The effect is to subordinate the poetry to Currie's sometimes prurient interest in Burns's private life. Currie's incorporation of the poetry in the biography was replicated in many collections, including Robert Chambers's important editions in 1852 and 1856. The standard twentieth-century scholarly edition of Burns is James Kinsley's from 1968, to which the present volume's notes are deeply indebted. But mid-twentieth-century literary scholarship was interested in reconstructing the order and contexts in which the poems were *written*, and so Kinsley ordered the texts along the same biographical narrative as did Currie and Chambers. Kinsley was also committed (again, following the established scholarly practice of the time) to constructing an 'ideal' version of each text by collating its various versions in manuscript as well as print, to the end of producing a poem that corresponded as closely as possible to the poet's 'final intentions'. The paradoxical effect of these procedures is to completely efface the poet's intentions regarding the context in which his work was to be *read*; the context in which the poems were eventually read; and that different versions of the same poem may have been written for different contexts. That Burns wrote 'Man was made to mourn' almost immediately after 'The Fornicator' is quite interesting, but should not obscure the fact that the former appeared in the celebrated volume that made Burns famous, and the latter only in a book printed for private circulation among his friends after the author's death.

The present volume, following the nineteenth-century precedent of William Scott Douglas's 1871 and 1876 editions, is organized on the principle that the context in which a poem or a song first found its public is an important fact about that poem or song. This principle finds expression in two ways. First, each text is generally based on the first published version, whatever form that publication took (see 'Note on the Text'). Second, the texts are presented in order of publication rather than composition, beginning with the complete text of the Kilmarnock *Poems* of 1786. By following this principle, this volume aims to return Burns to history; not as an object of merely antiquarian interest, but because for Burns, as I hope this introduction has shown, poetry and song provided a means of living in history, not a picture of it, or an escape from it. The history in which Burns lived was in many ways the beginning of our own; we do him fullest justice when we seek in his work the resources to do the same.

CHRONOLOGY

1759 25 January: B born in Alloway in Ayrshire to William Burnes and Agnes Broun.

Adam Smith, *The Theory of Moral Sentiments.*

1760 Accession of George III.

1763 (First) Peace of Paris ends Seven Years War between France and the United Kingdom.

1764 William Shenstone, *The Works in Verse and Prose.*

1765 B and brother Gilbert attend classes of John Murdoch.

James Macpherson, *Works of Ossian.*

1766 The Burns family move to a 70-acre farm, Mount Oliphant.

1768 Murdoch leaves for Dumfries: schooling is now at home.

Laurence Sterne, *A Sentimental Journey.*

1770 Oliver Goldsmith, *The Deserted Village.*

1771 Henry Mackenzie, *The Man of Feeling.*

1773 Robert Fergusson, *Poems.*

1774 Death of Fergusson in an Edinburgh asylum, aged 24.

1775 B spends the summer at Kirkoswald, his mother's home village, studying surveying.

1776 American Declaration of Independence; opening of the Revolutionary War.

Adam Smith, *An Enquiry into the Nature and Causes of the Wealth of Nations.*

1777 The Burns family move inland to Lochlie, a 130-acre farm in the parish of Tarbolton.

1780 B, Gilbert, and friends found the Tarbolton Batchelors' Club.

1781 B joins the Tarbolton Masonic Lodge; moves to Irvine for the rest of the year to learn flax-dressing.

1783 Begins keeping poetry and songs in a commonplace book.

(Second) Peace of Paris ends American Revolutionary War.

1784 13 February: death of William Burnes. Family moves to Mossgiel, a 118-acre farm near the village of Mauchline.

1785 May: birth of Elizabeth, Burns's child with Elizabeth Paton, who had been a servant at Lochlie.

B now engaged to Jean Armour, daughter of a Mauchline stonemason.

1786 March: Jean's parents discover her pregnancy and send her to stay with relatives in Paisley. This confirms B's plan to emigrate to Jamaica.

July: threatened with a suit for damages from James Armour, B transfers his share of the Mossgiel lease to Gilbert. Publication at Kilmarnock of *Poems, Chiefly in the Scottish Dialect.*

September: Jean gives birth to twins; the girl will die the following year.

November: travels to Edinburgh to arrange publication of a second edition.

1787 April: publication of the Edinburgh edition of *Poems.*

May: touring the Borders. *The Scots Musical Museum,* Volume I.

August–October: touring the Highlands.

1788 February: *The Scots Musical Museum,* Volume II.

March: Jean gives birth to twin girls who both die within a month.

June: B settles at Ellisland farm on the river Nith in Dumfriesshire.

July: B commissioned into the Excise; takes up part-time duties.

December: Jean joins B at Ellisland with their son Robert.

1789 June: in Paris, declaration of a National Assembly.

July 14: storming of the Bastille prison.

August: B and Jean have a second son, Francis.

1790 February: *The Scots Musical Museum,* Volume III.

Edmund Burke, *Reflections on the Revolution in France.*

1791 April: a third son, William, born at Ellisland.

Autumn: B gives up Ellisland and moves the family into an apartment in Dumfries to work full-time as an exciseman.

Thomas Paine, *The Rights of Man,* a reply to Burke's attack on the revolution.

1792 May: British government moves against 'seditious writings' such as *Rights of Man.*

August: *The Scots Musical Museum,* Volume IV.

September: victories of the recently declared French Republic spark street celebrations and demonstrations.

November: birth of Elizabeth, who survives infancy, the first daughter with Jean to do so.

December: B reported to his superiors in the Excise for his radical sympathies.

Mary Wollstonecraft, *A Vindication of the Rights of Woman.*

1793 January: execution in Paris of Louis XVI.

February: a third edition of *Poems,* now in two volumes. France declares war on the United Kingdom.

May: first half-volume of Thomson's *Select Collection of Original Scotish Airs*.

August: sedition trials begin in Scotland, with sentencing of lawyer Thomas Muir to 14 years transportation to Australia.

1794 May: British government suspends Habeas Corpus, allowing for detention without charge.

August: B and Jean have a fourth son, James.

Another two-volume edition of B's *Poems* published.

December: B takes on duties of acting supervisor.

1795 January: B is a founder member of the Royal Dumfries Volunteers, a home-defence unit.

A bad harvest exacerbates political discontent. Government passes the Seditious Meetings Act and the Treasonable Practices Act: more repressive legislation.

September: Elizabeth, B and Jean's only daughter, dies.

December: B too ill to work, creating real financial hardship in the household.

1796 21 July: B dies in Dumfries; buried with full military honours by the Volunteers.

December: *The Scots Musical Museum*, Volume V.

NOTE ON THE TEXT

THE aim of this edition is to present the poems and songs of Burns in a form as close as is practicable to that in which readers first encountered them in the public realm during Burns's lifetime and in the century after his death. The copy-text is accordingly the first published version of each work, unless there is a particular reason for choosing a later one, in which case this is explained in the notes. Substantial emendations to the copy-text are made only on the basis of manuscript sources or authorial changes to later editions. Such emendations are also annotated. The body of each text on the following pages generally follows its copy-text in accidentals of spelling and punctuation, although the inconsistent use of quotation marks has been regularized by adopting single marks throughout. Capitalization follows the copy-texts from the Kilmarnock and Edinburgh editions, but has been regularized elsewhere, including the capitalization of the first word of each poem; the use of italics in naming tunes has also been regularized. The title at the head of each poem or song is that used in the copy-text, although on the contents page, and in the notes and index, a more familiar alternative may accompany this for the sake of clarity. Similarly, the name of the addressee of a verse epistle may, following the copy-text, be obscured with asterisks at the head of the poem, but the name is completed on the contents page and in references elsewhere. The only footnotes that appear on the same page as the text are those that appear in the copy-text, and are the work of the poet unless otherwise stated. The only additions to the page are line numbers for ease of reference, and the degree sign (°) to indicate a note at the end of the book.

Applying these principles is mostly straightforward in the case of work published during the poet's lifetime, or sent for publication in *The Scots Musical Museum* or the *Select Collection* before his death. Occasionally, a question arises regarding what counts as 'publication'. One of the lifetime copy-texts ('Here Lies Robert Fergusson Poet') is a tombstone. Another ('Written on a window in Stirling') is an anti-Burns tract, which obtained *its* copy-text from the transcription into a tourist's notebook of some graffiti written by Burns and subsequently destroyed by him (in this case, the window was clearly the first published version, alas no longer available for use as copy-text). In the case of posthumously published work, the criteria are put under much more serious strain. Was *The Merry Muses of Caledonia* in the public realm in 1799? It was printed, certainly, but for private circulation; it could be argued that this was not publication, but a sophistication of the private circulation in manuscript that many Burns texts underwent *before* publication. I have allowed the printed nature of the text to sway me in this instance, and the suspicion that printed books tend to get borrowed and mislaid, and fall into the wrong hands, and generally get around in a way that makes them public, even if they are not on open sale; and in a way that manuscripts, more carefully attended to, more intimately consumed, do not.

The posthumously published work is also much more prone to textual corruption. In the decades after the poet's death, some of the transcription from manuscript sources for hasty printing in chapbooks and magazines was careless. In this case it seems justified to correct the copy-text with reference to other sources, while pointing out, in the notes, that the poem on the page of this volume is not *quite* the poem first encountered in her tuppenny tract or monthly magazine by a contemporary reader. The limit case for this procedure proved to be 'A poet's welcome to his love-begotten daughter'. This exists in several good holograph manuscripts, all of them different from each other; its first published version, in a chapbook from 1799, differs in many ways from all the manuscripts, at one point simply contradicting them, apparently due to corruption of the text during transcription. But so many are these corruptions that to correct them all with reference to the manuscripts is not to produce a good reading version of the first published text, but to produce yet another version of the poem, too distant from the printed copy *and* from the manuscripts to count as a version of either of them. In this case, instead, the copy-text is the first complete publication of a reliable manuscript copy, which does not come about until the centenary of the poet's death.

The music provides other challenges. Attending to the textual circumstances in which songs were first published means distinguishing those that appeared with no more than the name of a tune below their title from those that were published with a score. In the first instance, Burns clearly expected the reader to fit the words to the tune themselves. This volume makes the same demand in such cases; but if Burns relied on his reader's musical knowledge, here the tune is offered in the notes, adapted from a contemporary compendium (almost always *The Scots Musical Museum*). Where the song was published with a score, in the *Museum* or in *A Select Collection of Original Scotish Airs*, this volume follows its copy-text in placing words and music alongside one another. Just as the verbal text follows its copy-text in accidentals

of spelling, punctuation, and so on, so the scores here maintain acci-
dentals of annotation: the deployment of slurs and beams, for example,
will look odd to the modern musician's eye. On the other hand, Stephen
Clarke's transcriptions for the *Museum* sometimes struggled with its
small pages: syllables could not be arranged, or bass and treble notes
aligned, in any consistent way, and this has been tidied up for the
present volume. Without quite the same spatial restrictions, it has also
been possible to extract each first verse from the score and include it
also at the head of subsequent verses in the lyric, for easier appreciation
of the song as a whole.

Music was not the only accompaniment to which Burns set his
words. The self-conscious construction of a particular type of poetic
identity in the *Poems* finds its visual equivalent in the engraving of the
poet by John Beugo that appeared in the frontispiece of the Edinburgh
editions from 1787 onwards. 'Tam o' Shanter' was written as the com-
panion to a picture: an engraving of a ruin near the poet's birthplace, an
old church his father had worked to restore. These images, like the
tunes for the songs, shaped the way in which Burns's readers experi-
enced his words, and are included here as another aspect of the mater-
ial context in which his poetry was first encountered and enjoyed.

POEMS,

CHIEFLY IN THE

SCOTTISH DIALECT,

BY

ROBERT BURNS.

THE Simple Bard, unbroke by rules of Art,
He pours the wild effusions of the heart:
And if inspir'd, 'tis Nature's pow'rs inspire;
Her's all the melting thrill, and her's the kindling fire.

ANONYMOUS.°

KILMARNOCK:
PRINTED BY JOHN WILSON.
M,DCC,LXXXVI.

PREFACE

THE following trifles are not the production of the Poet, who, with all the advantages of learned art, and perhaps amid the elegancies and idlenesses of upper life, looks down for a rural theme, with an eye to Theocrites or Virgil.° To the Author of this, these and other celebrated names their countrymen are, in their original languages, 'A fountain shut up, and a book sealed.'° Unacquainted with the necessary requisites for commencing Poet by rule, he sings the sentiments and manners, he felt and saw in himself and his rustic compeers around him, in his and their native language. Though a Rhymer from his earliest years, at least from the earliest impulses of the softer passions, it was not till very lately, that the applause, perhaps the partiality, of Friendship, wakened his vanity so far as to make him think any thing of his was worth showing; and none of the following works were ever composed with a view to the press. To amuse himself with the little creations of his own fancy, amid the toil and fatigues of a laborious life; to transcribe the various feelings, the loves, the griefs, the hopes, the fears, in his own breast; to find some kind of counterpoise to the struggles of a world, always an alien scene, a task uncouth to the poetical mind; these were his motives for courting the Muses, and in these he found Poetry to be it's own reward.

Now that he appears in the public character of an Author, he does it with fear and trembling. So dear is fame to the rhyming tribe, that even he, an obscure, nameless Bard, shrinks aghast, at the thought of being branded as 'An impertinent blockhead, obtruding his nonsense on the world; and because he can make a shift to jingle a few doggerel, Scotch rhymes together, looks upon himself as a Poet of no small consequence forsooth.'

It is an observation of that celebrated Poet,[1] whose divine Elegies do honor to our language, our nation, and our species, that 'Humility has depressed many a genius to a hermit, but never raised one to fame.' If any Critic catches at the word *genius*, the Author tells him, once for all, that he certainly looks upon himself as possest of some poetic abilities, otherwise his publishing in the manner he has done, would be a manœuvre below the worst character, which, he hopes, his worst enemy will ever give him: but to the genius of a Ramsay,° or the glorious

---

[1] Shenstone.°

dawnings of the poor, unfortunate Ferguson,° he, with equal unaffected sincerity, declares, that, even in his highest pulse of vanity, he has not the most distant pretensions. These two justly admired Scotch Poets he has often had in his eye in the following pieces; but rather with a view to kindle at their flame, than for servile imitation.

To his Subscribers,° the Author returns his most sincere thanks. Not the mercenary bow over a counter, but the heart-throbbing gratitude of the Bard, conscious how much he is indebted to Benevolence and Friendship, for gratifying him, if he deserves it, in that dearest wish of every poetic bosom—to be distinguished. He begs his readers, particularly the Learned and the Polite, who may honor him with a perusal, that they will make every allowance for Education and Circumstances of Life: but, if after a fair, candid, and impartial criticism, he shall stand convicted of Dulness and Nonsense, let him be done by, as he would in that case do by others—let him be condemned, without mercy, to contempt and oblivion.

THE TWA DOGS, A TALE

'TWAS in that place o' Scotland's isle,
That bears the name o' auld king COIL,°
Upon a bonie day in June,
When wearing thro' the afternoon,
Twa Dogs, that were na thrang at hame,
Forgather'd ance upon a time.

The first I'll name, they ca'd him *Cæsar*,
Was keepet for His Honor's pleasure;
His hair, his size, his mouth, his lugs,
Shew'd he was nane o' Scotland's dogs,   10
But whalpet some place far abroad,
Where sailors gang to fish for Cod.°

His locked, letter'd, braw brass-collar
Shew'd him the *gentleman* an' *scholar*;
But tho' he was o' high degree,
The fient a pride na pride had he,
But wad hae spent an hour caressan,
Ev'n wi' a Tinkler-gipsey's *messan*:
At Kirk or Market, Mill or Smiddie,
Nae tawted *tyke*, tho' e'er sae duddie,   20
But he wad stan't, as glad to see him,
An' stroan't on stanes an' hillocks wi' him.

The tither was a *ploughman's collie*,
A rhyming, ranting, raving billie,
Wha for his friend an' comrade had him,
And in his freaks had *Luath* ca'd him,
After some dog in *Highland sang*,[1]
Was made lang syne, lord knows how lang.

He was a gash an' faithfu' *tyke*,
As ever lap a sheugh or dyke.   30
His honest, sonsie, baws'nt face,
Ay gat him friends in ilka place;

---

[1] Cuchullin's dog in Ossian's Fingal.°

His breast was white, his towzie back,
Weel clad wi' coat o' glossy black;
His gawsie tail, wi' upward curl,
Hung owre his hurdies wi' a swirl.

Nae doubt but they were fain o' ither,
An' unco pack an' thick thegither;
Wi' social nose whyles snuff'd an' snowket;
Whyles mice and modewurks they howket;   40
Whyles scour'd awa in lang excursion,
An' worry'd ither in diversion;
Till tir'd at last wi' mony a farce,
They set them down upon their arse,°
An' there began a lang digression
About the *lords o' the creation.*

CÆSAR

I've aften wonder'd, honest *Luath,*
What sort o' life poor dogs like you have;
An' when the *gentry's* life I saw,
What way *poor bodies* liv'd ava.   50

Our *Laird* gets in his racked rents,°
His coals, his kane, an' a' his stents:
He rises when he likes himsel;
His flunkies answer at the bell;
He ca's his coach; he ca's his horse;
He draws a bonie, silken purse
As lang's my tail, whare thro' the steeks,
The yellow letter'd *Geordie* keeks.°

Frae morn to een it's nought but toiling,
At baking, roasting, frying, boiling;   60
An' tho' the gentry first are steghan,
Yet ev'n the *ha' folk* fill their peghan
Wi' sauce, ragouts, an' sic like trashtrie,°
That's little short o' downright wastrie.
Our *Whipper-in,* wee, blastet wonner,°
Poor, worthless elf, it eats a dinner,
Better than ony *Tenant-man*
His Honor has in a' the lan':

An' what poor *Cot-folk* pit their painch in,°
I own it's past my comprehension.°   70

LUATH

Trowth, Cæsar, whyles they're fash't enough;°
A *Cotter* howkan in a sheugh,
Wi' dirty stanes biggan a dyke,
Bairan a quarry, an' sic like,°
Himsel, a wife, he thus sustains,
A smytrie o' wee, duddie weans,
An' nought but his han'-daurk, to keep
Them right an' tight in thack an' raep.

An' when they meet wi' sair disasters,
Like loss o' health or want o' masters,   80
Ye maist wad think, a wee touch langer,
An' they maun starve o' cauld and hunger:
But how it comes, I never kent yet,
They're maistly wonderfu' contented;
An' buirdly chiels, and clever hizzies,
Are bred in sic a way as this is.

CÆSAR

But then, to see how ye're negleket,
How huff'd, an' cuff'd, an' disrespeket!
L—d man, our gentry care as little
For *delvers*, *ditchers*, an' sic cattle;   90
They gang as saucy by poor folk,
As I wad by a stinkan brock.

I've notic'd, on our Laird's *court-day*,°
An' mony a time my heart's been wae,
Poor *tenant bodies*, scant o' cash,
How they maun thole a *factor's* snash;
He'll stamp an' threaten, curse an' swear,
He'll *apprehend* them, *poind* their gear;°
While they maun stan', wi' aspect humble,
An' hear it a', an' fear an' tremble!   100

I see how folk live that hae riches;
But surely poor-folk maun be wretches!

LUATH

They're no sae wretched 's ane wad think;
Tho' constantly on poortith's brink,
They're sae accustom'd wi' the sight,
The view o't gies them little fright.

Then chance and fortune are sae guided,
They're ay in less or mair provided;
An' tho' fatigu'd wi' close employment,
A blink o' rest 's a sweet enjoyment.   110

The dearest comfort o' their lives,
Their grushie weans an' faithfu' wives;
The *prattling things* are just their pride,
That sweetens a' their fire-side.

An' whyles twalpennie-worth o' *nappy*
Can mak the bodies unco happy;
They lay aside their private cares,
To mind the Kirk and State affairs;
They'll talk o' *patronage* an' *priests*,°
Wi' kindling fury i' their breasts,   120
Or tell what new taxation's comin,
An' ferlie at the folk in LON'ON.

As bleak-fac'd Hallowmass returns,°
They get the jovial, rantan *Kirns*,
When *rural life*, of ev'ry station,
Unite in common recreation;
Love blinks, Wit slaps, an' social Mirth
Forgets there's *care* upo' the earth.

That *merry day* the year begins,
They bar the door on frosty win's;   130
The nappy reeks wi' mantling ream,
An' sheds a heart-inspiring steam;
The luntan pipe, an' sneeshin mill,
Are handed round wi' right guid will;
The cantie, auld folks, crackan crouse,
The young anes rantan thro' the house—

My heart has been sae fain to see them,
That I for joy hae barket wi' them.

Still it's owre true that ye hae said,
Sic game is now owre aften play'd;   140
There's monie a creditable *stock*
O' decent, honest, fawsont folk,
Are riven out baith root an' branch,
Some rascal's pridefu' greed to quench,°
Wha thinks to knit himsel the faster
In favor wi' some *gentle Master*,
Wha aiblins thrang a *parliamentin*,
For Britain's guid his saul indentin—°

CÆSAR

Haith lad ye little ken about it;
For Britain's guid! guid faith! I doubt it.   150
Say rather, gaun as PREMIERS lead him,°
An' saying *aye* or *no*'s they bid him:
At Operas an' Plays parading,
Mortgaging, gambling, masquerading:
Or maybe, in a frolic daft,
To HAGUE or CALAIS takes a waft,
To make a *tour* an' tak a whirl,
To learn *bon ton* an' see the worl'.°

There, at VIENNA or VERSAILLES,
He rives his father's auld entails;°   160
Or by MADRID he takes the rout,
To thrum *guittars* an' fecht wi' nowt;
Or down *Italian Vista* startles,
Wh—re-hunting amang groves o' myrtles:°
Then bowses drumlie *German-water*,°
To mak himsel look fair and fatter,
An' purge the bitter ga's an' cankers,
O' curst *Venetian* b—res an' ch—ncres.°

For Britain's guid! for her destruction!
Wi' dissipation, feud an' faction!   170

LUATH

Hech man! dear sirs! is that the gate,
They waste sae mony a braw estate!
Are we sae foughten and harass'd
For gear to gang that gate at last!

O would they stay aback frae courts,
An' please themsels wi' countra sports,
It wad for ev'ry ane be better,
The *Laird*, the *Tenant*, an' the *Cotter!*
For thae frank, rantan, ramblan billies,
Fient haet o' them 's ill hearted fellows;   180
Except for breakin o' their timmer,
Or speakin lightly o' their *Limmer*,
Or shootin of a hare or moorcock,°
The ne'er-a-bit they're ill to poor folk.

But will ye tell me, master *Cæsar*,
Sure *great folk's* life's a life o' pleasure?
Nae cauld nor hunger e'er can steer them,
The vera thought o't need na fear them.

CÆSAR

L—d man, were ye but whyles where I am,
The *gentles* ye wad neer envy them!   190

It's true, they need na starve or sweat,
Thro' Winter's cauld, or Summer's heat;
They've nae sair-wark to craze their banes,
An' fill *auld-age* wi' grips an' granes;
But *human-bodies* are sic fools,
For a' their colledges an' schools,
That when nae *real* ills perplex them,
They *mak* enow themsels to vex them;
An' ay the less they hae to sturt them,
In like proportion, less will hurt them.   200

A country fellow at the pleugh,
His *acre's* till'd, he's right eneugh;
A country girl at her wheel,

Her *dizzen's* done, she's unco weel;°
But Gentlemen, an' Ladies warst,
Wi' ev'n down *want o' wark* are curst.
They loiter, lounging, lank an' lazy;
Tho' deil-haet ails them, yet uneasy;
Their days, insipid, dull an' tasteless,
Their nights, unquiet, lang an' restless.   210

    An' ev'n their sports, their balls an' races,
Their galloping thro' public places,
There's sic parade, sic pomp an' art,
The joy can scarcely reach the heart.

    The *Men* cast out in *party-matches*,°
Then sowther a' in deep debauches.
Ae night, they're mad wi' drink an' wh—ring,
Niest day their life is past enduring.

    The *Ladies* arm-in-arm in clusters,
As great an' gracious a' as sisters;   220
But hear their *absent thoughts* o' ither,
They're a' run deils an' jads thegither.
Whyles, owre the wee bit cup an' platie,
They sip the *scandal-potion* pretty;
Or lee-lang nights, wi' crabbet leuks,
Pore owre the devil's *pictur'd beuks*;°
Stake on a chance a farmer's stackyard,
An' cheat like ony *unhang'd blackguard*.

    There's some exceptions, man an' woman;
But this is Gentry's life in common.   230

    By this, the sun was out o' sight,
An' darker gloamin brought the night:
The *bum-clock* humm'd wi' lazy drone,
The kye stood rowtan i' the loan;
When up they gat an' shook their lugs,
Rejoic'd they were na *men* but *dogs*;
An' each took off his several way,
Resolv'd to meet some ither day.

SCOTCH DRINK

Gie him strong Drink *until he wink,*
That's sinking in despair;
An' liquor *guid to fire his bluid,*
That's prest wi' grief an' care:
There let him bowse an' deep carouse,
Wi' bumpers flowing o'er,
Till he forgets his loves *or debts,*
An' minds his griefs no more.

SOLOMON'S PROVERBS, xxxi. 6, 7.°

LET other Poets raise a fracas
'Bout vines, an' wines, an' druken *Bacchus,*°
An' crabbed names an' stories wrack us,
      An' grate our lug,
I sing the juice *Scotch bear* can mak us,
      In glass or jug.

O thou, my MUSE! guid, auld SCOTCH DRINK!
Whether thro' wimplin worms thou jink,°
Or, richly brown, ream owre the brink,
      In glorious faem,   10
Inspire me, till I *lisp* an' *wink,*
      To sing thy name!

Let husky Wheat the haughs adorn,
And Aits set up their awnie horn,
An' Pease an' Beans, at een or morn,
      Perfume the plain,
Leeze me on thee *John Barleycorn,*
      Thou king o' grain!

On thee aft Scotland chows her cood,
In souple scones, the wale o' food!°   20
Or tumbling in the boiling flood
      Wi' kail an' beef;
But when thou pours thy strong *heart's blood,*
      There thou shines chief.

Food fills the wame, an' keeps us livin;
Tho' life's a gift no worth receivin,
When heavy-dragg'd wi' pine an' grievin;
      But oil'd by thee,
The wheels o' life gae down-hill, scrievin,°
      Wi' rattlin glee.   30

Thou clears the head o' doited Lear;
Thou chears the heart o' drooping Care;
Thou strings the nerves o' Labor-sair,
      At's weary toil;
Thou ev'n brightens dark Despair,
      Wi' gloomy smile.

Aft, clad in massy, siller weed,
Wi' Gentles thou erects thy head;
Yet humbly kind, in time o' need,
      The *poor man's* wine;   40
His wee drap pirratch, or his bread,
      Thou kitchens fine.

Thou art the life o' public haunts;
But thee, what were our fairs and rants?
Ev'n godly meetings o' the saunts,°
      By thee inspir'd,
When gaping they besiege the *tents*,°
      Are doubly fir'd.

That *merry night* we get the corn in,
O sweetly, then, thou reams the horn in!   50
Or reekan on a *New-year-mornin*
      In cog or bicker,
An' just a wee drap *sp'ritual burn* in,°
      An' gusty sucker!

When Vulcan gies his bellys breath,°
An' Ploughmen gather wi' their graith,
O rare! to see thee fizz an' freath
      I' the lugget caup!
Then *Burnewin* comes on like Death
      At ev'ry chap.   60

Nae mercy, then, for airn or steel;
The brawnie, banie, ploughman-chiel
Brings hard owrehip, wi' sturdy wheel,
                    The strong forehammer,
Till block an' studdie ring an' reel
                    Wi' dinsome clamour.

When skirlin weanies see the light,
Thou maks the gossips clatter bright,°
How fumbling coofs their dearies slight,°
                    Wae worth them for't!   70
While healths gae round to him wha, *tight*,
                    Gies famous sport.°

When neebors anger at a plea,
An' just as wud as wud can be,
How easy can the *barley-brie*
                    Cement the quarrel!
It's aye the cheapest Lawyer's fee
                    To taste the barrel.

Alake! that e'er my *Muse* has reason,
To wyte her countrymen wi' treason!   80
But monie daily weet their weason
                    Wi' liquors nice,
An' hardly, in a winter season,
                    E'er spier her price.

Wae worth that *Brandy*, burnan trash!
Fell source o' monie a pain an' brash!
Twins monie a poor, doylt, druken hash
                    O' half his days;
An' sends, beside, auld *Scotland's* cash
                    To her warst faes.   90

Ye Scots wha wish auld Scotland well,
Ye chief, to you my tale I tell,
Poor, plackless devils like *mysel*,
                    It sets you ill,
Wi' bitter, dearthfu' *wines* to mell,°
                    Or foreign gill.

May *Gravels* round his blather wrench,
An' *Gouts* torment him, inch by inch,°
Wha twists his gruntle wi' a glunch
   O' sour disdain,   100
Out owre a glass o' *Whisky-punch*
   Wi' honest men!

O *Whisky!* soul o' plays an' pranks!
Accept a *Bardie's* gratefu' thanks!
When wanting thee, what tuneless cranks
   Are my poor Verses!
Thou comes—they rattle i' their ranks
   At ither's arses!

Thee *Ferintosh!* O sadly lost!°
Scotland lament frae coast to coast!   110
Now colic-grips, an' barkin hoast,
   May kill us a';
For loyal Forbes' *Charter'd boast*°
   Is ta'en awa!

Thae curst horse-leeches o' th' Excise,°
Wha mak the *Whisky stells* their prize!
Haud up thy han' *Deil!* ance, twice, *thrice!*
   There, sieze the blinkers!
An' bake them up in brunstane pies
   For poor d—n'd *Drinkers*.   120

Fortune, if thou'll but gie me still
Hale breeks, a scone, an' *whisky gill*,
An' rowth o' *rhyme* to rave at will,
   Tak a' the rest,
An' deal't about as thy blind skill
   Directs thee best.

THE AUTHOR'S EARNEST CRY AND PRAYER,
TO THE RIGHT HONORABLE AND HONORABLE,
THE SCOTCH REPRESENTATIVES IN THE
HOUSE OF COMMONS

Dearest of Distillation! last and best!——
——How art thou lost!——

PARODY ON MILTON°

YE *Irish lords*, ye *knights* an' *squires*,°
Wha *represent* our *Brughs* an' *Shires*,
An' dousely manage our affairs
   In *Parliament*,
To you a simple Bardie's pray'rs
   Are humbly sent.

  Alas! my roupet *Muse* is haerse!
Your Honor's hearts wi' grief 'twad pierce,
To see her sittan on her arse
   Low i' the dust,   10
An' scriechan out prosaic verse,
   An' like to brust!

  Tell them wha hae the chief direction,
Scotland an' *me's* in great affliction,
E'er sin' they laid that curst restriction
   On AQUAVITÆ;°
An' rouse them up to strong conviction,
   An' move their pity.

  Stand forth and tell yon PREMIER YOUTH,°
The honest, open, naked truth: 20
Tell him o' mine an' Scotland's drouth,
   His servants humble:
The muckle devil blaw you south,
   If ye dissemble!

  Does ony *great man* glunch an' gloom?°
Speak out an' never fash your thumb.
Let *posts* an' *pensions* sink or swoom

              Wi' them wha grant them:
If honestly they canna come,
              Far better want them.   30

    In gath'rin votes you were na slack,
Now stand as tightly by your tack:
Ne'er claw your lug, an' fidge your back,
              An' hum an' haw,
But raise your arm, an' tell your crack
              Before them a'.

    Paint Scotland greetan owre her thrissle;
Her *mutchkin stowp* as toom's a whissle;
An' d—mn'd Excise-men in a bussle,°
              Seizan a *Stell*,   40
Triumphant crushan't like a muscle
              Or laimpet shell.

    Then on the tither hand present her,
A blackguard *Smuggler*, right behint her,°
An' cheek-for-chow, a chuffie *Vintner*,
              Colleaguing join,
Picking her pouch as bare as Winter,
              Of a' kind coin.

    Is there, that bears the name o' SCOT,
But feels his heart's bluid rising hot,   50
To see his poor, auld Mither's *pot*,
              Thus dung in staves,°
An' plunder'd o' her hindmost groat,
              By gallows knaves?

    Alas! I'm but a nameless wight,
Trode i' the mire out o' sight!
But could I like MONTGOMERIES fight,°
              Or gab like BOSWELL,°
There's some *sark-necks* I wad *draw* tight,
              An' *tye* some *hose* well.   60

    God bless your Honors, can ye see't,
The kind, auld, cantie Carlin greet,

An' no get warmly to your feet,
                    An' gar them hear it,
An' tell them, wi' a patriot-heat,
                    Ye winna bear it?

Some o' you nicely ken the laws,
To round the period an' pause,
An' with rhetoric clause on clause
                    To mak harangues;   70
Then echo thro' Saint Stephen's wa's°
                    Auld Scotland's wrangs.

Dempster, a true-blue Scot I'se warran;°
Thee, aith-detesting, chaste *Kilkerran*;°
An' that glib-gabbet Highland Baron,
                    The Laird o' *Graham*;°
And ane, a chap that's d—mn'd auldfarren,
                    Dundas his name.°

Erskine, a spunkie norland billie;°
True Campbells, *Frederick* an' *Ilay*;°   80
An' Livistone, the bauld *Sir Willie*;°
                    An' monie ithers,
Whom auld Demosthenes or Tully°
                    Might own for brithers.

Arouse my boys! exert your mettle,
To get auld Scotland back her *kettle!*
Or faith! I'll wad my new pleugh-pettle,
                    Ye'll see't or lang,
She'll teach you, wi' a reekan whittle,
                    Anither sang.   90

This while she's been in crankous mood,
Her *lost Militia* fir'd her bluid;°
(Deil na they never mair do guid,
                    Play'd her that pliskie!)
An' now she's like to rin red-wud
                    About her *Whisky*.

An' L—d! if ance they pit her till't,
Her tartan petticoat she'll kilt,
An' durk an' pistol at her belt,°
      She'll tak the streets,°   100
An' rin her whittle to the hilt,
      I' th' first she meets!

For G—d-sake, Sirs! then speak her fair,
An' straik her cannie wi' the hair,
An' to the *muckle house* repair,°
      Wi' instant speed,
An' strive, wi' a' your Wit an' Lear,
      To get remead.

Yon ill-tongu'd tinkler, *Charlie Fox*,°
May taunt you wi' his jeers an' mocks;   110
But gie him't het, my hearty cocks!
      E'en cowe the cadie!°
An' send him to his dicing box,
      An' sportin lady.°

Tell yon guid bluid o' auld *Boconnock's*,°
I'll be his debt twa mashlum bonnocks,
An' drink his health in auld *Nanse Tinnock's*[1]°
      Nine times a week,
If he some scheme, like tea an' winnocks,°
      Wad kindly seek.   120

Could he some *commutation* broach,
I'll pledge my aith in guid braid Scotch,
He need na fear their foul reproach
      Nor erudition,
Yon mixtie-maxtie, queer hotch-potch,
      The *Coalition*.°

Auld Scotland has a raucle tongue;
She's just a devil wi' a rung;
An' if she promise auld or young

---

[1] A worthy old Hostess of the Author's in *Mauchline*, where he sometimes studies Politics over a glass of guid, auld *Scotch Drink*.

                    To tak their part,   130
Tho' by the neck she should be strung,
          She'll no desert.

    And now, ye chosen FIVE AND FORTY,°
May still your Mither's heart support ye;
Then, tho' a *Minister* grow dorty,
          An' kick your place,°
Ye'll snap your fingers, poor an' hearty,
          Before his face.

    God bless your Honors, a' your days,
Wi' sowps o' kail and brats o' claise,   140
In spite o' a' the thievish kaes
          That haunt St. *Jamie's!*°
Your humble Bardie sings an' prays
          While *Rab* his name is.

               POSTSCRIPT
    Let half-starv'd slaves in warmer skies,°
See future wines, rich-clust'ring, rise;
Their lot auld Scotland ne'er envies,
          But blythe an' frisky,
She eyes her freeborn, martial boys,
          Tak aff their Whisky.   150

    What tho' their Phœbus kinder warms,
While Fragrance blooms an' Beauty charms!
When wretches range, in famish'd swarms,
          The scented groves,
Or hounded forth, *dishonor* arms
          In hungry droves.

    Their *gun's* a burden on their shouther;
They downa bide the stink o' *powther*;
Their bauldest thought's a hank'ring swither,
          To stan' or rin,   160
Till skelp— a shot— they're aff, a' throw'ther,
          To save their skin.

But bring a SCOTCHMAN frae his hill,°
Clap in his cheek a *Highland gill*,
Say, such is royal GEORGE'S will,
        An' there's the foe,
He has nae thought but how to kill
        Twa at a blow.

Nae cauld, faint-hearted doubtings tease him;
Death comes, wi' fearless eye he sees him;   170
Wi' bluidy han' a welcome gies him;
        An' when he fa's,
His latest draught o' breathin lea'es him°
        In faint huzzas.

Sages their solemn een may steek,
An' raise a philosophic reek,
An' physically causes seek,
        In *clime* an' *season*,°
But tell me *Whisky's* name in Greek,
        I'll tell the reason.   180

SCOTLAND, my auld, respected Mither!
Tho' whyles ye moistify your leather,
Till whare ye sit, on craps o' heather,
        Ye tine your dam;°
FREEDOM and WHISKY gang thegither,
        Tak aff your *dram!*

THE HOLY FAIR

A robe of seeming truth and trust
  Hid crafty observation;
And secret hung, with poison'd crust,
  The dirk of Defamation:
A mask that like the gorget show'd,
  Dye-varying, on the pigeon;
And for a mantle large and broad,
  He wrapt him in Religion.
      HYPOCRISY A-LA-MODE.°

I

UPON a simmer Sunday morn,
    When Nature's face is fair,
I walked forth to view the corn,
    An' snuff the callor air.
The rising sun, owre GALSTON Muirs,°
    Wi' glorious light was glintan;
The hares were hirplan down the furrs,
    The lav'rocks they were chantan
                Fu' sweet that day.

II

As lightsomely I glowr'd abroad,   10
    To see a scene sae gay,
Three *hizzies*, early at the road,
    Cam skelpan up the way.
Twa had manteeles o' dolefu' black,
    But ane wi' lyart lining;
The third, that gaed a wee a-back,
    Was in the fashion shining
                Fu' gay that day.

III

The *twa* appear'd like sisters twin,
    In feature, form an' claes;   20
Their visage wither'd, lang an' thin,
    An' sour as ony slaes:
The *third* cam up, hap-step-an'-loup,
    As light as ony lambie,
An' wi' a curchie low did stoop,
    As soon as e'er she saw me,
                Fu' kind that day.

IV

Wi' bonnet aff, quoth I, 'Sweet lass,
    'I think ye seem to ken me;
'I'm sure I've seen that bonie face,   30
    'But yet I canna name ye.'
Quo' she, an' laughan as she spak,
    An' taks me by the han's,

'Ye, for my sake, hae gien the feck
  'Of a' the *ten comman's*
                A screed some day.'

V

'My name is FUN—your cronie dear,°
  'The nearest friend ye hae;
'An' this is SUPERSTITION here,
  'An' that's HYPOCRISY.   40
'I'm gaun to ********* *holy fair,*°
  'To spend an hour in daffin:
'Gin ye'll go there, yon runkl'd pair,
  'We will get famous laughin
                At them this day.'

VI

Quoth I, 'With a' my heart, I'll do't;
  'I'll get my sunday's sark on,
'An' meet you on the holy spot;
  'Faith, we'se hae fine remarkin!'
Then I gaed hame at crowdie-time,   50
  An' soon I made me ready;
For roads were clad, frae side to side,
  Wi' monie a wearie body,
                In droves that day.

VII

Here, farmers gash, in ridin graith,
  Gaed hoddan by their cotters;
There, swankies young, in braw braid-claith,
  Are springan owre the gutters.
The lasses, skelpan barefit, thrang,
  In silks an' scarlets glitter;   60
Wi' *sweet-milk cheese*, in monie a whang,
  An' *farls*, bak'd wi' butter,
                Fu' crump that day.

VIII

When by the *plate* we set our nose,
  Weel heaped up wi' ha'pence,
A greedy glowr *black-bonnet* throws,°

An' we maun draw our tippence.
Then in we go to see the show,
  On ev'ry side they're gath'ran;
Some carryan dails, some chairs an' stools,   70
  An' some are busy bleth'ran
        Right loud that day.

IX

Here stands a shed to fend the show'rs,
  An' screen our countra Gentry;
There, *racer Jess*, an' twathree wh—res,°
  Are blinkan at the entry.
Here sits a raw o' tittlan jads,
  Wi' heaving breasts an' bare neck;
An' there, a batch o' *Wabster lads*,
  Blackguarding frae K*******ck°   80
        For *fun* this day.

X

Here, some are thinkan on their sins,
  An' some upo' their claes;
Ane curses feet that fyl'd his shins,
  Anither sighs an' prays:
On this hand sits an *Elect* swatch,°
  Wi' screw'd-up, grace-proud faces;
On that, a set o' chaps, at watch,
  Thrang winkan on the lasses
        To *chairs* that day.   90

XI

O happy is that man, an' blest!
  Nae wonder that it pride him!
Whase ain dear lass, that he likes best,
  Comes clinkan down beside him!
Wi' arm repos'd on the *chair-back*,
  He sweetly does compose him;
Which, by degrees, slips round her *neck*,
  An's loof upon her *bosom*
        Unkend that day.

XII

Now a' the congregation o'er   100
   Is silent expectation;
For ****** speels the holy door,°
   Wi' tidings o' s—lv—t—n.°
Should *Hornie*, as in ancient days,°
   'Mang sons o' G— present him,
The vera sight o' ******'s face,
   To's ain *het hame* had sent him
         Wi' fright that day.

XIII

Hear how he clears the points o' Faith
   Wi' rattlin an' thumpin!   110
Now meekly calm, now wild in wrath,
   He's stampan, an' he's jumpan!
His lengthen'd chin, his turn'd up snout,
   His eldritch squeel an' gestures,
O how they fire the heart devout,
   Like *cantharidian* plaisters°
         On sic a day!

XIV

But hark! the *tent* has chang'd it's voice;°
   There's peace an' rest nae langer;
For a' the *real judges* rise,   120
   They canna sit for anger.
***** opens out his cauld harangues,°
   On *practice* and on *morals*;
An' aff the *godly* pour in thrangs,
   To gie the jars an' barrels
         A lift that day.

XV

What signifies his barren shine,
   Of *moral pow'rs* an' *reason*?
His English style, an' gesture fine,°
   Are a' clean out o' season.   130
Like SOCRATES or ANTONINE,°
   Or some auld pagan heathen,

The *moral man* he does define,
  But ne'er a word o' *faith* in
              That's right that day.

XVI

In guid time comes an antidote
  Against sic poosion'd nostrum;
For *******, frae the water-fit,°
  Ascends the *holy rostrum*:
See, up he's got the word o' G—,   140
  An' meek an' mim has view'd it,
While COMMON-SENSE has taen the road,°
  An' aff, an' up the *Cowgate*°
              Fast, fast that day.

XVII

Wee ****** neist, the Guard relieves,°
  An' Orthodoxy raibles,
Tho' in his heart he weel believes,
  An' thinks it auld wives' fables:
But faith! the birkie wants a *Manse*,
  So, cannilie he hums them;   150
Altho' his *carnal* Wit an' Sense
  Like hafflins-wise o'ercomes him
              At times that day.

XVIII

Now, butt an' ben, the Change-house fills,°
  Wi' *yill-caup* Commentators:
Here's crying out for bakes an' gills,
  An' there the pint-stowp clatters;
While thick an' thrang, an' loud an' lang,
  Wi' *Logic*, an' wi' *Scripture*,
They raise a din, that, in the end,   160
  Is like to breed a rupture
              O' wrath that day.

XIX

Leeze me on Drink! it gies us mair
  Than either School or Colledge:
It kindles Wit, it waukens Lear,

It pangs us fou o' Knowledge.
Be't *whisky-gill* or *penny-wheep*,
　Or ony stronger potion,
It never fails, on drinkin deep,
　To kittle up our *notion*,   170
　　　　By night or day.

XX

The lads an' lasses, blythely bent
　To mind baith *saul* an' *body*,
Sit round the table, weel content,
　An' steer about the *toddy*.
On this ane's dress, an' that ane's leuk,
　They're makin observations;
While some are cozie i' the neuk,
　An' forming *assignations*
　　　　To meet some day.   180

XXI

But now the L——'s ain trumpet touts,°
　Till a' the hills are rairan,
An' echos back return the shouts;
　Black ****** is na spairan:°
His piercin words, like Highlan swords,
　Divide the joints an' marrow;°
His talk o' H——ll, whare devils dwell,
　Our vera 'Sauls does harrow'[1]
　　　　Wi' fright that day!

XXII

A vast, unbottom'd, boundless *Pit*,   190
　Fill'd fou o' *lowan brunstane*,
Whase raging flame, an' scorching heat,
　Wad melt the hardest whun-stane!
The *half asleep* start up wi' fear,
　An' think they hear it roaran,
When presently it does appear,
　'Twas but some neebor *snoran*
　　　　Asleep that day.

[1] Shakespeare's Hamlet.

XXIII

'Twad be owre lang a tale to tell,
  How monie stories past,   200
An' how they crouded to the yill,
  When they were a' dismist:
How drink gaed round, in cogs an' caups,
  Amang the furms an' benches;
An' *cheese* an' *bread*, frae women's laps,
  Was dealt about in lunches,
                An' dawds that day.

XXIV

In comes a gawsie, gash *Guidwife*,
  An' sits down by the fire,
Syne draws her *kebbuck* an' her knife;   210
  The lasses they are shyer.
The auld *Guidmen*, about the *grace*,
  Frae side to side they bother,
Till some ane by his bonnet lays,
  An' gies them't, like a *tether*,
                Fu' lang that day.

XXV

Waesucks! for him that gets nae lass,
  Or lasses that hae naething!
Sma' need has he to say a grace,
  Or melvie his braw claithing!   220
O *Wives* be mindfu', ance yoursel,
  How bonie lads ye wanted,
An' dinna, for a *kebbuck-heel*,
  Let lasses be affronted
                On sic a day!

XXVI

Now *Clinkumbell*, wi' rattlan tow,
  Begins to jow an' croon;
Some swagger hame, the best they dow,
  Some wait the afternoon.
At slaps the billies halt a blink,   230
  Till lasses strip their shoon:

Wi' *faith* an' *hope*, an' *love* an' *drink*,
  They're a' in famous tune
          For crack that day.

XXVII

How monie hearts this day converts,
  O' sinners and o' Lasses!
Their hearts o' stane, gin night are gane,
  As saft as ony flesh is.
There's some are fou o' *love divine*;
  There's some are fou o' *brandy*;   240
An' monie jobs that day begin,
  May end in *Houghmagandie*
          Some ither day.

ADDRESS TO THE DEIL

O Prince, O chief of many throned pow'rs,
That led th'embattl'd Seraphim to war—

                    MILTON°

O Thou, whatever title suit thee!
Auld Hornie, Satan, Nick, or Clootie,°
Wha in yon cavern grim an' sootie,
          Clos'd under hatches,
Spairges about the brunstane cootie,
          To scaud poor wretches!

Hear me, *auld Hangie*, for a wee,
An' let poor, *damned bodies* bee;
I'm sure sma' pleasure it can gie,
          Ev'n to a *deil*,   10
To skelp an' scaud poor dogs like me,
          An' hear us squeel!

Great is thy pow'r, an' great thy fame;
Far kend an' noted is thy name;
An' tho' yon *lowan heugh's* thy hame,
          Thou travels far;

An' faith! thou's neither lag nor lame,
           Nor blate nor scaur.

Whyles, ranging like a roaran lion,°
For prey, a' holes an' corners tryin;   20
Whyles, on the strong-wing'd Tempest flyin,
           Tirlan the *kirks*;
Whyles, in the human bosom pryin,
           Unseen thou lurks.

I've heard my rev'rend *Graunie* say,
In lanely glens ye like to stray;
Or where auld, ruin'd castles, gray,
           Nod to the moon,
Ye fright the nightly wand'rer's way,
           Wi' eldritch croon.   30

When twilight did my *Graunie* summon,
To say her pray'rs, douse, honest woman!
Aft 'yont the dyke she's heard you bumman,
           Wi' eerie drone;
Or, rustling, thro' the boortries coman,
           Wi' heavy groan.

Ae dreary, windy, winter night,
The stars shot down wi' sklentan light,
Wi' you, *mysel*, I gat a fright,
           Ayont the lough;   40
Ye, like a *rash-buss*, stood in sight,
           Wi' waving sugh.

The cudgel in my nieve did shake,
Each bristl'd hair stood like a stake,
When wi' an eldritch, stoor *quaick, quaick*,
           Amang the springs,
Awa ye squatter'd like a *drake*,
           On whistling wings.

Let *Warlocks* grim, an' wither'd *Hags*,°
Tell how wi' you on ragweed nags,   50
They skim the muirs an' dizzy crags,

Wi' wicked speed;
And in kirk-yards renew their leagues,
        Owre howcket dead.

Thence, countra wives, wi' toil an' pain,
May plunge an' plunge the *kirn* in vain;
For Oh! the yellow treasure's taen
        By witching skill;
An' dawtet, twal-pint *Hawkie's* gane
        As yell's the Bill.   60

Thence, mystic knots mak great abuse,
On *Young-Guidmen*, fond, keen an' croose;
When the best *wark-lume* i' the house,
        By cantraip wit,
Is instant made no worth a louse,
        Just at the bit.

When thowes dissolve the snawy hoord,
An' float the jinglan icy boord,
Then, *Water-kelpies* haunt the foord,
        By your direction,   70
An' nighted Trav'llers are allur'd
        To their destruction.

An' aft your moss-traversing *Spunkies*
Decoy the wight that late an' drunk is:
The bleezan, curst, mischievous monkies
        Delude his eyes,
Till in some miry slough he sunk is,
        Ne'er mair to rise.

When MASONS' mystic *word* an' *grip*,°
In storms an' tempests raise you up,   80
Some cock or cat, your rage maun stop,
        Or, strange to tell!
The *youngest Brother* ye wad whip
        Aff straught to *H–ll*.

Lang syne in EDEN'S bonie yard,
When youthfu' lovers first were pair'd,

An' all the Soul of Love they shar'd,
          The raptur'd hour,
Sweet on the fragrant, flow'ry swaird,
          In shady bow'r.   90

Then you, ye auld, snick-drawing dog!
Ye cam to Paradise incog,
An' play'd on man a cursed brogue,
          (Black be your fa'!)
An' gied the infant warld a shog,
          'Maist ruin'd a'.

D'ye mind that day, when in a bizz,
Wi' reeket duds, an' reestet gizz,
Ye did present your smoutie phiz,
          'Mang better folk,   100
An' sklented on the *man of Uzz*,°
          Your spitefu' joke?

An' how ye gat him i' your thrall,
An' brak him out o' house an' hal',
While scabs an' botches did him gall,
          Wi' bitter claw,
An' lows'd his ill-tongu'd, wicked *Scawl*
          Was worst ava?

But a' your doings to rehearse,
Your wily snares an' fechtin fierce,
Sin' that day MICHAEL[1] did you pierce,°   110
          Down to this time,
Wad ding a *Lallan* tongue, or *Erse*,°
          In Prose or Rhyme.

An' now, auld *Cloots*, I ken ye're thinkan,
A certain *Bardie's* rantin, drinkin,
Some luckless hour will send him linkan,
          To your black pit;
But faith! he'll turn a corner jinkan,
          An' cheat you yet.   120

          [1] Vide Milton, Book 6th.

But fare-you-weel, auld *Nickie-ben*!
O wad ye tak a thought an' men'!
Ye aiblins might—I dinna ken—
      Still hae a *stake*—
I'm wae to think upo' yon den,
      Ev'n for your sake!

THE DEATH AND DYING WORDS OF POOR MAILIE,
THE AUTHOR'S ONLY PET YOWE.
AN UNCO MOURNFU' TALE

AS MAILIE, an' her lambs thegither,
Was ae day nibbling on the tether,
Upon her cloot she coost a hitch,
An' owre she warsl'd in the ditch:
There, groaning, dying, she did ly,
When *Hughoc*[1] he cam doytan by.

    Wi' glowrin een, an' lifted han's,
Poor *Hughoc* like a statue stan's;
He saw her days were near hand ended,
But, waes my heart! he could na mend it!   10
He gaped wide, but naething spak,
At length poor *Mailie* silence brak.

'O thou, whase lamentable face
Appears to mourn my woefu' case!
My *dying words* attentive hear,
An' bear them to my *Master* dear.

    Tell him, if e'er again he keep
As muckle gear as buy a *sheep*,
O, bid him never tye them mair,
Wi' wicked strings o' hemp or hair!°   20
But ca them out to park or hill,
An' let them wander at their will:
So, may his flock increase an' grow
To *scores* o' lambs, an' *packs* of woo'!°

            [1] A neibor herd-callan.

Tell him, he was a Master kin',
An' ay was guid to me an' mine;
An' now my *dying* charge I gie him,°
My helpless *lambs*, I trust them wi' him.

O, bid him save their harmless lives,
Frae dogs an' tods, an' butchers' knives!   30
But gie them guid *cow-milk* their fill,
Till they be fit to fend themsel;
An' tent them duely, e'en an' morn,
Wi' taets o' *hay* an' ripps o' *corn*.

An' may they never learn the gaets,
Of ither vile, wanrestfu' *Pets!*
To slink thro' slaps, an' reave an' steal,
At stacks o' pease, or stocks o' kail.
So may they, like their great *forbears*,
For monie a year come thro' the sheers: 40
So *wives* will gie them bits o' bread,
An' *bairns* greet for them when they're dead.

My poor *toop-lamb*, my son an' heir,
O, bid him breed him up wi' care!
An' if he live to be a beast,
To pit some havins in his breast!
An' warn him ay at ridin time,°
To stay content wi' *yowes* at hame;
An' no to rin an' wear his cloots,
Like ither menseless, graceless brutes.   50

An' niest my *yowie*, silly thing,
Gude keep thee frae a *tether string!*
O, may thou ne'er forgather up,
Wi' onie blastet, moorlan *toop*;
But ay keep mind to moop an' mell,
Wi' sheep o' credit like thysel!

And now, *my bairns*, wi' my last breath,
I lea'e my blessin wi' you baith:
An' when ye think upo' your Mither,
Mind to be kind to ane anither.   60

Now, honest Hughoc, dinna fail,
To tell my Master a' my tale;
An' bid him burn this cursed *tether*,
An' for thy pains thou'se get my blather.'°

This said, poor *Mailie* turn'd her head,
An' clos'd her een amang the dead!

POOR MAILIE'S ELEGY

LAMENT in rhyme, lament in prose,
Wi' saut tears trickling down your nose;
Our *Bardie's* fate is at a close,
    Past a' remead!
The last, sad cape-stane of his woes;
    Poor Mailie's dead!

It's no the loss o' warl's gear,
That could sae bitter draw the tear,
Or make our *Bardie*, dowie, wear
    The mourning weed: 10
He's lost a friend and neebor dear,
    In *Mailie* dead.

Thro' a' the town she trotted by him;
A lang half-mile she could descry him;
Wi' kindly bleat, when she did spy him,
    She ran wi' speed:
A friend mair faithfu' ne'er came nigh him,
    Than *Mailie* dead.

I wat she was a *sheep* o' sense,
An' could behave hersel wi' mense: 20
I'll say't, she never brak a fence,
    Thro' thievish greed.
Our *Bardie*, lanely, keeps the spence
    Sin' *Mailie's* dead.

Or, if he wanders up the howe,
Her living image in *her yowe*,

Comes bleating till him, owre the knowe,
      For bits o' bread;
An' down the briny pearls rowe
      For *Mailie* dead.   30

She was nae get o' moorlan tips,
Wi' tauted ket, an' hairy hips;
For her forbears were brought in ships,
      Frae 'yont the TWEED:°
A bonier *fleesh* ne'er cross'd the clips
      Than *Mailie's* dead.

Wae worth that man wha first did shape,
That vile, wanchancie thing—*a raep!*
It maks guid fellows girn an' gape,
      Wi' chokin dread;   40
An' *Robin's* bonnet wave wi' crape
      For *Mailie* dead.

O, a' ye *Bards* on bonie DOON!°
An' wha on AIRE your chanters tune!°
Come, join the melancholious croon
      O' *Robin's* reed!
His heart will never get aboon!
      His *Mailie's* dead!

TO J. S****

Friendship, mysterious cement of the soul!
Sweet'ner of Life, and solder of Society!
I owe thee much—

                 BLAIR.°

DEAR S****, the sleest, pawkie thief,
That e'er attempted stealth or rief,
Ye surely hae some warlock-breef
      Owre human hearts;
For ne'er a bosom yet was prief
      Against your arts.

For me, I swear by sun an' moon,
And ev'ry star that blinks aboon,
Ye've cost me twenty pair o' shoon
          Just gaun to see you;   10
And ev'ry ither pair that's done,
          Mair taen I'm wi' you.

That auld, capricious carlin, *Nature*,
To mak amends for scrimpet stature,
She's turn'd you off, a human-creature
          On her *first* plan,
And in her freaks, on ev'ry feature,
          She's wrote, *the Man*.

Just now I've taen the fit o' rhyme,°
My barmie noddle's working prime,   20
My fancy yerket up sublime
          Wi' hasty summon:
Hae ye a leisure-moment's time
          To hear what's comin?

Some rhyme a neebor's name to lash;
Some rhyme, (vain thought!) for needfu' cash;
Some rhyme to court the countra clash,
          An' raise a din;
For me, an *aim* I never fash;
          I rhyme for *fun*.   30

The star that rules my luckless lot,
Has fated me the russet coat,°
An' damn'd my fortune to the groat;°
          But, in requit,
Has blest me with a *random-shot*
          O' countra wit.

This while my notion's taen a sklent,
To try my fate in guid, black *prent*;°
But still the mair I'm that way bent,
          Something cries, 'Hoolie!   40
'I red you, honest man, tak tent!
          'Ye'll shaw your folly.

'There's ither Poets, much your betters,
'Far seen in *Greek*, deep men o' *letters*,
'Hae thought they had ensur'd their debtors,
          'A' future ages;
'Now moths deform in shapeless tatters,
                    'Their unknown pages.'

Then farewel hopes of Laurel-boughs,
To garland my poetic brows!   50
Henceforth, I'll rove where busy ploughs
          Are whistling thrang,
An' teach the lanely heights an' howes
                    My rustic sang.

I'll wander on with tentless heed,
How never-halting moments speed,
Till fate shall snap the brittle thread;
          Then, all unknown,
I'll lay me with th' *inglorious dead*,°
                    Forgot and gone!   60

But why, o' Death, begin a tale?
Just now we're living sound an' hale;
Then top and maintop croud the sail,
          Heave *Care* o'er-side!
And large, before Enjoyment's gale,
                    Let's tak the tide.

This life, sae far's I understand,
Is a' enchanted fairy-land,
Where Pleasure is the Magic-wand,
          That, wielded right,   70
Maks Hours like Minutes, hand in hand,
                    Dance by fu' light.

The *magic-wand* then let us wield;
For, ance that five an' forty's speel'd,
See, crazy, weary, joyless Eild,
          Wi' wrinkl'd face,
Comes hostan, hirplan owre the field,
                    Wi' creeping pace.

When ance *life's day* draws near the gloamin,
Then fareweel vacant, careless roamin;   80
An' fareweel cheerfu' tankards foamin,
          An' social noise;
An' fareweel dear, deluding woman,
          The joy of joys!

O *Life!* how pleasant in thy morning,
Young Fancy's rays the hills adorning!
Cold-pausing Caution's lesson scorning,
          We frisk away,
Like school-boys, at th' expected warning,
          To joy and play.   90

We wander there, we wander here,
We eye the *rose* upon the brier,
Unmindful that the *thorn* is near,
          Among the leaves;
And tho' the puny wound appear,
          Short while it grieves.

Some, lucky, find a flow'ry spot,
For which they never toil'd nor swat;
They drink the *sweet* and eat the *fat*,
          But care or pain;   100
And haply, eye the barren hut,
          With high disdain.°

With steady aim, some Fortune chase;
Keen hope does ev'ry sinew brace;
Thro' fair, thro' foul, they urge the race,
          And sieze the prey:
Then canie, in some cozie place,
          They close the *day*.

And others, like your humble servan',
Poor wights! nae rules nor roads observin;   110
To right or left, eternal swervin,
          They zig-zag on;
Till curst with Age, obscure an' starvin,
          They aften groan.

Alas! what bitter toil an' straining—
But truce with peevish, poor complaining!
Is Fortune's fickle *Luna* waning?°
        E'en let her gang!
Beneath what light she has remaining,
        Let's sing our Sang.   120

My pen I here fling to the door,
And kneel, ye *Pow'rs*, and warm implore,°
'Tho' I should wander *Terra* o'er,
        'In all her climes,
'Grant me but this, I ask no more,
        'Ay rowth o' rhymes.

'Gie dreeping roasts to *countra Lairds*,
'Till icicles hing frae their beards;
'Gie fine braw claes to fine *Life-guards*,
        'And *Maids of Honor*;   130
'And yill an' whisky gie to *Cairds*,
        'Until they sconner.

'A *Title*, DEMPSTER merits it;°
'A *Garter* gie to WILLIE PIT;°
'Gie Wealth to some be-ledger'd Cit,°
        'In cent per cent;
'But give me real, sterling Wit,
        'And I'm content.

'While ye are pleas'd to keep me hale,
'I'll sit down o'er my scanty meal,   140
'Be't *water-brose*, or *muslin-kail*,
        'Wi' cheerfu' face,
'As lang's the Muses dinna fail
        'To say the grace.'

An anxious e'e I never throws
Behint my lug, or by my nose;
I jouk beneath Misfortune's blows
        As weel's I may;
Sworn foe to *sorrow*, *care*, and *prose*,
        I rhyme away.   150

O ye, douse folk, that live by rule,
Grave, tideless-blooded, calm and cool,
Compar'd wi' you—O fool! fool! fool!
⠀⠀⠀⠀⠀⠀How much unlike!
Your hearts are just a standing pool,
⠀⠀⠀⠀⠀⠀Your lives, a dyke!

⠀⠀⠀Nae hare-brain'd, sentimental traces,°
In your unletter'd, nameless faces!
In *arioso* trills and graces°
⠀⠀⠀⠀⠀⠀Ye never stray,⠀⠀⠀⠀⠀⠀⠀⠀⠀160
But *gravissimo*, solemn basses°
⠀⠀⠀⠀⠀⠀Ye hum away.

⠀⠀⠀Ye are sae *grave*, nae doubt ye're *wise*;
Nae ferly tho' ye do despise
The hairum-scairum, ram-stam boys,°
⠀⠀⠀⠀⠀⠀The rambling squad:°
I see ye upward cast your eyes—
⠀⠀⠀⠀⠀⠀—Ye ken the road—

⠀⠀⠀Whilst I—but I shall haud me there—
Wi' you I'll scarce gang *ony where*—⠀⠀⠀⠀⠀170
Then *Jamie*, I shall say nae mair,
⠀⠀⠀⠀⠀⠀But quat my sang,
Content *with* YOU to mak a *pair*,
⠀⠀⠀⠀⠀⠀Whare'er I gang.

A DREAM

Thoughts, words and deeds, the Statute blames with reason;
But surely Dreams *were ne'er indicted Treason.*

ON READING, IN THE PUBLIC PAPERS, THE LAUREATE'S
ODE, WITH THE OTHER PARADE OF JUNE 4th, 1786, THE
AUTHOR WAS NO SOONER DROPT ASLEEP, THAN HE
IMAGINED HIMSELF TRANSPORTED TO THE BIRTH-DAY
LEVEE; AND, IN HIS DREAMING FANCY, MADE THE
FOLLOWING ADDRESS.

I

GUID-MORNIN to your MAJESTY!
  May heaven augment your blisses,
On ev'ry new *Birth-day* ye see,
  A humble Bardie wishes!°
My Bardship here, at your Levee,
  On sic a day as this is,
Is sure an uncouth sight to see,
  Amang thae Birth-day dresses
              Sae fine this day.

II

I see ye're complimented thrang,   10
  By many a *lord* an' *lady*;
'God save the King' 's a cukoo sang
  That's unco easy said ay:
The *Poets* too, a venal gang,
  Wi' rhymes weel-turn'd an' ready,
Wad gar you trow ye ne'er do wrang,
  But ay unerring steady,
              On sic a day.

III

For me! before a Monarch's face,
  Ev'n *there* I winna flatter;   20
For neither Pension, Post, nor Place,
  Am I your humble debtor:
So, nae reflection on YOUR GRACE,°
  Your Kingship to bespatter;
There's monie *waur* been o' the Race,
  And aiblins *ane* been better°
            Than You this day.

IV

'Tis very true, my sovereign King,
  My skill may weel be doubted;
But *Facts* are cheels that winna ding,   30
  An' downa be disputed:
Your *royal nest*, beneath *Your* wing,
  Is e'en right reft an' clouted,

And now the third part o' the string,
   An' less, will gang about it°
            Than did ae day.

V

Far be't frae me that I aspire
   To blame your Legislation,
Or say, ye wisdom want, or fire,
   To rule this mighty nation;   40
But faith! I muckle doubt, my SIRE,
   Ye've trusted 'Ministration,
To chaps, wha, in a *barn* or *byre*,
   Wad better fill'd their station
            Than *courts* yon day.

VI

And now Ye've gien auld *Britain* peace,
   Her broken shins to plaister;
Your sair taxation does her fleece,
   Till she has scarce a tester:
For me, thank God, my life's a *lease*,   50
   Nae *bargain* wearing faster,
Or faith! I fear, that, wi' the geese,
   I shortly boost to pasture
            I' the craft some day.°

VII

I'm no mistrusting *Willie Pit*,
   When taxes he enlarges,
(An' *Will's* a true guid fallow's get,°
   A Name not Envy spairges)
That he intends to pay your *debt*,°
   An' lessen a' your *charges*;   60
But, G—d-sake! let nae *saving-fit*
   Abridge your bonie *Barges*
            An' *Boats* this day.

VIII

Adieu, my LIEGE! may Freedom geck
   Beneath your high protection;
An' may Ye rax Corruption's neck,

And gie her for dissection!°
But since I'm here, I'll no neglect,
  In loyal, true affection,
To pay your QUEEN, with due respect,°   70
  My fealty an' subjection
          This great Birth-day.

IX

Hail, *Majesty most Excellent!*
  While Nobles strive to please Ye,
Will Ye accept a Compliment,
  A simple Bardie gies Ye?
Thae bonie Bairntime, Heav'n has lent,°
  Still higher may they heeze Ye
In bliss, till Fate some day is sent,
  For ever to release Ye   80
          Frae Care that day.

X

For you, young Potentate o' W—,°
  I tell your *Highness* fairly,
Down Pleasure's stream, wi' swelling sails,
  I'm tauld ye're driving rarely;
But some day ye may gnaw your nails,
  An' curse your folly sairly,
That e'er ye brak Diana's *pales*,°
  Or rattl'd dice wi' *Charlie*°
          By night or day.   90

XI

Yet aft a ragged *Cowte's* been known,
  To mak a noble *Aiver*;
So, ye may dousely fill a Throne,
  For a' their clish-ma-claver:
There, Him at *Agincourt* wha shone,
  Few better were or braver;
And yet, wi' funny, queer *Sir John*,[1]
  He was an unco shaver
          For monie a day.

---

[1] Sir John Falstaff, Vide Shakespeare.

XII

For you, right rev'rend O——,°   100
   Nane sets the *lawn-sleeve* sweeter,°
Altho' a ribban at your lug°
   Wad been a dress compleater:
As ye disown yon paughty dog,
   That *bears* the Keys of Peter,°
Then swith! an' get a *wife* to hug,
   Or trouth! ye'll stain the *Mitre*
           Some luckless day.

XIII

Young, royal TARRY-BREEKS,° I learn,
   Ye've lately come athwart her;   110
A glorious *Galley*,[1] stem and stern,
   Weel rigg'd for *Venus barter*;
But first hang out that she'll discern°
   Your *hymeneal Charter*,
Then heave aboard your *grapple airn*,
   An', large upon her *quarter*,
           Come full that day.

XIV

Ye lastly, bonie blossoms a',
   Ye *royal Lasses* dainty,°
Heav'n mak you guid as weel as braw,   120
   An' gie you *lads* a plenty:
But sneer na *British-boys* awa;
   For King's are unco scant ay,
An' German-Gentles are but *sma'*,°
   They're better just than *want ay*
           On onie day.

XV

God bless you a'! consider now,
   Ye're unco muckle dautet;
But ere the *course* o' life be through,
   It may be bitter sautet: 130

---

[1] Alluding to the Newspaper account of a certain royal Sailor's Amour.

An' I hae seen their *coggie* fou,
   That yet hae tarrow't at it,
But or the *day* was done, I trow,
   The laggen they hae clautet
             Fu' clean that day.

THE VISION

DUAN FIRST[1]

THE sun had clos'd the *winter-day*,
The Curlers quat their roaring play,°
And hunger'd Maukin taen her way
         To kail-yards green,°
While faithless snaws ilk step betray
         Whare she has been.

   The Thresher's weary *flingin-tree*,
The lee-lang day had tir'd me;
And when the Day had clos'd his e'e,
         Far i' the West,   10
Ben i' the *Spence*, right pensivelie,
         I gaed to rest.

   There, lanely, by the ingle-cheek,
I sat and ey'd the spewing reek,
That fill'd, wi' hoast-provoking smeek,
         The auld, clay biggin;°
And heard the restless rattons squeak
         About the riggin.

   All in this mottie, misty clime,
I backward mus'd on wasted time,   20
How I had spent my *youthfu' prime*,
         An' done nae-thing,
But stringing blethers up in rhyme
         For fools to sing.

---

[1] Duan, a term of Ossian's for the different divisions of a digressive Poem. See his Cath-Loda, Vol. 2 of McPherson's Translation.

Had I to guid advice but harket,
I might, by this, hae led a market,
Or strutted in a Bank and clarket
      My *Cash-Account*;
While here, half-mad, half-fed, half-sarket,
      Is a' th' amount.   30

I started, mutt'ring blockhead! coof!
And heav'd on high my wauket loof,
To swear by a' yon starry roof,
      Or some rash aith,
That I, henceforth, would be *rhyme-proof*
      Till my last breath—

When click! the *string* the *snick* did draw;°
And jee! the door gaed to the wa';
And by my ingle-lowe I saw,
      Now bleezan bright,   40
A tight, outlandish *Hizzie*, braw,
      Come full in sight.

Ye need na doubt, I held my whisht;
The infant aith, half-form'd, was crusht;
I glowr'd as eerie's I'd been dusht,
      In some wild glen;
When sweet, like *modest Worth*, she blusht,
      And stepped ben.

Green, slender, leaf-clad *Holly-boughs*°
Were twisted, gracefu', round her brows,   50
I took her for some SCOTTISH MUSE,
      By that same token;
And come to stop those reckless vows,
      Would soon been broken.

A 'hare-brain'd, sentimental trace'°
Was strongly marked in her face;
A wildly-witty, rustic grace
      Shone full upon her;
Her *eye*, ev'n turn'd on empty space,
      Beam'd keen with *Honor*.   60

Down flow'd her robe, a *tartan* sheen,°
Till half a leg was scrimply seen;
And such a *leg!* my BESS, I ween,°
      Could only peer it;
Sae straught, sae taper, tight and clean,
      Nane else came near it.

Her *Mantle* large, of greenish hue,
My gazing wonder chiefly drew;
Deep *lights* and *shades*, bold-mingling, threw
      A lustre grand;   70
And seem'd, to my astonish'd view,
      A *well-known* Land.

Here, rivers in the sea were lost;
There, mountains to the skies were tost:
Here, tumbling billows mark'd the coast,
      With surging foam;
There, distant shone, *Art's* lofty boast,
      The lordly dome.

Here, DOON pour'd down his far-fetch'd floods;
There, well-fed IRWINE stately thuds:°   80
Auld, hermit AIRE staw thro' his woods,°
      On to the shore;
And many a lesser torrent scuds,
      With seeming roar.

Low, in a sandy valley spread,
An ancient BOROUGH rear'd her head;°
Still, as in *Scottish Story* read,
      She boasts a *Race,*
To ev'ry nobler virtue bred,
      And polish'd grace.°   90

DUAN SECOND

With musing-deep, astonish'd stare,
I view'd the heavenly-seeming *Fair*;
A whisp'ring *throb* did witness bear
      Of kindred sweet,
When with an elder Sister's air
      She did me greet.

'All hail! *my own* inspired Bard!
'In me thy native Muse regard!
'Nor longer mourn thy fate is hard,
                    'Thus poorly low!   100
'I come to give thee such *reward*,
                    'As *we* bestow.

'Know, the great *Genius* of this Land,
'Has many a light, aerial band,°
'Who, all beneath his high command,
                    'Harmoniously,
'As *Arts* or *Arms* they understand,
                    'Their labors ply.

'They SCOTIA'S Race among them share;
'Some fire the *Sodger* on to dare;   110
'Some rouse the *Patriot* up to bare°
                    'Corruption's heart:
'Some teach the *Bard*, a darling care,
                    'The tuneful Art.

''Mong swelling floods of reeking gore,
'They ardent, kindling spirits pour;
'Or, mid the venal Senate's roar,
                    'They, sightless, stand,
'To mend the honest *Patriot-lore*,
                    'And grace the hand.°   120

'Hence, FULLARTON, the brave and young;°
'Hence, DEMPSTER'S truth-prevailing tongue;°
'Hence, sweet harmonious BEATTIE sung
                    'His "Minstrel lays;"°
'Or tore, with noble ardour stung,
                    'The *Sceptic's* bays.°

'To lower Orders are assign'd,
'The humbler ranks of Human-kind,
'The rustic Bard, the lab'ring Hind,°
                    'The Artisan;   130
'All chuse, as various they're inclin'd,
                    'The various man.

'When yellow waves the heavy grain,
'The threat'ning *Storm*, some, strongly, rein;
'Some teach to meliorate the plain,
          'With *tillage-skill*;°
'And some instruct the Shepherd-train,
          'Blythe o'er the hill.

'Some hint the Lover's harmless wile;
'Some grace the Maiden's artless smile;   140
'Some soothe the Lab'rer's weary toil,
          'For humble gains,
'And make his *cottage-scenes* beguile
          'His cares and pains.

'Some, bounded to a district-space,
'Explore at large Man's *infant race*,
'To mark the embryotic trace,
          'Of *rustic Bard*;
'And careful note each op'ning grace,
          'A guide and guard.   150

'*Of these am I*—COILA my name;°
'And this district as mine I claim,
'Where once the *Campbell's*, chiefs of fame,°
          'Held ruling pow'r:
'I mark'd thy embryo-tuneful flame,
          'Thy natal hour.

'With future hope, I oft would gaze,
'Fond, on thy little, early ways,
'Thy rudely-caroll'd, chiming phrase,
          'In uncouth rhymes,   160
'Fir'd at the simple, artless lays
          'Of other times.

'I saw thee seek the sounding shore,
'Delighted with the dashing roar;
'Or when the *North* his fleecy store
          'Drove thro' the sky,
'I saw grim Nature's visage hoar,
          'Struck thy young eye.

'Or when the deep-green-mantl'd Earth,
'Warm-cherish'd ev'ry floweret's birth,   170
'And joy and music pouring forth,
          'In ev'ry grove,
'I saw thee eye the gen'ral mirth
          'With boundless love.

'When ripen'd fields, and azure skies,
'Call'd forth the *Reaper's* rustling noise,
'I saw thee leave their ev'ning joys,
          'And lonely stalk,
'To vent thy bosom's swelling rise,
          'In pensive walk.   180

'When *youthful Love*, warm-blushing, strong,
'Keen-shivering shot thy nerves along,
'Those accents, grateful to thy tongue,
          'Th' adored *Name*,
'I taught thee how to pour in song,
          'To soothe thy flame.

'I saw thy pulse's maddening play,
'Wild-send thee Pleasure's devious way,
'Misled by Fancy's *meteor-ray*,
          'By Passion driven;   190
'But yet the *light* that led astray,
          'Was *light* from Heaven.

'I taught thy manners-painting strains,
'The *loves*, the *ways* of simple swains,
'Till now, o'er all my wide domains,
          'Thy fame extends;
'And some, the pride of *Coila's* plains,
          'Become thy friends.

'Thou canst not learn, nor I can show,
'To paint with *Thomson's* landscape-glow;°   200
'Or wake the bosom-melting throe,
          'With *Shenstone's* art;°
'Or pour, with *Gray*, the moving flow,°
          'Warm on the heart.

'Yet all beneath th'unrivall'd Rose,
'The lowly Daisy sweetly blows;
'Tho' large the forest's Monarch throws
　　　　'His army shade,
'Yet green the juicy Hawthorn grows,
　　　　'Adown the glade.　　　　　　　210

'Then never murmur nor repine;
'Strive in thy *humble sphere* to shine;
'And trust me, not *Potosi's mine*,°
　　　　'Nor *Kings regard*,
'Can give a bliss o'ermatching thine,
　　　　'A *rustic Bard*.

'To give my counsels all in one,
'Thy *tuneful flame* still careful fan;
'Preserve *the dignity of Man*,
　　　　'With Soul erect;　　　　　　　220
'And trust, the UNIVERSAL PLAN
　　　　'Will all protect.

'*And wear thou this*'—She solemn said,
And bound the *Holly* round my head:
The polish'd leaves, and berries red,
　　　　Did rustling play;
And, like a passing thought, she fled,
　　　　In light away.

THE following POEM will, by many Readers, be well
enough understood; but, for the sake of those who are unac-
quainted with the manners and traditions of the country
where the scene is cast, Notes are added, to give some account
of the principal Charms and Spells of that Night, so big with
Prophecy to the Peasantry in the West of Scotland. The pas-
sion of prying into Futurity makes a striking part of the his-
tory of Human-nature, in it's rude state, in all ages and nations;
and it may be some entertainment to a philosophic mind, if
any such should honor the Author with a perusal, to see the
remains of it, among the more unenlightened in our own.

HALLOWEEN[1]

Yes! let the Rich deride, the Proud disdain,
The simple pleasures of the lowly train;
To me more dear, congenial to my heart,
One native charm, than all the gloss of art.

GOLDSMITH.°

I

UPON that *night*, when Fairies light,
  On *Cassilis Downans*[2] dance,°
Or owre the lays, in splendid blaze,
  On sprightly coursers prance;
Or for *Colean*,° the rout is taen,
  Beneath the moon's pale beams;
There, up the *Cove*,[3] to stray an' rove,
  Amang the rocks an' streams
            To sport that night.

II

Amang the bonie, winding banks,   10
  Where *Doon* rins, wimplin, clear,
Where BRUCE[4] ance rul'd the martial ranks,°
  An' shook his *Carrick* spear,
Some merry, friendly, countra folks,
  Together did convene,
To *burn* their nits, an' *pou* their stocks,
  An' haud their *Halloween*
            Fu' blythe that night.

[1] Is thought to be a night when Witches, Devils, and other mischief-making beings, are all abroad on their baneful, midnight errands: particularly, those aerial people, the Fairies, are said, on that night, to hold a grand Anniversary.

[2] Certain little, romantic, rocky, green hills, in the neighbourhood of the ancient seat of the Earls of Cassilis.

[3] A noted cavern near Colean-house, called the Cove of Colean; which, as well as Cassilis Downans, is famed, in country story, for being a favourite haunt of Fairies.

[4] The famous family of that name, the ancestors of ROBERT the great Deliverer of his country, were Earls of Carrick.

III

The lasses feat, an' cleanly neat,
    Mair braw than when they're fine;°   20
Their faces blythe, fu' sweetly kythe,
    Hearts leal, an' warm, an' kin':
The lads sae trig, wi' wooer-babs,
    Weel knotted on their garten,
Some unco blate, an' some wi' gabs,
    Gar lasses hearts gang startin
                  Whyles fast at night.

IV

Then, first an' foremost, thro' the kail,
    Their *stocks*[1] maun a' be sought ance;
They steek their een, an' grape an' wale,   30
    For muckle anes, an' straught anes.
Poor hav'rel *Will* fell aff the drift,°
    An' wander'd thro' the *Bow-kail*,
An' pow't, for want o' better shift,
    A *runt* was like a sow-tail
                  Sae bow't that night.

V

Then, straught or crooked, yird or nane,
    They roar an' cry a' throw'ther;
The vera *wee-things*, toddlan, rin,
    Wi' stocks out owre their shouther:
An' gif the *custock's* sweet or sour,   40
    Wi' joctelegs they taste them;
Syne coziely, aboon the door,
    Wi' cannie care, they've plac'd them
                  To lye that night.

[1] The first ceremony of Halloween, is, pulling each a *Stock*, or plant of kail. They must go out, hand in hand, with eyes shut, and pull the first they meet with: its being big or little, straight or crooked, is prophetic of the size and shape of the grand object of all their Spells—the husband or wife. If any *yird*, or earth, stick to the root, that is *tocher*, or fortune; and the taste of the *custoc*, that is, the heart of the stem, is indicative of the natural temper and disposition. Lastly, the stems, or to give them their ordinary appellation, the *runts*, are placed somewhere above the head of the door; and the christian names of the people whom chance brings into the house, are, according to the priority of placing the *runts*, the names in question.

VI

The lasses staw frae 'mang them a',
    To pou their *stalks o' corn*;[1]
But *Rab* slips out, an' jinks about,
    Behint the muckle thorn:
He grippet *Nelly* hard an' fast;   50
    Loud skirl'd a' the lasses;
But her *tap-pickle* maist was lost,
    When kiutlan in the *Fause-house*[2]
            Wi' him that night.

VII

The auld Guidwife's weel-hoordet *nits*[3]
    Are round an' round divided,
An' monie lads an' lasses fates
    Are there that night decided:
Some kindle, couthie, side by side,
    An' *burn* thegither trimly;   60
Some start awa, wi' saucy pride,
    An' jump out owre the chimlie
            Fu' high that night.

VIII

Jean slips in twa, wi' tentie e'e;
    Wha 'twas, she wadna tell;
But this is *Jock*, an' this is *me*,
    She says in to hersel:
He bleez'd owre her, an' she owre him,
    As they wad never mair part,
Till fuff! he started up the lum,
    An' *Jean* had e'en a sair heart   70
            To see't that night.

[1] They go to the barn-yard, and pull each, at three several times, a stalk of Oats. If the third stalk wants the *top-pickle*, that is, the grain at the top of the stalk, the party in question will want the Maidenhead.

[2] When the corn is in a doubtful state, by being too green, or wet, the Stack-builder, by means of old timber, &c. makes a large apartment in his stack, with an opening in the side which is fairest exposed to the wind: this he calls a *Fause-house*.

[3] Burning the nuts is a favourite charm. They name the lad and lass to each particular nut, as they lay them in the fire; and according as they burn quietly together, or start from beside one another, the course and issue of the Courtship will be.

IX

Poor Willie, wi' his *bow-kail runt*,
   Was *brunt* wi' primsie *Mallie*;
An' *Mary*, nae doubt, took the drunt,
   To be compar'd to *Willie*:
Mall's nit lap out, wi' pridefu' fling,
   An' her ain fit, it brunt it;
While *Willie* lap, and swore by *jing*,
   'Twas just the way he wanted   80
           To be that night.

X

Nell had the *Fause-house* in her min',
   She pits hersel an' *Rob* in;
In loving bleeze they sweetly join,
   Till white in ase they're sobbin:
Nell's heart was dancin at the view;
   She whisper'd *Rob* to leuk for't:
Rob, stownlins, prie'd her bonie mou,
   Fu' cozie in the neuk for't,
           Unseen that night.   90

XI

But *Merran* sat behint their backs,
   Her thoughts on *Andrew Bell*;
She lea'es them gashan at their cracks,
   An' slips out by hersel:
She thro' the yard the nearest taks,
   An' for the *kiln* she goes then,°
An' darklins grapet for the *bauks*,
   And in the *blue-clue*[1] throws then,
           Right fear't that night.

---

[1] Whoever would, with success, try this spell, must strictly observe these directions. Steal out, all alone, to the *kiln*, and, darkling, throw into the *pot*, a clew of blue yarn; wind it in a new clew off the old one; and towards the latter end, something will hold the thread: demand, *wha hauds?* i.e. who holds? and answer will be returned from the kiln-pot, by naming the christian and sirname of your future Spouse.

XII

An' ay she *win't*, an' ay she swat,   100
   I wat she made nae jaukin;
Till something *held* within the *pat*,
   Good L——d! but she was quaukin!
But whether 'twas the *Deil* himsel,
   Or whether 'twas a *bauk-en'*,
Or whether it was *Andrew Bell*,
   She did na wait on talkin
           To spier that night.

XIII

Wee *Jenny* to her Graunie says,
   'Will ye go wi' me Graunie?   110
'I'll *eat the apple*[1] at the *glass*,
   'I gat frae uncle Johnie:'
She fuff't her pipe wi' sic a lunt,
   In wrath she was sae vap'rin,
She notic't na, an aizle brunt
   Her braw, new, worset apron
           Out thro' that night.

XIV

'Ye little Skelpie-limmer's-face!
   'I daur you try sic sportin,
'As seek the *foul Thief* onie place,   120
   'For him to spae your fortune:
'Nae doubt but ye may get a *sight!*
   'Great cause ye hae to fear it;
'For monie a ane has gotten a fright,
   'An' liv'd an' di'd deleeret,
           'On sic a night.

XV

'Ae Hairst afore the *Sherra-moor*,°
   'I mind't as weel's yestreen,

---

[1] Take a candle, and go, alone, to a looking glass; eat an apple before it, and some traditions say you should comb your hair all the time: the face of your conjugal companion, *to be*, will be seen in the glass, as if peeping over your shoulder.

'I was a gilpey then, I'm sure,
  'I was na past fyfteen: 130
'The Simmer had been cauld an' wat,
  'An' *Stuff* was unco green;
'An' ay a rantan *Kirn* we gat,
  'An' just on *Halloween*
        'It fell that night.

XVI

'Our *Stibble-rig* was *Rab McGraen*,
  'A clever, sturdy fallow;
'His Sin gat *Eppie Sim* wi' wean,
  'That liv'd in Achmacalla:°
'He gat *hemp-seed*,[1] I mind it weel, 140
  'An' he made unco light o't;
'But monie a day was *by himsel*,
  'He was sae sairly frighted
        'That vera night.'

XVII

Then up gat fechtan *Jamie Fleck*,
  An' he swoor by his conscience,
That he could *saw hemp-seed* a peck;
  For it was a' but nonsense:
The auld guidman raught down the pock,
  An' out a handfu' gied him; 150
Syne bad him slip frae 'mang the folk,
  Sometime when nae ane see'd him,
        An' try't that night.

XVIII

He marches thro' amang the stacks,
  Tho' he was something sturtan;
The *graip* he for a *harrow* taks,

[1] Steal out, unperceived, and sow a handful of hemp seed; harrowing it with any thing you can conveniently draw after you. Repeat, now and then, 'Hemp-seed I saw thee, Hemp-seed I saw thee; and him (or her) that is to be my true-love, come after me and pou thee.' Look over your left shoulder, and you will see the appearance of the person invoked, in the attitude of pulling hemp. Some traditions say, 'come after me and shaw thee,' that is, show thyself; in which case it simply appears. Others omit the harrowing, and say, 'come after me and harrow thee.'

An' haurls at his curpan:
And ev'ry now an' then, he says,
  'Hemp-seed I saw thee,
'An' her that is to be my lass,   160
  'Come after me an' draw thee
         'As fast this night.'

XIX

He whistl'd up *lord Lenox' march*,°
  To keep his courage cheary;
Altho' his hair began to arch,
  He was sae fley'd an' eerie:
Till presently he hears a squeak,
  An' then a grane an' gruntle;
He by his showther gae a keek,
  An' tumbl'd wi' a wintle   170
        Out owre that night.

XX

He roar'd a horrid murder-shout,
  In dreadfu' desperation!
An' young an' auld come rinnan out,
  An' hear the sad narration:
He swoor 'twas hilchan *Jean McCraw*,
  Or crouchie *Merran Humphie*,
Till stop! she trotted thro' them a';
  An' wha was it but *Grumphie*
        Asteer that night?   180

XXI

Meg fain wad to the *Barn* gaen,
  To *winn three wechts o' naething*;[1]
But for to meet the Deil her lane,

---

[1] This charm must likewise be performed, unperceived and alone. You go to the *barn*, and open both doors; taking them off the hinges, if possible; for there is danger, that the Being, about to appear, may shut the doors, and do you some mischief. Then take that instrument used in winnowing the corn, which, in our country-dialect, we call a *wecht;* and go thro' all the attitudes of letting down corn against the wind. Repeat it three times; and the third time, an apparition will pass thro' the barn, in at the windy door, and out at the other, having both the figure in question and the appearance or retinue, marking the employment or station in life.

                    She pat but little faith in:
                 She gies the Herd a pickle nits,
                    An' twa red cheeket apples,
                 To watch, while for the *Barn* she sets,
                    In hopes to see *Tam Kipples*
                             That vera night.

                             XXII

                 She turns the key, wi' cannie thraw,   190
                    An' owre the threshold ventures;
                 But first on *Sawnie* gies a ca',
                    Syne bauldly in she enters:
                 A *ratton* rattl'd up the wa',
                    An' she cry'd, L——d preserve her!
                 An' ran thro' midden-hole an' a',
                    An' pray'd wi' zeal and fervour,
                             Fu' fast that night.

                             XXIII

                 They hoy't out Will, wi' sair advice;
                    They hecht him some fine braw ane;   200
                 It chanc'd the *Stack* he *faddom't thrice*,[1]°
                    Was timmer-propt for thrawin:°
                 He taks a swirlie, auld *moss-oak*,
                    For some black, grousome *Carlin;*
                 An' loot a winze, an' drew a stroke,
                    Till skin in blypes cam haurlin
                             Aff's nieves that night.

                             XXIV

                 A wanton widow *Leezie* was,
                    As cantie as a kittlen;
                 But Och! that night, amang the shaws,   210
                    She gat a fearfu' settlin!
                 She thro' the whins, an' by the cairn,
                    An' owre the hill gaed scrievin,

    ¹ Take an opportunity of going, unnoticed, to a *Bear-stack*, and fathom it three times
round. The last fathom of the last time, you will catch in your arms, the appearance of
your future conjugal yoke-fellow.

Whare *three Lairds' lan's met at a burn*,[1]
   To dip her *left sark-sleeve* in,
            Was bent that night.

XXV

Whyles owre a linn the burnie plays,
   As thro' the glen it wimpl't;
Whyles round a rocky scar it strays;
   Whyles in a wiel it dimpl't;   220
Whyles glitter'd to the nightly rays,
   Wi' bickerin, dancin dazzle;
Whyles cooket underneath the braes,
   Below the spreading hazle
            Unseen that night.

XXVI

Amang the brachens, on the brae,
   Between her an' the moon,
The Deil, or else an outler Quey,
   Gat up an' gae a croon:
Poor *Leezie's* heart maist lap the hool;   230
   Near lav'rock-height she jumpet,
But mist a fit, an' in the *pool*,
   Out owre the lugs she plumpet,
            Wi' a plunge that night.

XXVII

In order, on the clean hearth-stane,
   The *Luggies*[2] three are ranged;
And ev'ry time great care is taen,
   To see them duely changed:

[1] You go out, one or more, for this is a social spell, to a south-running spring or rivulet, where 'three Lairds' lands meet,' and dip your left shirt sleeve. Go to bed in sight of a fire, and hang your wet sleeve before it to dry. Ly awake; and sometime near midnight, an apparition, having the exact figure of the grand object in question, will come and turn the sleeve, as if to dry the other side of it.

[2] Take three dishes; put clean water in one, foul water in another, and leave the third empty: blindfold a person, and lead him to the hearth where the dishes are ranged; he (or she) dips the left hand: if by chance in the clean water, the future husband or wife will come to the bar of Matrimony, a Maid; if in the foul, a widow; if in the empty dish, it foretells, with equal certainty, no marriage at all. It is repeated three times; and every time the arrangement of the dishes is altered.

Auld, uncle *John*, wha *wedlock's joys*,
    Sin' *Mar's-year* did desire,°   240
Because he gat the toom dish thrice,
    He heav'd them on the fire,
                In wrath that night.

XXVIII

Wi' merry sangs, an' friendly cracks,
    I wat they did na weary;
And unco tales, an' funnie jokes,
    Their sports were cheap an' cheary:
Till *butter'd So'ns*,[1] wi' fragrant lunt,
    Set a' their gabs a steerin;
Syne, wi' a social glass o' strunt,   250
    They parted aff careerin
                Fu' blythe that night.

THE AULD FARMER'S NEW-YEAR-MORNING SALUTATION TO HIS AULD MARE, MAGGIE, ON GIVING HER THE ACCUSTOMED RIPP OF CORN TO HANSEL IN THE NEW-YEAR

A *Guid New-year* I wish you Maggie!
Hae, there's a ripp to thy auld baggie:
Tho' thou's howe-backet, now, an' knaggie,
            I've seen the day,
Thou could hae gaen like ony staggie
            Out owre the lay.

Tho' now thou's dowie, stiff an' crazy,
An' thy auld hide as white's a daisie,
I've seen thee dappl't, sleek an' glaizie,
            A bonie gray: 10
He should been tight that daur't to *raize* thee,
            Ance in a day.

Thou ance was i' the foremost rank,
A *filly* buirdly, steeve an' swank,

---

[1] Sowens, with butter instead of milk to them, is always the *Halloween Supper*.

An' set weel down a shapely shank,
      As e'er tread yird;
An' could hae flown out owre a stank,
      Like onie bird.

It's now some nine-an'-twenty-year,
Sin' thou was my *Guidfather's Meere*;   20
He gied me thee, o' tocher clear,
      An' fifty mark;°
Tho' it was sma', 'twas *weel-won* gear,
      An' thou was stark.

When first I gaed to woo my *Jenny*,
Ye then was trottan wi' your Minnie:
Tho' ye was trickie, slee an' funnie,
      Ye ne'er was donsie;
But hamely, tawie, quiet an' cannie,
      An' unco sonsie.   30

That *day*, ye pranc'd wi' muckle pride,
When ye bure hame my bonie *Bride*:
An' sweet an' gracefu' she did ride
      Wi' maiden air!
KYLE-STEWART I could bragged wide,°
      For sic a *pair*.

Tho' now ye dow but hoyte and hoble,
An' wintle like a saumont-coble,
That day, ye was a jinker noble,
      For heels an' win'!   40
An' ran them till they a' did wauble,
      Far, far behin'!

When thou an' I were young an' skiegh,
An' *Stable-meals* at Fairs were driegh,°
How thou wad prance, an' snore, an' scriegh,
      An' tak the road!
Towns-bodies ran, an' stood abiegh,
      An' ca't thee mad.

When thou was corn't, an' I was mellow,°
We took the road ay like a Swallow: 50
At *Brooses* thou had ne'er a fellow,
        For pith an' speed;
But ev'ry tail thou pay't them hollow,°
        Whare'er thou gaed.

The sma', droop-rumpl't, hunter cattle,°
Might aiblins waur't thee for a brattle;
But *sax Scotch mile*, thou try't their mettle,°
        An' gart them whaizle:
Nae whip nor spur, but just a wattle
        O' saugh or hazle.   60

Thou was a noble *Fittie-lan'*,
As e'er in tug or tow was drawn!
Aft thee an' I, in aught hours gaun,
        On guid March-weather,
Hae turn'd *sax rood* beside our han',°
        For days thegither.

Thou never braing't, an' fetch't, an' flisket,
But thy *auld tail* thou wad hae whisket,
An' spread abreed thy weel-fill'd *brisket*,
        Wi' pith an' pow'r,   70
Till sprittie knowes wad rair't an' risket,
        An' slypet owre.

When frosts lay lang, an' snaws were deep,
An' threaten'd *labor* back to keep,
I gied thy *cog* a wee-bit heap
        Aboon the timmer;°
I ken'd my *Maggie* wad na sleep,
        For that, or Simmer.

In *cart* or *car* thou never reestet;
The steyest brae thou wad hae fac't it;   80
Thou never lap, an' sten't, an' breastet,
        Then stood to blaw;
But just thy step a wee thing hastet,
        Thou snoov't awa.

My Pleugh is now thy *bairn-time* a';°
Four gallant brutes, as e'er did draw;
Forby sax mae, I've sell't awa,
          That thou hast nurst:
They drew me thretteen pund an' twa,
          The vera warst.   90

Monie a sair daurk we twa hae wrought,
An' wi' the weary warl' fought!
An' monie an *anxious day*, I thought
          We wad be beat!
Yet here to *crazy Age* we're brought,
          Wi' something yet.

An' think na', my auld, trusty *Servan'*,
That now perhaps thou's less deservin,
An' thy *auld days* may end in starvin',
          For my last fow,   100
A heapet *Stimpart*, I'll reserve ane
          Laid by for you.

We've worn to crazy years thegither;
We'll toyte about wi' ane anither;
Wi' tentie care I'll flit thy tether,
          To some hain'd rig,°
Whare ye may nobly rax your leather,
          Wi' sma' fatigue.

THE COTTER'S SATURDAY NIGHT
INSCRIBED TO R. A****, ESQ;

Let not Ambition mock their useful toil,
    Their homely joys, and destiny obscure;
Nor Grandeur hear, with a disdainful smile,
    The short and simple annals of the Poor.

                                          GRAY.°

I

MY lov'd, my honor'd, much respected friend,
    No mercenary Bard his homage pays;

With honest pride, I scorn each selfish end,
    My dearest meed, a friend's esteem and praise:
To you I sing, in simple Scottish lays,
    The *lowly train* in life's sequester'd scene;
The native feelings strong, the guileless ways,
    What A**** in a *Cottage* would have been;
Ah! tho' his worth unknown, far happier there I ween!

II

November chill blaws loud wi' angry sugh;°   10
    The short'ning winter-day is near a close;
The miry beasts retreating frae the pleugh;
    The black'ning trains o' craws to their repose:
The toil-worn COTTER frae his labor goes,
    This night his weekly moil is at an end,
Collects his *spades*, his *mattocks* and his *hoes*,
    Hoping the *morn* in ease and rest to spend,
And weary, o'er the moor, his course does hameward
    bend.°

III

At length his lonely *Cot* appears in view,
    Beneath the shelter of an aged tree;   20
The expectant *wee-things*, toddlan, stacher through
    To meet their *Dad*, wi' flichterin noise and glee.
His wee-bit ingle, blinkan bonilie,
    His clean hearth-stane, his thrifty *Wifie's* smile,
The *lisping infant*, prattling on his knee,
    Does a' his weary *kiaugh* and care beguile,°
And makes him quite forget his labor and his toil.

IV

Belyve, the *elder bairns* come drapping in,
    At *Service* out, amang the Farmers roun';°
Some ca' the pleugh, some herd, some tentie rin   30
    A cannie errand to a neebor town:
Their eldest hope, their *Jenny*, woman-grown,
    In youthfu' bloom, Love sparkling in her e'e,
Comes hame, perhaps, to shew a braw new gown,
    Or deposite her sair-won penny-fee,
To help her *Parents* dear, if they in hardship be.

V

With joy unfeign'd, *brothers* and *sisters* meet,
  And each for other's weelfare kindly spiers:
The social hours, swift-wing'd, unnotic'd fleet;
  Each tells the uncos that he sees or hears.   40
The Parents partial eye their hopeful years;
  Anticipation forward points the view;
The *Mother*, wi' her needle and her sheers,
  Gars auld claes look amaist as weel's the new;
The *Father* mixes a' wi' admonition due.

VI

Their Master's and their Mistress's command,
  The *youngkers* a' are warned to obey;
And mind their labors wi' an eydent hand,
  And ne'er, tho' out o' sight, to jauk or play:
'And O! be sure to fear the LORD alway!   50
  'And mind your *duty*, duely, morn and night!
'Lest in temptation's path ye gang astray,
  'Implore his *counsel* and assisting *might*:
'They never sought in vain that sought the LORD aright.'

VII

But hark! a rap comes gently to the door;
  Jenny, wha kens the meaning o' the same,
Tells how a neebor lad came o'er the moor,
  To do some errands, and convoy her hame.
The wily Mother sees the *conscious flame*
  Sparkle in *Jenny's* e'e, and flush her cheek,   60
With heart-struck, anxious care enquires his name,
  While *Jenny* hafflins is afraid to speak;
Weel-pleas'd the Mother hears, it's nae wild, worthless
    Rake.°

VIII

With kindly welcome, *Jenny* brings him ben;
  A *strappan youth*; he takes the Mother's eye;
Blythe *Jenny* sees the *visit's* no ill taen;
  The Father cracks of horses, pleughs and kye.
The *Youngster's* artless heart o'erflows wi' joy,

But blate and laithfu', scarce can weel behave;
The Mother, wi' a woman's wiles, can spy   70
    What makes the *youth* sae bashfu' and sae grave;
Weel-pleas'd to think her *bairn's* respected like the lave.

IX

O happy love! where love like this is found!
    O heart-felt raptures! bliss beyond compare!
I've paced much this weary, *mortal round*,
    And sage EXPERIENCE bids me this declare—
'If Heaven a draught of heavenly pleasure spare,
    'One *cordial* in this melancholy *Vale*,
''Tis when a youthful, loving, *modest* Pair,
    'In other's arms, breathe out the tender tale,   80
'Beneath the milk-white thorn that scents the ev'ning gale.'

X.

Is there, in human form, that bears a heart—
    A Wretch! a Villain! lost to love and truth!
That can, with studied, sly, ensnaring art,
    Betray sweet Jenny's unsuspecting youth?
Curse on his perjur'd arts! dissembling smooth!
    Are *Honor*, *Virtue*, *Conscience*, all exil'd?
Is there no Pity, no relenting Ruth,
    Points to the Parents fondling o'er their Child?
Then paints the *ruin'd Maid*, and *their* distraction wild!   90

XI

But now the Supper crowns their simple board,
    The healsome *Porritch*, chief of SCOTIA'S food:
The soupe their *only Hawkie* does afford,
    That 'yont the hallan snugly chows her cood:
The *Dame* brings forth, in complimental mood,
    To grace the lad, her weel-hain'd kebbuck, fell,
And aft he's prest, and aft he ca's it guid;
    The frugal *Wifie*, garrulous, will tell,
How 'twas a towmond auld, sin' Lint was i' the bell.

XII

The chearfu' Supper done, wi' serious face,   100
    They, round the ingle, form a circle wide;

The Sire turns o'er, with patriarchal grace,
    The big *ha'-Bible*, ance his *Father's* pride:
His bonnet rev'rently is laid aside,
    His *lyart haffets* wearing thin and bare;
Those strains that once did sweet in ZION glide,°
    He wales a portion with judicious care;
'*And let us worship GOD!*' he says with solemn air.

XIII

They chant their artless notes in simple guise;
    They tune their *hearts*, by far the noblest aim: 110
Perhaps *Dundee's* wild-warbling measures rise,
    Or plaintive *Martyrs*, worthy of the name;
Or noble *Elgin* beets the heaven-ward flame,°
    The sweetest far of SCOTIA'S holy lays:
Compar'd with these, *Italian trills* are tame;°
    The tickl'd ears no heart-felt raptures raise;
Nae unison hae they, with our CREATOR'S praise.

XIV

The priest-like Father reads the sacred page,
    How *Abram* was the Friend of GOD on high;
Or, *Moses* bade eternal warfare wage,   120
    With *Amalek's* ungracious progeny;°
Or how the *royal Bard* did groaning lye,
    Beneath the stroke of Heaven's avenging ire;°
Or *Job's* pathetic plaint, and wailing cry;°
    Or rapt *Isaiah's* wild, seraphic fire;
Or other *Holy Seers* that tune the *sacred lyre*.°

XV

Perhaps the *Christian Volume* is the theme,°
    How *guiltless blood* for *guilty man* was shed;
How HE, who bore in heaven the second name,
    Had not on Earth whereon to lay His head:°   130
How His first *followers* and *servants* sped;°
    The *Precepts sage* they wrote to many a land:°
How *he*, who lone in *Patmos* banished,°
    Saw in the sun a mighty angel stand;
And heard great *Bab'lon's* doom pronounc'd by
    Heaven's command.

XVI

Then kneeling down to HEAVEN'S ETERNAL
    KING,
  The *Saint*, the *Father*, and the *Husband* prays:
Hope 'springs exulting on triumphant wing,'[10]
  That *thus* they all shall meet in future days:
There, ever bask in *uncreated rays*,°   140
  No more to sigh, or shed the bitter tear,
Together hymning their CREATOR'S praise,°
  In *such society*, yet still more dear;
While circling Time moves round in an eternal sphere.

XVII

Compar'd with *this*, how poor Religion's pride,
  In all the pomp of *method*, and of *art*,
When men display to congregations wide,
  Devotion's ev'ry grace, except the *heart!*
The POWER, incens'd, the Pageant will desert,
  The pompous strain, the sacredotal stole;   150
But haply, in some *Cottage* far apart,
  May hear, well pleas'd, the language of the *Soul*;
And in His *Book of Life* the Inmates poor enroll.°

XVIII

Then homeward all take off their sev'ral way;
  The youngling *Cottagers* retire to rest:
The Parent-pair their *secret homage* pay,
  And proffer up to Heaven the warm request,
That HE who stills the *raven's* clam'rous nest,
  And decks the *lily* fair in flow'ry pride,°
Would, in the way *His Wisdom* sees the best,   160
  For *them* and for their *little ones* provide;
But chiefly, in their hearts with *Grace divine* preside.

XIX

From scenes like these, old SCOTIA'S grandeur springs,°
  That makes her lov'd at home, rever'd abroad:
Princes and lords are but the breath of kings,°
  'An honest man's the noble work of GOD:'°

---

[1] Pope's Windsor Forest.

And *certes*, in fair Virtue's heavenly road,
  The *Cottage* leaves the *Palace* far behind:
What is a lordling's pomp? a cumbrous load,
  Disguising oft the *wretch* of human kind,   170
Studied in arts of Hell, in wickedness refin'd!

XX

O SCOTIA! my dear, my native soil!
  For whom my warmest wish to heaven is sent!
Long may thy hardy sons of *rustic toil*,
  Be blest with health, and peace, and sweet content!
And O may Heaven their simple lives prevent
  From *Luxury's* contagion, weak and vile!
Then howe'er *crowns* and *coronets* be rent,
  A *virtuous Populace* may rise the while,°
And stand a wall of fire around their much-lov'd
  ISLE.   180

XXI

O THOU! who pour'd the *patriotic tide*,°
  That stream'd thro' great, unhappy WALLACE'
          heart;°
Who dar'd to, nobly, stem tyrannic pride,
  Or *nobly die*, the second glorious part:
(The Patriot's GOD, peculiarly thou art,
  His *friend, inspirer, guardian* and *reward!*)
O never, never SCOTIA'S realm desert,
  But still the *Patriot*, and the *Patriot-Bard*,
In bright succesion raise, her *Ornament* and *Guard!*°

TO A MOUSE,
*On turning her up in her Nest, with the Plough,
November, 1785*

WEE, sleeket, cowran, tim'rous *beastie*,
O, what a panic's in thy breastie!
Thou need na start awa sae hasty,
          Wi' bickering brattle!
I wad be laith to rin an' chase thee,
          Wi' murd'ring *pattle!*

I'm truly sorry Man's dominion
Has broken Nature's social union,°
An' justifies that ill opinion,
        Which makes thee startle,   10
At me, thy poor, earth-born companion,
        An' *fellow-mortal!*

I doubt na, whyles, but thou may *thieve*;
What then? poor beastie, thou maun live!
A *daimen-icker* in a *thrave*
        'S a sma' request:
I'll get a blessin wi' the lave,
        An' never miss't!

Thy wee-bit *housie*, too, in ruin!
It's silly wa's the win's are strewin!   20
An' naething, now, to big a new ane,
        O' foggage green!
An' bleak *December's winds* ensuin,
        Baith snell an' keen!

Thou saw the fields laid bare an' wast,
An' weary *Winter* comin fast,
An' cozie here, beneath the blast,
        Thou thought to dwell,
Till crash! the cruel *coulter* past°
        Out thro' thy cell.   30

That wee-bit heap o' leaves an' stibble,
Has cost thee monie a weary nibble!
Now thou's turn'd out, for a' thy trouble,
        But house or hald,
To thole the Winter's *sleety dribble*,
        An' *cranreuch* cauld!

But Mousie, thou art no thy-lane,
In proving *foresight* may be vain:
The best laid schemes o' *Mice* an' *Men*,
        Gang aft agley,°   40
An' lea'e us nought but grief an' pain,
        For promis'd joy!

Still, thou art blest, compar'd wi' *me!*
The *present* only toucheth thee:
But Och! I *backward* cast my e'e,
                    On prospects drear!
An' *forward*, tho' I canna *see*,
                    I *guess* an' *fear!*°

EPISTLE TO DAVIE,
A BROTHER POET
January—

I

WHILE winds frae off BEN-LOMOND blaw,°
And bar the doors wi' driving snaw,
    And hing us owre the ingle,
I set me down, to pass the time,
And spin a verse or twa o' rhyme,
    In hamely, *westlin* jingle.
While frosty winds blaw in the drift,
    Ben to the chimla lug,
I grudge a wee the *Great-folk's* gift,
    That live sae bien an' snug:
        I tent less, and want less   10
            Their roomy fire-side;
        But hanker, and canker,
            To see their cursed pride.

II

It's hardly in a body's pow'r,
To keep, at times, frae being sour,
    To see how things are shar'd;
How *best o' chiels* are whyles in want,
While *Coofs* on countless thousands rant,°
    And ken na how to wair't;   20
But DAVIE lad, ne'er fash your head,
    Tho' we hae little gear,
We're fit to win our daily bread,
    As lang's we're hale and fier:

'Mair spier na, nor fear na,'[1]°
    Auld age ne'er mind a feg;
The last o't, the warst o't,
    Is only but to beg.

III

To lye in kilns and barns at e'en,°
When banes are craz'd, and bluid is thin,   30
    Is, doubtless, great distress!
Yet then *content* could make us blest;
Ev'n then, sometimes we'd snatch a taste
    Of truest happiness.
The honest heart that's free frae a'
    Intended fraud or guile,
However Fortune kick the ba',
    Has ay some cause to smile:
        And mind still, you'll find still,
            A comfort this nae sma';   40
        Nae mair then, we'll care then,
            Nae *farther* we can *fa'*.

IV

What tho', like Commoners of air,
We wander out, we know not where,
    But either house or hal'?
Yet *Nature's* charms, the hills and woods,
The sweeping vales, and foaming floods,
    Are free alike to all.
In days when Daisies deck the ground,
    And Blackbirds whistle clear,   50
With honest joy, our hearts will bound,
    To see the *coming* year:
        On braes when we please then,
            We'll sit and *sowth* a tune;
        Syne *rhyme* till't, we'll time till't,°
            And sing't when we hae done.

V

It's no in titles nor in rank;
It's no in wealth like *Lon'on Bank*,

[1] Ramsay.

To purchase peace and rest;°
It's no in makin muckle, *mair:*   60
It's no in books; it's no in Lear,
    To make us truly blest:
If Happiness hae not her seat
    And center in the breast,
We may be *wise*, or *rich*, or *great*,
    But never can be *blest*:
       Nae treasures, nor pleasures
          Could make us happy lang;
       The *heart* ay's the part ay,
          That makes us right or wrang.   70

VI

Think ye, that sic as *you* and *I*,
Wha drudge and drive thro' wet and dry,
    Wi' never-ceasing toil;
Think ye, are we less blest than they,
Wha scarcely tent us in their way,
    As hardly worth their while?
Alas! how aft, in haughty mood,
    GOD'S creatures they oppress!
Or else, neglecting a' that's guid,
    They riot in excess!   80
       Baith careless, and fearless,
          Of either Heaven or Hell;
       Esteeming, and deeming,
          It a' an idle tale!

VII

Then let us chearfu' acquiesce;
Nor make our scanty Pleasures less,
    By pining at our state:
And, ev'n should Misfortunes come,
I, here wha sit, hae met wi' some,
    An's thankfu' for them yet.   90
They gie the wit of *Age* to *Youth;*
    They let us ken oursel;
They make us see the naked truth,
    The *real* guid and ill.
       Tho' losses, and crosses,

Be lessons right severe,
There's *wit* there, ye'll get there,
Ye'll find nae other where.

VIII

But tent me, DAVIE, *Ace o' Hearts!*
(To say aught less wad wrang the *cartes*,   100
    And flatt'ry I detest)
This life has joys for you and I;
And joys that riches ne'er could buy;
    And joys the very best.
There's a' the *Pleasures o' the Heart*,
    The *Lover* and the *Frien'*;
Ye hae your MEG, your dearest part,°
    And I my darling JEAN!
        It warms me, it charms me,
            To mention but her *name*:   110
        It heats me, it beets me,
            And sets me a' on flame!

IX

O, all ye *Pow'rs* who rule above!
O THOU, whose very self art *love!*
    THOU know'st my words sincere!
The *life blood* streaming thro' my heart,
Or my more dear *Immortal part*,
    Is not more fondly dear!
When heart-corroding care and grief
    Deprive my soul of rest,   120
Her dear idea brings relief,
    And solace to my breast.°
        Thou BEING, Allseeing,
            O hear my fervent pray'r!
        Still take her, and make her,
            THY most peculiar care!

X

All hail! ye tender feelings dear!
The smile of love, the friendly tear,
    The sympathetic glow!
Long since, this world's thorny ways   130

Had number'd out my weary days,°
   Had it not been for you!
Fate still has blest me with a friend,
   In ev'ry care and ill;
And oft a more *endearing* band,
   A *tye* more tender still.
     It lightens, it brightens,
      The tenebrific scene,°
     To meet with, and greet with,
      My DAVIE or my JEAN!   140

XI

O, how that *name* inspires my style!
The words come skelpan, rank and file,
   Amaist before I ken!
The ready measure rins as fine,
As *Phœbus* and the famous *Nine*°
   Were glowran owre my pen.
My spavet *Pegasus* will limp,°
   Till ance he's fairly het;
And then he'll hilch, and stilt, and jimp,
   And rin an unco fit: 150
     But least then, the beast then,
      Should rue this hasty ride,
     I'll light now, and dight now,
      His sweaty, wizen'd hide.

THE LAMENT

OCCASIONED BY THE UNFORTUNATE ISSUE
OF A FRIEND'S AMOUR

Alas! how oft does goodness wound itself!
And sweet Affection *prove the spring of Woe!*
                    HOME.°

I

O Thou pale Orb, that silent shines,
   While care-untroubled mortals sleep!
Thou seest a *wretch*, who inly pines,
   And wanders here to wail and weep!

With Woe I nightly vigils keep,
 Beneath thy wan, unwarming beam;
And mourn, in lamentation deep,
 How *life* and *love* are all a dream!

II

I joyless view thy rays adorn,
 The faintly-marked, distant hill:
I joyless view thy trembling horn,   10
 Reflected in the gurgling rill.
My fondly-fluttering heart, be still!
 Thou busy pow'r, Remembrance, cease!
Ah! must the agonizing thrill,
 For ever bar returning Peace!

III

No idly-feign'd, poetic pains,
 My sad, lovelorn lamentings claim:
No shepherd's pipe—Arcadian strains;
 No fabled tortures, quaint and tame.   20
The *plighted faith*; the *mutual flame*;
 The *oft-attested Powers above*;
The *promis'd Father's tender name*;
 These were the pledges of my love!

IV

Encircled in her clasping arms,
 How have the raptur'd moments flown!
How have I wish'd for Fortune's charms,
 For her dear sake, and her's alone!
And, must I think it! is she gone,
 My secret-heart's exulting boast?   30
And does she heedless hear my groan?
 And is she ever, ever lost?

V

Oh! can she bear so base a heart,
 So lost to Honor, lost to Truth,
As from the *fondest lover* part,
 The *plighted husband* of her youth?
Alas! Life's path may be unsmooth!

Her way may lie thro' rough distress!
Then, who her pangs and pains will soothe,
   Her sorrows share and make them less?   40

VI

Ye winged Hours that o'er us past,
   Enraptur'd more, the more enjoy'd,
Your dear remembrance in my breast,
   My fondly-treasur'd thoughts employ'd.
That breast, how dreary now, and void,
   For her too scanty once of room!
Ev'n ev'ry *ray* of *Hope* destroy'd,
   And not a *Wish* to gild the gloom!

VII

The morn that warns th'approaching day,
   Awakes me up to toil and woe: 50
I see the hours, in long array,
   That I must suffer, lingering, slow.
Full many a pang, and many a throe,
   Keen Recollection's direful train,°
Must wring my soul, ere Phœbus, low,
   Shall kiss the distant, western main.

VIII

And when my nightly couch I try,
   Sore-harass'd out, with care and grief,
My toil-beat nerves, and tear-worn eye,
   Keep watchings with the nightly thief: 60
Or if I slumber, Fancy, chief,
   Reigns, hagard-wild, in sore afright:
Ev'n day, all-bitter, brings relief,
   From such a horror-breathing night.

IX

O! thou bright Queen, who, o'er th'expanse,
   Now highest reign'st, with boundless sway!
Oft has thy silent-marking glance
   Observ'd us, fondly-wand'ring, stray!
The time, unheeded, sped away,
   While Love's *luxurious pulse* beat high,   70

Beneath thy silver-gleaming ray,
  To mark the mutual-kindling eye.

X

Oh! scenes in strong remembrance set!
  Scenes, never, never to return!
Scenes, if in stupor I forget,
  Again I feel, again I burn!
From ev'ry joy and pleasure torn,
  Life's weary vale I'll wander thro';
And hopeless, comfortless, I'll mourn
  A faithless woman's broken vow.   80

DESPONDENCY, AN ODE

I

OPPRESS'D with grief, oppress'd with care,
A burden more than I can bear,
  I set me down and sigh:
O Life! Thou art a galling load,
Along a rough, a weary road,
  To wretches such as I!
Dim-backward as I cast my view,
  What sick'ning Scenes appear!
What Sorrows *yet* may pierce me thro',
  Too justly I may fear!   10
    Still caring, despairing,
      Must be my bitter doom;
    My woes here, shall close ne'er,
      But with the *closing tomb!*

II

Happy! ye sons of Busy-life,
Who, equal to the bustling strife,
  No other view regard!
Ev'n when the wished *end's* deny'd,
Yet while the busy *means* are ply'd,
  They bring their own reward: 20
Whilst I, a hope-abandon'd wight,

Unfitted with an *aim*,°
Meet ev'ry sad-returning night,
    And joyless morn the same.
        You, bustling and justling,
            Forget each grief and pain;
        I, listless, yet restless,
            Find ev'ry prospect vain.

III

How blest the Solitary's lot,
Who, all-forgetting, all-forgot,°   30
    Within his humble cell,
The cavern wild with tangling roots,
Sits o'er his newly-gather'd fruits,
    Beside his crystal well!°
Or haply, to his ev'ning thought,
    By unfrequented stream,
The *ways of men* are distant brought,
    A faint-collected dream:
        While praising, and raising
            His thoughts to Heaven on high,   40
        As wand'ring, meand'ring,
            He views the solemn sky.

IV

Than I, no *lonely Hermit* plac'd
Where never human footstep trac'd,
    Less fit to play the part,
The *lucky moment* to improve,
And *just* to stop, and *just* to move,
    With *self-respecting* art:
But ah! those pleasures, Loves and Joys,
    Which I too keenly taste,   50
The *Solitary* can despise,
    Can want, and yet be blest!
        He needs not, he heeds not,
            Or human love or hate;°
        Whilst I here, must cry here,
            At perfidy ingrate!

V

Oh, enviable, early days,
When dancing thoughtless Pleasure's maze,
    To Care, to Guilt unknown!
How ill exchang'd for riper times,   60
To feel the follies, or the crimes,
    Of others, or my own!
Ye tiny elves that guiltless sport,
    Like linnets in the bush,
Ye little know the ills ye court,
    When Manhood is your wish!
        The losses, the crosses,
            That *active man* engage;
        The fears all, the tears all,
            Of dim declining *Age!*   70

MAN WAS MADE TO MOURN, A DIRGE

I

WHEN chill November's surly blast
    Made fields and forests bare,
One ev'ning, as I wand'red forth,
    Along the banks of AIRE,
I spy'd a man, whose aged step
    Seem'd weary, worn with care;
His face was furrow'd o'er with years,°
    And hoary was his hair.

II

Young stranger, whither wand'rest thou?
    Began the rev'rend Sage;   10
Does thirst of wealth thy step constrain,°
    Or youthful Pleasure's rage?
Or haply, prest with cares and woes,
    Too soon thou hast began,
To wander forth, with me, to mourn
    The miseries of Man.

III

The Sun that overhangs yon moors,
    Out-spreading far and wide,
Where hundreds labour to support
    A haughty lordling's pride;   20
I've seen yon weary winter-sun
    Twice forty times return;
And ev'ry time has added proofs,
    That Man was made to mourn.

IV

O Man! while in thy early years,
    How prodigal of time!
Mispending all thy precious hours,
    Thy glorious, youthful prime!
Alternate Follies take the sway;
    Licentious Passions burn;   30
Which tenfold force gives Nature's law,
    That Man was made to mourn.

V

Look not alone on youthful Prime,
    Or Manhood's active might;°
Man then is useful to his kind,
    Supported is his right:
But see him on the edge of life,
    With Cares and Sorrows worn,°
Then Age and Want, Oh! ill-match'd pair!°
    Show Man was made to mourn.   40

VI

A few seem favourites of Fate,
    In Pleasure's lap carest;
Yet, think not all the Rich and Great,
    Are likewise truly blest.
But Oh! what crouds in ev'ry land,
    All wretched and forlorn,
Thro' weary life this lesson learn,
    That Man was made to mourn!

VII

Many and sharp the num'rous Ills
    Inwoven with our frame!°   50
More pointed still we make ourselves,
    Regret, Remorse and Shame!
And Man, whose heav'n-erected face,
    The smiles of love adorn,°
Man's inhumanity to Man°
    Makes countless thousands mourn!

VIII

See, yonder poor, o'erlabour'd wight,
    So abject, mean and vile,
Who begs a brother of the earth
    To give him leave to toil;   60
And see his lordly *fellow-worm*,
    The poor petition spurn,
Unmindful, tho' a weeping wife,
    And helpless offspring mourn.

IX

If I'm design'd yon lordling's slave,
    By Nature's law design'd,
Why was an independent wish
    E'er planted in my mind?°
If not, why am I subject to
    His cruelty, or scorn?   70
Or why has Man the will and pow'r
    To make his fellow mourn?

X

Yet, let not this too much, my Son,
    Disturb thy youthful breast:
This partial view of human-kind
    Is surely not the *last!*
The poor, oppressed, honest man
    Had never, sure, been born,
Had there not been some recompence
    To comfort those that mourn!   80

XI

O Death! the poor man's dearest friend,
   The kindest and the best!
Welcome the hour, my aged limbs
   Are laid with thee at rest!
The Great, the Wealthy fear thy blow,
   From pomp and pleasure torn;
But Oh! a blest relief for those°
   That weary-laden mourn!

WINTER, A DIRGE

I

THE Wintry West extends his blast,
   And hail and rain does blaw;
Or, the stormy North sends driving forth,
   The blinding sleet and snaw:
While, tumbling brown, the Burn comes down,
   And roars frae bank to brae;
And bird and beast, in covert, rest,
   And pass the heartless day.

II

'The sweeping blast, the sky o'ercast,'[1]°
   The joyless *winter-day*,   10
Let others fear, to me more dear,
   Than all the pride of May:
The Tempest's howl, it *soothes* my soul,
   My *griefs* it seems to join;
The leafless trees my fancy please,
   Their *fate* resembles mine!

III

Thou POW'R SUPREME, whose mighty Scheme,
   These *woes* of mine fulfil;
Here, firm, I rest, they *must* be best,
   Because they are *Thy* Will!   20

[1] Dr. Young.

Then all I want (Oh, do thou grant
  This one request of mine!)
Since to *enjoy* Thou dost deny,
  Assist me to *resign!*

A PRAYER,
IN THE PROSPECT OF DEATH

I

O THOU unknown, Almighty Cause°
  Of all my hope and fear!
In whose dread Presence, ere an hour,
  Perhaps I must appear!

II

If I have wander'd in those paths
  Of life I ought to shun;
As *Something*, loudly, in my breast,
  Remonstrates I have done;

III

Thou know'st that Thou hast formed me,
  With Passions wild and strong;
And list'ning to their witching voice
  Has often led me wrong.

10

IV

Where human *weakness* has come short,
  Or *frailty* stept aside,
Do Thou, ALL-GOOD, for such Thou art,
  In shades of darkness hide.

V

Where with *intention* I have err'd,
  No other plea I have,
But, *Thou art good*; and Goodness still°
  Delighteth to forgive.

20

your thought,
s attained;
come to nought,°
s strained.

III

llains a';
d wicked,
but *human law*,
ricked:
d are unco weak,
trusted;
ing balance shake,
ht adjusted!

IV

fa' in Fortune's strife,
we should na censure,
important end of life,
ally may answer:
hae an *honest heart*,
ortith hourly stare him;
ay tak a neebor's part,
e nae *cash* to spare him.

V

, aff han', your story tell,
en wi' a bosom crony;
till keep something to yoursel
e scarcely tell to ony.
ceal yoursel as weel's ye can
rae critical dissection;
t keek thro' ev'ry other man,
Wi' sharpen'd, sly inspection.

VI

he *sacred lowe* o' weel plac'd love,
Luxuriantly indulge it;
ut never tempt th'*illicit rove*,°
Tho' naething should divulge it:
ave the quantum o' the sin;

20

30

40

TO A MOUNTAIN-DAISY,

On turning one down, with the Plough, in April— 1786

WEE, modest, crimson-tipped flow'r,
Thou's met me in an evil hour;
For I maun crush amang the stoure
            Thy slender stem:
To spare thee now is past my pow'r,
            Thou bonie gem.

Alas! it's no thy neebor sweet,
The bonie *Lark*, companion meet!
Bending thee 'mang the dewy weet!
            Wi's spreckl'd breast,   10
When upward-springing, blythe, to greet
            The purpling East.°

Cauld blew the bitter-biting *North*
Upon thy early, humble birth;
Yet chearfully thou glinted forth
            Amid the storm,
Scarce rear'd above the *Parent-earth*
            Thy tender form.

The flaunting *flow'rs* our Gardens yield,
High-shelt'ring woods and wa's maun shield,   20
But thou, beneath the random bield
            O' clod or stane,
Adorns the histie *stibble-field*,
            Unseen, alane.

There, in thy scanty mantle clad,
Thy snawie bosom sun-ward spread,°
Thou lifts thy unassuming head
            In humble guise;
But now the *share* uptears thy bed,°
            And low thou lies!   30

Such is the fate of artless Maid,
Sweet *flow'ret* of the rural shade!

By Love's simplicity betray'd,
            And guileless trust,
Till she, like thee, all soil'd, is laid
            Low i' the dust.

Such is the fate of simple Bard,
On Life's rough ocean luckless starr'd!
Unskilful he to note the card
            Of *prudent Lore*,   40
Till billows rage, and gales blow hard,
            And whelm him o'er!

Such fate to *suffering worth* is giv'n,
Who long with wants and woes has striv'n,
By human pride or cunning driv'n
            To Mis'ry's brink,
Till wrench'd of ev'ry stay but HEAV'N,°
            He, ruin'd, sink!

Ev'n thou who mourn'st the *Daisy's* fate,
That fate is thine—no distant date;   50
Stern Ruin's *plough-share* drives, elate,°
            Full on thy bloom,
Till crush'd beneath the *furrow's* weight,
            Shall be thy doom!

TO RUIN

I

ALL hail! inexorable lord!
At whose destruction-breathing word,
   The mightiest empires fall!
Thy cruel, woe-delighted train,
The ministers of Grief and Pain,
   A sullen welcome, all!
With stern-resolv'd, despairing eye,
   I see each aimed dart;
For one has cut my *dearest tye*,
   And quivers in my heart.   10

TO A MOUNTAIN-DAISY,
*On turning one down, with the Plough, in April—*1786

WEE, modest, crimson-tipped flow'r,
Thou's met me in an evil hour;
For I maun crush amang the stoure
    Thy slender stem:
To spare thee now is past my pow'r,
    Thou bonie gem.

 Alas! it's no thy neebor sweet,
The bonie *Lark*, companion meet!
Bending thee 'mang the dewy weet!
    Wi's spreckl'd breast,   10
When upward-springing, blythe, to greet
    The purpling East.°

 Cauld blew the bitter-biting *North*
Upon thy early, humble birth;
Yet chearfully thou glinted forth
    Amid the storm,
Scarce rear'd above the *Parent-earth*
    Thy tender form.

 The flaunting *flow'rs* our Gardens yield,
High-shelt'ring woods and wa's maun shield, 20
But thou, beneath the random bield
    O' clod or stane,
Adorns the histie *stibble-field*,
    Unseen, alane.

 There, in thy scanty mantle clad,
Thy snawie bosom sun-ward spread,°
Thou lifts thy unassuming head
    In humble guise;
But now the *share* uptears thy bed,°
    And low thou lies!   30

 Such is the fate of artless Maid,
Sweet *flow'ret* of the rural shade!

By Love's simplicity betray'd,
       And guileless trust,
Till she, like thee, all soil'd, is laid
       Low i' the dust.

Such is the fate of simple Bard,
On Life's rough ocean luckless starr'd!
Unskilful he to note the card
       Of *prudent Lore*,   40
Till billows rage, and gales blow hard,
       And whelm him o'er!

Such fate to *suffering worth* is giv'n,
Who long with wants and woes has striv'n,
By human pride or cunning driv'n
       To Mis'ry's brink,
Till wrench'd of ev'ry stay but HEAV'N,°
       He, ruin'd, sink!

Ev'n thou who mourn'st the *Daisy's* fate,
That fate is thine—no distant date;   50
Stern Ruin's *plough-share* drives, elate,°
       Full on thy bloom,
Till crush'd beneath the *furrow's* weight,
       Shall be thy doom!

TO RUIN

I

ALL hail! inexorable lord!
At whose destruction-breathing word,
   The mightiest empires fall!
Thy cruel, woe-delighted train,
The ministers of Grief and Pain,
   A sullen welcome, all!
With stern-resolv'd, despairing eye,
   I see each aimed dart;
For one has cut my *dearest tye*,
   And quivers in my heart.   10

Then low'ring, and pouring,
 The *Storm* no more I dread;
Tho' thick'ning, and black'ning,
 Round my devoted head.

II

And thou grim Pow'r, by Life abhorr'd,
While Life a *pleasure* can afford,
 Oh! hear a wretch's pray'r!
Nor more I shrink appall'd, afraid;
I court, I beg thy friendly aid,
 To close this scene of care!   20
When shall my soul, in silent peace,
 Resign Life's *joyless* day?
My weary heart it's throbbings cease,
 Cold mould'ring in the clay?
  No fear more, no tear more,
   To stain my lifeless face,
  Enclasped, and grasped,
   Within thy cold embrace!

EPISTLE TO A YOUNG FRIEND

May—1786

I

I Lang hae thought, my youthfu' friend,
 A Something to have sent you,
Tho' it should serve nae other end
 Than just a kind memento;
But how the subject theme may gang,
 Let time and chance determine;
Perhaps it may turn out a Sang;
 Perhaps, turn out a Sermon.

II

Ye'll try the world soon my lad,
 And ANDREW dear believe me,   10
Ye'll find mankind an unco squad,
 And muckle they may grieve ye:

For care and trouble set your thought,
    Ev'n when your end's attained;
And a' your views may come to nought,°
    Where ev'ry nerve is strained.

III

I'll no say, men are villains a';
    The real, harden'd wicked,
Wha hae nae check but *human law*,
    Are to a few restricked: 20
But Och, mankind are unco weak,
    An' little to be trusted;
If *Self* the wavering balance shake,
    It's rarely right adjusted!

IV

Yet they wha fa' in Fortune's strife,
    Their fate we should na censure,
For still th' *important end* of life,
    They equally may answer:
A man may hae an *honest heart*,
    Tho' Poortith hourly stare him;   30
A man may tak a neebor's part,
    Yet hae nae *cash* to spare him.

V

Ay free, aff han', your story tell,
    When wi' a bosom crony;
But still keep something to yoursel
    Ye scarcely tell to ony.
Conceal yoursel as weel's ye can
    Frae critical dissection;
But keek thro' ev'ry other man,
    Wi' sharpen'd, sly inspection.   40

VI

The *sacred lowe* o' weel plac'd love,
    Luxuriantly indulge it;
But never tempt th'*illicit rove*,°
    Tho' naething should divulge it:
I wave the quantum o' the sin;

The hazard of concealing;
But Och! it hardens *a' within*,
    And petrifies the feeling!

VII

To catch Dame Fortune's golden smile,
    Assiduous wait upon her;   50
And gather gear by ev'ry wile,
    That's justify'd by Honor:
Not for to *hide* it in a *hedge*,
    Nor for a *train-attendant*;
But for the glorious priviledge
    Of being *independant*.

VIII

The *fear o' Hell's* a hangman's whip,
    To haud the wretch in order;
But where ye feel your *Honor* grip,
    Let that ay be your border: 60
It's slightest touches, instant pause—
    Debar a' side-pretences;
And resolutely keep it's laws,
    Uncaring consequences.

IX

The great CREATOR to revere,
    Must sure become the *Creature*;
But still the preaching cant forbear,
    And ev'n the rigid feature:
Yet ne'er with Wits prophane to range,
    Be complaisance extended;   70
An *athiest-laugh's* a poor exchange
    For *Deity offended!*

X

When ranting round in Pleasure's ring,
    Religion may be blinded;
Or if she gie a *random-sting*,
    It may be little minded;
But when on Life we're tempest-driven,
    A Conscience but a canker—

A correspondence fix'd wi' Heav'n,
    Is sure a noble *anchor!*   80

XI

Adieu, dear, amiable Youth!
    Your *heart* can ne'er be wanting!
May Prudence, Fortitude and Truth
    Erect your brow undaunting!
In *ploughman phrase* 'GOD send you speed,'
    Still daily to grow wiser;
And may ye better reck the *rede*,
    Than ever did th' *Adviser!*°

ON A SCOTCH BARD
GONE TO THE WEST INDIES

A' Ye wha live by sowps o' drink,
A' ye wha live by crambo-clink,
A' ye wha live and never think,
                    Come, mourn wi' me!
Our *billie's* gien us a' a jink,
                    An' owre the Sea.

    Lament him a' ye rantan core,
Wha dearly like a random-splore;
Nae mair he'll join the *merry roar*,
                    In social key;   10
For now he's taen anither shore,
                    An' owre the Sea!

    The bonie lasses weel may wiss him,
And in their dear *petitions* place him:°
The widows, wives, an' a' may bless him,
                    Wi' tearfu' e'e;
For weel I wat they'll sairly miss him
                    That's owre the Sea!

    O Fortune, they hae room to grumble!
Hadst thou taen aff some drowsy bummle,°   20
Wha can do nought but fyke an' fumble,°

          'Twad been nae plea;
But he was gleg as onie wumble,°
          That's owre the Sea!

   Auld, cantie KYLE may weepers wear,°
An' stain them wi' the saut, saut tear:
'Twill mak her poor, auld heart, I fear,
          In flinders flee:°
He was her *Laureat* monie a year,
          That's owre the Sea!   30

   He saw Misfortune's cauld *Nor-west*
Lang-mustering up a bitter blast;
A Jillet brak his heart at last,
          Ill may she be!
So, took a birth afore the mast,
          An' owre the Sea.

   To tremble under Fortune's cummock,
On scarce a bellyfu' o' *drummock*,
Wi' his proud, independant stomach,
          Could ill agree;   40
So, row't his hurdies in a *hammock*,
          An' owre the Sea.

   He ne'er was gien to great misguidin,
Yet coin his pouches wad na bide in;
Wi' him it ne'er was *under hidin*;
          He dealt it free:
The *Muse* was a' that he took pride in,
          That's owre the Sea.

   Jamaica bodies, use him weel,
An' hap him in a cozie biel:
Ye'll find him ay a dainty chiel,   50
          An' fou o' glee:
He wad na wrang'd the vera *Diel*,
          That's owre the Sea.

   Fareweel, my *rhyme-composing billie!*
Your native soil was right ill-willie;

But may ye flourish like a lily,
                    Now bonilie!
I'll toast you in my hindmost *gillie*,
                    Tho' owre the Sea!   60

A DEDICATION

TO G**** H******** Esq;

EXPECT na, Sir, in this narration,
A fleechan, fleth'ran *Dedication*,
To roose you up, an' ca' you guid,
An' sprung o' great an' noble bluid;
Because ye're sirnam'd like *His Grace*,°
Perhaps related to the race:
Then when I'm tir'd—and sae are *ye*,
Wi' monie a fulsome, sinfu' lie,
Set up a face, how I stop short,
For fear your modesty be hurt.   10

This may do—maun do, Sir, wi' them wha
Maun please the Great-folk for a wamefou;
For me! sae laigh I need na bow,
For, LORD be thanket, *I can plough*;
And when I downa yoke a naig,
Then, LORD be thanket, *I can beg*;°
Sae I shall say, an' that's nae flatt'rin,
It's just *sic Poet* an' *sic Patron*.

The Poet, some guid Angel help him,
Or else, I fear, some *ill ane* skelp him!
He may do weel for a' he's done yet,
But only—he's no just begun yet.   20

The Patron, (Sir, ye maun forgie me,
I winna lie, come what will o' me)
On ev'ry hand it will allow'd be,
He's just—nae better than he should be.

I readily and freely grant,
He downa see a poor man want;
What's no his ain, he winna tak it;
What ance he says, he winna break it;   30
Ought he can lend he'll no refus't,
Till aft his guidness is abus'd;
And rascals whyles that do him wrang,
Ev'n *that*, he does na mind it lang:
As Master, Landlord, Husband, Father,°
He does na fail his part in either.

But then, nae thanks to him for a' that;
Nae *godly symptom* ye can ca' that;
It's naething but a milder feature,
Of our poor, sinfu', corrupt Nature:°   40
Ye'll get the best o' moral works,
'Mang black *Gentoos*, and Pagan *Turks*,°
Or Hunters wild on *Ponotaxi*,°
Wha never heard of Orth–d–xy.°
That he's the poor man's friend in need,
The GENTLEMAN in word and deed,
It's no through terror of D–mn–t–n; ⎫
It's just a carnal inclination,   ⎬
And Och! that's nae r–g–n–r–t–n!° ⎭

Morality, thou deadly bane,°   50
Thy tens o' thousands thou hast slain!
Vain is his hope, whase stay an' trust is,
In *moral* Mercy, Truth, and Justice!

No—stretch a point to catch a plack;°
Abuse a Brother to his back;
Steal through the *winnock* frae a wh–re,
But point the Rake that taks the *door*;°
Be to the Poor like onie whunstane,
And haud their noses to the grunstane;
Ply ev'ry art o' *legal* thieving;   60
No matter—stick to *sound believing*.

Learn three-mile pray'rs, an' half-mile graces,
Wi' weel-spread looves, an' lang, wry faces;

Grunt up a solemn, lengthen'd groan,
And damn a' Parties but your own;°
I'll warrant then, ye're nae Deceiver,
A steady, sturdy, staunch *Believer*.

O ye wha leave the springs o' C–lv–n,°
For *gumlie dubs* of your ain delvin!
Ye sons of Heresy and Error,   70
Ye'll *some day* squeel in quaking terror!
When Vengeance draws the sword in wrath,°
And in the fire throws the *sheath*;
When Ruin, with his sweeping *besom*,°
Just frets till Heav'n commission gies him;
While o'er the *Harp* pale Misery moans,
And strikes the ever-deep'ning tones,
Still louder shrieks, and heavier groans!°

Your pardon, Sir, for this digression,
I maist forgat my *Dedication*;   80
But when Divinity comes cross me,
My readers then are sure to lose me.°

So Sir, you see 'twas nae daft vapour,
But I maturely thought it proper,
When a' my works I did review,
To *dedicate* them, Sir, to YOU:
Because (ye need na tak it ill)
I thought them something like *yoursel*.

Then patronize them wi' your favor,
And your Petitioner shall ever—   90
I had amaist said, *ever pray*,
But that's a word I need na say:
For prayin I hae little skill o't;
I'm baith dead-sweer, an' wretched ill o't;
But I'se repeat each poor man's *pray'r*,
That kens or hears about you, Sir—

'May ne'er Misfortune's gowling bark,
'Howl thro' the dwelling o' the CLERK!°
'May ne'er his gen'rous, honest heart,

'For that same gen'rous spirit smart!   100
'May K******'s far-honor'd name°
'Lang beet his hymeneal flame,
'Till H*******'s, at least a diz'n,
'Are frae their nuptial labors risen:
'Five bonie Lasses round their table,
'And sev'n braw fellows, stout an' able,
'To serve their King an' Country weel,
'By word, or pen, or pointed steel!
'May Health and Peace, with mutual rays,
'Shine on the ev'ning o' his days;   110
'Till his wee, curlie *John's* ier-oe,
'When ebbing life nae mair shall flow,
'The last, sad, mournful rites bestow!'

    I will not wind a lang conclusion,
With complimentary effusion:
But whilst your wishes and endeavours,
Are blest with Fortune's smiles and favours,
I am, Dear Sir, with zeal most fervent,
Your much indebted, humble servant.

    But if, which Pow'rs above prevent,   120
That iron-hearted Carl, *Want*,
Attended, in his grim advances,
By *sad mistakes*, and *black mischances*,
While hopes, and joys, and pleasures fly him,
Make you as poor a dog as I am,
Your *humble servant* then no more;
For who would humbly serve the Poor?
But by a poor man's hopes in Heav'n!
While recollection's pow'r is giv'n,
If, in the vale of humble life,   130
The victim sad of Fortune's strife,
I, through the tender-gushing tear,
Should recognise my *Master dear*,
If friendless, low, we meet together,
Then, Sir, your hand—my FRIEND and BROTHER.

TO A LOUSE,
On Seeing one on a Lady's Bonnet at Church

HA! whare ye gaun, ye crowlan ferlie!
Your impudence protects you sairly:
I canna say but ye strunt rarely,
   Owre *gawze* and *lace*;
Tho' faith, I fear ye dine but sparely,
   On sic a place.

Ye ugly, creepan, blastet wonner,
Detested, shunn'd, by saunt an' sinner,
How daur ye set your fit upon her,
   Sae fine a *Lady!*   10
Gae somewhere else and seek your dinner,
   On some poor body.

Swith, in some beggar's haffet squattle;
There ye may creep, and sprawl, and sprattle,°
Wi' ither kindred, jumping cattle,
   In shoals and nations;
Whare *horn* nor *bane* ne'er daur unsettle,°
   Your thick plantations.

Now haud you there, ye're out o' sight,
Below the fatt'rels, snug and tight,   20
Na faith ye yet! ye'll no be right,°
   Till ye've got on it,
The vera tapmost, towrin height
   O' *Miss's bonnet.*

My sooth! right bauld ye set your nose out,
As plump an' gray as onie grozet:
O for some rank, mercurial rozet,
   Or fell, red smeddum,°
I'd gie you sic a hearty dose o't,
   Wad dress your droddum!   30

I wad na been surpriz'd to spy
You on an auld wife's *flainen toy*;

Or aiblins some bit duddie boy,
    On's *wylecoat*;
But Miss's fine *Lunardi*, fye!°
    How daur ye do't?

O *Jenny* dinna toss your head,
An' set your beauties a' abread!
Ye little ken what cursed speed
    The blastie's makin!   40
Thae *winks* and *finger-ends*, I dread,
    Are notice takin!°

O wad some Pow'r the giftie gie us
To see oursels as others see us!°
It wad frae monie a blunder free us
    An' foolish notion:
What airs in dress an' gait wad lea'e us,
    And ev'n Devotion!

EPISTLE TO J. L*****K,
AN OLD SCOTCH BARD
April 1st, 1785

WHILE briers an' woodbines budding green,
An' Paitricks scraichan loud at e'en,
And morning Poossie whiddan seen,
    Inspire my Muse,
This freedom, in an *unknown* frien',
    I pray excuse.

On Fasteneen we had a rockin,°
To ca' the crack and weave our stockin;
And there was muckle fun and jokin,
    Ye need na doubt;   10
At length we had a hearty yokin,
    At *sang about*.

There was ae *sang*, amang the rest,°
Aboon them a' it pleas'd me best,
That some kind husband had addrest,

To some sweet wife:
It thirl'd the heart-strings thro' the breast,°
A' to the life.

I've scarce heard ought describ'd sae weel,
What gen'rous, manly bosoms feel;
Thought I, 'Can this be *Pope*, or *Steele*,
Or *Beattie's* wark;'°
They told me 'twas an odd kind chiel
About *Muirkirk*.

It pat me fidgean-fain to hear't,
An' sae about him there I spier't;
Then a' that kent him round declar'd,
He had *ingine*,
That nane excell'd it, few cam near't,
It was sae fine.

That set him to a pint of ale,
An' either douse or merry tale,
Or rhymes an' sangs he'd made himsel,
Or witty catches,
'Tween Inverness and Tiviotdale,°
He had few matches.

Then up I gat, an' swoor an aith,
Tho' I should pawn my pleugh an' graith,
Or die a cadger pownie's death,
At some dyke-back,
A *pint* an' *gill* I'd gie them *baith*,
To hear your crack.

But first an' foremost, I should tell,
Amaist as soon as I could spell,
I to the *crambo-jingle* fell,
Tho' rude an' rough,
Yet crooning to a body's sel,
Does weel eneugh.

I am nae *Poet*, in a sense,
But just a *Rhymer* like by chance,

20

30

40

50

An' hae to Learning nae pretence,
    Yet, what the matter?
Whene'er my Muse does on me glance,
    I jingle at her.

Your Critic-folk may cock their nose,
And say, 'How can you e'er propose,
'You wha ken hardly *verse* frae *prose*,
    'To mak a *sang?*
But by your leaves, my learned foes,
    Ye're maybe wrang.   60

What's a' your jargon o' your Schools,°
Your Latin names for horns an' stools;
If honest Nature made you *fools*,
    What sairs your Grammars?
Ye'd better taen up *spades* and *shools*,
    Or *knappin-hammers.*

A set o' dull, conceited Hashes,
Confuse their brains in *Colledge-classes!*
They *gang in* Stirks, and *come out* Asses,
    Plain truth to speak;   70
An' syne they think to climb Parnassus°
    By dint o' Greek!

Gie me ae spark o' Nature's fire,°
That's a' the learning I desire;
Then tho' I drudge thro' dub an' mire
    At pleugh or cart,
My Muse, tho' hamely in attire,
    May touch the heart.

O for a spunk o' ALLAN'S glee,°
Or FERGUSON'S, the bauld an' slee,°   80
Or bright L*****K'S, my friend to be,
    If I can hit it!
That would be *lear* eneugh for me,
    If I could get it.

Now, Sir, if ye hae friends enow,
Tho' *real friends* I b'lieve are few,

Yet, if your catalogue be fow,
        I'se no insist;
But gif ye want ae friend that's true,
        I'm on your list.   90

I winna blaw about *mysel*,
As ill I like my fauts to tell;
But friends an' folk that wish me well,
        They sometimes roose me;
Tho' I maun own, as monie still,
        As far abuse me.

There's ae *wee faut* they whiles lay to me,
I like the lasses—Gude forgie me!
For monie a Plack they wheedle frae me,
        At dance or fair: 100
Maybe some *ither thing* they gie me
        They weel can spare.

But MAUCHLINE Race or MAUCHLINE Fair,°
I should be proud to meet you there;
We'se gie ae night's discharge to *care*,
        If we forgather,
An' hae a swap o' *rhymin-ware*,°
        Wi' ane anither.

The *four-gill chap*, we'se gar him clatter,
An' kirs'n him wi' reekin water;   110
Syne we'll sit down an' tak our whitter,
        To chear our heart;
An' faith, we'se be *acquainted* better
        Before we part.

Awa ye selfish, warly race,
Wha think that havins, sense an' grace,
Ev'n love an' friendship should give place
        To *catch-the-plack!*°
I dinna like to see your face,
        Nor hear your crack.   120

But ye whom social pleasure charms,
Whose hearts the *tide of kindness* warms,

Who hold your *being* on the terms,
       'Each aid the others,'
Come to my bowl, come to my arms,
       My friends, my brothers!

But to conclude my lang epistle,
As my auld pen's worn to the grissle;
Twa lines frae you wad gar me fissle,
       Who am, most fervent,   130
While I can either sing, or whissle,
       Your friend and servant.

TO THE SAME

April 21st, 1785

WHILE new-ca'd kye rowte at the stake,°
An' pownies reek in pleugh or braik,
This hour on e'enin's edge I take,
       To own I'm debtor,
To honest-hearted, auld L******K,
       For his kind *letter*.

Forjesket sair, with weary legs,
Rattlin the corn out-owre the rigs,
Or dealing thro' amang the naigs
       Their ten-hours bite,   10
My awkart Muse sair pleads and begs,°
       I would na write.

The tapetless, ramfeezl'd hizzie,
She's saft at best an' something lazy,
Quo' she, 'Ye ken we've been sae busy
       'This month an' mair,
'That trouth, my head is grown right dizzie,
       'An' something sair.'

Her dowf excuses pat me mad;
'Conscience,' says I, 'ye thowless jad!   20
'I'll write, an' that a hearty blaud,

'This vera night;
'So dinna ye affront your trade,
        'But rhyme it right.

'Shall bauld L*****K, the *king o' hearts*,
'Tho' mankind were a *pack o' cartes*,
'Roose you sae weel for your deserts,
        'In terms sae friendly,
'Yet ye'll neglect to shaw your parts
        'An' thank him kindly?'°   30

Sae I gat paper in a blink,
An' down gaed *stumpie* in the ink:°
Quoth I, 'Before I sleep a wink,
        'I vow I'll close it;
'An' if ye winna mak it clink,
        'By Jove I'll prose it!'

Sae I've begun to scrawl, but whether
In rhyme, or prose, or baith thegither,
Or some hotch-potch that's rightly neither,
        Let time mak proof;   40
But I shall scribble down some blether
        Just clean aff-loof.

My worthy friend, ne'er grudge an' carp,
Tho' Fortune use you hard an' sharp;
Come, kittle up your *moorlan harp*°
        Wi' gleesome touch!
Ne'er mind how Fortune *waft* an' *warp*;°
        She's but a b–tch.

She's gien me monie a jirt an' fleg,
Sin I could striddle owre a rig;   50
But by the L—d, tho' I should beg
        Wi' lyart pow,
I'll laugh, an' sing, an' shake my leg,
        As lang's I dow!

Now comes the *sax an' twentieth* simmer,
I've seen the bud upo' the timmer,

Still persecuted by the limmer
　　　　　Frae year to year;
But yet, despite the kittle kimmer,
　　　　　I, *Rob*, am here.　　　　　　　60

Do ye envy the *city-gent*,
Behint a kist to lie an' sklent,
Or purse-proud, big wi' cent per cent,
　　　　　An' muckle wame,
In some bit *Brugh* to represent°
　　　　　A *Bailie's* name?°

Or is't the paughty, feudal *Thane*,°
Wi' ruffl'd sark an' glancin cane,
Wha thinks himsel nae *sheep-shank bane*,
　　　　　But lordly stalks,　　　　　　　70
While caps an' bonnets aff are taen,
　　　　　As by he walks?

'O *Thou* wha gies us each guid gift!
'Gie me o' *wit* an' *sense* a lift,
'Then turn me, if *Thou* please, *adrift*,
　　　　　'Thro' Scotland wide;
'Wi' *cits* nor *lairds* I wadna shift,°
　　　　　'In a' their pride!'

Were this the *charter* of our state,
'On pain o' *hell* be rich an' great,'　　　80
Damnation then would be our fate,
　　　　　Beyond remead;
But, thanks to *Heav'n*, that's no the gate
　　　　　We learn our *creed*.

For thus the royal *Mandate* ran,
When first the human race began,
'The social, friendly, honest man,
　　　　　'Whate'er he be,
''Tis *he* fulfils *great Nature's plan*,
　　　　　'And none but *he*.'　　　　　　90

O *Mandate,* glorious and divine!
The followers o' the ragged Nine,°
Poor, thoughtless devils! yet may shine
   In glorious light,
While sordid sons o' Mammon's line
   Are dark as night!

 Tho' here they scrape, an' squeeze, an' growl,
Their worthless nievefu' of a *soul*
May in some *future carcase* howl,°
   The forest's fright;   100
Or in some day-detesting *owl*
   May shun the light.

 Then may L*****K and B**** arise,
To reach their native, kindred skies,
And *sing* their pleasures, hopes an' joys,
   In some mild sphere,
Still closer knit in friendship's ties
   Each passing year!

TO W. S*****N, OCHILTREE

May——1785

I Gat your letter, winsome Willie;
Wi' gratefu' heart I thank you brawlie;
Tho' I maun say't, I wad be silly,
   An' unco vain,
Should I believe, my coaxin billie,
   Your flatterin strain.

 But I'se believe ye kindly meant it,
I sud be laith to think ye hinted
Ironic satire, sidelins sklented,
   On my poor Musie;   10
Tho' in sic phraisin terms ye've penn'd it,
   I scarce excuse ye.

 My senses wad be in a creel,°
Should I but dare a *hope* to speel,

Wi' *Allan*, or wi' *Gilbertfield*,°
    The braes o' fame;
Or *Ferguson*, the writer-chiel,°
    A deathless name.

(O *Ferguson!* thy glorious *parts*,
Ill-suited *law's* dry, musty arts!   20
My curse upon your whunstane hearts,
    Ye Enbrugh Gentry!
The tythe o' what ye waste at *cartes*
    Wad stow'd his pantry!)

Yet when a tale comes i' my head,
Or lasses gie my heart a screed,
As whiles they're like to be my dead,
    (O sad disease!)
I kittle up my *rustic reed*;
    It gies me ease.   30

Auld COILA, now, may fidge fu' fain,°
She's gotten *Bardies* o' her ain,
Chiels wha their chanters winna hain,°
    But tune their lays,
Till echoes a' resound again
    Her weel-sung praise.

Nae *Poet* thought her worth his while,
To set her name in measur'd style;
She lay like some unkend-of isle
    Beside *New Holland*,°   40
Or whare wild-meeting oceans *boil*
    Besouth *Magellan*.°

Ramsay an' famous *Ferguson*
Gied *Forth* an' *Tay* a lift aboon;
Yarrow an' *Tweed*, to monie a tune,°
    Owre Scotland rings;
While *Irwin*, *Lugar*, *Aire* an' *Doon*,
    Naebody sings.°

Th' *Illissus, Tiber, Thames* an' *Seine,*°
Glide sweet in monie a tunefu' line;   50
But *Willie* set your fit to mine,
                    An' cock your crest,°
We'll gar our streams an' burnies shine
                    Up wi' the best.

We'll sing auld COILA'S plains an' fells,
Her moors red-brown wi' heather bells,
Her banks an' braes, her dens an' dells,
                    Where glorious WALLACE°
Aft bure the gree, as story tells,
                    Frae Suthron billies.   60

At WALLACE' name, what Scottish blood,
But boils up in a spring-tide flood!
Oft have our fearless fathers strode
                    By WALLACE' side,
Still pressing onward, red-wat-shod,
                    Or glorious dy'd!

O sweet are COILA'S haughs an' woods,
When lintwhites chant amang the buds,
And jinkin hares, in amorous whids,
                    Their loves enjoy,   70
While thro' the braes the cushat croods
                    With wailfu' cry!

Ev'n winter bleak has charms to me,°
When winds rave thro' the naked tree;
Or frosts on hills of *Ochiltree*
                    Are hoary gray;
Or blinding drifts wild-furious flee,
                    Dark'ning the day!

O NATURE! a' thy shews an' forms
To feeling, pensive hearts hae charms!   80
Whether the Summer kindly warms,
                    Wi' life an' light,
Or Winter howls, in gusty storms,
                    The lang, dark night!

The *Muse*, nae *Poet* ever fand her,
Till by himsel he learn'd to wander,
Adown some trottin burn's meander,
   An' no think lang;
O sweet, to stray an' pensive ponder
   A heart-felt sang!   90

 The warly race may drudge an' drive,
Hog-shouther, jundie, stretch an' strive,
Let me fair NATURE'S face descrive,
   And I, wi' pleasure,
Shall let the busy, grumbling hive
   Bum owre their treasure.

Fareweel, 'my rhyme-composing brither!'°
We've been owre lang unkenn'd to ither:
Now let us lay our heads thegither,
   In love fraternal: 100
May *Envy* wallop in a tether,
   Black fiend, infernal!

While Highlandmen hate tolls an' taxes;
While moorlan herds like guid, fat braxies;
While Terra firma, on her axis,
   Diurnal turns,
Count on a friend, in faith an' practice,
   In ROBERT BURNS.

POSTSCRIPT

My memory's no worth a preen;
I had amaist forgotten clean,   110
Ye bad me write you what they mean
   By this *new-light*,[1]
'Bout which our *herds* sae aft hae been
   Maist like to fight.

In days when mankind were but callans,
At *Grammar*, *Logic*, an' sic talents,

[1] A cant-term for those religious opinions, which Dr. TAYLOR of Norwich has defended so strenuously.

They took nae pains their speech to balance,
      Or rules to gie,
But spak their thoughts in plain, braid lallans,
      Like you or me.   120

  In thae auld times, they thought the *Moon*,
Just like a sark, or pair o' shoon,
Woor by degrees, till her last roon
          Gaed past their viewin,
An' shortly after she was done
          They gat a new ane.

  This past for certain, undisputed;
It ne'er cam i' their heads to doubt it,
Till chiels gat up an' wad confute it,
          An' ca'd it wrang;   130
An' muckle din there was about it,
          Baith loud an' lang.

  Some *herds*, weel learn'd upo' the beuk,°
Wad threap auld folk the thing misteuk;
For 'twas the *auld moon* turn'd a newk
          An' out o' sight,
An' backlins-comin, to the leuk,
          She grew mair bright.

  This was deny'd, it was affirm'd;
The *herds* an' *hissels* were alarm'd;   140
The rev'rend gray-beards rav'd an' storm'd,
          That beardless laddies
Should think they better were inform'd,
          Than their auld dadies.

  Frae less to mair it gaed to sticks;°
Frae words an' aiths to clours an' nicks;
An' monie a fallow gat his licks,
          Wi' hearty crunt;
An' some, to learn them for their tricks,
          Were hang'd an' brunt.   150

This game was play'd in monie lands,
An' *auld-light* caddies bure sic hands,
That faith, the *youngsters* took the sands°
      Wi' nimble shanks,
Till *Lairds* forbad, by strict commands,
      Sic bluidy pranks.

But *new-light herds* gat sic a cowe,
Folk thought them ruin'd stick-an-stowe,
Till now amaist on ev'ry *knowe*
      Ye'll find ane plac'd;   160
An' some, their *New-light* fair avow,
      Just quite barefac'd.

Nae doubt the *auld-light flocks* are bleatan;
Their zealous *herds* are vex'd an' sweatan;
Mysel, I've ev'n seen them greetan
      Wi' girnan spite,
To hear the *Moon* sae sadly lie'd on
      By word an' write.°

But shortly they will cowe the louns!
Some *auld-light herds* in neebor towns   170
Are mind't, in things they ca' *balloons*,°
      To tak a flight,
An' stay ae month amang the *Moons*
      An' see them right.

Guid observation they will gie them;
An' when the *auld Moon's* gaun to lea'e them,
The hindmost *shaird*, they'll fetch it wi' them,
      Just i' their pouch,
An' when the *new-light* billies see them,
      I think they'll crouch!   180

Sae, ye observe that a' this clatter
Is naething but a 'moonshine matter;'°
But tho' dull *prose-folk* latin splatter
      In logic tulzie,
I hope we, *Bardies*, ken some better
      Than mind sic brulzie.

EPISTLE TO J. R******,
ENCLOSING SOME POEMS

O Rough, rude, ready-witted R******,
The wale o' cocks for fun an' drinkin!°
There's monie godly folks are thinkin,
     Your *dreams*[1] an' tricks°
Will send you, Korah-like, a sinkin,°
     Straught to auld Nick's.

Ye hae sae monie cracks an' cants,
And in your wicked, druken rants,
Ye mak a devil o' the *Saunts*,°
     An' fill them fou;   10
And then their failings, flaws an' wants,
     Are a' seen thro'.

Hypocrisy, in mercy spare it!
That *holy robe*, O dinna tear it!
Spare't for their sakes wha aften wear it,
     The lads in *black*;
But your curst wit, when it comes near it,
     Rives't aff their back.

Think, wicked Sinner, wha ye're skaithing:
It's just the *Blue-gown* badge an' claithing,   20
O' Saunts; tak that, ye lea'e them naething,
     To ken them by,
Frae ony unregenerate Heathen,°
     Like you or I.

I've sent you here, some rhymin ware,
A' that I bargain'd for, an' mair;
Sae when ye hae an hour to spare,
     I will expect,
Yon *Sang*[2] ye'll sen't, wi' cannie care,
     And no neglect.   30

---

[1] A certain humorous *dream* of his was then making a noise in the world.
[2] A *Song* he had promised the Author.

Tho' faith, sma' heart hae I to sing!
My Muse dow scarcely spread her wing:
I've play'd mysel a bonie *spring*,
        An' *danc'd* my fill!
I'd better gaen an' sair't the king,
        At Bunker's hill.°

'Twas ae night lately, in my fun,°
I gaed a rovin wi' the gun,
An' brought a *Paitrick* to the *grun'*,
        A bonie *hen*,   40
And, as the twilight was begun,
        Thought nane wad ken.

The poor, wee thing was *little hurt*;
I *straiket* it a wee for sport,
Ne'er thinkan they wad fash me for't;
        But, Deil-ma-care!
Somebody tells the *Poacher-Court*,°
        The hale affair.

Some auld, us'd hands had taen a note,
That *sic a hen* had got a *shot*;   50
I was suspected for the plot;
        I scorn'd to lie;
So gat the whissle o' my groat,
        An' pay't the *fee*.°

But by my *gun*, o' guns the wale,
An' by my *pouther* an' my *hail*,
An' by my *hen*, an' by her *tail*,
        I vow an' swear!
The *Game* shall pay, ower moor an' *dail*,
        For this, niest year.   60

As soon's the *clockin-time* is by,°
An' the *wee powts* begun to cry,
L—d, I'se hae sportin by an' by,
        For my *gowd guinea*;
Tho' I should herd the *buckskin* kye°
        For't, in Virginia!

Trowth, they had muckle for to blame!
'Twas neither broken wing nor limb,
But twa-three *draps* about the *wame*
Scarce thro' the *feathers*;
An' baith a *yellow George* to claim,°
An' *thole* their *blethers!*

It pits me ay as mad's a hare;
So I can rhyme nor write nae mair;
But *pennyworths* again is fair,°
When time's expedient:
Meanwhile I am, respected Sir,
Your most obedient.

SONG

Tune—*Corn Rigs are bonie*

I

IT was upon a Lammas night,
When corn rigs are bonie,
Beneath the moon's unclouded light,
I held awa to Annie:°
The time flew by, wi' tentless heed,°
Till 'tween the late and early;
Wi' sma' persuasion she agreed,
To see me thro' the barley.

II

The sky was blue, the wind was still,
The moon was shining clearly;
I set her down, wi' right good will,
Amang the rigs o' barley:
I ken't her heart was a' my ain;
I lov'd her most sincerely;
I kiss'd her owre and owre again,
Amang the rigs o' barley.

III

I lock'd her in my fond embrace;
Her heart was beating rarely:

My blessings on that happy place,   20
    Amang the rigs o' barley!
But by the moon and stars so bright,
    That shone that hour so clearly!°
She ay shall bless that happy night,
    Amang the rigs o' barley.

IV

I hae been blythe wi' Comrades dear;
    I hae been merry drinking;
I hae been joyfu' gath'rin gear;
    I hae been happy thinking: 30
But a' the pleasures e'er I saw,
    Tho' three times doubl'd fairly,
That happy night was worth them a',
    Amang the rigs o' barley.

CHORUS

    Corn rigs, an' barley rigs,
        An' corn rigs are bonie:
    I'll ne'er forget that happy night,
        Amang the rigs wi' Annie.

SONG,
COMPOSED IN AUGUST
Tune—*I had a horse, I had nae mair*

I

NOW westlin winds, and slaught'ring guns
    Bring Autumn's pleasant weather;°
And the moorcock springs, on whirring wings,°
    Amang the blooming heather:
Now waving grain, wide o'er the plain,
    Delights the weary Farmer;
And the moon shines bright, when I rove at night,
    To muse upon my Charmer.

II

The Partridge loves the fruitful fells;°
    The Plover loves the mountains;°   10

The Woodcock haunts the lonely dells;°
    The soaring Hern the fountains:
Thro' lofty groves, the Cushat roves,
    The path of man to shun it;°
The hazel bush o'erhangs the Thrush,
    The spreading thorn the Linnet.

III

Thus ev'ry kind their pleasure find,
    The savage and the tender;
Some social join, and leagues combine;
    Some solitary wander: 20
Avaunt, away! the cruel sway,
    Tyrannic man's dominion;
The Sportsman's joy, the murd'ring cry,°
    The flutt'ring, gory pinion!°

IV

But PEGGY dear, the ev'ning's clear,
    Thick flies the skimming Swallow;
The sky is blue, the fields in view,
    All fading-green and yellow:
Come let us stray our gladsome way,
    And view the charms of Nature;°   30
The rustling corn, the fruited thorn,
    And ev'ry happy creature.°

V

We'll gently walk, and sweetly talk,
    Till the silent moon shine clearly;°
I'll grasp thy waist, and fondly prest,°
    Swear how I love thee dearly:°
Not vernal show'rs to budding flow'rs,
    Not Autumn to the Farmer,
So dear can be, as thou to me,
    My fair, my lovely Charmer!   40

SONG
Tune—*Gilderoy*

I

FROM thee, ELIZA, I must go,
  And from my native shore:
The cruel fates between us throw
  A boundless ocean's roar;
But boundless oceans, roaring wide,
  Between my Love and me,
They never, never can divide
  My heart and soul from thee.

II

Farewell, farewell, ELIZA dear,
  The maid that I adore!   10
A boding voice is in mine ear,
  We part to meet no more!
But the latest throb that leaves my heart,°
  While Death stands victor by,
That throb, ELIZA, is thy part,
  And thine that latest sigh!

THE FAREWELL.
TO THE BRETHREN OF ST. JAMES'S LODGE, TARBOLTON
Tune—*Goodnight and joy be wi' you a'*

I

ADIEU! a heart-warm, fond adieu!
  Dear brothers of the *mystic tye!*
Ye favored, ye *enlighten'd* Few,°
  Companions of my social joy!
Tho' I to foreign lands must hie,
  Pursuing Fortune's slidd'ry ba',
With melting heart, and brimful eye,
  I'll mind you still, tho' far awa.

II

Oft have I met your social Band,
 And spent the chearful, festive night;   10
Oft, honor'd with supreme command,°
 Presided o'er the *Sons of light*:
And by that *Hieroglyphic* bright,°
 Which none but *Craftsmen* ever saw!
Strong Mem'ry on my heart shall write
 Those happy scenes when far awa!

III

May Freedom, Harmony and Love
 Unite you in the *grand Design*,
Beneath th' Omniscient Eye above,
 The glorious ARCHITECT Divine!°   20
That you may keep th' *unerring line*,
 Still rising by the *plummet's law*,
Till *Order* bright, completely shine,
 Shall be my Pray'r when far awa.

IV

And *YOU*, farewell! whose merits claim,°
 Justly that *highest badge* to wear!
Heav'n bless your honor'd, noble Name,
 To MASONRY and SCOTIA dear!
A last request, permit me here,
 When yearly ye assemble a',   30
One *round*, I ask it with a *tear*,
 To him, *the Bard, that's far awa*.

EPITAPHS AND EPIGRAMS°

EPITAPH ON A HENPECKED COUNTRY SQUIRE

As father Adam first was fool'd,
 A case that's still too common,
Here lyes a man a woman rul'd,
 The devil rul'd the woman.

EPIGRAM ON SAID OCCASION

O Death, hadst thou but spar'd his life,
  Whom we, this day, lament!
We freely wad exchang'd the *wife*,
  An' a' been weel content.

Ev'n as he is, cauld in his graff,
  The *swap* we yet will do't;
Tak thou the Carlin's carcase aff,
  Thou'se get the *saul o' boot*.

ANOTHER

One Queen Artemisa, as old stories tell,
When depriv'd of her husband she loved so well,
In respect for the love and affection he'd show'd her,
She reduc'd him to dust, and she drank up the Powder.

But Queen N**********, of a diff'rent complexion,
When call'd on to order the fun'ral direction,
Would have *eat* her dead lord, on a slender pretence,
Not to show her respect, but—*to save the expense*.

EPITAPHS

ON A CELEBRATED RULING ELDER

Here Sowter **** in Death does sleep;°
  To H—ll, if he's gane thither,
Satan, gie him thy gear to keep,
  He'll haud it weel thegither.

ON A NOISY POLEMIC

Below thir stanes lie Jamie's banes;
  O Death, it's my opinion,
Thou ne'er took such a bleth'ran b—tch,
  Into thy dark dominion!

ON WEE JOHNIE
Hic jacet wee *Johnie*

Whoe'er thou art, O reader, know,
    That Death has murder'd Johnie;
An' here his *body* lies fu' low——
    For *saul* he ne'er had ony.

FOR THE AUTHOR'S FATHER

O ye whose cheek the tear of pity stains,
    Draw near with pious rev'rence and attend!
Here lie the loving Husband's dear remains,
    The tender Father, and the gen'rous Friend.

The pitying Heart that felt for human Woe;
    The dauntless heart that fear'd no human Pride;
The Friend of Man, to vice alone a foe;
    'For ev'n his failings lean'd to Virtue's side.'[1]

FOR R.A. ESQ;

Know thou, O stranger to the fame
Of this much lov'd, much honor'd name!
(For none that knew him need be told)
A warmer heart Death ne'er made cold.

FOR G.H. ESQ;

The poor man weeps—here G——N sleeps,
    Whom canting wretches blam'd:°
But with *such as he*, where'er he be,
    May I be *sav'd* or *d——'d!*

[1] Goldsmith.

A BARD'S EPITAPH

IS there a whim-inspir'd fool,
Owre fast for thought, owre hot for rule,
Owre blate to seek, owre proud to snool,
      Let him draw near;
And o'er this grassy heap sing dool,
      And drap a tear.

Is there a Bard of rustic song,
Who, noteless, steals the crouds among,°
That weekly this area throng,
      O, pass not by!
But with a frater-feeling strong,°
      Here, heave a sigh.

Is there a man whose judgment clear,
Can others teach the course to steer,
Yet runs, himself, life's mad career,
      Wild as the wave,
Here pause—and thro' the starting tear,
      Survey this grave.

The poor Inhabitant below
Was quick to learn and wise to know,
And keenly felt the friendly glow,
      And *softer flame*;
But thoughtless follies laid him low,
      And stain'd his name!

Reader attend—whether thy soul
Soars fancy's flights beyond the pole,
Or darkling grubs this earthly hole,
      In low pursuit,
Know, prudent, cautious, *self-controul*
      Is Wisdom's root.

10

20

FINIS

A. Nasmyth pinxt.   I. Beugo sculp.

ROBERT   BURNS

POEMS,

CHIEFLY IN THE

SCOTTISH DIALECT.

BY

ROBERT BURNS.

EDINBURGH:
PRINTED FOR THE AUTHOR,
AND SOLD BY WILLIAM CREECH.
M,DCC,LXXXVII.

DEDICATION.

TO THE

NOBLEMEN AND GENTLEMEN

OF THE

CALEDONIAN HUNT.

My Lords, and Gentlemen,

A Scottish Bard, proud of the name, and whose highest ambition is to sing in his Country's service, where shall he so properly look for patronage as to the illustrious Names of his native Land; those who bear the honours and inherit the virtues of their Ancestors?—The Poetic Genius of my Country found me as the prophetic bard Elijah did Elisha—at the plough; *and threw her inspiring* mantle *over me.° She bade me sing the loves, the joys, the rural scenes and rural pleasures of my natal Soil, in my native tongue: I tuned my wild, artless notes, as she inspired.—She whispered me to come to this ancient metropolis of Caledonia, and lay my Songs under your hon-oured protection: I now obey her dictates.*

Though much indebted to your goodness, I do not approach you, my Lords and Gentlemen, in the usual stile of dedication, to thank you for past favours; that path is so hackneyed by prostituted Learning, that honest Rusticity is ashamed of it.—Nor do I present this Address with the venal soul of a servile Author, looking for a continuation of those favours: I was bred to the Plough, and am independent. I come to claim the common Scottish name with you, my illustrious Countrymen; and to tell the world that I glory in the title.—I come to congratulate my Country, that the blood of her ancient heroes still runs uncontaminated; and that from your courage, knowledge, and public spirit, she may expect protection, wealth, and liberty.—In the last place, I come to proffer my warmest wishes to the Great Fountain of Honour, the Monarch of the Universe, for your welfare and happiness.

When you go forth to waken the Echoes, in the ancient and favourite amusement of your Forefathers, may Pleasure ever be of your party; and may Social-joy await your return! When harassed in courts or camps with the justlings of bad men and bad measures, may the honest consciousness of injured Worth attend your return to your native Seats; and may Domestic Happiness, with a smiling welcome, meet you at your gates! May Corruption shrink at your kindling indignant glance; and may tyranny in the Ruler and licentiousness in the People equally find you an inexorable foe!

I have the honour to be,

   With the sincerest gratitude and highest respect,
   MY LORDS AND GENTLEMEN,
   Your most devoted humble servant,

          ROBERT BURNS.

EDINBURGH,
April 4. 1787.

THE BRIGS OF AYR

A POEM

Inscribed to J. B*********, Esq; AYR

THE simple Bard, rough at the rustic plough,
Learning his tuneful trade from ev'ry bough;
The chanting linnet, or the mellow thrush,
Hailing the setting sun, sweet, in the green thorn bush,
The soaring lark, the perching red-breast shrill,
Or deep-ton'd plovers, grey, wild-whistling o'er the hill;
Shall he, nurst in the Peasant's lowly shed,
To hardy Independence bravely bred,
By early Poverty to hardship steel'd,
And train'd to arms in stern Misfortune's field,   10
Shall he be guilty of their hireling crimes,
The servile, mercenary Swiss of rhymes?°
Or labour hard the panegyric close,°
With all the venal soul of dedicating Prose?
No! though his artless strains he rudely sings,
And throws his hand uncouthly o'er the strings,
He glows with all the spirit of the Bard,
Fame, honest fame, his great, his dear reward.°
Still, if some Patron's gen'rous care he trace,
Skill'd in the secret, to bestow with grace;   20
When B********* befriends his humble name,
And hands the rustic Stranger up to fame,
With heartfelt throes his grateful bosom swells,
The godlike bliss, to give, alone excels.

'Twas when the stacks get on their winter-hap,
And thack and rape secure the toil-won crap;
Potatoe-bings are snugged up frae skaith
Of coming Winter's biting, frosty breath;
The bees, rejoicing o'er their summer-toils,
Unnumber'd buds an' flow'rs' delicious spoils,   30
Seal'd up with frugal care in massive, waxen piles,
Are doom'd by Man, that tyrant o'er the weak,
The death o' devils, smoor'd wi' brimstone reek:°

The thund'ring guns are heard on ev'ry side,
The wounded coveys, reeling, scatter wide;
The feather'd field-mates, bound by Nature's tie,
Sires, mothers, children, in one carnage lie:
(What warm, poetic heart but inly bleeds,
And execrates man's savage, ruthless deeds!)
Nae mair the flow'r in field or meadow springs;   40
Nae mair the grove with airy concert rings,
Except perhaps the Robin's whistling glee,
Proud o' the height o' some bit half-lang tree:
The hoary morns precede the sunny days,
Mild, calm, serene, wide-spreads the noontide blaze,
While thick the gossamour waves wanton in the rays.

'Twas in that season; when a simple Bard,
Unknown and poor, simplicity's reward,
Ae night, within the ancient brugh of *Ayr*,
By whim inspir'd, or haply prest wi' care,   50
He left his bed and took his wayward rout,
And down by *Simpson's*[1] wheel'd the left about:
(Whether impell'd by all-directing Fate,
To witness what I after shall narrate;
Or whether, rapt in meditation high,
He wander'd out he knew not where nor why)
The drowsy *Dungeon-clock* had number'd two,°
And *Wallace-Tow'r*[2] had sworn the fact was true:°
The tide-swoln Firth, with sullen-sounding roar,
Through the still night dash'd hoarse along the shore: 60
All else was hush'd as Nature's closed e'e;
The silent moon shone high o'er tow'r and tree:°
The chilly Frost, beneath the silver beam,
Crept, gently-crusting, o'er the glittering stream.——

When, lo! on either hand the list'ning Bard,
The clanging sugh of whistling wings is heard;°
Two dusky forms dart thro' the midnight air,
Swift as the *Gos*[3] drives on the wheeling hare;
Ane on th' *Auld Brig* his airy shape uprears,

[1] A noted tavern at the *Auld Brig* end.   [2] The two steeples.
[3] The gos-hawk, or falcon.

The ither flutters o'er the *rising piers*:   70
Our warlock Rhymer instantly descry'd°
The Sprites that owre the *Brigs of Ayr* preside.
(That Bards are second-sighted is nae joke,
And ken the lingo of the sp'ritual folk;°
Fays, Spunkies, Kelpies, a', they can explain them,°
And ev'n the vera deils they brawly ken them).
Auld Brig appear'd of ancient Pictish race,
The vera wrinkles Gothic in his face:°
He seem'd as he wi' Time had warstl'd lang,
Yet, teughly doure, he bade an unco bang.   80
New Brig was buskit in a braw, new coat,
That he, at *Lon'on*, frae ane *Adams* got;°
In's hand five taper staves as smooth's a bead,°
Wi' virls an' whirlygigums at the head.°
The Goth was stalking round with anxious search,
Spying the time-worn flaws in ev'ry arch;
It chanc'd his new-come neebor took his e'e,
And e'en a vex'd and angry heart had he!
Wi' thieveless sneer to see his modish mien,
He, down the water, gies him this guid-een——   90

AULD BRIG

I doubt na, frien', ye'll think ye're nae sheep-shank,
Ance ye were streekit owre frae bank to bank!
But gin ye be a Brig as auld as me,
Tho' faith, that date, I doubt, ye'll never see;
There'll be, if that date come, I'll wad a boddle,
Some fewer whigmeleeries in your noddle.

NEW BRIG

Auld Vandal, ye but show your little mense,°
Just much about it wi' your scanty sense;
Will your poor, narrow foot-path of a street,
Where twa wheel-barrows tremble when they meet,   100
Your ruin'd, formless bulk o' stane and lime,
Compare wi' bonie *Brigs* o' modern time?
There's men of taste wou'd tak the *Ducat-stream*,[1]
Tho' they should cast the vera sark and swim,

[1] A noted ford, just above the Auld Brig.

E'er they would grate their feelings wi' the view
Of sic an ugly, Gothic hulk as you.

AULD BRIG

Conceited gowk! puff'd up wi' windy pride!
This mony a year I've stood the flood an' tide;
And tho' wi' crazy eild I'm sair forfairn,
I'll be a *Brig* when ye're a shapeless cairn!   110
As yet ye little ken about the matter,
But twa-three winters will inform ye better.
When heavy, dark, continued, a'-day rains
Wi' deepening deluges o'erflow the plains;
When from the hills where springs the brawling *Coil*,
Or stately *Lugar's* mossy fountains boil,
Or where the *Greenock* winds his moorland course,
Or haunted *Garpal*[1] draws his feeble source,°
Arous'd by blustering winds an' spotting thowes,
In mony a torrent down the snaw-broo rowes;   120
While crashing ice, borne on the roaring speat,
Sweeps dams, an' mills, an' brigs, a' to the gate;
And from *Glenbuck*,[2] down to the *Ratton-key*,[3]
Auld *Ayr* is just one lengthen'd, tumbling sea;
Then down ye'll hurl, deil nor ye never rise!
And dash the gumlie jaups up to the pouring skies.
A lesson sadly teaching, to your cost,
That Architecture's noble art is lost!

NEW BRIG

Fine *architecture*, trowth, I needs must say't o't!
The L—d be thankit that we've tint the gate o't!   130
Gaunt, ghastly, ghaist-alluring edifices,
Hanging with threat'ning jut like precipices;
O'er-arching, mouldy, gloom-inspiring coves,
Supporting roofs, fantastic, stony groves:°
Windows and doors in nameless sculptures drest,
With order, symmetry, or taste unblest;
Forms like some bedlam Statuary's dream,

---

[1] The banks of the *Garpal Water* is one of the few places in the West of Scotland where those fancy-scaring beings, known by the name of *Ghaists*, still continue pertinaciously to inhabit.

[2] The source of the river of Ayr.   [3] A small landing-place above the large key.

The craz'd creations of misguided whim;
Forms might be worshipp'd on the bended knee,
And still the *second dread command* be free,°
Their likeness is not found on earth, in air, or sea.

Mansions that would disgrace the building-taste
Of any mason reptile, bird, or beast;
Fit only for a doited Monkish race,
Or frosty maids forsworn the dear embrace,
Or Cuifs of later times, wha held the notion,
That sullen gloom was sterling, true devotion:
Fancies that our guid Brugh denies protection,
And soon may they expire, unblest with resurrection!°

AULD BRIG

O ye, my dear-remember'd, ancient yealings,°   150
Were ye but here to share my wounded feelings!
Ye worthy *Proveses*, an' mony a *Bailie*,°
Wha in the paths o' righteousness did toil ay;
Ye dainty *Deacons*, an' ye douce *Conveeners*,°
To whom our moderns are but causey-cleaners;
Ye godly *Councils* wha hae blest this town;
Ye godly *Brethren* o' the sacred gown,
Wha meekly gae your *hurdies* to the *smiters*;
And (what would now be strange) ye *godly Writers*:°
A' ye douce folk I've borne aboon the broo,   160
Were ye but here, what would ye say or do!
How would your spirits groan in deep vexation,
To see each melancholy alteration;
And, agonising, curse the time and place
When ye begat the base, degen'rate race!
Nae langer Rev'rend Men, their country's glory,
In plain, braid Scots hold forth a plain, braid story:
Nae langer thrifty Citizens, an' douce,
Meet owre a pint, or in the Council-house;
But staumrel, corky-headed, graceless Gentry,   170
The herryment and ruin of the country;
Men, three-parts made by Taylors and by Barbers,
Wha waste your weel-hain'd gear on d——d *new Brigs*
    and *Harbours!*°

NEW BRIG

Now haud you there! for faith ye've said enough,
And muckle mair than ye can mak to through.°
As for your Priesthood, I shall say but little,
Corbies and *Clergy* are a shot right kittle:°
But, under favor o' your langer beard,
Abuse o' Magistrates might weel be spar'd;
To liken them to your auld-warld squad,   180
I must needs say, comparisons are odd.
In *Ayr*, Wag-wits nae mair can have a handle
To mouth 'A Citizen,' a term o' scandal:°
Nae mair the Council waddles down the street,
In all the pomp of ignorant conceit;
Men wha grew wise priggin owre hops an' raisins,
Or gather'd lib'ral views in Bonds and Seisins.°
If haply Knowledge, on a random tramp,
Had shor'd them with a glimmer of his lamp,
And would to Common-sense for once betray'd them,   190
Plain, dull Stupidity stept kindly in to aid them.

————

What farther clishmaclaver might been said,
What bloody wars, if Spirites had blood to shed,
No man can tell; but, all before their sight,
A fairy train appear'd in order bright:
Adown the glittering stream they featly danc'd;°
Bright to the moon their various dresses glanc'd:
They footed o'er the wat'ry glass so neat,
The infant ice scarce bent beneath their feet:
While arts of Minstrelsy among them rung,   200
And soul-ennobling Bards heroic ditties sung.

O had *McLauchlan*,[1] thairm-inspiring Sage,°
Been there to hear this heavenly band engage,
When thro' his dear *Strathspeys* they bore with Highland rage;
Or when they struck old Scotia's melting airs,
The lover's raptur'd joys or bleeding cares;
How would his Highland lug been nobler fir'd,

---

[1] A well known performer of Scottish music on the violin.

And ev'n his matchless hand with finer touch inspir'd!
No guess could tell what instrument appear'd,
But all the soul of Music's self was heard;   210
Harmonious concert rung in every part,
While simple melody pour'd moving on the heart.

The Genius of the Stream in front appears,°
A venerable Chief advanc'd in years;
His hoary head with water-lilies crown'd,
His manly leg with garter tangle bound.°
Next came the loveliest pair in all the ring,
Sweet Female Beauty hand in hand with Spring;
Then, crown'd with flow'ry hay, came Rural Joy,
And Summer, with his fervid-beaming eye: 220
All-chearing Plenty, with her flowing horn,
Led yellow Autumn wreath'd with nodding corn;
Then Winter's time-bleach'd locks did hoary show,
By Hospitality with cloudless brow.°
Next follow'd Courage with his martial stride,
From where the *Feal* wild-woody coverts hide:°
Benevolence, with mild, benignant air,
A female form, came from the tow'rs of *Stair*:°
Learning and Worth in equal measures trode,
From simple *Catrine*, their long-lov'd abode:°   230
Last, white-rob'd Peace, crown'd with a hazle wreath,
To rustic Agriculture did bequeath
The broken, iron instruments of Death,°
At sight of whom our Sprites forgat their kindling wrath.

ADDRESS TO THE UNCO GUID,
OR THE
RIGIDLY RIGHTEOUS

My Son, these maxims make a rule,
And lump them ay thegither;
The Rigid Righteous *is a fool,*
The Rigid Wise *anither:*
The cleanest corn that e'er was dight

May hae some pyles o' caff in;
So ne'er a fellow-creature slight
For random fits o' daffin.

SOLOMON. — Eccles. ch. vii. vers. 16.°

I

O YE wha are sae guid yoursel,
    Sae pious and sae holy,
Ye've nought to do but mark and tell
    Your Neebours' fauts and folly!
Whase life is like a weel-gaun mill,
    Supply'd wi' store o' water,
The heaped happer's ebbing still,
    And still the clap plays clatter.°

II

Hear me, ye venerable Core,
    As counsel for poor mortals,   10
That frequent pass douce Wisdom's door
    For glaikit Folly's portals;
I, for their thoughtless, careless sakes
    Would here propone defences,
Their donsie tricks, their black mistakes,
    Their failings and mischances.

III

Ye see your state wi' theirs compar'd,
    And shudder at the niffer,
But cast a moment's fair regard
    What maks the mighty differ;   20
Discount what scant occasion gave,
    That purity ye pride in,
And (what's aft mair than a' the lave)
    Your better art o' hiding.

IV

Think, when your castigated pulse
    Gies now and then a wallop,
What ragings must his veins convulse,
    That still eternal gallop:
Wi' wind and tide fair i' your tail,

Right on ye scud your sea-way;   30
But, in the teeth o' baith to sail,
   It maks an unco leeway.

V

See Social-life and Glee sit down,
   All joyous and unthinking,
Till, quite transmugrify'd, they're grown
   Debauchery and Drinking:
O would they stay to calculate
   Th' eternal consequences;
Or your more dreaded h–ll to state,
   D–mnation of expences!   40

VI

Ye high, exalted, virtuous Dames,
   Ty'd up in godly laces,
Before ye gie poor *Frailty* names,
   Suppose a change o' cases;
A dear-lov'd lad, convenience snug,
   A treacherous inclination——
But, let me whisper i' your lug,
   Ye're aiblins nae temptation.

VII

Then gently scan your brother Man,°
   Still gentler sister Woman;   50
Tho' they may gang a kennin wrang,
   To step aside is human:
One point must still be greatly dark,
   The moving *Why* they do it;
And just as lamely can ye mark,
   How far perhaps they rue it.

VIII

Who made the heart, 'tis *He* alone
   Decidedly can try us,
He knows each chord its various tone,
   Each spring its various bias: 60
Then at the balance let's be mute,
   We never can adjust it;

What's *done* we partly may compute,
But know not what's *resisted*.

TO A HAGGIS

FAIR fa' your honest, sonsie face,
Great Chieftan o' the Puddin-race!
Aboon them a' ye tak your place,
                    Painch, tripe, or thairm:°
Weel are ye wordy of a *grace*
                    As lang's my arm.

The groaning trencher there ye fill,
Your hurdies like a distant hill,
Your *pin* wad help to mend a mill°
                    In time o' need,   10
While thro' your pores the dews distil
                    Like amber bead.°

His knife see Rustic-labour dight,
An' cut you up wi' ready slight,
Trenching your gushing entrails bright
                    Like onie ditch;
And then, O what a glorious sight,
                    Warm-reekin, rich!

Then, horn for horn they stretch an' strive,°
Deil tak the hindmost, on they drive,   20
Till a' their weel-swall'd kytes belyve
                    Are bent like drums;
Then auld Guidman, maist like to rive,
                    Bethankit hums.°

Is there that owre his French *ragout*,
Or *olio* that wad staw a sow,
Or *fricassee* wad mak her spew°
                    Wi' perfect sconner,
Looks down wi' sneering, scornfu' view
                    On sic a dinner?   30

Poor devil! see him owre his trash,
As feckless as a wither'd rash,
His spindle shank a guid whip-lash,
      His nieve a nit;
Thro' bluidy flood or field to dash,
      O how unfit!

But mark the Rustic, *haggis-fed*,
The trembling earth resounds his tread,
Clap in his walie nieve a blade,
      He'll mak it whissle;   40
An' legs, an' arms, an' heads will sned,
      Like taps o' thrissle.°

Ye Pow'rs wha mak mankind your care,
And dish them out their bill o' fare,
Auld Scotland wants nae skinking ware
      That jaups in luggies;
But, if ye wish her gratefu' pray'r,
      Gie her a *Haggis!*°

JOHN BARLEYCORN[1]
A BALLAD

I

THERE was three kings into the east,
  Three kings both great and high,
And they hae sworn a solemn oath
  John Barleycorn should die.

II

They took a plough and plough'd him down,
  Put clods upon his head,
And they hae sworn a solemn oath
  John Barleycorn was dead.

---

[1] This is partly composed on the plan of an old song known by the same name.

III

But the chearful Spring came kindly on,
   And show'rs began to fall;   10
John Barleycorn got up again,
   And sore surpris'd them all.

IV

The sultry suns of Summer came,
   And he grew thick and strong,
His head weel arm'd wi' pointed spears,
   That no one should him wrong.

V

The sober Autumn enter'd mild,
   When he grew wan and pale;
His bending joints and drooping head
   Show'd he began to fail.   20

VI

His colour sicken'd more and more,
   He faded into age;
And then his enemies began
   To show their deadly rage.

VII

They've taen a weapon, long and sharp,
   And cut him by the knee;
Then ty'd him fast upon a cart,
   Like a rogue for forgerie.

VIII

They laid him down upon his back,
   And cudgell'd him full sore;°
They hung him up before the storm,   30
   And turn'd him o'er and o'er.°

IX

They filled up a darksome pit
   With water to the brim,°

They heaved in John Barleycorn,
　There let him sink or swim.

X

They laid him out upon the floor,
　To work him farther woe,
And still, as signs of life appear'd,
　They toss'd him to and fro.°　　　　　　40

XI

They wasted, o'er a scorching flame,°
　The marrow of his bones;
But a Miller us'd him worst of all,
　For he crush'd him between two stones.°

XII

And they hae taen his very heart's blood,
　And drank it round and round;
And still the more and more they drank,
　Their joy did more abound.

XIII

John Barleycorn was a hero bold,
　Of noble enterprise,　　　　　　　　　50
For if you do but taste his blood,
　'Twill make your courage rise.

XIV

'Twill make a man forget his woe;
　'Twill heighten all his joy:
'Twill make the widow's heart to sing,
　Tho' the tear were in her eye.

XV

Then let us toast John Barleycorn,
　Each man a glass in hand;
And may his great posterity
　Ne'er fail in old Scotland!　　　　　　60

A FRAGMENT

Tune—*Gilliecrankie*

I

WHEN *Guilford* good our Pilot stood,°
    An' did our hellim thraw, man,°
Ae night, at tea, began a plea,
    Within *America*, man:
Then up they gat the maskin-pat,
    And in the sea did jaw, man;°
An' did nae less, in full Congress,°
    Than quite refuse our law, man.

II

Then thro' the lakes *Montgomery* takes,°
    I wat he was na slaw, man;   10
Down *Lowrie's burn* he took a turn,
    And *C–rl–t–n* did ca', man:°
But yet, whatreck, he, at *Quebec*,
    Montgomery-like did fa', man,
Wi' sword in hand, before his band,
    Amang his en'mies a', man.°

III

Poor *Tammy G–ge* within a cage°
    Was kept at *Boston-ha'*, man;
Till *Willie H——e* took o'er the knowe°
    For *Philadelphia*, man: 20
Wi' sword an' gun he thought a sin
    Guid Christian bluid to draw, man;
But at *New-York*, wi' knife an' fork,
    Sir Loin he hacked sma', man.°

IV

B–rg——ne gaed up, like spur an' whip,°
    Till *Fraser* brave did fa', man;
Then lost his way, ae misty day,
    In *Saratoga* shaw, man.
C–rnw–ll–s fought as lang's he dought,°

An' did the Buckskins claw, man;°   30
But *Cl–nt–n's* glaive frae rust to save°
   He hung it to the wa', man.

V

Then *M–nt–gue*, an' *Guilford* too,°
   Began to fear a fa', man;
And *S–ckv–lle* doure, wha stood the stoure,°
   The German Chief to thraw, man:°
For Paddy *B–rke*, like ony Turk,°
   Nae mercy had at a', man;
An' *Charlie F–x* threw by the box,°
   An' lows'd his tinkler jaw, man.   40

VI

Then *R–ck–ngh–m* took up the game;°
   Till Death did on him ca', man;
When *Sh–lb–rne* meek held up his cheek,°
   Conform to Gospel law, man:
Saint Stephen's boys, wi' jarring noise,
   They did his measures thraw, man,
For *N–rth* an' *F–x* united stocks,°
   An' bore him to the wa', man.

VII

Then Clubs an' Hearts were *Charlie's* cartes,°
   He swept the stakes awa', man,   50
Till the Diamond's Ace, of *Indian* race,
   Led him a sair *faux pas*, man:°
The Saxon lads, wi' loud placads,°
   On *Chatham's Boy* did ca', man;°
An' Scotland drew her pipe an' blew,
   'Up, Willie, waur them a', man!'°

VIII

Behind the throne then *Gr–nv–lle's* gone,°
   A secret word or twa, man;
While slee *D–nd–s* arous'd the class°
   Be-north the Roman wa', man: 60
An' *Chatham's* wraith, in heav'nly graith,
   (Inspired Bardies saw, man)

Wi' kindling eyes cry'd, '*Willie*, rise!
'Would I hae fear'd them a', man!'

IX

But, word an' blow, *N–rth, F–x, and Co.*
   Gowff'd *Willie* like a ba', man,°
Till *Suthron* raise, an' coost their claise
   Behind him in a raw, man:°
An' *Caledon* threw by the drone,
   An' did her whittle draw, man;   70
An' swoor fu' rude, thro' dirt an' blood,
   To mak it guid in law, man.°

* * * * * * *

Songs from *The Scots Musical Museum*

GREEN GROWS THE RASHES

There's nought but care on ev'-ry han', In ev'-ry hour that pas-ses, O: What

sig-ni-fies the life o' man, An' twere not for the las-ses, O?

Chorus

Green grow the rash-es, O; Green grow the rash-es, O; The

sweet-est hours that e'er I spend, Are spent a-mang the las-ses, O.

There's nought but care on ev'ry han',
  In ev'ry hour that passes, O:
What signifies the life o' man,
  An' twere not for the lasses, O?

CHORUS: Green grow the rashes, O;
         Green grow the rashes, O;
         The sweetest hours that e'er I spend,
         Are spent amang the lasses, O.

The warly race may riches chase,
  An' riches still may fly them, O;   10
An' tho' at last they catch them fast,
  Their hearts can ne'er enjoy them, O.
         Green grow, &c.

But gie me a canny hour at e'en,
  My arms about my Dearie, O;
An' warly cares, an' warly men,
  May a' gae tapsalteerie, O!
         Green grow, &c.

For you sae douse! ye sneer at this,
  Ye'er nought but senseless asses, O:
The wisest Man the warl' saw,°
  He dearly lov'd the lasses, O.   20
         Green grow, &c.

Auld Nature swears, the lovely Dears
  Her noblest work she classes, O:
Her prentice han' she try'd on man,
  An' then she made the lasses, O.
         Green grow, &c.

THE BIRKS OF ABERFELDY

CHORUS: Bonny lassie, will ye go,
     will ye go, will ye go,
     bonny lassie, will ye go
     to the Birks of Aberfeldy?

Now Simmer blinks on flowery braes,
And o'er the chrystal streamlets plays;
Come let us spend the lightsome days
  In the birks of Aberfeldy.
    Bonny lassie, &c.

The little birdies blythely sing,
While o'er their heads the hazels hing;   10
Or lightly flit on wanton wing
  In the birks of Aberfeldy.
    Bonny lassie, &c.

The braes ascend like lofty wa's,
The foamy stream deep-roaring fa's,
O'er-hung wi' fragrant-spreading shaws,
  The birks of Aberfeldy.
    Bonny lassie, &c.

The hoary cliffs are crown'd wi' flowers,
White o'er the linns the burnie pours,
And rising weets wi' misty showers
  The birks of Aberfeldy.   20
    Bonny lassie, &c.

Let Fortune's gifts at random flee,
They ne'er shall draw a wish frae me.
Supremely blest wi' love and thee
  In the birks of Aberfeldy.
    Bonny lassie, &c.

THE PLOUGHMAN

The Ploughman he's a bony lad,
His mind is ever true, jo,
His garters knit below his knee,
His bonnet it is blue, jo.°

CHORUS: Then up wi't a', my Ploughman lad,
And hey, my merry Ploughman;
Of a' the trades that I do ken,
Commend me to the Ploughman.

My Ploughman he comes hame at e'en,
    He's aften wat and weary: 10
Cast off the wat, put on the dry,
    And gae to bed, my Dearie.
        Up wi't a' &c.

I will wash my Ploughman's hose,
    And I will dress his o'erlay;
I will mak my Ploughman's bed,
    And chear him late and early.
        Up wi't a' &c.

I hae been east, I hae been west,
    I hae been at Saint Johnston,°
The boniest sight that e'er I saw
    Was th' Ploughman laddie dancin.   20
        Up wi't a' &c.

Snaw-white stockins on his legs,
    And siller buckles glancin;
A gude blue bannet on his head,
    And O but he was handsome!
        Up wi't a' &c.

Commend me to the Barn yard,
    And the Corn-mou, man;°
I never gat my Coggie fou
    Till I met wi' the Ploughman.
        Up wi't a' &c.

RATTLIN, ROARIN WILLIE

Lively

O Rat-tlin, roa-rin Wil-lie, O he held to the fair, An' for to sell his fid-dle And buy some o-ther ware; But par-ting wi' his fid-dle, The saut tear blin't his e'e; And Rat-tlin, roar-in Wil-lie Ye're wel-come hame to me.

O Rattlin, roarin Willie,
  O he held to the fair,
An' for to sell his fiddle
  And buy some other ware;
But parting wi' his fiddle,
  The saut tear blin't his e'e;°
And Rattlin, roarin Willie
  Ye're welcome hame to me.

O Willie, come sell your fiddle,
  O sell your fiddle sae fine;   10
O Willie, come sell your fiddle,
  And buy a pint o' wine;
If I should sell my fiddle,
  The warl' would think I was mad,
For mony a rantin day
  My fiddle and I hae had.

As I cam by Crochallan°
  I cannily keekit ben,
Rattlin, roarin Willie
  Was sitting at yon boord-en',   20
Sitting at yon boord-en',
  And amang guid companie;
Rattlin, roarin Willie,
  Ye're welcome hame to me!

TIBBIE, I HAE SEEN THE DAY

Slowish

O Tib-bie, I hae seen the day, Ye would na been sae shy; For laik o' gear ye light-ly me, But trowth, I care na by. Yes-treen I met you on the moor, Ye spak na, but gaed by like stoure; Ye geck at me be-cause I'm poor, But fient a hair care I.

Chorus

O Tib-bie, I hae seen the day, Ye would na been sae shy; For laik o' gear ye light-ly me, But trowth I care na by.

CHORUS: O Tibbie, I hae seen the day,
            Ye would na been sae shy;
            For laik o' gear ye lightly me,
            But trowth, I care na by.

Yestreen I met you on the moor,
Ye spak na, but gaed by like stoure;
Ye geck at me because I'm poor,
    But fient a hair care I.
      Tibbie, I hae &c.

I doubt na, lass, but ye may think,
Because ye hae the name o' clink,   10
That ye can please me at a wink,
    Whene'er ye like to try.
      Tibbie, I hae &c.

But sorrow tak him that's sae mean,
Altho' his pouch o' coin were clean,
Wha follows ony saucy quean
    That looks sae proud and high.
      Tibbie, I hae &c.

Altho' a lad were e'er sae smart,
If that he want the yellow dirt,
Ye'll cast your head anither airt,
    And answer him fu' dry.   20
      Tibbie, I hae &c.

But if he hae the name o' gear,
Ye'll fasten to him like a brier,
Tho' hardly he for sense or lear
    Be better than the kye.
      Tibbie, I hae &c.

But, Tibbie, lass, tak my advice,
Your daddie's gear maks you sae nice;
The deil a ane wad spier your price,
    Were ye as poor as I.
      Tibbie, I hae &c.

AY WAUKIN, O

Sim-mer's a plea-sant time, Flowers of ev'-ry co-lour; The wa-ter rins o'er the heugh, And I long for my true lo-ver!

Ay wau-kin, O, Wau-kin still and wea-ry: Sleep I can get nane, For think-ing on my Dear-ie.

Simmer's a pleasant time,
    Flowers of ev'ry colour;
The water rins o'er the heugh,
    And I long for my true lover!

CHORUS: Ay waukin, O,
        Waukin still and weary:
        Sleep I can get nane,
        For thinking on my Dearie.

When I sleep I dream,
    When I wauk I'm irie;   10
Sleep I can get nane
    For thinking on my Dearie.
        Ay waukin &c.

Lanely night comes on,
    A' the lave are sleepin:
I think on my bony lad
    And I bleer my een wi' greetin.
        Ay waukin &c.

MY LOVE SHE'S BUT A LASSIE YET

My love she's but a las-sie yet, My love she's but a las-sie yet, We'll let her stand a year or twa, She'll no be half sae sau-cy yet. I rue the day I sought her O, I rue the day I sought her O, Wha gets her needs na say he's woo'd, But he may say he's bought her O.

My love she's but a lassie yet,
My love she's but a lassie yet,
We'll let her stand a year or twa,
    She'll no be half sae saucy yet.

I rue the day I sought her O,
I rue the day I sought her O,
Wha gets her needs na say he's woo'd,
    But he may say he's bought her O.

Come draw a drap o' the best o't yet,
Come draw a drap o' the best o't yet: 10
Gae seek for pleasure whare ye will,
    But here I never misst it yet.

We're a' dry wi' drinking o't,
We're a' dry wi' drinking o't:
The minister kisst the fidler's wife,
    He could na preach for thinkin o't.

I LOVE MY JEAN

Of a' the airts the wind can blaw, I dear-ly like the west, For
there the bo-ny Las-sie lives, The Las-sie I lo'e best: There's
wild-woods grow, and ri-vers row, And mony a hill be-tween; But
day and night my fan-cy's flight Is ever wi' my Jean. I
see her in the de-wy flowers, I see her sweet and fair; I
hear her in the tune-fu' birds, I hear her charm the air: There's

not a bo - ny flower, that springs By foun - tain, shaw, or green, There's

not a bo - ny bird that sings, But minds me o' my Jean.

Of a' the airts the wind can blaw,
   I dearly like the west,
For there the bony Lassie lives,
   The Lassie I lo'e best:
There's wild-woods grow, and rivers row,
   And mony a hill between;
But day and night my fancy's flight
   Is ever wi' my Jean.

I see her in the dewy flowers,
   I see her sweet and fair;
I hear her in the tunefu' birds,   10
   I hear her charm the air:
There's not a bony flower, that springs
   By fountain, shaw, or green,
There's not a bony bird that sings,
   But minds me o' my Jean.

JOHN ANDERSON MY JO

John An-der-son my jo, John, When we were first ac-quent; Your

locks were like the ra-ven, Your bo-ny brow was brent; But

now your brow is beld, John, Your locks are like the snaw; But

bles-sings on your fro-sty pow, John An-der-son my Jo.

John Anderson my jo, John,
 When we were first acquent;
Your locks were like the raven,
 Your bony brow was brent;
But now your brow is beld, John,
 Your locks are like the snaw;
But blessings on your frosty pow,
 John Anderson my Jo.

John Anderson my jo, John,
 We clamb the hill the gither;   10
And mony a canty day John,
 We've had wi' ane anither:
Now we maun totter down, John,
 And hand in hand we'll go;
And sleep the gither at the foot,
 John Anderson my Jo.

CA' THE EWES TO THE KNOWES

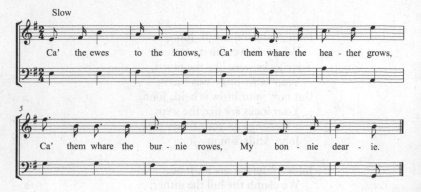

CHORUS: Ca' the ewes to the knows,
     Ca' them whare the heather grows,
     Ca' them whare the burnie rowes,
     My bonnie dearie.

 As I gaed down the water-side,
  There I met my shepherd-lad,
He row'd me sweetly in his plaid,
  An he ca'd me his dearie.
    Ca' the ewes &c.

 Will ye gang down the water-side
  And see the waves sae sweetly glide 10
Beneath the hazels spreading wide,
  The moon it shines fu' clearly.
    Ca' the ewes &c.

 I was bred up at nae sic school,
  My shepherd-lad, to play the fool,
And a' the day to sit in dool,
  And nae body to see me.
    Ca' the ewes &c.

Ye sall get gowns and ribbons meet,
  Cauf-leather shoon upon your feet,
And in my arms ye'se lie and sleep,
    And ye sall be my dearie.   20
      Ca' the ewes &c.

If ye'll but stand to what ye've said,
  I'se gang wi' you, my shepherd-lad,
And ye may rowe me in your plaid,
    And I sall be your dearie.
      Ca' the ewes &c.

While waters wimple to the sea;
  While day blinks in the lift sae hie;
Till clay-cauld death sall blin' my e'e,
    Ye sall be my dearie.   30
      Ca' the ewes &c.

THE RANTIN DOG THE DADDIE O'T

O wha my babie-clouts will buy,
O wha will tent me when I cry;
Wha will kiss me where I lie.
The rantin dog the daddie o't.

O wha will own he did the faut,
O wha will buy the groanin maut,°
O wha will tell me how to ca't.
The rantin dog the daddie o't.

When I mount the Creepie-chair,°
Wha will sit beside me there,   10
Gie me Rob, I'll seek nae mair,
The rantin dog the Daddie o't.

Wha will crack to me my lane;
Wha will mak me fidgin fain;
Wha will kiss me o'er again.
The rantin dog the Daddie o't.

TAM GLEN

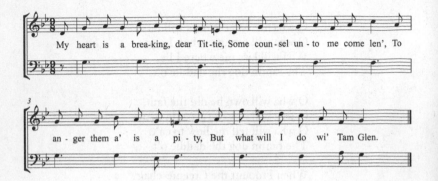

My heart is a brea-king, dear Tit-tie, Some coun-sel un-to me come len', To
an-ger them a' is a pi-ty, But what will I do wi' Tam Glen.

My heart is a breaking, dear Tittie,
   Some counsel unto me come len',
To anger them a' is a pity,
   But what will I do wi' Tam Glen.

I'm thinking, wi' sic a braw fellow,
   In poortith I might mak a fen:
What care I in riches to wallow,
   If I mauna marry Tam Glen.

There's Lowrie the laird o' Dumeller,
   'Gude day to you brute' he comes ben: 10
He brags and he blaws o' his siller,
   But when will he dance like Tam Glen.

My Minnie does constantly deave me,
   And bids me beware o' young men;
They flatter, she says, to deceive me,
   But wha can think sae o' Tam Glen.

My Daddie says, gin I'll forsake him,
  He'll gie me gude hunder marks ten:°
But, if it's ordain'd I maun take him,
  O wha will I get but Tam Glen.   20

Yestreen at the Valentines' dealing,°
  My heart to my mou gied a sten;
For thrice I drew ane without failing,
  And thrice it was written, Tam Glen.

The last Halloween I was waukin
  My droukit sark-sleeve, as ye ken;°
His likeness cam up the house staukin,
  And the very grey breeks o' Tam Glen!

Come counsel, dear Tittie, don't tarry;
  I'll gie you my bonie black hen,   30
Gif ye will advise me to Marry
  The lad I lo'e dearly, Tam Glen.

MY TOCHERS THE JEWEL

O mei-kle thinks my Luve o' my beau-ty, And mei-kle thinks my Luve o' my kin; But

lit-tle thinks my Luve, I ken braw-lie, My toch-er's the jew-el has charms for him. It's

a' for the ap-ple he'll nour-ish the tree; It's a' for the hin-ey he'll che-rish the bee, My

laddie's sae meik-le in love wi' the sil-ler, He can-na hae luve to spare for me.

O meikle thinks my Luve o' my beauty,
    And meikle thinks my Luve o' my kin;
But little thinks my Luve, I ken brawlie,
    My tocher's the jewel has charms for him.
It's a' for the apple he'll nourish the tree;
    It's a' for the hiney he'll cherish the bee,
My laddie's sae meikle in love wi' the siller,
    He canna hae luve to spare for me.

Your proffer o' luve's an airle-penny,°
    My tocher's the bargain ye wad buy;   10
But an ye be crafty, I am cunnin,
    Sae ye wi' anither your fortune maun try.
Ye're like to the timmer o' yon rotten wood,
    Ye're like to the bark o' yon rotten tree.
Ye'll slip frae me like a knotless thread,
    And ye'll crack your credit wi' mae nor me.

THERE'LL NEVER BE PEACE TILL JAMIE COMES HAME

By yon cas-tle wa' at the close of the day, I heard a man sing tho' his head it was grey; And as he was sing-ing the tears down came, There'll ne-ver be peace till Jam-ie comes hame. The Church is in ru-ins, the state is in jars, De-lu-sions, op-pres-sions, and mur-der-ous wars, We dare na weel say't, but we ken wha's to blame, There'll ne-ver be peace till Jam-ie comes hame.

By yon castle wa' at the close of the day,
I heard a man sing tho' his head it was grey;
And as he was singing the tears down came,
There'll never be peace till Jamie comes hame.
The Church is in ruins, the state is in jars,°
Delusions, oppressions, and murderous wars,
We dare na weel say't, but we ken wha's to blame,°
There'll never be peace till Jamie comes hame.

My seven braw sons for Jamie drew sword,°
And now I greet round their green beds in the yerd;   10
It brak the sweet heart of my faithfu' auld Dame,
There'll never be peace till Jamie comes hame.
Now life is a burden that bows me down,
Sin I tint my bairns, and he tint his crown;
But till my last moments my words are the same,
There'll never be peace till Jamie comes hame.

RORY DALL'S PORT

Slow and tender

Ae fond kiss, and then we se - ver; Ae fare-well and then for ev - er!

Deep in heart-wrung tears I'll pledge thee, War - ring sighs and groans I'll wage thee.

Who shall say that for - tune grieves him While the star of hope she leaves him?

Me, nae chear-fu' twin - kle lights me; Dark de - spair a - round be-nights me.

Ae fond kiss, and then we sever;
Ae farewell and then for ever!
Deep in heart-wrung tears I'll pledge thee,
Warring sighs and groans I'll wage thee.
Who shall say that fortune grieves him
While the star of hope he leaves him?
Me, nae chearfu' twinkle lights me;
Dark despair around benights me.

I'll ne'er blame my partial fancy,
Naething could resist my Nancy: 10
But to see her, was to love her;
Love but her, and love for ever.
Had we never lov'd sae kindly,
Had we never lov'd sae blindly,
Never met—or never parted,
We had ne'er been broken-hearted.

Fare thou weel, thou first and fairest!
Fare thee weel, thou best and dearest!
Thine be ilka joy and treasure,
Peace, Enjoyment, Love and Pleasure!   20
Ae fond kiss, and then we sever;
Ae fareweel, Alas! for ever!
Deep in heart-wrung tears I'll pledge thee,
Warring sighs and groans I'll wage thee.

BESS AND HER SPINNING WHEEL

Slow

O Leeze me on my spin - ning wheel, And leeze me on my rock and reel; Frae

tap to tae that cleeds me bien, And haps me fiel and warm at e'en! I'll

set me down and sing and spin, While laigh de - scends the sim - mer sun, Blest

wi' con - tent, and milk and meal, O leeze me on my spin - nin wheel.

O Leeze me on my spinning wheel,
And leeze me on my rock and reel;°
Frae tap to tae that cleeds me bien,
And haps me fiel and warm at e'en!
I'll set me down and sing and spin,
While laigh descends the simmer sun,
Blest wi' content, and milk and meal,
O leeze me on my spinnin wheel.

On ilka hand the burnies trot,°
And meet below my theekit cot;   10
The scented birk and hawthorn white
Across the pool their arms unite,
Alike to screen the birdie's nest,
And little fishes caller rest:
The sun blinks kindly in the biel',
Where, blythe I turn my spinnin wheel.

On lofty aiks the cushats wail,
And Echo cons the doolfu' tale;
The lintwhites in the hazel braes,
Delighted, rival ithers lays: 20
The craik amang the claver hay,°
The pairtrick whirrin o'er the ley,
The swallow jinkin round my shiel,
Amuse me at my spinnin wheel.

Wi' sma' to sell, and less to buy,
Aboon distress, below envy,
O wha wad leave this humble state,
For a' the pride of a' the great?
Amid their flairing, idle toys,
Amid their cumbrous, dinsome joys,   30
Can they the peace and pleasure feel
Of Bessy at her spinnin wheel!

YE JACOBITES BY NAME

Ye Ja-co-bites by name give an ear, give an ear; Ye

Ja - co - bites by name, give an ear; Ye

Ja - co - bites by name Your fautes I will pro-claim Your

doc - trines I maun blame, you shall hear.

Ye Jacobites by name give an ear, give an ear;
  Ye Jacobites by name, give an ear;
    Ye Jacobites by name
      Your fautes I will proclaim
        Your doctrines I maun blame,
          You shall hear.

What is Right, and what is Wrang, by the law, by the law?
  What is Right, and what is Wrang, by the law?
    What is Right, and what is Wrang?
      A short sword, and a lang,   10
        A weak arm, and a strang
          For to draw.

What makes heroic strife, fam'd a far, fam'd a far?
  What makes heroic strife, fam'd a far?
    What makes heroic strife?
      To whet th' assassin's knife,
        Or hunt a Parent's life
          Wi' bludie war.

Then let your schemes alone, in the state, in the state,
  Then let your schemes alone, in the state,   20
    Then let your schemes alone,
      Adore the rising sun,
        And leave a man undone
          To his fate.

THE BANKS O' DOON

Slow and tender

Ye Banks and braes o' bo - nie Doon, How can ye bloom sae fresh and fair; How

can ye chant, ye lit - tle birds, And I sae wea - ry fu' o' care! Thou'll

break my heart thou warb - ling bird, That wan - tons thro' the flower-ing thorn: Thou

minds me o' de - par - ted joys, De - par - ted ne - ver to re - turn.

Ye Banks and braes o' bonie Doon,
   How can ye bloom sae fresh and fair;
How can ye chant, ye little birds,
   And I sae weary fu' o' care!
Thou'll break my heart thou warbling bird,
   That wantons thro' the flowering thorn:
Thou minds me o' departed joys,
   Departed never to return.°

Oft hae I rov'd by bonie Doon,
   To see the rose and woodbine twine;   10
And ilka bird sang o' its luve,
   And fondly sae did I o' mine.
Wi' lightsome heart I pu'd a rose,
   Fu' sweet upon its thorny tree;
And my fause luver staw my rose,
   But, ah! he left the thorn wi' me.

SUCH A PARCEL OF ROGUES IN A NATION

Fare-weel to a' our Sco-tish fame, Fare-weel our an-cient glo-ry; Fare-weel ev-en to the Sco-tish name, Sae fam'd in mar-tial sto-ry. Now Sark rins o'er the Sol-way sands, And Tweed rins to the oc-ean To mark where Eng-land's pro-vince stands, Such a par-cel of rogues in a na-tion.

Fareweel to a' our Scotish fame,
　　Fareweel our ancient glory;
Fareweel even to the Scotish name,
　　Sae fam'd in martial story.
Now Sark runs o'er the Solway sands,
　　And Tweed rins to the ocean°
To mark where England's province stands,
Such a parcel of rogues in a nation.

What force or guile could not subdue,
　　Thro' many warlike ages,　　　　　　　　　　　　10
Is wrought now by a coward few,
　　For hireling traitors wages.
The English steel we could disdain,
　　Secure in valour's station;
But English gold has been our bane,
Such a parcel of rogues in a nation!

O would, or I had seen the day
　　That treason thus could fell us,
My auld grey head had lien in clay,
　　Wi' Bruce and loyal Wallace!°　　　　　　　　　　20
But pith and power, till my last hour,
　　I'll mak this declaration;
We're bought and sold for English gold
Such a parcel of rogues in a nation.

AFTON WATER

Slow & tender

Flow gent-ly sweet A-fton a-mong thy green braes, Flow gent-ly, I'll sing thee a song in thy praise; My Ma-ry's a-sleep by thy mur-mur-ing stream, Flow gent-ly, sweet A-fton, dis-turb not her dream.

Flow gently sweet Afton among thy green braes,
Flow gently, I'll sing thee a song in thy praise;
My Mary's asleep by thy murmuring stream,
Flow gently, sweet Afton, disturb not her dream.

Thou stock dove whose echo resounds thro' the glen,
Ye wild whistling blackbirds in yon thorny den,°
Thou green crested lapwing thy screaming forbear,
I charge you disturb not my slumbering Fair.

How lofty, sweet Afton, thy neighbouring hills,
Far mark'd with the courses of clear, winding rills;   10
There daily I wander as noon rises high,
My flocks and my Mary's sweet Cot in my eye.

How pleasant thy banks and green vallies below,
Where wild in the woodlands the primroses blow;
There oft as mild ev'ning weeps over the lea,
The sweet scented birk shades my Mary and me.

Thy chrystal stream, Afton, how lovely it glides,
And winds by the cot where my Mary resides;
How wanton thy waters her snowy feet lave,
As gathering sweet flowerets she stems thy clear wave.   20

Flow gently, sweet Afton, among thy green braes,
Flow gently, sweet River, the theme of my lays;
My Mary's asleep by thy murmuring stream,
Flow gently, sweet Afton, disturb not her dream.

THE DEIL'S AWA WI' TH' EXCISEMAN

The deil cam fiddlin thro' the town,
   And danc'd awa wi' th' Exciseman;
And ilka wife cries, auld Mahoun,°
   I wish you luck o' the prize, man.

CHORUS: The deil's awa the deil's awa
         The deil's awa wi' the Exciseman,
         He's danc'd awa he's danc'd awa
         He's danc'd awa wi' the Exciseman.

We'll mak our maut and we'll brew our drink,
   We'll laugh, sing, and rejoice, man;   10
And mony braw thanks to the meikle black deil,
   That danc'd awa wi' th' Exciseman.
     The deil's awa, &c.

There's threesome reels, there's foursome reels,
   There's hornpipes and strathspeys, man,
But the ae best dance e'er cam to the Land°
   Was, the deil's awa wi' th' Exciseman.
     The deil's awa, &c.

A RED RED ROSE

Slow

O my Luve's like a red, red rose, That's new-ly sprung in June; O
My Luve's like the me-lo-die That's sweet-ly play'd in tune. As
fair art thou, my bon-ie lass, So deep in luve am I; And
I will luve thee still, my dear, Till a' the seas gang dry. Till
a' the seas gang dry, my Dear, And the rocks melt wi' the sun: O
I will love thee still my dear, While the sands o' life shall run.

O my Luve's like a red, red rose,
 That's newly sprung in June;
O my Luve's like the melodie
 That's sweetly play'd in tune.

As fair art thou, my bonie lass,
 So deep in luve am I;
And I will luve thee still, my Dear,
 Till a' the seas gang dry.

Till a' the seas gang dry, my Dear,
 And the rocks melt wi' the sun: 10
O I will love thee still my dear,
 While the sands o' life shall run.

And fare thee weel, my only Luve!
 And fare thee weel, a while!
And I will come again, my Luve,
 Tho' it were ten thousand mile!

AULD LANG SYNE

Should auld ac-quain-tance be for-got And ne-ver brought to mind? Should

auld ac-quain-tance be for-got, And auld lang syne! For

Chorus

auld lang syne my jo, For auld lang syne, We'll

tak a *cup o' kind-ness yet for auld lang syne.

* Some Sing Kiss in place of Cup.

Should auld acquaintance be forgot
    And never brought to mind?
Should auld acquaintance be forgot,
    And auld lang syne!

CHORUS: For auld lang syne my jo,
        For auld lang syne,
        We'll tak a cup o' kindness yet
        For auld lang syne.

And surely ye'll be your pint stowp!
    And surely I'll be mine!   10
And we'll tak a cup o' kindness yet,
    For auld lang syne.
        For auld &c.

We twa hae run about the braes,
    And pou'd the gowans fine;
But we've wander'd mony a weary fitt,
    Sin auld lang syne.
        For auld &c.

We twa hae paidl'd in the burn,
    Frae morning sun till dine;
But seas between us braid hae roar'd,
    Sin auld lang syne.   20
        For auld &c.

And there's a hand, my trusty fiere!
    And gie's a hand o' thine!
And we'll tak a right gude-willie-waught,
    For auld lang syne.
        For auld &c.

COMIN THRO' THE RYE

Very Slow

Co - min thro' the rye, poor bo - dy, Co - min thro' the rye She

drai - gl't a' her pet - ti - coa - tie Co - min thro' the rye. Oh

part repeated in Chorus

Jen - ny's a' weet poor bo - dy, Jen - ny's sel - dom dry She

drai - gl't a' her pet - ti - coa - tie Co - min thro' the rye.

Comin thro' the rye, poor body,
    Comin thro' the rye
She draigl't a' her petticoatie
    Comin thro' the rye.

CHORUS: Oh Jenny's a' weet poor body
        Jenny's seldom dry
        She draigl't a' her petticoatie
        Comin thro' the rye.

Gin a body meet a body
    Comin thro' the rye,   10
Gin a body kiss a body
    Need a body cry.
        Oh Jenny's a' weet &c.

Gin a body meet a body
    Comin thro' the glen;
Gin a body kiss a body
    Need the warld ken!
        Oh Jenny's a' weet &c.

O LEAVE NOVELS &c

Lively

O leave no - vels, ye Mauch-line belles, Ye're sa - fer at your spin - ning wheel; Such witch - ing books, are bai - ted hooks for rak - ish rooks like Rob Moss - giel. Your fine Tom Jones and Grand - i - sons they make your youth - ful fan - cies reel they heat your brains, and fire your veins and then you're prey for Rob Moss - giel.

O leave novels, ye Mauchline belles,
    Ye're safer at your spinning wheel;
Such witching books, are baited hooks
    For rakish rooks like Rob Mossgiel.
Your fine Tom Jones and Grandisons°
    They make your youthful fancies reel
They heat your brains, and fire your veins
    And then you're prey for Rob Mossgiel.

Beware a tongue that's smoothly hung;
    A heart that warmly seems to feel;   10
That feelin heart but acks a part,
    'Tis rakish art in Rob Mossgiel.
The frank address, the soft caress,
    Are worse than poisoned darts of steel,
The frank address, and politesse,
    Are all finesse in Rob Mossgiel.

Songs from *A Select Collection of Original Scotish Airs, for the Voice*

DUNCAN GRAY CAME HERE TO WOO

Air—*Duncan Gray*

Dun-can Gray came here to woo, Ha ha the woo-ing o't On

new year's night when we were fou, Ha ha the woo-ing o't.

Mag-gie coost her head fu' high, Look'd asklent and un-co skeigh

Gart poor Dun-can stand a-biegh Ha ha the woo-ing o't.

DUNCAN GRAY came here to woo,
  Ha, ha, the wooing o't;
On new-year's night, when we were fow,
  Ha, ha, the wooing o't.
MAGGIE coost her head fu' high,
  Look'd asklent and unco skeigh,
Gart poor Duncan stand abiegh;
  Ha, ha, the wooing o't.

Duncan fleech'd, and Duncan pray'd,
  Ha, ha, the wooing o't;   10
Meg was deaf as AILSA Craig,[1]
  Ha, ha, the wooing o't.
Duncan sigh'd, baith out and in,
  Grat his een baith blear't and blin',
Spak o' louping o'er a linn;
  Ha, ha, the wooing o't.

Time and chance are but a tide,
  Ha, ha, the wooing o't;
Slighted love is sair to bide,
  Ha, ha, the wooing o't.   20
Shall I like a fool, quoth he,
  For a haughty hizzie die?
She may gae to—France for me!
  Ha, ha, the wooing o't.

How it comes, let Doctors tell,
  Ha, ha, the wooing o't;
Meg grew sick,—as he grew heal,
  Ha, ha, the wooing o't.
Something in her bosom wrings,
  For relief a sigh she brings;   30
And oh! her een they spak sic things!
  Ha, ha, the wooing o't.

---

[1] A great insulated rock to the south of the island of Arran. [note in Thomson]

Duncan was a lad o' grace,
   Ha, ha, the wooing o't;
Maggie's was a piteous case,
   Ha, ha, the wooing o't.
Duncan cou'd na be her death,
   Swelling pity smoor'd his wrath;
Now they're crouse and canty baith!
   Ha, ha, the wooing o't.   40

O WHISTLE, AND I'LL COME TO YOU, MY LAD

Air—*O whistle, and I'll come to you, my lad*

whis-tle and I'll come to you my lad O whis-tle and I'll come to you my lad; Tho'

fa-ther and mo-ther and a' shou'd gae mad O whist-le and I'll come to you my lad. But

wa - ri - ly tent when ye come to court me And come na un - less the back

yett be a jee Syne up the back style and let nae bo - dy see And

come as ye were na com-ing to me And come as ye were na com - ing to me.

O WHISTLE, and I'll come to you, my lad,
O whistle, and I'll come to you, my lad;
Tho' father and mother and a' should gae mad,
O whistle and I'll come to you my lad.
But warily tent, when you come to court me,
And come na unless the back-yett be a-jee;
Syne up the back-style, and let naebody see,
And come, as ye were na coming to me,
And come, as ye were na coming to me.

O whistle, and I'll come to you, my lad,   10
O whistle, and I'll come to you, my lad;
Tho' father and mother and a' should gae mad,
O whistle and I'll come to you my lad.
At kirk, or at market, whene'er ye meet me,
Gang by me as tho' that ye car'd nae a flie;
But steal me a blink o' your bonie black e'e,
Yet look as ye were na looking at me,
Yet look as ye were na looking at me.

O whistle, and I'll come to you, my lad,
O whistle, and I'll come to you, my lad;   20
Tho' father and mother and a' should gae mad,
O whistle and I'll come to you my lad.
Ay vow and protest that ye carena for me,
And *whyles* ye may lightly my beauty a wee;
But court nae anither, tho' joking ye be,
For fear that she wyle your fancy frae me,
For fear that she wyle your fancy frae me.

Other poems and songs published in Burns's lifetime

WRITTEN ON A WINDOW IN STIRLING

HERE STEWARTS once in triumph reign'd,°
And laws for Scotia well ordain'd.°
But now unroof'd their palace stands;°
Their sceptre's fall'n to other's hands.°
The injur'd STEWART's Line is gone,
A Race, outlandish, fills the throne:°
An ideot Race to honour lost,°
Who know them best despise them most.°

Here Lies
ROBERT FERGUSSON POET
Born September 5th 1751
Died October 16th 1774

No sculptur'd Marble here nor pompous lay°
No storied Urn nor animated Bust°
This simple Stone directs Pale Scotia's way
To pour her Sorrows o'er her Poets Dust.

ELEGY,
On the departed Year 1788

FOR lords or kings I dinna mourn,
E'en let them die—for that they're born:
But Oh! prodigious to reflect!
A TOWMONT, Sirs, is gane to wreck!
O EIGHTY-EIGHT, in thy sma' space,
What dire events hae taken place!
Of what enjoyments thou has reft us,
In what a pickle thou has left us!

The Spanish empire's tint a head;°
And my auld teethless Bautie's dead:°   10
The tulzie's teugh 'tween PITT and FOX,°
And our gudewife's wee birdy cocks;
The tane is game, a bludie devil,
But to the *hen birds* unco civil;°
The tither's dour, has nae sic breedin,
But better stuff ne'er claw'd a midden.

Ye *Ministers*, come mount the pupit,
And cry till ye be haerse and rupet;
For EIGHTY-EIGHT he wish'd you weel,
And gied you a' baith gear and meal;   20
E'en mony a plack and mony a peck,°
Ye ken yoursels, for little feck.

Ye *bonnie lasses*, dight your een
For some o' you hae tint a frien';
In EIGHTY-EIGHT, ye ken, was taen,
What ye'll ne'er hae to gie again.

Observe the vera nowt and sheep,
How dowf an' dowielie they creep;°
Nay even the yirth itsel does cry,
For *Embrugh* wells are grutten dry.°   30

O EIGHTY-NINE, thou'se but a bairn,
And no o'er auld, I hope, to learn!
Thou beardless boy, I pray tak care;
Thou now has got thy *Daddie's* chair;
Nae hand-cuff'd, mizzl'd, half-shackl'd *Regent*,°
But like himsel, a full free agent,
Be sure ye follow out the plan,
Nae waur than he did—honest man! }
As muckle better as you can.

JANUARY 1, 1789

ON CAPTAIN GROSE'S PRESENT
PEREGRINATIONS THROUGH SCOTLAND,
COLLECTING THE ANTIQUITIES OF THAT KINGDOM

HEAR, Land o' Cakes, and brither Scots,°
Frae Maiden-kirk to Johnie Groat's,°
If there's a hole in a' your coats,
      I rede you tent it;
A chield's amang you taking notes,
      And faith, he'll prent it.

If in your bounds ye chance to light
Upon a fine, fat, fodgel wight,
O' stature short, but genius bright,
      That's he—mark weel!   10
And wow! he has an unco slight
      O' cawk and keel.°

At some auld houlet-haunted biggin,
Or kirk deserted by its riggin,
It's ten to ane ye'll find him snug in
      Some eldritch part,
Wi' deils, they say, Lord safe's, colleaguin
      At some black art.

Ilk ghaist that haunts auld ha' or chamer,
Ye gipsey-gang that deal in glamor,°
And you deep-read in Hell's black grammer,   20
      Warlocks and witches,
Ye'll quake at his conjuring hammer,
      Ye midnight bitches.

It's tauld he was a sodger bred,°
And ane would rather fa'n than fled;
But now he's quat the spurtle blade,°
      And dog-skin wallet,
And ta'en the—Antiquarian trade,
      I think they call it.   30

He hath a fouth o' auld nick-nackets;
Rousty airn-caps and gingling jackets,°
Would haud the Lothians three in tackets
             A towmont gude;
And parritch-pots and auld saut-backets,
             Afore the flood.

Of Eve's first fire he has a cinder;
Auld Tubalcain's fire-shool and fender;°
That which distinguished the gender
             O' Balaam's ass;°   40
A broomstick o' the Witch of Endor,°
             Weel shod wi' brass.

Besides, he'll cut you off fu' gleg
The shape of Adam's philibeg:°
The knife that cutet Abel's craig,°
             He'll prove you fully,
It was a faulding jockteleg,
             Or lang kail gully.

But would you see him in his glee,
(For meikle glee and fun has he),   50
Then set him down, and twa or three
             Gude fellows wi' him!
And port, O port! shine thou a wee,
             And then ye'll see him!

Now, by the powers o' verse and prose,
Thou art a dainty chield, O Gr——:
Whae'er o' thee shall ill suppose,
             They sair misca' thee:
I'd take the rascal by the nose,
             Would say, shame fa' thee.   60

August 11.

ALLOA CHURCH AIRSHIRE.

TAM O' SHANTER. A TALE

WHEN chapmen billies leave the street,°
And drouthy neebors, neebors meet,
As market-days are wearing late,
And folk begin to tak the gate;
While we sit bowsing at the nappy,
And gettin fou, and unco happy,
We think na on the long Scots miles,°
The waters, mosses, slaps and styles,
That lie between us and our hame,
Where sits our sulky, sullen dame,   10
Gathering her brows, like gathering storm,
Nursing her wrath to keep it warm.

   This truth fand honest Tam o' Shanter,
As he frae Ayr ae night did canter;
(Auld Ayr, whom ne'er a town surpasses
For honest men and bonnie lasses.)

O Tam! hadst thou but been sae wise
As taen thy ain wife Kate's advice!
She tauld thee weel, thou was a skellum,
A bletherin, blusterin, drunken blellum;   20
That frae November till October,
Ae market-day thou was na sober;
That ilka melder, wi' the miller,°
Thou sat as long as thou had siller;
That every naig was ca'd a shoe on,
The smith and thee gat roarin fou on;
That at the L——d's house, even on Sunday,°
Thou drank wi' Kirkton Jean till Monday.——
She prophesied that, late or soon,
Thou wad be found deep-drown'd in Doon;   30
Or catch'd wi' warlocks in the mirk
By Aloway's old haunted kirk.

Ah, gentle dames! it gars me greet,
To think how mony counsels sweet,
How mony lengthen'd sage advices,
The husband frae the wife despises!

But to our tale:——Ae market-night,
Tam had got planted unco right,
Fast by an ingle bleezing finely,
Wi' reamin swats that drank divinely;°   40
And at his elbow, souter Johnie,
His ancient, trusty, drouthy cronie;
Tam lo'ed him like a vera brither,
They had been fou for weeks thegither.——
The night drave on wi' sangs and clatter,
And ay the ale was growing better:
The landlady and Tam grew gracious,
Wi' favors secret, sweet, and precious:
The souter tauld his queerest stories;
The landlord's laugh was ready chorus: 50
The storm without might rair and rustle,
Tam did na mind the storm a whistle.——
Care, mad to see a man sae happy,
E'en drown'd himself amang the nappy:
As bees flee hame, wi' lades o' treasure,

The minutes wing'd their way wi' pleasure:
Kings may be blest, but Tam was glorious;
O'er a' the ills o' life victorious!

But pleasures are like poppies spread,
You seize the flower, its bloom is shed;   60
Or like the snow falls in the river,
A moment white—then melts for ever;
Or like the borealis race,°
That flit ere you can point their place;
Or like the rainbow's lovely form,
Evanishing amid the storm.—°
Nae man can tether time or tide,
The hour approaches Tam maun ride;
That hour o' night's black arch the key-stane,
That dreary hour he mounts his beast in;   70
And sic a night he taks the road in
As ne'er poor sinner was abroad in.

The wind blew, as 'twad blawn its last;
The rattling showers rose on the blast;
The speedy gleams the darkness swallow'd
Loud, deep, and lang, the thunder bellow'd:
That night, a child might understand
The deil had business on his hand.

Weel mounted on his grey meare, Meg,
A better never lifted leg,   80
Tam skelpit on thro' dub and mire,
Despising wind, and rain, and fire:
Whyles holding fast his gude blue bonnet;°
Whyles crooning o'er an auld Scots sonnet;°
Whyles glowring round wi' prudent cares,
Lest bogles catch him unawares;
Kirk-Aloway was drawing nigh,
Where ghaists and houlets nightly cry.°

By this time he was cross the ford,
Where in the snaw the chapman smoor'd;   90
And past the birks and meikle stane,
Where drunken Charlie brak's neck-bane;

And thro' the whins, and by the cairn,
Where hunters fand the murder'd bairn;
And near the tree, aboon the well,
Where Mungo's mither hang'd hersel:°
Before him, Doon pours all his floods;
The doubling storm roars thro' the woods;°
The light'nings flash from pole to pole;
Near, and more near, the thunders roll:°   100
When, glimmering thro' groaning trees,
Kirk-Aloway seem'd in a bleeze;
Thro' ilka bore the beams were glancing,
And loud resounded mirth and dancing.

   Inspiring, bold John Barleycorn!
What dangers thou canst make us scorn:
Wi' tippeny, we fear nae evil;
Wi' usquabae, we'll face the devil!
The swats sae ream'd in Tammie's noddle,
Fair-play, he car'd na deils a boddle:°   110
But Maggy stood, right sair astonish'd,
Till by the heel and hand admonish'd,
She ventur'd forward on the light,
And, wow! Tam saw an unco sight!

   Warlocks and witches in a dance,
Nae cotillon brent new frae France,°
But hornpipes, jigs, strathspeys and reels,
Put life and mettle in their heels.—
A winnock-bunker in the East,°
There sat auld Nick in shape o' beast;   120
A towzie tyke, black, grim, and large;
To gie them music was his charge:
He screw'd the pipes and gart them skirl,°
Till roof and rafters a' did dirl.—
Coffins stood round, like open presses,
That shaw'd the dead in their last dresses;
And (by some devilish cantraip slight)
Each in its cauld hand held a light;
By which heroic Tam was able
To note upon the haly table,   130
A murderer's banes, in gibbet-airns;°

Twa span-lang, wee, unchristen'd bairns;°
A thief, new cutted frae a rape,
Wi' his last gasp his gab did gape;
Five tomahawks, wi' blood red-rusted;
Five scymitars, wi' murder crusted;
A garter which a babe had strangled;
A knife a father's throat had mangled,
Whom his ain son of life bereft,
The grey hairs yet stak to the heft: 140
Wi' mair of horrible and awefu',
That even to name wad be unlawfu':—°
Three lawyers' tongues, turn'd inside out,
Wi' lies seam'd like a beggar's clout;
Three priests' hearts, rotten, black as muck,
Lay stinking, vile, in every neuk.°

     As Tammie glowr'd, amaz'd and curious,
The mirth and fun grew fast and furious:
The piper loud and louder blew;
The dancers quick and quicker flew;   150
They reel'd, they set, they cross'd, they cleekit,
Till ilka Carlin swat and reekit,
And coost her duddies on the wark,
And linkit at it in her sark.—

     Now Tam! O Tam! had they been queans,
A' plump and strappin in their teens!
Their sarks, instead o' creeshie flainen,
Been snaw-white, seventeen-hunder linen;°
Thir breeks o' mine, my only pair,
That ance were plush o' gude blue hair,   160
I wad hae gien them off my hurdies
For ae blink o' the bonie burdies!
But withered beldams, auld and droll,
Rigwoodie hags wad spean a foal,°
Loupin and flingin on a crummock,
I wonder did na turn thy stomach.—

     But Tam kend what was what fu' brawlie;
There was ae winsome wench and walie,°
That night enlisted in the core,

(Lang after kend on Carrick shore;   170
For mony a beast to dead she shot,
And perish'd mony a bonnie boat,
And shook baith meikle corn and bear
And kept the country-side in fear)—°
Her cutty-sark o' Paisley harn,°
That while a lassie she had worn,
In longitude tho' sorely scanty,
It was her best, and she was vauntie.—
Ah! little thought thy reverend graunie,
That sark she coft for her wee Nannie   180
Wi' twa pund Scots ('twas a' her riches)°
Should ever grac'd a dance o' witches!

    But here my Muse her wing maun cour,
Sic flights are far beyond her power;
To sing how Nannie lap and flang,
(A souple jad she was and strang,)
And how Tam stood like ane bewitch'd,
And thought his vera een enrich'd;
Even Satan glowr'd, and fidg'd fu' fain,
And hotch'd, and blew wi' might and main;   190
Till first ae caper—syne anither—
Tam lost his reason a' thegither,
And roars out—'Weel done, cutty-sark!'
And in an instant all was dark;
And scarcely had he Maggie rallied,
When out the hellish legion sallied.—

    As bees bizz out wi' angry fyke,
When plundering herds assail their byke;
As open pussie's mortal foes,°
When, pop, she starts before their nose;   200
As eager rins the market-croud,
When 'catch the thief!' resounds aloud;°
So Maggy rins, the witches follow,
Wi' mony an eldritch shout and hollo.—

    Ah Tam! ah Tam! thou'll get thy fairin!
In hell they'll roast thee like a herrin!
In vain thy Kate awaits thy comin,

Kate soon will be a woefu' woman!!!
Now, do thy speedy utmost, Meg!
And win the key-stane o' the brig;°   210
There at them thou thy tail may toss,
A running stream they dare na cross!
But ere the key-stane she could make,
The fient a tail she had to shake;
For Nannie, far before the rest,
Hard upon noble Maggy prest,
And flew at Tam with furious ettle,
But little kend she Maggy's mettle!
Ae spring brought off her master hale,
But left behind her ain gray tail: 220
The carlin claught her by the rump,
And left poor Maggy scarce a stump.

Now wha this Tale o' truth shall read,
Ilk man and mother's son, take heed:
Whene'er to drink you are inclin'd,
Or cutty-sarks rin in your mind,
Think, ye may buy the joys o'er dear;
Remember TAM O' SHANTER'S MEARE!

EXTEMPORE
ON SOME LATE COMMEMORATIONS OF THE POET THOMSON

DOST thou not rise, indignant shade,
    And smile with spurning scorn,
When they wha would hae starv'd thy life,
    Thy senseless turf adorn?

They, wha about thee mak sic fyke,
    Now thou art but a name,
Wad seen thee d—n'd ere they had spar'd
    Ae plack to fill thy wame.

Helpless, alane, thou clamb the brae,
    Wi' meikle, meikle toil;   10

And claucht th' unfading garland there,
  Thy sair-won rightfu' spoil.°

And wear it there! and call aloud
  This axiom undoubted—
'Would'st thou hae Nobles' patronage?
  'First learn to live without it!!!'

'To wham hae routh, shall yet be given'—°
  Is every Patron's faith;
'But he, the friendless, needy wretch,
  'Shall lose the mite he hath.'   20

THE RIGHTS OF WOMAN

AN OCCASIONAL ADDRESS
SPOKEN, ON HER BENEFIT NIGHT, NOV. 26, AT DUMFRIES, BY MISS FONTENELLE

WHILE Europe's eye is fix'd on mighty things,
The fate of empires, and the fall of kings;°
While quacks of state must each produce his plan,°
And even children lisp, The Rights of Man;°
Amid the mighty fuss, just let me mention,
The RIGHTS of WOMAN merit some attention—

First, in the sexes' intermix'd connection,
One sacred Right of Woman is, PROTECTION.
The tender flower that lifts its head, elate,
Helpless, must fall before the blasts of fate,   10
Sunk on the earth, deface'd its lovely form,
Unless your shelter ward th' impending storm.

Our second Right, but needless here is caution,
To keep that Right inviolate 's the fashion:
Each man of sense has it so full before him,
He'd die before he'd wrong it——'tis DECORUM.
There was indeed, in far less polish'd days,
A time when rough, rude man had naughty ways:
Would swagger, swear, get drunk, kick up a riot,°
Nay even thus invade a Lady's quiet.   20

Now, thank our stars! these Gothic times are fled;°
Now well-bred men—and you are all well-bred—
Most justly think (and we are much the gainers)
Such conduct neither spirit, wit, nor manners.°

For Right the third, our last, our best, our dearest,
That right to flutt'ring female hearts the nearest,
Which even the Rights of Kings in low prostration
Most humbly own——'tis dear, dear ADMIRATION!
In that blest sphere alone we live and move,
There taste that life of life, immortal Love!   30
Smiles, glances, tears, sighs, fits, flirtations, airs,
'Gainst such an host, what flinty savage dares—
When awful beauty joins with all her charms,
Who is so rash as rise in rebel arms?

Then truce with Kings, and truce with Constitutions,
With bloody armaments and revolutions;
Let MAJESTY your first attention summon,
Ah! cà ira! The Majesty of Woman!!!°

LAMENT
FOR
JAMES, EARL OF GLENCAIRN

THE wind blew hollow frae the hills,°
    By fits the sun's departing beam
Look'd on the fading yellow woods
    That wav'd o'er Lugar's winding stream:°
Beneath a craigy steep, a Bard,
    Laden with years and meikle pain,
In loud lament bewail'd his lord,
    Whom death had all untimely taen.

He lean'd him to an ancient aik,°
    Whose trunk was mould'ring down with years;   10
His locks were bleached white with time,
    His hoary cheek was wet wi' tears;
And as he touch'd his trembling harp,
    And as he tuned his doleful sang,

The winds, lamenting thro' their caves,
  To echo bore the notes alang.

'Ye scatter'd birds that faintly sing
  'The reliques of the vernal quire;
'Ye woods that shed on a' the winds
  'The honours of the aged year,°   20
'A few short months, and glad and gay,
  'Again ye'll charm the ear and e'e;
'But nocht in all-revolving time
  'Can gladness bring again to me.

'I am a bending aged tree,
  'That long has stood the wind and rain;
'But now has come a cruel blast,
  'And my last hald of earth is gane:
'Nae leaf o' mine shall greet the spring,
  'Nae simmer sun exalt my bloom;   30
'But I maun lie before the storm,
  'And ithers plant them in my room.

'I've seen sae mony changefu' years,
  'On earth I am a stranger grown;
'I wander in the ways of men,
  'Alike unknowing and unknown:°
'Unheard, unpitied, unreliev'd,
  'I bear alane my lade o' care,
'For silent, low, on beds of dust,
  'Lie a' that would my sorrows share.°   40

'And last, (the sum of a' my griefs!)
  'My noble master lies in clay;
'The flower amang our barons bold,
  'His country's pride, his country's stay:
'In weary being now I pine,
  'For all the life of life is dead,°
'And hope has left my aged ken,
  'On forward wing for ever fled.

'Awake thy last sad voice, my harp!
  'The voice of woe and wild despair!   50

'Awake, resound thy latest lay,
  'Then sleep in silence evermair!
'And thou, my last, best, only friend,
  'That fillest an untimely tomb,
'Accept this tribute from the Bard
  'Thou brought from fortune's mirkest gloom.

'In Poverty's low barren vale,
  'Thick mists, obscure, involv'd me round;
'Though oft I turned the wistful eye,
  'Nae ray of fame was to be found: 60
'Thou found'st me, like the morning sun
  'That melts the fogs in limpid air,°
'The friendless Bard and rustic song,
  'Became alike thy fostering care.

'O! why has Worth so short a date!
  'While villains ripen grey with time!
'Must thou, the noble, generous, great,
  'Fall in bold manhood's hardy prime!
'Why did I live to see that day?
  'A day to me so full of woe?   70
'O! had I met the mortal shaft
  'Which laid my benefactor low!

'The bridegroom may forget the bride,
  'Was made his wedded wife yestreen;
'The monarch may forget the crown
  'That on his head an hour has been;
'The mother may forget the child
  'That smiles sae sweetly on her knee;
'But I'll remember thee, Glencairn,°
  'And a' that thou hast done for me!'   80

BRUCE'S ADDRESS
TO HIS TROOPS, AT THE BATTLE OF BANNOCKBURN

SCOTS, wha hae wi' Wallace bled,
Scots, wham BRUCE has aften led,
Welcome to your gory bed,
 Or to glorious victorie!°

Now's the day, and now's the hour!
See the front o' battle lour!
See approach proud EDWARD's pow'r!
 EDWARD, chains and slaverie!°

Wha will be a traitor knave?
Wha can fill a coward's grave?   10
Wha sae base as be a slave?
 Traitor, coward, turn and flie!°

Wha for Scotland's King and Law,
FREEDOM's sword will strongly draw,°
Freeman stand or Freeman fa?
 CALEDONIAN! on wi' me!°

By Oppression's woes and pains!
By your sons in servile chains!
We will drain our dearest veins—
 But they shall—they SHALL *be free!*° 20

Lay the proud usurpers low;
Tyrants fall in every foe;
LIBERTY's in every blow!°
 Forward let us do or die!°

THE ELECTION: A NEW SONG
Tune—*Fy, let us a' to the Bridal*

FY, let us a' to K————,°
 For there will be bickerin there;
For *M——'s light horse* are to muster,°

And O, how the heroes will swear!
And there will be *M——* commander,
    And *G——* the battle to win;°
Like brothers they'll stand by each other,
    Sae knit in alliance and kin.°

And there will be black-nebbit *Johnie*,°
    The tongue o' the trump to them a';   10
An he get na H–ll for his haddin,
    The Deil gets nae justice ava.
And there will be *K————'s* birkie,°
    A boy no sae black at the bane;
But as to his fine *Nabob* fortune,
    We'll e'en let the subject alane.

And there will be *W——'s* new *Sh——ff*,°
    Dame Justice fu' brawlie has sped;
She's gotten the heart of a *B——*,
    But, Lord! what's become o' the head?   20
And there will be *C————*, Esquire,°
    Sae mighty in *C————'s* eyes:
A wight that will weather d–mn–tion,
    The Devil the prey will despise.

And there will be ————*ses* doughty,°
    New-christening towns far and near;°
Abjuring their democrat doings
    By kissin the a— of a *Peer*.°
And there will be *K————*, sae gen'rous,°
    Whase honour is proof to the storm;   30
To save them from stark reprobation,
    He lent them his name to the *Firm*.

But we winna mention *R——stle*,°
    The *body*, e'en let him escape:
He'd venture the gallows for siller,
    An 'twere na the cost o' the rape.
And where is our King's *L—— L————t*,°
    Sae fam'd for his *gratefu'* return?°
The billie is gettin his questions
    To say in *S–nt St–ph–n's* the morn.°   40

And there will be Lads o' the g–sp–l,
   M————, wha's as *gude* as he's *true*:°
And there will be B——'s *Apostle*,°
   Wha's mair o' the *black* than the *blue*:°
And there will be Folk frae *Saint MARY'S*,°
   A *house* o' great merit and note;
The deil ane but honours them highly,
   Tho' deil ane will gie them his vote.°

And there will be wealthy young *RICHARD*—°
   Dame Fortune should hing by the neck   50
For prodigal thriftless bestowing—
   His merit had won him respect.
And there will be rich brother *Nabobs*,°
   Tho' *Nabobs*, yet men of the first:
And there will be *C–ll–st–n's* whiskers,°
   And *Quintin*, o' lads not the warst.°

And there will be *Stamp-office Johnie*,°
   Tak tent how ye purchase a dram:
And there will be gay *C–ss–nc–ry*,°
   And there will be gleg *Colonel Tam*.°   60
And there will be trusty *KIROCHTREE*,°
   Whase honour was ever his law;
If the VIRTUES were packt in a parcel
   His WORTH might be sample for a'.

And can we forget the auld MAJOR,°
   Wha'll ne'er be forgot in the *Greys*;°
Our flatt'ry we'll keep for some other,
   HIM, only it's justice to praise.
And there will be maiden *K–lk–rr–n*,°
   And also *B–rsk–m–n's* gude Knight;°   70
And there will be roaring *B–rtwh–stle*,°
   Yet, luckily roars in the right.

And there, frae the *N–ddisd–le* border,°
   Will mingle the *M–xw–lls* in droves;
Teugh *Jockie*, staunch *Geordie*, and *Walie*,°
   That griens for the fishes and loaves.°
And there will be *L–g–n M——d–w–l*,°

Sculdudry—and he will be there;°
And also the *Wild Scot o' Galloway*,
Sogering, gunpowder *Bl—r*.°   80

Then hey the *chaste Int'rest* o' *B*——,°
 And hey for the blessins 'twill bring:
It may send *B*—— to the *C*————ns,°
 In *S–d–m* 'twould make him a King.°
And hey for the sanctified *M*——,°
 Our land wha wi' *Ch–p–ls* has stor'd:°
He founder'd his horse amang harlots,
 But gied the auld naig to the *L–rd*!

THE DUMFRIES VOLUNTEERS—A BALLAD

Tune—*Push about the jorum*

Does haughty Gaul invasion threat,
 Then let the louns bewaure, Sir,
There's WOODEN WALLS upon our seas,°
 And VOLUNTEERS on shore, Sir:
The Nith shall run to Corsincon,[1]°
 And Criffell[2] sink in Solway,
Ere we permit a foreign foe
 On British ground to rally.

O let us not, like snarling tykes,
 In wrangling be divided,   10
Till, slap! come in an *unco loun*,
 And wi' a rung decide it!
Be Britain still to Britain true,
 Amang oursels united;
For never but by British hands
 Must British wrongs be righted.

The *kettle* o' the Kirk and State,
 Perhaps a clout may fail in't,
But de'il a foreign tinkler loun
 Shall ever ca' a nail in't: 20

---

[1] A high hill at the source of the Nith.
[2] A high hill at the confluence of the Nith with Solway Firth.

Our FATHERS BLUDE the *kettle* bought,°
   And wha wad dare to spoil it,
By Heavens! the sacrilegious dog
   Shall fuel be to boil it!

The wretch that would a *tyrant* own,
   And th' wretch his true-sworn brother,
Who'd set the *mob* above the *throne*,°
   May they be damn'd together!
Who will not sing, GOD SAVE THE KING,
   Shall hang as high's the steeple;   30
But while we sing, GOD SAVE THE KING,
   We'll ne'er forget THE PEOPLE.°

SONG

Tune—*For a' that, and a' that*

WHAT tho' on hamely fare we dine,
   Wear hodden grey, and a' that:°
Gie fools their silk, and knaves their wine,
   A man's a man for a' that.
For a' that, and a' that,
   Their tinsel shew, and a' that;
An honest man, tho' ne'er sae poor,
   Is chief o' men for a' that.

Ye see yon birkie ca'd a lord,
   Wha struts and stares, and a' that,   10
Tho' hundreds worship at his word,
   He's but a cuif for a' that.
For a' that, and a' that,
His ribband, star, and a' that;°
A man of independent mind,
   Can look, and laugh at a' that.

The king can make a belted knight,°
   A marquis, duke, and a' that,
But an honest man's aboon his might,
   Guid faith, he manna fa' that!   20
For a' that, and a' that,

His dignities, and a' that;°
The pith o' sense, and pride o' worth,
Are grander far than a' that.

Then let us pray, that come it may,
    As come it shall, for a' that;
When sense and worth, o'er a' the earth,
    Shall bear the gree, and a' that;
For a' that, and a' that,
It's coming yet, for a' that;   30
And man, and man, the world o'er,
Shall brothers be, for a' that.

Other poems and songs published posthumously

JOLLY BEGGARS:
A CANTATA

RECITATIVO

WHEN lyart leaves bestrow the yird,
Or wavering like the Bauckie bird,[1]°
  Bedim cauld Boreas' blast;°
When hailstanes drive wi' bitter skyte,
And infant frosts begin to bite,
  In hoary cranreuch drest;
Ae night at e'en a merry core
  O' randie, gangrel bodies,
In Poosie-Nansie's held the splore,°
  To drink their orra duddies: 10
      Wi' quaffing and laughing,
        They ranted and they sang;
      Wi' jumping and thumping,
        The vera girdle rang.

First, neist the fire, in auld red rags,°
Ane sat; weel brac'd wi' mealy bags,°
  And knapsack a' in order;
His doxy lay within his arm,
Wi' usquebae an' blankets warm,
  She blinket on her sodger: 20
An' ay he gies the tozie drab
  The tither skelpin' kiss,
While she held up her greedy gab
  Just like an aumos dish.°
      Ilk smack still, did crack still,
        Just like a cadger's whip,
      Then staggering and swaggering°
        He roar'd this ditty up—

---

[1] The old Scotch name for the Bat.

AIR
Tune—*Soldier's Joy*°

I

I am a son of Mars who have been in many wars,
And show my cuts and scars wherever I come;   30
This here was for a wench, and that other in a trench,
When welcoming the French at the sound of the drum.
                    Lal de daudle, &c.

II

My prenticeship I past where my leader breath'd his last,
When the bloody die was cast on the heights of Abram;°
I served out my trade when the gallant game was play'd,°
And the Moro low was laid at the sound of the drum.°
                    Lal de daudle, &c.

III

I lastly was with Curtis, among the floating batt'ries,
And there I left for witness an arm and a limb;
Yet let my country need me, with Elliot to head me,°
I'd clatter on my stumps at the sound of a drum.   40
                    Lal de daudle, &c.

IV

And now tho' I must beg with a wooden arm and leg,
And many a tatter'd rag hanging over my bum,
I'm as happy with my wallet, my bottle and my callet,°
As when I us'd in scarlet to follow a drum.
                    Lal de daudle, &c.

V

What tho' with hoary locks, I must stand the winter shocks,
Beneath the woods and rocks oftentimes for a home,
When the tother bag I sell, and the tother bottle tell,°
I could meet a troop of hell, at the sound of a drum.
                    Lal de daudle, &c.

RECITATIVO

He ended; and the kebars sheuk,
    Aboon the chorus roar;   50

While frighted rattons backward leuk,
   And seek the benmost bore:
A fairy fiddler frae the neuk,°
   He skirl'd out encore!
But up arose the martial chuck,
   And laid the loud uproar.

AIR

Tune—Soldier Laddie°

I

I once was a maid, tho' I cannot tell when,
And still my delight is in proper young men;
Some one of a troop of dragoons was my daddie,
No wonder I'm fond of a sodger laddie.   60
            Sing, Lal de lal, &c.

II

The first of my loves was a swaggering blade,
To rattle the thundering drum was his trade;
His leg was so tight, and his cheek was so ruddy,
Transported I was with my sodger laddie.
            Sing, Lal de lal, &c.

III

But the godly old chaplain left him in the lurch,
The sword I forsook for the sake of the church;
He ventur'd the soul, and I risked the body,
'Twas then I prov'd false to my sodger laddie.
            Sing, Lal de lal, &c.

IV

Full soon I grew sick of my sanctified sot,
The regiment at large for a husband I got;   70
From the gilded spontoon to the fife I was ready,°
I asked no more but a sodger laddie.
            Sing, Lal de lal, &c.

V

But the peace it reduc'd me to beg in despair,°
Till I met my old boy at a Cunningham fair;°

His *rags regimental* they flutter'd so gaudy,
My heart it rejoic'd at my sodger laddie.
                    Sing, Lal de lal, &c.

VI

And now I have lived—I know not how long,
And still I can join in a cup or a song;
But whilst with both hands I can hold the glass steady,
Here's to thee, my hero, my sodger laddie.°   80
                    Sing, Lal de lal, &c.

RECITATIVO

Then neist outspak a raucle carlin,
Wha kent fu' weel to cleek the sterling,
For mony a pursie she had hooked,
And had in mony a well been douked.°
Her love had been a Highland laddie,°
But weary fa' the waefu' woodie!
Wi' sighs and sobs she thus began
To wail her braw John Highlandman.

AIR
Tune—*O an ye were dead gudeman*°

I

A Highland lad my love was born,
The Lalland laws he held in scorn;   90
But he still was faithfu' to his clan,
My gallant, braw John Highlandman.

CHORUS

Sing, hey my braw John Highlandman!
Sing, ho my braw John Highlandman!
There's not a lad in a' the lan'
Was match for my John Highlandman.

II

With his philibeg an' tartan plaid,°
An' gude claymore down by his side,°
The ladies' hearts he did trepan,°

My gallant, braw John Highlandman.
> Sing, hey, &c.

III

We ranged a' from Tweed to Spey,°
An' liv'd like lords and ladies gay;
For a Lalland face he feared none,
My gallant, braw John Highlandman.
> Sing, hey, &c.

IV

They banish'd him beyond the sea,
But ere the bud was on the tree,
Adown my cheeks the pearls ran,
Embracing my John Highlandman.
> Sing, hey, &c.

V

But, oh! they catch'd him at the last,
And bound him in a dungeon fast;   110
My curse upon them every one,
They've hang'd my braw John Highlandman.
> Sing, hey, &c.

VI

And now a widow, I must mourn
The pleasures that will ne'er return;
No comfort but a hearty can,
When I think on John Highlandman.
> Sing, hey, &c.

RECITATIVO

A pigmy scraper wi' his fiddle,
Wha us'd to trysts and fairs to driddle,
Her strappan limb and gausy middle
> He reach'd nae higher,   120
Had hol'd his heartie like a riddle,
> An' blawn't on fire.

Wi' hand on haunch, an' upward e'e,
He croon'd his gamut, one, two, three,

Then in an Arioso key,°
   The wee Apollo°
Set off wi' *Allegretto* glee°
   His giga solo.°

AIR

Tune—*Whistle owre the lave o't*°

I

Let me ryke up to dight that tear,
An' go wi' me to be my dear,   130
An' then your every care and fear
  May whistle owre the lave o't.

CHORUS

I am a fiddler to my trade,
 An' a' the tunes that e'er I play'd,
The sweetest still to wife or maid,
   Was whistle owre the lave o't.

II

At kirns an' weddings we'se be there,
An' O! sae nicely's we will fare;
We'll bouse about till Daddie Care
  Sing, whistle owre the lave o't.   140
     I am, &c.

III

Sae merrily's the banes we'll pyke,
An' sun oursells about the dyke,
An' at our leisure when ye like,
  We'll whistle owre the lave o't.
     I am, &c.

IV

But bless me wi' your heaven o' charms,
And while I kittle hair on thairms,°
Hunger, cauld, an' a' sic harms,
  May whistle owre the lave o't.
     I am, &c.

RECITATIVO

Her charms had struck a sturdy Caird,
   As weel as poor Gutscraper;   150
He taks the fiddler by the beard,
   And draws a roosty rapier.—
He swoor by a' was swearing worth,
   To speet him like a pliver,
Unless he wou'd from that time forth,
   Relinquish her for ever.

Wi' ghastly e'e, poor tweedle-dee
   Upon his hunkers bended,°
And pray'd for grace wi' ruefu' face,
   An' so the quarrel ended.   160
But tho' his little heart did grieve,
   When round the tinker prest her,
He feign'd to snirtle in his sleeve,
   When thus the Caird address'd her.

AIR

Tune—*Clout the caudron*°

I

My bonny lass I work in brass,
   A tinker is my station;
I've travell'd round all Christian ground
   In this my occupation.
I've ta'en the gold, I've been enroll'd°
   In many a noble squadron;   170
But vain they search'd, when off I march'd
   To go an' clout the caudron.
                     I've ta'en the gold, &c.

II

Despise that shrimp, that wither'd imp,
   Wi' a' his noise an' caprin',
An' tak' a share wi' those that bear
   The *budget* an' the *apron*.
An' *by* that stowp! my faith an' houpe,

An' *by* that dear Kilbaigie,[10]
If e'er ye want, or meet wi' scant,
May I ne'er weet my craigie.   180
                        An' by that stowp, &c.

RECITATIVO

The Caird prevail'd—th' unblushing fair°
    In his embraces sunk,
Partly wi' love o'ercome sae sair,
    An' partly she was drunk.
Sir Violino with an air,
    That show'd a man of spunk,
Wish'd *unison* between the pair,
    An' made the bottle clunk
            To their health that night.

But hurchin Cupid shot a shaft   190
    That play'd a dame a shavie,
The fiddler rak'd her fore and aft,
    Behint the chicken cavie.
Her lord, a wight o' Homer's[2] craft,
    Tho' limping wi' the spavie,
He hirpl'd up, an' lap like daft,
    An' shor'd them Dainty Davie
            O boot that night.°

He was a care-defying blade
    As ever Bacchus listed,°   200
Tho' Fortune sair upon him laid,
    His heart she ever miss'd it.
He had no wish but—to be glad,
    Nor want but—when he thristed;
He hated nought but—to be sad,
    And thus the muse suggested
            His sang that night.

---

[1] A peculiar sort of whisky so called: a great favourite with Poosie-Nansie's clubs.
[2] Homer is allowed to be the oldest ballad singer on record.

AIR

Tune—*For a' that, an' a' that*°

I

I am a bard of no regard,
  Wi' gentle folks, an' a' that;
But *Homer-like*, the glowran byke,   210
  Frae town to town I draw that.

CHORUS

For a' that, an' a' that,
  An' twice as muckle's a' that;
I've lost but ane, I've twa behin',
  I've *wife eneugh* for a' that.

II

I never drank the Muses' stank,
  Castalia's burn, an' a' that;°
But there it streams, and richly reams,°
  My *Helicon* I ca' that.
                    For a' that, &c.

III

Great love I bear to a' the fair,   220
  Their humble slave, an' a' that;
But lordly will, I hold it still°
  A mortal sin to thraw that.
                    For a' that, &c.

IV

In raptures sweet, this hour we meet,
  Wi' mutual love an' a' that;
But for how lang the *flie may stang*,
  Let *inclination* law that.
                    For a' that, &c.

V

Their tricks and craft have put me daft,
  They've ta'en me in, an' a' that;
But clear your decks, an' here's the *sex!* °   230
  I like the jads for a' that.

For a' that, an' a' that,
    An' twice as muckle's a' that;
My *dearest bluid*, to do them guid,
    They're welcome till't for a' that.

RECITATIVO

So sung the bard—and Nansie's wa's
Shook with a thunder of applause,
    Re-echo'd from each mouth;
They toom'd their pocks, an' pawn'd their duds,
They scarcely left to coor their fuds,   240
    To quench their lowan drouth.°
Then owre again, the jovial thrang,
    The poet did request
To lowse his pack an' wale a sang,
    A ballad o' the best:
        He, rising, rejoicing
            Between his twa *Deborahs*,°
        Looks round him, an' found them
            Impatient for the chorus.

AIR

Tune—*Jolly mortals fill your glasses*°

I

See! the smoking bowl before us,   250
    Mark our jovial ragged ring!
Round and round take up the chorus,
    And in raptures let us sing.

CHORUS

    A fig for those by law protected!
    Liberty's a glorious feast!
    Courts for cowards were erected,
        Churches built to please the priest.

II

What is title? what is treasure?
    What is reputation's care?
If we lead a life of pleasure,   260

'Tis no matter *how* or *where!*
   A fig, &c.

III

With the ready trick and fable,
 Round we wander all the day;
And at night, in barn or stable,
 Hug our doxies on the hay.
   A fig, &c.

IV

Does the train-attended *carriage*
 Through the country lighter rove?
Does the sober bed of marriage
 Witness brighter scenes of love?
   A fig, &c.

V

Life is all a *variorum,*°
 We regard not how it goes;
Let them cant about *decorum*
 Who have character to lose.°
   A fig, &c.

VI

Here's to budgets, bags and wallets!
 Here's to all the wandering train!
Here's our ragged *brats* and *callets!*
 One and all cry out, Amen!

A fig for those by law protected!
 Liberty's a glorious feast!
Courts for cowards were erected,
 Churches built to please the priest.

HOLY WILLIE'S PRAYER:
A POEM

O THOU, wha in the heavens dost dwell,
Wha, as it pleases best thysel',

270

280

Sends ane to heaven and ten to hell,
   A' for thy glory,°
And no for ony guid or ill
    They've done afore thee!°

I bless and praise thy matchless might,
Whan thousands thou hast left in night,
That I am here afore thy sight,
    For gifts an' grace°   10
A burnin' an' a shinin' light,°
    To a' this place.

What was I, or my generation,°
That I should get such exaltation,
I wha deserve sic just damnation,
    For broken laws,
Five thousand years 'fore my creation,°
    Thro' Adam's cause.

When frae my mither's womb I fell,
Thou might hae plunged me in hell,   20
To gnash my gums, to weep and wail,
    In burnin' lake,°
Whar damned devils roar and yell,
    Chain'd to a stake.

Yet I am here a chosen sample,°
To show thy grace is great an' ample;
I'm here a pillar in thy temple,°
    Strong as a rock,
A guide, a buckler an' example°
    To a' thy flock.°   30

But yet, O L—d! confess I must,
At times I'm fash'd wi' fleshly lust;°
An' sometimes too, wi' warldly trust°
    Vile self gets in;
But thou remembers we are dust,°
    Defil'd in sin.

O L—d! yestreen, thou kens, wi' Meg,
Thy pardon I sincerely beg,
O! may it ne'er be a livin' plague
          To my dishonour,°   40
An' I'll ne'er lift a lawless l–g°
          Again upon her.

Besides, I farther maun allow,
Wi' Lizie's lass, three times I trow;
But, L—d, that Friday I was fow,
          When I came near her,
Or else, thou kens, thy *servant true*
          Wad ne'er hae steer'd her.°

Maybe thou lets this *fleshly thorn*°
Beset thy servant e'en and morn,   50
Lest he o'er high and proud shou'd turn,°
          'Cause he's sae *gifted*;
If sae, thy han' maun e'en be borne,°
          Until thou lift it.

L—d bless thy chosen in this place,
For *here* thou hast a *chosen race*;°
But G–d confound their stubborn face,
          And blast their name,°
Wha bring thy elders to disgrace
          An' public shame.   60

L—d mind G——n H———n's deserts,°
He drinks, an' swears, an' plays at cartes,°
Yet has sae mony takin' arts,°
          Wi' grit an' sma',
Frae G–d's ain priest the people's hearts°
          He steals awa'.

An' whan we chasten'd him therefore,
Thou kens how he bred sic a splore,
As set the warld in a roar
          O' laughin' at us;   70
Curse thou his basket and his store,°
          Kail an' potatoes.

L—d hear my earnest cry an' pray'r,
Against that presbyt'ry o' Ayr;
Thy strong right hand, L—d make it bare,°
        Upo' their heads,
L—d weigh it down, and dinna spare,
        For their misdeeds.

O L—d my G—d, that glib-tongu'd A——n,°   80
My very heart an' saul are quakin',
To think how we stood sweatin', shakin',°
        An' p—d wi' dread,
While he wi' hingin' lips and snakin'
        Held up his head.°

L—d in the day of vengeance try him,°
L—d visit them wha did employ him,°
An' pass not in thy mercy by 'em,°
        Nor hear their pray'r;
But for thy people's sake destroy 'em,
        And dinna spare.   90

But, L—d remember me and mine
Wi' mercies temp'ral and divine,
That I for gear and grace may shine,
        Excell'd by nane,
An' a' the glory shall be thine,
        Amen, Amen!

EXTEMPORE VERSES
ON
DINING WITH LORD DAER
Mossgiel, October 25ᵗʰ

THIS wot all ye whom it concerns,
I, rhymer Rab, alias BURNS,
        October twenty-third,
A ne'er to be forgotten day!
Sae far I sprachl'd up the brae,
        I dinner'd with a LORD.

I've been at drucken Writer's feasts;°
Nay, been bitch-fou 'mang godly Priests,
        (Wi' rev'rence be it spoken!)
I've even join'd the honour'd jorum,   10
When mighty Squireships o' the Quorum,°
        Their hydra drouth did sloken.

But wi' a LORD!—stand out my shin!°
A LORD—a PEER—an EARL'S SON—
        Up higher yet, my bonnet!
An' such a LORD—lang Scotch ell twa;°
Our PEERAGE he looks o'er them a',
        As I look o'er my sonnet.°

But, O! for Hogarth's magic pow'r,°
To shew Sir Bardie's willyart glowr,   20
        An' how he star'd an' stammer'd!
When goavan 's he'd been led wi' branks,
An' stumpan on his ploughman shanks,
        He in the parlour hammer'd.

'To meet good Stuart little pain is,°
'Or Scotia's sacred Demosthenes,'°
        Thinks I, 'They are but men!'
But 'Burns, my Lord'—Guid G–d! I doited;
My knees on ane anither knoited,
        As faultering I gaed ben!   30

I sidling shelter'd in a neuk,
An' at his Lordship staw a leuk,
        Like some portentous omen:
Except GOOD SENSE, an' SOCIAL GLEE,
An' (what surpris'd me) MODESTY,
        I marked nought uncommon.

I watch'd the symptoms o' the GREAT,°
The GENTLE PRIDE, the LORDLY STATE,
        The arrogant assuming;
The fient a pride, nae pride had he,   40
Nor sauce, nor state, that I could see,
        Mair than an honest Ploughman.

Then from his Lordship I shall learn,
Henceforth to meet with unconcern,
    One rank as well's another:
Nae honest, worthy man need care,
To meet wi' NOBLE, youthfu' DAER,
    For he but meets a BROTHER.

THE FORNICATER

Tune—*Clout the Cauldron*

YOU Jovial boys who love the joys,
    The blessfu' joys of lovers;
An' dare avow't wi daintless brow,°
    Whate'er the lass discovers;°
I pray draw near, and you shall hear,
    An' welcome in a *frater*,°
I've lately been on quarintine,
    A proven Fornicater.

Before the congregation wide,°
    I past the muster fairly;   10
My handsome Betsey by my side,
    We gat our ditty rarely.°
My downcast eye, by chance did spy,
    What made my mouth to water,
Those limbs sae clean, where I between°
    Commenced Fornicater.

Wi' ruefu' face and signs o' grace,
    I paid the buttock hire;°
The night was dark, and thro the park
    I cou'dna but convoy her;°   20
A parting kiss, what cou'd I less,
    My vows began to scatter;
Sweet Betsey fell, fal lal de ral!
    I am a Fornicater.

But, by the sun an' moon I swear,
    An' I'll fulfil ilk hair o't,

That while I own a single crown,
    She's welcome to a share o't;
My rogish boy, his mother's joy,
    An' darling of his *pater*,°   30
I for his sake the name will take,
    A harden'd Fornicater.°

NINE INCH WILL PLEASE A LADY

Tune—The Quaker's wife

COME rede me dame, come tell me, dame,
    My dame, come tell me truly,
What length o' graith, when weel ca'd hame,°
    Will sair a woman duly?
The carlin clew her wanton tail,
    Her wanton tail sae ready;
I learn't a sang in Annandale,°
    Nine inch will please a lady.

But for a coontrie c—t like mine,
    In sooth we're nae sae gentle;   10
We'll tak' twa thumb-bread to the nine,
    And that's a sonsie p——e.°
O leeze me on my Charlie-lad!
    I'll ne'er forget my Charlie!
Twa roarin handfu' and a daud,°
    He nidg't it in fu' rarely.°

But weary fa' the laithron doup,°
    And may it ne'er ken thrivin';
It's no the length that gars me loup,
    But its the double drivin'.   20
Come nidge me Tam, come nodge me Tam,
    Come nidge me o'er the nyvle;°
Come louse and lug your batterin' ram,
    And thrash him at my gyvel.°

POOR BODIES DO NAETHING BUT M–W

Tune—The Campbells are commin'

WHEN princes an' prelates,°
An' hot-headed zealates,
A' Europe had set in a low, a low,°
   The poor man lies down,
   Nor envies a crown,
But comforts himsel' wi' a m–w, a m–w.

   An' why shou'd na poor bodies m–w, m–w, m–w;
   An' why shou'd na poor bodies m–w;
   The rich they hae siller, an' houses, an' land,
   Poor bodies hae naething but m–w.   10

When B—s—k's great prince°
Gade a cruizin' to France,°
Republican billies to cow, cow, cow;
   Great B—s—k's strang prince
   Wadda shown better sense,
At hame wi his prin—ss to m–w, m–w, m–w.
       An' why, &c.

The E–p——r swore,°
By sea an' by shore,
At Paris to kick up a row, a row;
   But Paris ay ready,
   Just leugh at the laddie,   20
An' bade him gae hame an' gae m–w, m–w, m–w.
       An' why, &c.

When the brave duke of Y—k°
The Rhine first did pass,°
Republican armies to cow, cow, cow,
   They bade him gae hame,
   To his P—ss—n dame,°
An' gie her a kiss an' a m–w, a m–w.
       An' why, &c.

Out over the Rhine,
Proud P—ss—a did shine,°   30
To spend his last blood he did vow, vow, vow;
But F—d——k had better,°
Ne'er forded the water,
But spent as he dought at a m—w, a m—w.
                    An' why, &c.

The black-headed eagle,°
As keen as a beagle,
He hunted o'er height an' o'er howe, howe, howe,
In the braes of Gemap,°
He fell in trap,
E'en let him come out as he dow, dow, dow.   40
                    An' why, &c.

When Kate laid her claws,
On poor St——l—s,°
An' Poland was bent like a bow, a bow;°
May the diel in her a—e,
Ram a huge p—k o' brass,
An' d—n her to h—ll wi' a m—w.
                    An' why, &c.°

POEM

ON PASTORAL POETRY

HAIL Poesie! thou Nymph reserv'd!
In chase o' thee, what crouds hae swerv'd
Frae common sense, or sunk enerv'd
                    'Mang heaps o' clavers;
And och! o'er aft thy joes hae starv'd,
                    Mid a' thy favors!

Say, Lassie, why thy train amang,
While loud, the trump's heroic clang,
And sock or buskin skelp alang°
                    To death or marriage;   10
Scarce ane has tried the shepherd-sang
                    But wi' miscarriage?

In Homer's craft Jock Milton thrives;°
Eschylus' pen Will Shakespeare drives;°
Wee Pope, the knurlin, 'till him rives
          Horatian fame;°
In thy sweet sang, Barbauld, survives
          Even Sappho's flame.°

But thee, Theocritus, wha matches?°
They're no herd's ballats, Maro's catches;°   20
Squire Pope but busks his skinklin patches
          O' heathen tatters:°
I pass by hunders, nameless wretches,
          That ape their betters.

In this braw age o' wit and lear,
Will nane the Shepherd's whistle mair
Blaw sweetly in its native air
          And rural grace;
And wi' the far-fam'd Grecian share
          A rival place?   30

Yes! there is ane; a Scottish callan!
There's ane; come forrit, honest Allan!°
Thou need na jouk behint the hallan,
          A chiel sae clever;
The teeth o' time may gnaw Tamtallan,°
          But thou's for ever.

Thou paints auld nature to the nines,
In thy sweet Caledonian lines;
Nae gowden stream thro' myrtles twines,
          Where Philomel,°   40
While nightly breezes sweep the vines,
          Her griefs will tell!

In gowany glens thy burnie strays,
Where bonnie lasses bleach their claes;
Or trots by hazelly shaws and braes,
          Wi' hawthorns gray,
Where blackbirds join the shepherd's lays
          At close o' day.

Thy rural loves are nature's sel;
Nae bombast spates o' nonsense swell;   50
Nae snap conceits, but that sweet spell
   O' witchin love,
That charm, that can the strongest quell,
    The sternest move.°

POETICAL INSCRIPTION,
FOR AN ALTAR TO INDEPENDENCE
*At Kerrouchtry, the seat of Mr. Heron, written in
Summer 1795.*

THOU of an independent mind
With soul resolved, with soul resigned;
Prepar'd power's proudest frown to brave,
Who wilt not be, nor have a slave;
Virtue alone who dost revere,
Thy own reproach alone dost fear,
Approach this shrine, and worship here.

ADDRESS TO A LADY

OH wert thou in the cauld blast,
 On yonder lea, on yonder lea;
My plaidie to the angry airt,
 I'd shelter thee, I'd shelter thee:
Or did misfortune's bitter storms
 Around thee blaw, around thee blaw,
Thy bield should be my bosom,
 To share it a', to share it a'.

Or were I in the wildest waste,
 Sae black and bare, sae black and bare,   10
The desart were a paradise,
 If thou wert there, if thou wert there.
Or were I monarch o' the globe,
 Wi' thee to reign, wi' thee to reign;
The brightest jewel in my crown,
 Wad be my queen, wad be my queen.

LINES

WRITTEN EXTEMPORE IN A LADY'S POCKET-BOOK

GRANT me, indulgent heaven, that I may live
To see the miscreants feel the pains they give;
Deal Freedom's sacred treasures free as air,
Till slave and despot be but things which were.

VERSES

*Written under the Portrait of Fergusson the Poet, in a copy of
that author's works presented to a young Lady, Edinburgh 19ᵗʰ
March, 1787, by the late celebrated Robert Burns.*

CURSE on ungrateful man that can be pleased,
And yet can starve the author of the pleasure!°
O thou my elder brother in misfortune,
By far my elder brother in the muse,°
With tears I pity thy unhappy fate!
Why is the bard unfitted for the world°
Yet has so keen a relish of its pleasures?

SONG

Tune—*The Weaver and his Shuttle, O*

MY father was a farmer upon the Carrick border, O°
And carefully he bred me in decency and order, O
He bade me act a manly part, though I had ne'er a farthing, O
For without an honest manly heart, no man was worth regarding, O.

Then out into the world my course I did determine, O
Tho' to be rich was not my wish, yet to be great was charming, O
My talents they were not the worst; nor yet my education: O
Resolv'd was I, at least to try, to mend my situation, O.

In many a way, and vain essay, I courted fortune's favor; O
Some cause unseen, still stept between, to frustrate each
     endeavour; O

10

Sometimes by foes I was o'erpower'd; sometimes by friends
    forsaken; O
And when my hope was at the top, I still was worst mistaken, O.

Then sore harrass'd, and tir'd at last, with fortune's vain delusion; O
I dropt my schemes, like idle dreams, and came to this
    conclusion; O
The past was bad, and the future hid; its good or ill untryed; O
But the present hour was in my pow'r, and so I would enjoy it, O.

No help, nor hope, nor view had I; nor person to befriend me; O
So I must toil, and sweat and moil, and labor to sustain me, O°
To plough and sow, to reap and mow, my father bred
    me early; O
For one, he said, to labor bred, was a match for fortune
    fairly, O.   20

Thus all obscure, unknown, and poor, thro' life I'm doom'd
    to wander, O
Till down my weary bones I lay in everlasting slumber: O
No view nor care, but shun whate'er might breed me pain
    or sorrow; O
I live to day, as well's I may, regardless of tomorrow, O.

But chearful still, I am as well, as a monarch in a palace, O
Tho' fortune's frown still hunts me down, with all her
    wonted malice; O
I make indeed, my daily bread, but ne'er can make it farther; O
But as daily bread is all I need, I do not much regard her, O.

When sometimes by my labor I earn a little money, O
Some unforeseen misfortune comes generally upon me; O   30
Mischance, mistake, or by neglect, or my good-natur'd folly; O
But come what will, I've sworn it still, I'll ne'er be
    melancholy, O.

All you who follow wealth and power with unremitting ardor, O
The more in this you look for bliss, you leave your view
    the farther; O
Had you the wealth Potosi boasts, or nations to adore you, O°
A chearful honest hearted clown I will prefer before you, O.

FRAGMENT

Tune—*Dainty Davie*

THERE was a lad was born in Kyle,[1]
But what na day o' what na style°
I doubt its hardly worth the while
   To be sae nice wi' *Robin*.°

Robin was a rovin' Boy,
   Rantin' rovin', rantin' rovin';
Robin was a rovin' Boy,
   Rantin' rovin' Robin.

Our monarch's hindmost year but ane°
Was five and twenty days begun,   10
'Twas then a blast o' Janwar Win'°
   Blew hansel in on *Robin*.°

The gossip keekit in his loof,°
Quo' scho wha lives will see the proof,
This waly boy will be nae coof,
   I think we'll ca' him *Robin*.

He'll hae misfortunes great and sma',
But ay a heart aboon them a';
He'll be a credit 'till us a',
   We'll a' be proud o' *Robin*.   20

But sure as three times three mak nine,
I see by ilka score and line,
This chap will dearly like our kin',
   So leeze me on thee *Robin*.

Guid faith quo' scho I doubt you Sir,
Ye'll gar the lasses lie aspar;°
But twenty fauts ye may hae waur
   So blessin's on thee, *Robin!*

[1] *Kyle*—a district of Ayrshire. [note in Cromek 1808]

Robin was a rovin' Boy,
Rantin' rovin', rantin' rovin';
Robin was a rovin' Boy,
Rantin' rovin' Robin.   30

ELEGY
On the Death Of Robert Ruisseaux[1]

Now Robin lies in his last lair,°
He'll gabble rhyme, nor sing nae mair,
Cauld poverty, wi' hungry stare,
            Nae mair shall fear him;
Nor anxious fear, nor cankert care
            E'er mair come near him.

To tell the truth, they seldom fash't him,
Except the moment that they crush't him;
For sune as chance or fate had husht 'em
            Tho' e'er sae short,   10
Then wi' a rhyme or song he lasht 'em,
            And thought it sport.—

Tho' he was bred to kintra wark,
And counted was baith wight and stark,
Yet that was never Robin's mark
            To mak a man;
But tell him, he was learn'd and clark,
            Ye roos'd him then![2]

SKETCH OF AN EPISTLE TO R. GRAHAM, Esq.
OF FINTRAY

Fintray, my stay in worldly strife,
Friend o' my muse, friend o' my life,
      Are ye as idle 's I am?
Come then, wi' uncouth, kintra fleg,

---

[1] *Ruisseaux*—a play on his own name. [note in Cromek 1808]
[2] *Ye roos'd*—ye prais'd. [note in Cromek 1808]

O'er Pegasus I'll fling my leg,
  And ye shall see me try him.

I'll sing the zeal Drumlanrig bears,°
Who left the all-important cares
  Of fiddles, whores and hunters;°
And bent on buying borough towns,°   10
Came shaking hands wi' wabster louns,°
  And kissing barefit bunters.°

Combustion through our boroughs rode,°
Whistling his roaring pack abroad,
  Of mad, unmuzzled lions;
As Queensberry buff and blue unfurled,°
And Westerha' and Hopeton hurled°
  To every Whig defiance.°

But Queensberry, cautious, left the war,
Th' unmanner'd dust might soil his star,°   20
  Besides, he hated bleeding;
But left behind him heroes bright,
Heroes in Cesarean fight,
  Or Ciceronian pleading.°

O, for a throat like huge Monsmeg,°
To muster o'er each ardent Whig°
  Beneath Drumlanrig's banner.
Heroes and heroines commix
All in the field of politics,
  To win immortal honour.   30

McM—rdo and his lovely spouse,°
(Th' enamour'd laurels kiss her brows),
  Led on the loves and graces;
She won each gaping Burgess' heart;°
While he, sub rosa, play'd his part°
  Among their wives and lasses.

Craigdarroch led a light-arm'd corps,°
Tropes, metaphors and figure pours,
  Like Hecla streaming thunder;°

Glenriddel, skill'd in rusty coins,°   40
Blew up each Tory's dark designs,°
　　And bar'd the treason under.

In either wing two champions fought,
Redoubted Staig who set at nought°
　　The wildest savage Tory;
And Walsh, who ne'er yet flinch'd his ground,°
High-wav'd his magnum-bonum round
　　With Cyclopean fury.°

Miller brought up th' artillery ranks,°
The many-pounders of the Banks,   50
　　Resistless desolation;
While Maxwelton, that baron bold,°
Mid Lawson's port entrench'd his hold,°
　　And threaten'd worse damnation.

To these, what Tory hosts oppos'd;
With these, what Tory warriors clos'd,
　　Surpasses my descriving.
Squadrons, extended long and large,
With furious speed rush'd to the charge,
　　Like raging devils driving.   60

What verse can sing!—what prose narrate!
The butcher deeds of bloody fate
　　Amid this mighty tulzie?
Grim horror girn'd; pale terror roar'd
As murther at his thrapple shor'd;
　　And hell mixt in the brulzie!

As Highland craigs, by thunder cleft,
When light'nings fire the stormy lift,
　　Hurl down wi' crashing rattle;
As flames amang a hundred woods;   70
As headlong foam a hundred floods;
　　Such is the rage of battle.°

The stubborn Tories dare to die:
As soon the rooted oaks would fly,

Before th' approaching fellers,
The Whigs come on like ocean's roar,
When all his wintry billows pour
    Against the Buchan bullers.°

Lo, from the shades of death's deep night,
Departed Whigs enjoy the fight,   80
    And think on former daring!
The muffled murtherer of Charles
The Magna Charta flag unfurls,°
    All deadly gules its bearing.

Nor wanting ghosts of Tory fame;
Bold Scrimgeour follows gallant Graham:—°
    Auld Covenanters shiver—
(Forgive, forgive, much-wrong'd Montrose!°
While death and hell ingulph thy foes,
    Thou liv'st on high for ever!)   90

Still o'er the field the combat burns;
The Tories, Whigs, give way by turns;—
    But fate the word has spoken—
For woman's wit, or strength of man,
Alas! can do but what they can——
    The Tory ranks are broken!

O, that my e'en were flowing burns!
My voice a lioness that mourns
    Her darling cub's undoing!
That I might greet, that I might cry,   100
While Tories fall, while Tories fly,
    And furious Whigs pursuing!

What Whig but wails the good Sir James;
Dear to his country, by the names
    Friend, Patron, Benefactor!
Not Pulteney's wealth can Pulteney save!°
And Hopetoun falls, the generous, brave!
    And Stewart, bold as Hector!°

Thou, Pitt, shalt rue this overthrow;°
And Thurlow growl a curse of woe,°   110
  And Melville melt in wailing!°
Now Fox and Sheridan rejoice!°
And Burke shall sing, 'O Prince arise!°
  Thy power is all-prevailing!'

For your poor friend, the Bard, afar
He only hears and sees the war,°
  A cool spectator purely:°
So, when the storm the forest rends,
The robin in the hedge descends,
  And sober chirps securely.   120

Now for my friends and brethren's sakes,
And for my dear-lov'd land o' cakes,°
  I pray with holy fire:
Lord send a rough-shod troop o' hell,
O'er a' wad Scotland buy or sell,
  To grind them in the mire.

EPISTLE TO THE PRESIDENT OF THE HIGHLAND SOCIETY,
RESPECTING FIVE HUNDRED HIGHLANDERS ATTEMPTING TO EMIGRATE TO AMERICA·

To the Right Honourable the Earl of B ****, President of
the Right Honourable and Honourable the Highland Society,
which met on the 23d of May last, at the Shakespeare,
Covent-Garden, to concert ways and means to frustrate the
designs of FIVE HUNDRED HIGHLANDERS who, as the
Society were informed by Mr. Mᶜ—— of A **** s, were so
audacious as to attempt an escape from their lawful lords
and masters, whose property they are, by emigrating from
the lands of Mr Macdonald of Glengary to the wilds of
Canada, in search of that fantastic thing—LIBERTY!

  Long life, my Lord, an' health be yours,
  Unskaith'd by hunger'd Highlan' boors!
  Lord grant nae duddie, desperate beggar,

Wi' durk, claymore, or rusty trigger
May twin auld Scotland o' a life,
She likes—as *butchers* like a *knife!*

Faith, you and A **** s were right°
To keep the Highlan' hounds in sight!
I doubt na! they wad bid nae better
Than let them ance out owre the water;
Then up amang thae lakes and seas   10
They'll mak what rules an' laws they please.
Some daring Hancocke, or a Franklin,°
May set their Highlan' bluid a-ranklin;
Some Washington again may head them,°
Or some Montgomery, fearless, lead them;°
Till God knows what may be effected,
When by such heads an' hearts directed:
Poor dunghill sons of dirt and mire,
May to Patrician rights aspire!   20
Nae sage North, now, nor sager Sackville,°
To watch an' premier owre the pack vile!
An' whare will ye get Howes and Clintons°
To bring them to a right repentance?
To cowe the rebel generation,
An' save the *honour* o' the nation!

They! an' be d——d! what right hae they
To meat, or sleep, or light o' day?
Far less to riches, pow'r, or freedom,
But what your Lordships please to gie them?   30

But hear, my Lord! G **** hear!°
Your *hand's owre light on them*, I fear;
Your factors, grieves, trustees an' bailies,
I canna say but they do gailies;
They lay aside a' tender mercies,
An' tirl the hallions to the birsies;
Yet, while they're only poin'd and herriet,
They'll keep their stubborn Highland spirit:
But smash them! crash them a' to spails!
An' rot the dyvors i' the jails!   40
The young dogs, swinge them to the labour,

Let wark an' hunger mak them sober!
The hizzies, if they're oughtlins faussont,
Let them in Drury Lane be lesson'd!°
An' if the wives, an' dirty brats
Come thiggan at your doors an' yetts,
Flaffan wi' duds, an' grey wi' beese,°
Frightan awa your deucks and geese;
Get out a horse-whip, or a jowler,
The langest thong, the fiercest growler,   50
An' gar the tatter'd gipsies pack
Wi' a' their bastarts on their back!

Go on, my lord! I lang to meet you,
An' in my *house at hame* to greet you!
Wi' common lords ye shanna mingle,
The benmost newk beside the ingle
At my right hand assign'd your seat,
'Tween Herod's hip an' Polycrate,—°
Or, if ye on your station tarrow,
Between Almagro an' Pizarro;°   60
A seat, I'm sure ye're weel deservin't;
An' till ye come—your humble servant,
                         BEELZEBUB.°

    June 1,
Anno Mundi 5790°

THE SELKIRK GRACE

SOME hae meat and canna eat,
    And some wad eat that want it.
But we hae meat and we can eat,
    And sae the Lord be thanket.

THE TREE OF LIBERTY

HEARD ye o' the tree o' France,
    I watna what's the name o't;
Around it a' the patriots dance,°
    Weel Europe kens the fame o't.

It stands where ance the Bastile stood,°
    A prison built by kings, man,
When Superstition's hellish brood°
    Kept France in leading strings, man.

Upo' this tree there grows sic fruit,
    Its virtues a' can tell, man;   10
It raises man aboon the brute,
    It maks him ken himsel, man.
Gif ance the peasant taste a bit,
    He's greater than a lord, man,
And wi' the beggar shares a mite
    O' a' he can afford, man.

This fruit is worth a' Afric's wealth,
    To comfort us 'twas sent, man:
To gie the sweetest blush o' health,
    And mak us a' content, man.   20
It clears the een, it cheers the heart,
    Maks high and low gude friends, man;
And he wha acts the traitor's part,
    It to perdition sends, man.

My blessings aye attend the chiel,
    Wha pitied Gallia's slaves, man,°
And staw'd a branch, spite o' the deil,
    Frae yont the western waves, man.°
Fair Virtue water'd it wi' care,
    And now she sees wi' pride, man,   30
How weel it buds and blossoms there,
    Its branches spreading wide, man.

But vicious folk aye hate to see
    The works o' Virtue thrive, man;
The courtly vermin's banned the tree,
    And grat to see it thrive, man;
King Loui' thought to cut it down,°
    When it was unco sma', man;
For this the watchman cracked his crown,
    Cut aff his head and a', man.°   40

A wicked crew syne, on a time,°
　　Did tak a solemn aith, man,
It ne'er should flourish to its prime,
　　I wat they pledged their faith, man,
Awa they gaed wi' mock parade,
　　Like beagles hunting game, man,
But soon grew weary o' the trade,
　　And wished they'd been at hame, man.

For Freedom, standing by the tree,
　　Her sons did loudly ca', man;°   50
She sang a sang o' liberty,
　　Which pleased them ane and a', man.
By her inspired, the new-born race
　　Soon drew the avenging steel, man;
The hirelings ran—her foes gied chase,°
　　And banged the despot weel, man.

Let Britain boast her hardy oak,
　　Her poplar and her pine, man,
Auld Britain ance could crack her joke,
　　And o'er her neighbours shine, man.   60
But seek the forest round and round,
　　And soon 'twill be agreed, man,
That sic a tree can not be found,
　　'Twixt London and the Tweed, man.°

Without this tree, alake this life
　　Is but a vale o' woe, man;
A scene o' sorrow mixed wi' strife,
　　Nae real joys we know, man.
We labour soon, we labour late,
　　To feed the titled knave, man;   70
And a' the comfort we're to get,
　　Is that ayont the grave, man.

Wi' plenty o' sic trees, I trow,
　　The warld would live in peace, man;
The sword would help to mak a plough,
　　The din o' war wad cease, man.
Like brethren in a common cause,

We'd on each other smile, man;
And equal rights and equal laws
   Wad gladden every isle, man. 80

Wae worth the loon wha wadna eat
   Sic halesome dainty cheer, man;
I'd gie the shoon frae aff my feet,
   To taste sic fruit, I swear, man.
Syne let us pray, auld England may
   Sure plant this far-famed tree, man;
And blythe we'll sing, and hail the day
   That gave us liberty, man.

'Ill-fated genius' [on Robert Fergusson]

ILL-FATED genius! Heaven-taught Fergusson!°
   What heart that feels and will not yield a tear,
To think life's sun did set ere well begun
   To shed its influence on thy bright career.
O why should truest worth and genius pine,
   Beneath the iron grasp of Want and Wo,
While titled knaves and idiot greatness shine
   In all the spendour Fortune can bestow!

A FRAGMENT—
ON GLENRIDDEL'S FOX BREAKING HIS CHAIN

THOU, Liberty, thou art my theme,
Not such as idle Poets dream,
Who trick thee up a Heathen goddess
That a fantastic cap and rod has:°
Such stale conceits are poor and silly;
I paint thee out, a Highland filly,
A sturdy, stubborn, handsome dapple,
As sleek's a mouse, as round's an apple,
That when thou pleasest can do wonders;
But when thy luckless rider blunders, 10
Or if thy fancy should demur there,
Wilt break thy neck ere thou go further.—

These things premis'd, I sing a fox,
Was caught among his native rocks,
And to a dirty kennel chain'd,
How he his liberty regain'd.——

Glenriddel, a Whig without a stain,°
A Whig in principle and grain,
Couldst thou enslave a free-born creature,
A native denizen of Nature?   20
How couldst thou with a heart so good,
(A better ne'er was sluic'd with blood)
Nail a poor devil to a tree,
That ne'er did harm to thine or thee?

The staunchest Whig Glenriddel was,
Quite frantic in his Country's cause;°
And oft was Reynard's prison passing,
And with his brother Whigs canvassing
The Rights of Men, the Powers of Women,°
With all the dignity of Freemen.——   30

Sir Reynard daily heard debates
Of Princes' kings' and Nations' fates;
With many rueful, bloody stories
Of tyrants, Jacobites and tories:°
From liberty how angels fell,
That now are galley slaves in hell;
How Nimrod first the trade began°
Of binding Slavery's chains on man;
How fell Semiramis, G–d d–mn her!°
Did first with sacreligious hammer,   40
(All ills till then were trivial matters)
For Man dethron'd forge hen-peck fetters;
How Xerxes, that abandon'd tory,°
Thought cutting throats was reaping glory,
Untill the stubborn Whigs of Sparta°
Taught him great Nature's Magna charta;°
How mighty Rome her fiat hurl'd,
Resistless o'er a bowing world,
And kinder than they did desire,
Polish'd mankind with sword and fire: 50

With much too tedious to relate,
Of Ancient and of Modern date,
But ending still how Billy Pit,
(Unlucky boy!) with wicked wit,
Has gagg'd old Britain, drain'd her coffer,°
As butchers bind and bleed a heifer.—

    Thus wily Reynard by degrees,
In kennel listening at his ease,
Suck'd in a mighty stock of knowledge,
As much as some folks at a college.—   60
Knew Britain's rights and constitution,
Her aggrandizement, diminution,
How fortune wrought us good from evil;
Let no man then despise the devil,
As who should say, I ne'er can need him;
Since we to scoundrels owe our freedom.—

ODE [FOR GENERAL WASHINGTON'S BIRTHDAY]

No Spartan tube, no Attic shell,°
  No lyre Eolian I awake;°
'Tis Liberty's bold note I swell,
  Thy harp, Columbia, let me take.°
See gathering thousands, while I sing,
A broken chain, exulting, bring,
And dash it in a tyrant's face!°
And dare him to his very beard,
And tell him, he no more is feared,
  No more the Despot of Columbia's race.   10
A tyrant's proudest insults braved,
They shout, a People freed! They hail an Empire saved.

    Where is Man's godlike form?
Where is that brow erect and bold,
That eye that can, unmoved, behold
The wildest rage, the loudest storm,
That e'er created fury dared to raise!
Avaunt! thou caitiff, servile, base,
That tremblest at a Despot's nod,

Yet, crouching under th' iron rod,   20
Canst laud the arm that struck th' insulting blow!
Art thou of man's imperial line?
Dost boast that countenance divine?
Each sculking feature answers, No!
But come, ye sons of Liberty,
Columbia's offspring, brave as free,
In danger's hour still flaming in the van:
Ye know, and dare maintain, The Royalty of Man.

Alfred, on thy starry throne,°
Surrounded by the tuneful choir,   30
The Bards that erst have struck the patriot lyre,°
And roused the freeborn Briton's soul of fire,
    No more thy England own.—
Dare injured nations form the great design,
    To make detested tyrants bleed?°
Thy England execrates the glorious deed!
    Beneath her hostile banners waving,
    Every pang of honor braving,
England in thunder calls—'The Tyrant's cause is mine!'°
That hour accurst, how did the fiends rejoice,   40
And hell thro' all her confines raise th' exulting voice,
That hour which saw the generous English name°
Linkt with such damned deeds of everlasting shame!

Thee, Caledonia, thy wild heaths among,
Famed for the martial deed, the heaven-taught song,
    To thee, I turn with swimming eyes.—
Where is that soul of Freedom fled?
Immingled with the mighty Dead!
    Beneath that hallowed turf where WALLACE lies!°
Hear it not, Wallace, in thy bed of death!   50
    Ye babbling winds in silence sweep;
    Disturb not ye the hero's sleep,
Nor give the coward secret breath.—
Is this the ancient Caledonian form,
Firm as her rock, resistless as her storm?
Shew me that eye which shot immortal hate,
    Blasting the Despot's proudest bearing:
Shew me that arm which, nerved with thundering fate,

Braved Usurpation's boldest daring!°
Dark-quenched as yonder sinking star,   60
No more that glance lightens afar;
That palsied arm no more whirls on the waste of war.

A POET'S WELCOME TO HIS
LOVE-BEGOTTEN DAUGHTER
THE FIRST INSTANCE THAT ENTITLED HIM TO THE
VENERABLE APPELLATION OF FATHER

Thou's welcome, wean! Mishanter fa' me,
If thoughts o' thee or yet thy mammie
Shall ever daunton me or awe me,
    My sweet, wee lady,
Or if I blush when thou shalt ca' me
    Tyta or daddie!

What tho' they ca' me fornicator,°
An' tease my name in kintra clatter?
The mair they talk, I'm kend the better;
    E'en let them clash!   10
An auld wife's tongue 's a feckless matter
    To gie ane fash.

Welcome, my bonie, sweet, wee dochter!
Tho' ye come here a wee unsought for,
And tho' your comin I hae fought for
    Baith kirk and queir;°
Yet, by my faith, ye're no unwrought for—
    That I shall swear!

Sweet fruit o' monie a merry dint,
My funny toil is no a' tint: 20
Tho' thou cam to the warl' asklent,
    Which fools may scoff at,
In my last plack thy part 's be in't
    The better half o't.

Tho' I should be the waur bestead,
Thou 's be as braw and bienly clad,

And thy young years as nicely bred
   Wi' education,
As onie brat o' wedlock's bed
   In a' thy station.   30

Wee image o' my bonie Betty,°
As fatherly I kiss and daut thee,
As dear and near my heart I set thee,
   Wi' as guid will,
As a' the priests had seen me get thee
   That's out o' Hell.

Gude grant that thou may ay inherit
Thy mither's looks an' gracefu' merit,
An' thy poor, worthless daddie's spirit
   Without his failins!   40
'Twill please me mair to see thee heir it
   Than stocket mailins.°

And if thou be what I wad hae thee,
An' tak the counsel I shall gie thee,
I'll never rue my trouble wi' thee—
   The cost nor shame o't—
But be a loving father to thee,
   And brag the name o't.

APPENDIX 1

FROM THE LETTERS

[L125. To Dr John Moore, London]

Sir

For some months past I have been rambling over the country, partly on account of some little business I have to settle° in various places; but of late I have been confined with some lingering complaints originating as I take it in the stomach.—To divert my spirits a little in this miserable fog of Ennui, I have taken a whim to give you a history of MYSELF.—My name has made a small noise in the country; you have done me the honor to interest yourself very warmly in my behalf; and I think a faithful account of, what character of a man I am, and how I came by that character, may perhaps amuse you in an idle moment.—I will give you an honest narrative, though I know it will be at the expence of frequently being laughed at; for I assure you, Sir, I have, like Solomon whose character, excepting the trifling affair of WISDOM, I sometimes think I resemble, I have, I say, like him 'Turned my eyes to behold Madness and Folly;'° and like him too, frequently shaken hands with their intoxicating friendship.—In the very polite letter Miss Williams° did me the honor to write me, she tells me you have got a complaint in your eyes.—I pray God that it may be removed; for considering that lady and you are my common friends, you will probably employ her to read this letter; and then goodnight to that esteem with which she was pleased to honor the Scotch Bard.—After you have perused these pages, should you think them trifling and impertinent, I only beg leave to tell you that the poor Author wrote them under some very twitching qualms of conscience, that, perhaps he was doing what he ought not to do: a predicament he has more than once been in before.—

I have not the most distant pretensions to what the pye-coated guardians of escutcheons° call, A Gentleman.—When at Edin^r last winter, I got acquainted in the Herald's Office, and looking through that granary of Honors I there found almost every name in the kingdom; but for me,

> '—My ancient but ignoble blood
> Has crept thro' Scoundrels ever since the flood'—°

Gules, Purpure, Argent,° &c. quite disowned me.—My Fathers rented land of the noble Kieths of Marshal,° and had the honor to share their fate.—I do not use the word, Honor, with any reference to Political principles; loyal and disloyal I take to be merely relative terms in that ancient and formidable court known in this Country by the name of CLUB-LAW.—Those who dare welcome Ruin and shake hands with Infamy for what they sincerely believe to be the cause of their God or their King—'Brutus and Cassius are honorable men.'°—I mention this circumstance because it threw my father on the world at large; where after many years' wanderings and sojournings, he pickt up a pretty large quantity of Observation and Experience, to which I am indebted for most of my little pretensions to wisdom.—I have met with few who understood 'Men, their manners and their ways'° equal to him; but stubborn, ungainly Integrity, and headlong, ungovernable Irrascibillity are disqualifying circumstances: consequently I was born a very poor man's son.—For the first six or seven years of my life, my father was gardiner to a worthy gentleman of small estate in the neighbourhood of Ayr.—Had my father continued in that situation, I must have marched off to be one of the little underlings about a farm-house; but it was his dearest wish and prayer to have it in his power to keep his children under his own eye till they could discern between good and evil; so with the assistance of his generous Master my father ventured on a small farm in his estate.°—At these years I was by no means a favorite with any body.—I was a good deal noted for a retentive memory, a stubborn, sturdy something in my disposition, and an enthusiastic, idiot piety.—I say idiot piety, because I was then but a child.—Though I cost the schoolmaster some thrashings, I made an excellent English scholar; and against the years of ten or eleven, I was absolutely a Critic in substantives, verbs and particles.—In my infant and boyish days too, I owed much to an old Maid of my Mother's, remarkable for her ignorance, credulity and superstition.—She had, I suppose, the largest collection in the county of tales and songs concerning devils, ghosts, fairies, brownies, witches, warlocks, spunkies,° kelpies, elf-candles,° dead-lights,° wraiths, apparitions, cantraips, giants, inchanted towers, dragons and other trumpery.—This cultivated the latent seeds of Poesy; but had so strong an effect on my imagination, that to this hour, in my nocturnal rambles, I sometimes keep a sharp look-out in suspicious places; and though nobody can be more sceptical in these matters than I, yet it often takes an effort of Philosophy to shake off these idle terrors.—The earliest thing of Composition that I recollect taking pleasure in was, The vision of Mirza° and a hymn of Addison's beginning—'How are Thy servants blest, O Lord!' I particularly remember one half-stanza which was music to my boyish ear—

'For though in dreadful whirls we hung,
'High on the broken wave'—°

I met with these pieces in Mason's English Collection,° one of my schoolbooks.—The two first books I ever read in private, and which gave me more pleasure than any two books I ever read again, were, the life of Hannibal and the history of Sir William Wallace.°—Hannibal gave my young ideas such a turn that I used to strut in raptures up and down after the recruiting drum and bagpipe, and wish myself tall enough to be a soldier; while the story of Wallace poured a Scotish prejudice in my veins which will boil along there till the floodgates of life shut in eternal rest.—Polemical divinity about this time was putting the country half-mad; and I, ambitious of shining in conversation parties on sundays between sermons, funerals, &c. used in a few years more to puzzle

Calvinism with so much heat and indiscretion that I raised a hue and cry of heresy against me which has not ceased to this hour.—My vicinity to Ayr was of great advantage to me.—My social disposition, when not checked by some modification of spited pride, like our catechism definition of Infinitude, was 'without bounds or limits.'°—I formed many connections with other Youngkers who possessed superiour advantages; the youngling Actors who were busy with the rehearsal of PARTS in which they were shortly to appear on that STAGE where, Alas! I was destined to druge behind the SCENES.—It is not commonly at these green years that the young Noblesse and Gentry have a just sense of the immense distance between them and their ragged Playfellows.—It takes a few dashes into the world to give the young Great man that proper, decent, unnoticing disregard for the poor, insignificant, stupid devils, the mechanics and peasantry around him; who perhaps were born in the same village.—My young Superiours never insulted the clouterly appearance of my ploughboy carcase, the two extremes of which were often exposed to all the inclemencies of all the seasons.—They would give me stray volumes of books; among them, even then, I could pick up some observations; and ONE, whose heart I am sure not even the MUNNY BEGUM'S scenes have tainted,° helped me to a little French.—Parting with these, my young friends and benefactors, as they dropped off for the east or west Indies, was often to me a sore affliction; but I was soon called to more serious evils.—My father's generous Master died; the farm proved a ruinous bargain; and, to clench the curse, we fell into the hands of a Factor who sat for the picture I have drawn of one in my Tale of two dogs.°—My father was advanced in life when he married; I was the eldest of seven children; and he, worn out by early hardship, was unfit for labour.—My father's spirit was soon irritated, but not easily broken.—There was a freedom in his lease in two years more, and to weather these two years we retrenched expences.—We lived very poorly; I was a dextrous Ploughman for my years; and the next eldest to me was a brother, who could drive the plough very well and help me to thrash.—A Novel-Writer might perhaps have viewed these scenes with some satisfaction, but so did not I: my indignation yet boils at the recollection of the scoundrel tyrant's insolent, threatening epistles, which used to set us all in tears.—

This kind of life, the chearless gloom of a hermit with the unceasing moil of a galley-slave, brought me to my sixteenth year; a little before which period I first committed the sin of RHYME. You know our country custom of coupling a man and woman together as Partners in the labors of Harvest.—In my fifteenth autumn, my Partner was a bewitching creature who just counted an autumn less.—My scarcity of English denies me the power of doing her justice in that language; but you know the Scotch idiom, She was a bonie, sweet, sonsie lass.—In short, she altogether unwittingly to herself, initiated me in a certain delicious Passion, which in spite of acid Disappointment, gin-horse Prudence° and bookworm Philosophy, I hold to be the first of human joys, our dearest pleasure here below.—How she caught the contagion I can't say; you medical folks talk much of infection by breathing the same air, the touch, &c.

but I never expressly told her that I loved her.—Indeed I did not well know myself, why I liked so much to loiter behind with her, when returning in the evening from our labors; why the tones of her voice made my heartstrings thrill like an Eolian harp;° and particularly, why my pulse beat such a furious ratann when I looked and fingered over her hand, to pick out the nettle-stings and thistles.—Among her other love-inspiring qualifications, she sung sweetly; and 'twas her favorite reel to which I attempted giving an embodied vehicle in rhyme.—I was not so presumtive as to imagine that I could make verses like printed ones, composed by men who had Greek and Latin; but my girl sung a song which was said to be composed by a small country laird's son, on one of his father's maids, with whom he was in love; and I saw no reason why I might not rhyme as well as he, for excepting smearing sheep and casting peats, his father living in the moors, he had no more Scholarcraft than I had.—

Thus with me began Love and Poesy; which at times have been my only, and till within this last twelvemonth have been my highest enjoyment.—My father struggled on till he reached the freedom in his lease, when he entered on a larger farm° about ten miles farther in the country.—The nature of the bargain was such as to throw a little ready money in his hand at the commencement, otherwise the affair would have been impractible.—For four years we lived comfortably here; but a lawsuit between him and his Landlord commencing, after three years tossing and whirling in the vortex of Litigation, my father was just saved from absorption in a jail by phthisical° consumption, which after two years promises, kindly stept in and snatch'd him away—'To where the wicked cease from troubling, and where the weary be at rest.'—°

It is during this climacterick° that my little story iš most eventful.—I was, at the beginning of this period, perhaps the most ungainly, aukward being in the parish.—No Solitaire° was less acquainted with the ways of the world.—My knowledge of ancient story was gathered from Salmon's and Guthrie's geographical grammars;° my knowledge of modern manners, and of literature and criticism, I got from the Spectator.°—These, with Pope's works, some plays of Shakespear, Tull and Dickson on Agriculture,° The Pantheon,° Locke's Essay on the human understanding,° Stackhouse's history of the bible,° Justice's British Gardiner's directory,° Boyle's lectures,° Allan Ramsay's works,° Taylor's scripture doctrine of original sin,° a select Collection of English songs,° and Hervey's meditations° had been the extent of my reading.—The Collection of Songs was my vade mecum.°—I pored over them, driving my cart or walking to labor, song by song, verse by verse; carefully noting the true tender or sublime from affectation and fustian.—I am convinced I owe much to this for my critic-craft such as it is.—

In my seventeenth year, to give my manners a brush, I went to a country dancing school.—My father had an unaccountable antipathy against these meetings; and my going was, what to this hour I repent, in absolute defiance of his commands.—My father, as I said before, was the sport of strong passions: from that instance of rebellion he took a kind of dislike to me, which, I believe was one cause of that dissipation which marked my future years.—I only say,

Dissipation, comparative with the strictness and sobriety of Presbyterean country life; for though the will-o'-wisp meteors of thoughtless Whim were almost the sole lights of my path, yet early ingrained Piety and Virtue never failed to point me out the line of Innocence.—The great misfortune of my life was, never to have AN AIM.—I had felt early some stirrings of Ambition, but they were the blind gropings of Homer's Cyclops° round the walls of his cave: I saw my father's situation entailed on me perpetual labor.—The only two doors by which I could enter the fields of fortune were, the most niggardly economy, or the little chicaning art of bargain-making; the first is so contracted an aperture, I never could squeeze myself into it; the last, I always hated the contamination of the threshold.—Thus, abandoned of aim or view in life; with a strong appetite for sociability, as well from native hilarity as from a pride of observation and remark; a constitutional hypochondriac taint which made me fly solitude; add to all these incentives to social life, my reputation for bookish knowledge, a certain wild, logical talent, and a strength of thought something like the rudiments of good sense, made me generally a welcome guest; so 'tis no great wonder that always 'where two or three were met together, there was I in the midst of them.'° But far beyond all the other impulses of my heart was, un penchant á l'adorable moitiée du genre humain.°—My heart was compleatly tinder, and was eternally lighted up by some Goddess or other; and like every warfare in this world, I was sometimes crowned with success, and sometimes mortified with defeat.—At the plough, scythe or reap-hook I feared no competitor, and set Want at defiance: and as I never cared farther for my labors than while I was in actual exercise, I spent the evening in the way after my own heart.—A country lad rarely carries on an amour without an assisting confident.—I possessed a curiosity, zeal and intrepid dexterity in these matters which recommended me a proper Second in duels of that kind; and I dare say, I felt as much pleasure at being in the secret of half the amours in the parish, as ever did Premier at knowing the intrigues of half the courts of Europe.—

The very goosefeather in my hand seems instinctively to know the well-worn path of my imagination, the favorite theme of my song; and is with difficulty restrained from giving you a couple of paragraphs on the amours of my Compeers, the humble Inmates of the farm-house and cottage; but the grave sons of Science, Ambition or Avarice baptize these things by the name of Follies.—To the sons and daughters of labor and poverty they are matters of the most serious nature: to them, the ardent hope, the stolen interview, the tender farewell, are the greatest and most delicious part of their enjoyments.—

Another circumstance in my life which made very considerable alterations in my mind and manners was, I spent my seventeenth summer on a smuggling coast° a good distance from home at a noted school, to learn Mensuration, Surveying, Dialling,° &c. in which I made a pretty good progress.—But I made greater progress in the knowledge of mankind.—The contraband trade was at that time very successful; scenes of swaggering riot and roaring dissipation were as yet new to me; and I was no enemy to social life.—Here, though I learned to look unconcernedly on a large tavern-bill, and mix without fear in

a drunken squabble, yet I went on with a high hand in my Geometry, till the
sun entered Virgo,° a month which is always a carnival in my bosom, a charm-
ing Fillette who lived next door to the school overset my Trigonometry, and
set me off in a tangent from the sphere of my studies.—I struggled on with my
Sines and Co-sines for a few days more; but stepping out to the garden one
charming noon, to take the sun's altitude, I met with my Angel,

> —'Like Proserpine gathering flowers,
> 'Herself a fairer flower'—°

It was vain to think of doing any more good at school.—The remaining week I
staid, I did nothing but craze the faculties of my soul about her, or steal out to
meet with her; and the two last nights of my stay in the country, had sleep been
a mortal sin, I was innocent.—

I returned home very considerably improved.—My reading was enlarged
with the very important addition of Thomson's and Shenstone's works; I had
seen mankind in a new phasis;° and I engaged several of my schoolfellows to
keep up a literary correspondence with me.—This last helped me much on in
composition.—I had met with a collection of letters by the Wits of Queen
Ann's reign,° and I pored over them most devoutly. I kept copies of any of my
own letters that pleased me, and a comparison between them and the compos-
ition of most of my correspondents flattered my vanity.—I carried this whim
so far that though I had not three farthings worth of business in the world, yet
every post brought me as many letters as if I had been a broad, plodding son of
Day-book & Ledger.—

My life flowed on much in the same tenor till my twenty third year.—Vive
l'amour et vive la bagatelle,° were my sole principles of action.—The addition of
two more Authors to my library gave me great pleasure; Sterne and Mᶜkenzie.—
Tristram Shandy° and the Man of Feeling° were my bosom favorites.—Poesy
was still a darling walk for my mind, but 'twas only the humour of the hour.—I
had usually half a dozen or more pieces on hand; I took up one or other as it
suited the momentary tone of the mind, and dismissed it as it bordered on
fatigue.—My Passions when once they were lighted up, raged like so many
devils, till they got vent in rhyme; and then conning over my verses, like a spell,
soothed all into quiet.—None of the rhymes of those days are in print, except,
Winter, a dirge,° the eldest of my printed pieces; The death of Poor Mailie,°
John Barleycorn,° And songs first, second and third:° song second was the ebul-
lition of that passion which ended the forementioned school-business.—

My twenty third year was to me an important era.—Partly thro' whim, and
partly that I wished to set about doing something in life, I joined with a flax-dresser
in a neighbouring town,° to learn his trade and carry on the business of manufac-
turing and retailing flax.—This turned out a sadly unlucky affair.—My Partner
was a scoundrel of the first water who made money by the mystery of thieving;
and to finish the whole, while we were given a welcoming carousal to the New year,
our shop, by the drunken carelessness of my Partner's wife, took fire and was burnt
to ashes;° and left me like a true Poet, not worth sixpence.—I was oblidged to give

up business; the clouds of misfortune were gathering thick round my father's head, the darkest of which was, he was visibly far gone in a consumption; and to crown all, a belle-fille° whom I adored and who had pledged her soul to meet me in the field of matrimony, jilted me with peculiar circumstances of mortification.—The finishing evil that brought up the rear of this infernal file was my hypochondriac complaint being irritated to such a degree, that for three months I was in diseased state of body and mind, scarcely to be envied by the hopeless wretches who have just got their mittimus, 'Depart from me, ye Cursed.'—°

From this adventure I learned something of a town-life.—But the principal thing which gave my mind a turn was, I formed a bosom-friendship with a young fellow, the first created being I had ever seen, but a hapless son of misfortune.—He was the son of a plain mechanic; but a great Man in the neighbourhood taking him under his patronage gave him a genteel education with a view to bettering his situation in life.—The Patron dieing just as he was ready to launch forth into the world, the poor fellow in despair went to sea; where after a variety of good and bad fortune, a little before I was acquainted with him, he had been set ashore by an American Privateer on the wild coast of Connaught, stript of every thing.—I cannot quit this poor fellow's story without adding that he is at this moment Captain of a large westindiaman belonging to the Thames.—

This gentleman's mind was fraught with courage, independance, Magnanimity, and every noble, manly virtue.—I loved him, I admired him, to a degree of enthusiasm; and I strove to imitate him.—In some measure I succeeded: I had the pride before, but he taught it to flow in proper channels.—His knowledge of the world was vastly superiour to mine, and I was all attention to learn.— He was the only man I ever saw who was a greater fool than myself when WOMAN was the presiding star; but he spoke of a certain fashionable failing with levity, which hitherto I had regarded with horror.—Here his friendship did me a mischief; and the consequence was, that soon after I resumed the plough, I wrote the WELCOME inclosed.°—My reading was only encreased by two stray volumes of Pamela,° and one of Ferdinand Count Fathom,° which gave me some idea of Novels.—Rhyme, except some religious pieces which are in print, I had given up; but meeting with Fergusson's Scotch Poems,° I strung anew my wildly-sounding, rustic lyre with emulating vigour.—When my father died, his all went among the rapacious hell-hounds that growl in the kennel of justice; but we made a shift to scrape a little money in the family amongst us, with which, to keep us together, my brother and I took a neighbouring farm.°—My brother wanted my harebrained imagination as well as my social and amorous madness, but in good sense and every sober qualification he was far my superiour.—

I entered on this farm with a full resolution, 'Come, go to, I will be wise!'°— I read farming books; I calculated crops; I attended markets; and in short, in spite of 'The devil, the world and the flesh,' I believe I would have been a wise man; but the first year from unfortunately buying in bad seed, the second from a late harvest, we lost half of both our crops: this overset all my wisdom, and I returned 'Like the dog to his vomit, and the sow that was washed to her wallowing in the mire.'—°

I now began to be known in the neighbourhood as a maker of rhymes. The first of my poetic offspring that saw the light was a burlesque lamentation on a quarrel between two rev^d Calvinists,° both of them dramatis personae in my Holy Fair.—I had an idea myself that the piece had some merit; but to prevent the worst, I gave a copy of it to a friend who was very fond of these things, and told him I could not guess who was the Author of it, but that I thought it pretty clever.—With a certain side of both clergy and laity it met with a roar of applause.— Holy Willie's Prayer° next made its appearance, and alarmed the kirk-Session so much that they held three several meetings to look over their holy artillery, if any of it was pointed against profane Rhymers.—Unluckily for me, my idle wanderings led me, on another side, point blank within the reach of their heaviest metal.—This is the unfortunate story alluded to in my printed poem, The Lament.°—'Twas a shocking affair, which I cannot yet bear to recollect; and had very nearly given me one or two of the principal qualifications for a place among those who have lost the chart and mistake the reckoning of Rationality.—I gave up my part of the farm to my brother, as in truth it was only nominally mine; and made what little preparation was in my power for Jamaica.—Before leaving my native country for ever, I resolved to publish my Poems.—I weighed my productions as impartially as in my power; I thought they had merit; and 'twas a delicious idea that I would be called a clever fellow, even though it should never reach my ears a poor Negro-driver, or perhaps a victim to that inhospitable clime gone to the world of Spirits.— I can truly say that pauvre Inconnu° as I then was, I had pretty nearly as high an idea of myself and my works as I have at this moment.—It is ever my opinion that the great, unhappy mistakes and blunders, both in a rational and religious point of view, of which we see thousands daily guilty, are owing to their ignorance, or mistaken notions of themselves.—To know myself had been all along my constant study.—I weighed myself alone; I balanced myself with others; I watched every means of information how much ground I occupied both as a Man and as a Poet: I studied assiduously Nature's DESIGN where she seem'd to have intended the various LIGHTS and SHADES in my character.— I was pretty sure my Poems would meet with some applause; but at the worst, the roar of the Atlantic would deafen the voice of Censure, and the novelty of west-Indian scenes make me forget Neglect.—

I threw off six hundred copies, of which I had got subscriptions for about three hundred and fifty. My vanity was highly gratified by the reception I met with from the Publick; besides pocketing, all expences deducted, near twenty pounds.—This last came very seasonable, as I was about to indent myself° for want of money to pay my freight.—So soon as I was master of nine guineas, the price of wafting me to the torrid zone, I bespoke a passage in the very first ship that was to sail, for

'Hungry ruin had me in the wind'—°

I had for some time been sculking from covert to covert under all the terrors of a Jail; as some ill-advised, ungrateful people° had uncoupled the merciless legal Pack at my heels.—I had taken the last farewel of my few friends; my chest was on the road to Greenock;° I had composed my last song I should ever measure in Caledonia, 'The gloomy night is gathering fast,'° when a letter from Dr Blacklock to a friend of mine° overthrew all my schemes by rousing my poetic ambition.—The Doctor belonged to a set of Critics for whose applause I had not even dared to hope. His idea that I would meet with every encourage-ment for a second edition fired me so much that away I posted to Edinburgh without a single acquaintance in town, or a single letter of introduction in my pocket.—The baneful Star that had so long shed its blasting influence in my Zenith, for once made a revolution to the Nadir;° and the providential care of a good God placed me under the patronage of one of his noblest creatures, the Earl of Glencairn:° 'Oublie moi, Grand Dieu, si jamais je l'oublie!'—°

I need relate no farther.—At Edin^r I was in a new world: I mingled among many classes of men, but all of them new to me; and I was all attention 'to catch the manners living as they rise.'—°

You can now, Sir, form a pretty near guess what sort of a Wight° he is whom for some time you have honored with your correspondence.—That Fancy & Whim, keen Sensibility and riotous Passions may still make him zig-zag in his future path of life, is far from being improbable; but come what will, I shall answer for him the most determinate integrity and honor; and though his evil star should again blaze in his meridian with tenfold more direful influence, he may reluctantly tax Friendship with Pity but no more.—

My most respectful Compliments to Miss Williams.—Her very elegant and friendly letter I cannot answer at present, as my presence is requisite in Edinburgh, and I set off tomorrow.—

If you will oblidge me so highly and do me so much honor as now and then to drop me a letter, Please direct to me at Mauchline, Ayrshire.—

I have the honor to be, Sir,
your ever grateful humble serv^t
Rob^T Burns

Mauchline 2^d August 1787

[L515]

Mr Willm Johnston, *Proprietor of the Edin^r Gazetteer*°
Care of Mr Elliot, Bookseller Parliament-Square—Edin^r

Sir,

I have just read your Prospectus of the Edin^r Gazetteer.—If you go on in your Paper with the same spirit, it will, beyond all comparison, be the first Composition of the kind in Europe.—I beg leave to insert my name as a Subscriber; & if you have already published any papers, please send me them from the beginning.—Point out your own way of settling payments in this place, or I shall settle with you through the medium of my friend, Peter Hill, Bookseller in Edin^r.—

Go on, Sir! Lay bare, with undaunted heart & steady hand, that horrid mass of corruption called Politics & State-Craft! Dare to draw in their native colors these

'Calm, thinking VILLAINS whom no faith can fix'—°

whatever be the shiboleth of their pretended Party.—

The address, to me at Dumfries, will find,

Sir, your very humble Servt
ROB^T BURNS

Dumfries 13th Nov 1792

[L524. To Mrs Frances Dunlop]

Dumfries 6th Decr 1792°

I shall be in Ayrshire I think, next week; & if at all possible, I shall certainly, my much esteemed Friend, have the pleasure of visiting at Dunlop house.°— Alas, Madam! how seldom do we meet in this world that we have reason to congratulate ourselves on accessions of happiness!—I have not passed half the ordinary term of an old man's life, & yet I scarcely look over the obituary of a Newspaper that I do not see some names that I have known, & which I, & other acquaintances, little thought to meet with there so soon.—Every other instance of the mortality of our kind, makes us cast a horrid anxious look into the dreadful abyss of uncertainty, & shudder with apprehension for our own fate.—But of how different importance are the lives of different Individuals? Nay, of what importance is one period of the same life, more than another? A few years ago, I could have lain down in the dust, careless, as the book of Job elegantly says, 'Careless of the voice of the morning';° & now, not a few, & these most help-less, individuals, would, on losing me & my exertions, lose both their 'Staff & Shield.'°—By the way, these helpless ones have lately got an addition; M^{rs} B— having given me a fine girl° since I wrote you.—There is a charming passage in Thomson's Edward & Eleonora—

'The valiant, *in himself*, what can he suffer?
Or what does he regard his single woes?
But when, alas, he multiplies himself
To dearer selves, to the loved tender Fair,
To those whose bliss, whose beings hang upon him,
To helpless children! then, O then! he feels
The point of misery festering in his heart,
And weakly weeps his fortune like a coward'—°

As I am got in the way of quotations, I shall give you another from the same piece, peculiarly—Alas, too peculiarly apposite, my dear Madam, to your present frame of mind.—

'Who so unworthy but may proudly deck him
With his fair-weather virtue, that exults,

Glad, o'er the summer main? the tempest comes,
The rough winds rage aloud; when from the helm
This virtue shrinks, & in a corner lies
Lamenting—Heavens! if privileged from trial,
How cheap a thing were virtue!'—°

I do not remember to have heard you mention Thomson's Dramas, as favorite
walks of your reading.—Do you know, I pick up favorite quotations, & store
them in my mind as ready armour, offensive, or defensive, amid the struggle of
this turbulent existence.—Of these is one, a very favorite one, from Thomson's
Alfred—

'Attach thee firmly to the virtuous deeds
And offices of life: to life itself,
With all its vain & transient joys, sit loose'—°

Probably I have quoted some of these to you formerly, as indeed when I write
from the heart, I am apt to be guilty of these repetitions.—The compass of the
heart, in the musical style of expression, is much more bounded, than the
[illegible] reach of invention; so the notes of the former are extremely apt to
run into similar passages; but in return for the paucity of its compass, its few
notes are much more sweet.—I must still give you another quotation, which
I am almost sure I have given you before, but I cannot resist the tempta-
tion.—The subject is Religion.—Speaking of its importance to mankind, the
Author says,

''Tis this, my Friend, that streaks our morning bright;
'Tis this that gilds the horrors of our night.—
When wealth forsakes us, & when friends are few;
When friends are faithless, & when foes pursue;
'Tis this that wards the blow, or stills the smart,
Disarms affliction, or repels its dart:
Within the breast bids purest raptures rise,
Bids smiling conscience spread her cloudless skies'—°

I see you are in for double Postage, so I shall e'en scribble out t'other
sheet.—We, in this country, here have many alarms of the Reform, or rather
the Republican spirit, of your part of the kingdom.—Indeed, we are a good
deal in commotion ourselves, & in our Theatre here,° 'God save the king' has
met with some groans & hisses, while Ça ira° has been repeatedly called
for.—For me, I am a *Placeman*,° you know; a very humble one indeed, Heaven
knows, but still so much so as to gag me from joining in the cry.—What my
private sentiments are, you will find out without an Interpreter.—In the mean
time, I have taken up the subject in another view, and the other day, for a pretty
Actress's benefit-night, I wrote an Address, which I will give on the other page,
called *The Rights of Woman*.°
I shall have the honour of receiving your criticisms in person at Dunlop.

[L528]

ROBERT GRAHAM Esquire *of Fintry Excise Office Edin^r*

Dumfries Decr 31st [1792]

Sir,

I have been surprised, confounded & distracted by Mr Mitchel, the Collector,° telling me just now, that he has received an order from your Honble Board to enquire into my political conduct, & blaming me as a person disaffected to Government.—Sir, you are a Husband—& a father—you know what you would feel, to see the much-loved wife of your bosom, & your helpless, prattling little ones, turned adrift into the world, degraded & disgraced from a situation in which they had been respectable & respected, & left almost without the necessary support of a miserable existence.—Alas, Sir! must I think that such, soon, will be my lot! And from the damned, dark insinuations of hellish, groundless Envy too!—I believe, Sir, I may aver it, & in the sight of Omnipotence, that I would not tell a deliberate Falsehood, no, not though even worse horrors, if worse can be, than those I have mentioned, hung over my head; & I say, that the allegation, whatever villain has made it, is a LIE! To the British Constitution, on Revolution principles,° next after my God, I am most devoutly attached!—

You, Sir, have been much & generously my Friend—Heaven knows how warmly I have felt the obligation, how gratefully I have thanked you.—Fortune, Sir, has made you powerful, & me impotent; has given you patronage, & me dependence.—I would not for my *single Self* call on your Humanity; were such my insular, unconnected situation, I would despise the tear that now swells in my eye—I could brave Misfortune, I could face Ruin: for at the worst, 'Death's thousand doors stand open;'° but, Good God! the tender concerns that I have mentioned, the claims & ties that I, at this moment, see & feel around me, how they ennerve Courage, & wither Resolution! To your patronage, as a man of some genius, you have allowed me a claim; & your esteem, as an honest Man, I know is my due: to these, Sir, permit me to appeal; & by these may I adjure you to save me from that misery which threatens to overwhelm me, & which, with my latest breath I will say it, I have not deserved.

Pardon this confused scrawl.—Indeed I know not well what I have written.—

I have the honor to be, Sir,
your deeply indebted
& ever grateful humble serv^t
ROB^T BURNS

[L530. To Robert Graham of Fintry]

Dumfries 5th Jan^ry 1793°

Sir,

I am this moment honored with your letter: with what feelings I received this other instance of your goodness, I shall not pretend to describe.—

Now, to the charges which Malice & Misrepresentation have brought against me.——

It has been said, it seems, that I not only belong to, but head a disaffected party in this place.——I know of no party in this place, either Republican or Reform, except an old party of Borough-Reform;° with which I never had any thing to do.——Individuals, both Republican & Reform, we have, though not many of either; but if they have associated, it is more than I have the least knowledge of: & if there exists such an association, it must consist of such obscure, nameless beings, as precludes any possibility of my being known to them, or they to me.——

I was in the playhouse one night, when Çà ira° was called for.——I was in the middle of the pit, & from the Pit the clamour arose.——One or two individuals with whom I occasionally associate were of the party, but I neither knew of the Plot, nor joined in the Plot; nor ever opened my lips to hiss, or huzza, that, or any other Political tune whatever.——I looked on myself as far too obscure a man to have any weight in quelling a Riot; at the same time, as a character of higher respectability, than to yell in the howlings of a rabble.——This was the conduct of all the first Characters in this place; & these Characters know, & will avow, that such was my conduct.——

I never uttered any invectives against the king.——His private worth, it is altogether impossible that such a man as I, can appreciate; and in his Public capacity, I always revered, & ever will, with the soundest loyalty, revere, the Monarch of Great-britain, as, to speak in Masonic, the sacred KEYSTONE OF OUR ROYAL ARCH CONSTITUTION.——

As to REFORM PRINCIPLES, I look upon the British Constitution, as settled at the Revolution, to be the most glorious Constitution on earth, or that perhaps the wit of man can frame; at the same time, I think, & you know what High and distinguished Characters have for some time thought so, that we have a good deal deviated from the original principles of that Constitution; particularly, that an alarming System of Corruption has pervaded the connection between the Executive Power and the House of Commons.——This is the Truth, the Whole truth, of my Reform opinions; opinions which, before I was aware of the complection of these innovating times, I too unguardedly (now I see it) sported with: but henceforth, I seal up my lips.——However, I never dictated to, corresponded with, or had the least connection with, any political association whatever—except, that when the Magistrates & principal inhabitants of this town, met to declare their attachment to the Constitution, & their abhorrence of Riot, which declaration you would see in the Papers, I, as I thought my duty as a Subject at large, & a Citizen in particular, called upon me, subscribed the same declaratory Creed.——

Of Johnston, the publisher of the Edin^r Gazetteer,° I know nothing.—— One evening in company with four or five friends, we met with his prospectus which we thought manly & independant; & I wrote to him, ordering his paper for us.——If you think that I act improperly in allowing his Paper to come addressed to me, I shall immediately countermand it.——I never, so judge me, God! wrote a line of prose for the Gazetteer in my life.—An occasional address, spoken by Miss Fontenelle on her benefit-night here, which I called, the Rights of Woman,° I sent to the Gazetteer; as also, some extempore stanzas on the Commemoration of Thomson:° both these I will subjoin for your perusal.—You will see they have nothing whatever to do with Politics.—At the time when I sent Johnston one of these poems, but which one, I do not remember, I inclosed, at the request of my warm & worthy friend, Robt Riddel Esq: of Glenriddel,° a prose Essay, signed Cato, written by him, & addressed to the delegates for the County Reform,° of which he was one for this County.—With the merits, or demerits, of that Essay I have nothing to do, farther than transmitting it in the same Frank,° which Frank he had procured me.—

As to France, I was her enthusiastic votary in the beginning of the business.—When she came to shew her old avidity for conquest, in annexing Savoy,° &c. to her dominions, & invading the rights of Holland,° I altered my sentiments.—A tippling Ballad which I made on the Prince of Brunswick's breaking up his camp,° & sung one convivial evening, I shall likewise send you, sealed up, as it is not every body's reading.—This last is not worth your perusal; but lest Mrs FAME should, as she has already done, use, & even abuse, her old priviledge of lying, you shall be the master of every thing, le pour et le contre, of my political writings & conduct.—

This, my honored Patron, is all.—To this statement I challenge disquisition.—Mistaken Prejudice, or unguarded Passion, may mislead, & often have misled me; but when called on to answer for my mistakes, though, I will say it, no man can feel keener compunction for his errors, yet, I trust, no man can be more superiour to evasion or disguise.—

I shall do myself the honor to thank Mrs Graham for her goodness, in a separate letter.—

If, Sir, I have been so fortunate as to do away these misapprehensions of my conduct & character, I shall with the confidence which you were wont to allow me, apply to your goodness on every opening in the way of business, where I think I with propriety may offer myself.—An instance that occurs just now; M^r M^{c}farlane, Supervisor of the Galloway District is & has been for some time, very ill.—I spoke to Mr Mitchel as to his wishes to forward my application for the job, but though he expressed & ever does express every kindness for me, he hesitates, in hopes that the disease may be of short continuance.—However, as it seems to be a paralytic affection, I fear that it may be some time ere he can take charge of so extended a District.—There is a great deal of fatigue, & very little business in the District; two things suitable enough to my hardy constitution, & inexperience in that line of life.—

I have the honor to be, Sir,

your ever grateful, as highly obliged humble serv^t
ROB^T BURNS

[L531]

Mʳˢ GRAHAM *of Fintry* [Dumfries, 5 January 1793]

To Mʳˢ Graham of Fintry, this little poem,° written in haste on the spur of the
occasion, & therefore inaccurate; but a sincere Compliment to that Sex, the
most amiable of the works of God—is most respectfully presented by—

THE AUTHOR

[L558]

JOHN FRANCIS ERSKINE of Mar

In the year 1792/93, when Royalist & Jacobin had set all Britain by the ears,
because I unguardedly, rather under the temptation of being witty than disaf-
fected, had declared my sentiments in favor of Parliamentary Reform, in the
manner of that time, I was accused to the Board of Excise of being a Republican;
& was very near being turned adrift in the wide world on that account.—
Mʳ Erskine of Mar, *a gentleman indeed*, wrote to my friend Glenriddell° to
know if I was really out of place on account of my Political principles; & if so,
he proposed a Subscription among the friends of Liberty for me, which he
offered to head, that I might be no pecuniary loser by my political
Integrity.—This was the more generous, as I had not the honor of being known
to Mʳ Erskine. I wrote him as follows.—

[Dumfries, 13 April 1793]
Sir,
degenerate as Human Nature is said to be, & in many instances, worthless &
unprincipled it certainly is; still there are bright examples to the contrary;
examples, that even in the eye of Superiour Beings must shed a lustre on
the name of Man.—Such an example have I now before me, when you, Sir,
came forward to patronise & befriend a distant, obscure stranger; merely
because Poverty had made him helpless, & his British hardihood of mind had
provoked the arbitrary wantonness of Power.—My much esteemed friend,
Mʳ Riddell of Glenriddell, has just read me a paragraph of a letter he had from
you.—Accept, Sir, of the silent throb of gratitude; for words would but mock
the emotions of my soul.—
You have been misinformed, as to my final dismission from the Excise: I still
am in the service.—Indeed, but for the exertions of a gentleman who must be
known to you, Mʳ Graham of Fintry, a gentleman who has ever been my warm
& generous friend, I had, without so much as a hearing, or the smallest previ-
ous intimation, been turned adrift, with my helpless family, to all the horrors
of Want.—Had I had any other resource, probably I might have saved them
the trouble of a dismissal; but the little money I gained by my Publication, is
almost every guinea embarked, to save from ruin an only brother;° who, though
one of the worthiest, is by no means one of the most fortunate of men.—

In my defence to their accusations, I said, that whatever might be my sentiments of Republics, ancient or modern, as to Britain, I abjured the idea.—That a Constitution which, in its original principles, experience had proved to be every way fitted for our happiness in society, it would he insanity to sacrifice to an untried, visionary theory.—That, in consideration of my being situated in a department, however humble, immediately in the hands of the people in power, I had forborne taking any active part, either personally, or as an author, in the present business of Reform.—But that, where I must declare my sentiments, I would say that there existed a system of corruption between the Executive Power & the Representative part° of the Legislature, which boded no good to our glorious Constitution; & which every patriotic Briton must wish to see amended.—Some such Sentiments as these I stated in a letter to my generous Patron, M[r] Graham, which he laid before the Board at large, where it seems my last remark gave great offence; & one of our Supervisors general, a M[r] Corbet, was instructed to enquire, on the spot, into my conduct, & to document me—'that *my* business was to *act*, not to think; & that whatever might be Men or Measures, it was my business to be silent & obedient'—M[r] Corbet was likewise my steady friend; so, between M[r] Graham & him, I have been partly forgiven: only, I understand that all hopes of my getting officially forward are blasted.—

Now, Sir, to the business in which I would more immediately interest you.—The partiality of my Countrymen has brought me forward as a man of genius, & has given me a Character to support.—In the Poet, I have avowed manly & independant sentiments, which I trust will be found in the Man.— Reasons of no less weight than the support of a wife & children have pointed out as the eligible, & indeed the only eligible line of life for me, my present occupation.—Still, my honest fame is my dearest concern; & a thousand times have I trembled at the idea of the degrading epithets that Malice, or Misrepresentation may affix to my name.—I have often, in blasting anticipation, listened to some future hackney Magazine Scribbler, with the heavy malice of savage stupidity, exulting in his hireling paragraphs that 'Burns, notwithstanding the fanfaronade of independance to be found in his works, & after having been held forth to Public View & Public Estimation as a man of some genius, yet, quite destitute of resources within himself to support this borrowed dignity, he dwindled into a paltry Exciseman; & slunk out the rest of his insignificant existence in the meanest of pursuits & among the vilest of mankind.'—

In your illustrious hands, Sir, permit me to lodge my strong disavowal & defiance of these slanderous falsehoods.—BURNS was a poor man, from birth; & an Exciseman, by necessity: but—I will say it!—the sterling of his honest worth, no poverty could debase; & his independant British mind, Oppression might bend, but could not subdue!—Have not I, to me, a more precious stake in my Country's welfare, than the richest Dukedom in it?— I have a large family of children, & the probability of more. I have three sons, whom, I see already, have brought with them into the world souls ill qualified to inhabit the bodies of Slaves.—Can I look tamely on, & see any machination to wrest from them, the birthright of my boys,° the little independant Britons in whose veins runs my own blood?—No! I will not!—should my heart stream around my attempt to defend it!—

Does any man tell me, that my feeble efforts can be of no service; & that it does not belong to my humble station to meddle with the concerns of a People?—I tell him, that it is on such individuals as I, that for the hand of support & the eye of intelligence, a Nation has to rest.—The uninformed mob may swell a Nation's bulk; & the titled, tinsel Courtly throng may be its feathered ornament, but the number of those who are elevated enough in life, to reason & reflect; & yet low enough to keep clear of the venal contagion of a Court; these are a Nation's strength.—

One small request more: when you have honored this letter with a perusal, please commit it to the flames.—BURNS, in whose behalf you have so generously interested yourself, I have here, in his native colours, drawn *as he is*; but should any of the people in whose hands is the very bread he eats, get the least knowledge of the picture, it would ruin the poor Bard for ever.—

My Poems having just come out in another edition, I beg leave to present you with a copy; as a small mark of that high esteem & ardent gratitude with which I have the honor to be—
Sir,

Your deeply indebted,
And ever devoted humble servant

APPENDIX 2

CONTEMPORARY REVIEWS OF THE
KILMARNOCK *POEMS* (1786)

1. From *The Edinburgh Magazine, or Literary Miscellany,
for October 1786*, pp. 284–5.

Poems, chiefly in the Scottish Dialect. By ROBERT BURNS, *Kilmarnock*

WHEN an author we know nothing of solicits our attention, we are but too apt to treat him with the same reluctant civility we show to a person who has come unbidden into company. Yet talents and address will gradually diminish the distance of our behaviour, and when the first unfavourable impression has worn off, the author may become a favourite, and the stranger a friend. The poems we have just announced may probably have to struggle with the pride of learning and the partiality of refinement; yet they are intitled to particular indulgence.

Who are you, Mr Burns? will some surly critic say. At what university have you been educated? what languages do you understand? what authors have you particularly studied? whether has Aristotle or Horace° directed your taste? who has praised your poems, and under whose patronage are they published? In short, what qualifications intitle you to instruct and entertain us? To the questions of such a catechism, perhaps honest Robert Burns would make no satisfactory answers. 'My good Sir, he might say, I am a poor country man; I was bred up at the school of Kilmarnock; I understand no languages but my own; I have studied Allan Ramsay and Ferguson.° My poems have been praised at many a fire-side; and I ask no patronage for them, if they deserve none. I have not looked on mankind *through the spectacle of books*. An ounce of mother-wit, you know, is worth a pound of clergy; and Homer and Ossian,° for any thing that I have heard, could neither write nor read.' The author is indeed a striking example of native genius bursting through the obscurity of poverty and the obstructions of laborious life. He is said to be a common ploughman; and when we consider him in this light, we cannot help regretting that wayward fate had not placed him in a more favoured situation. Those who view him with the severity of lettered criticism, and judge him by the fastidious rules of art, will discover that he has not the doric simplicity° of Ramsay, nor the brilliant imagination of Ferguson; but to those who admire the exertions of untutored fancy, and are blind to many faults for the sake of numberless beauties, his poems will afford singular gratification. His observations on human characters are acute and sagacious, and his descriptions are lively and just. Of rustic pleasantry he has a rich fund; and some of his softer scenes are touched with inimitable delicacy. He seems to be a boon companion, and often startles us with a dash of libertinism, which will keep some readers at a distance. Some of his subjects are serious, but those of the humorous kind are the best. It is not meant, however, to enter into a minute investigation of his merits, as the copious extracts we have subjoined will enable our readers to judge for themselves. The Character Horace gives to Osellus is particularly applicable to him.

Rusticus abnormis sapiens, crassaque Minerva.°

2. [Henry Mackenzie,] *The Lounger* No XCVII. *Saturday, Dec.* 9. 1786.

To the feeling and the susceptible there is something wonderfully pleasing in the contemplation of genius, of that supereminent reach of mind by which some men are distinguished. In the view of highly superior talents, as in that of great and stupendous natural objects, there is a sublimity which fills the soul with wonder and delight, which expands it, as it were, beyond its usual bounds, and which, investing our nature with extraordinary powers, and extraordinary honours, interests our curiosity, and flatters our pride.

This divinity of genius, however, which admiration is fond to worship, is best arrayed in the darkness of distant and remote periods, and is not easily acknowledged in the present times, or in places with which we are perfectly acquainted. Exclusive of all the deductions which envy or jealousy may sometimes be supposed to make, there is a familiarity in the near approach of persons around us, not very consistent with the lofty ideas which we wish to form of him who has led captive our imagination in the triumph of his fancy, overpowered our feelings with the tide of passion, or enlightened our reason with the investigation of hidden truths. It may be true, that 'in the olden time' genius had some advantages which tended to its vigour and its growth;° but it is not unlikely that, even in these degenerate days, it rises much oftener than it is observed; that in 'the ignorant present time' our posterity may find names which they will dignify, though we neglected, and pay to their memory those honours which their contemporaries had denied them.

There is, however, a natural, and indeed a fortunate vanity in trying to redress this wrong which genius is exposed to suffer. In the discovery of talents generally unknown, men are apt to indulge the same fond partiality as in all other discoveries which themselves have made; and hence we have had repeated instances of painters and of poets, who have been drawn from obscure situations, and held forth to public notice and applause by the extravagant encomiums of their introductors, yet in a short time have sunk again to their former obscurity; whose merit, though perhaps somewhat neglected, did not appear to have been much undervalued by the world, and could not support, by its own intrinsic excellence, that superior place which the enthusiasm of its patrons would have assigned it.

I know not if I shall be accused of such enthusiasm and partiality, when I introduce to the notice of my readers a poet of our own country, with whose writings I have lately become acquainted; but if I am not greatly deceived, I think I may safely pronounce him a genius of no ordinary rank. The person to whom I allude, is ROBERT BURNS, an *Ayrshire* Ploughman, whose poems were some time ago published in a country-town in the west of Scotland, with no other ambition, it would seem, than to circulate among the inhabitants of the county where he was born, to obtain a little fame from those who had heard of his talents. I hope I shall not be thought to assume too much, if I endeavour to place him in a higher point of view, to call for a verdict of his country on the merit of his works, and to claim for him those honours which their excellence appears to deserve.

In mentioning the circumstances of his humble station, I mean not to rest his pretensions solely on that title, or to urge the merits of his poetry when considered in relation to the lowness of his birth, and the little opportunity of improvement which his education could afford. These particulars, indeed, might excite our wonder at his productions; but his poetry, considered abstractedly, and without the apologies arising from his situation, seems to me fully intitled to command our feelings, and to obtain our applause. One bar, indeed, his birth and education have opposed to his fame, the language in which most of his poems are written. Even in Scotland, the provincial dialect which Ramsay and he have used is now read with a difficulty which greatly damps the pleasure of the reader: in England it cannot be read at all, without such a constant reference to a glossary, as nearly to destroy that pleasure.

Some of his productions, however, especially those of the grave style, are almost English. From one of those I shall first present my readers with an extract, in which I think they will discover a high tone of feeling, a power and energy of expression, particularly and strongly characteristic of the mind and the voice of the poet. 'Tis from his poem intitled the *Vision*, in which the genius of his native county, *Ayrshire*, is thus supposed to address him:

[quotes 'The Vision', ll. 205–40]

Of strains like the above, solemn and sublime, with that rapt and inspired melancholy in which the Poet lifts his eye 'above this visible diurnal sphere,' the Poems intitled, *Despondency*, the *Lament*, *Winter, a Dirge*, and the Invocation to *Ruin*, afford no less striking examples. Of the tender and the moral, specimens equally advantageous might be drawn from the elegiac verses, intitled *Man was made to mourn*, from *The Cottar's Saturday Night*, the Stanzas *To a Mouse*, or those *To a Mountain-Daisy*, on turning it down with the plough in April 1786. This last Poem I shall insert entire, not from its superior merit, but because its length suits the bounds of my Paper.

[quotes 'To a Mountain-Daisy' complete, glossing Scots words with English equivalents]

I have seldom met with an image more truly pastoral than that of the lark, in the second stanza. Such strokes as these mark the pencil of the poet, which delineates Nature with the precision of intimacy, yet with the delicate colouring of beauty and of taste.

The power of genius is not less admirable in tracing the manners, than in painting the passions, or in drawing the scenery of Nature. That intuitive glance with which a writer like *Shakespeare* discerns the characters of men, with which he catches the many-changing hues of life, forms a sort of problem in the science of mind, of which it is easier to see the truth than to assign the cause. Though I am very far from meaning to compare our rustic bard to Shakespeare, yet whoever will read his lighter and more humorous poems, his *Dialogue of the Dogs*, his *Dedication to G—— H——, Esq*; his *Epistles to a young Friend*, and to *W. S——n*, will perceive with what uncommon penetration and sagacity this Heaven-taught ploughman, from his humble and unlettered station, has looked upon men and manners.

Against some passages of those last-mentioned poems it has been objected, that they breathe a spirit of libertinism and irreligion. But if we consider the ignorance and fanaticism of the lower class of people in the country where these poems were written, a fanaticism of that pernicious sort which sets *faith* in opposition to *good works*,° the fallacy and danger of which, a mind so enlightened as our Poet's could not but perceive; we shall look upon his lighter Muse, not as the enemy of religion, (of which in several places he expresses the justest sentiments), but as the champion of morality, and the friend of virtue.

There are, however, it must be allowed, some exceptionable parts of the volume he has given to the public, which caution would have suppressed, or correction struck out; but Poets are seldom cautious, and our Poet had, alas! no friends or companions from whom correction could be obtained. When we reflect on his rank in life, the habits to which he must have been subject, and the society in which he must have mixed, we regret perhaps more than wonder, that delicacy should be so often offended in perusing a volume in which there is so much to interest and please us.

Burns possesses the spirit as well as the fancy of a Poet. That honest pride and independence of soul which are sometimes the Muse's only dower, break forth on every occasion in his works. It may be, then, I shall wrong his feelings, while I indulge my own, in calling the attention of the public to his situation and circumstances. That condition, humble as it was, in which he found content, and wooed the Muse, might not have been deemed uncomfortable; but grief and misfortunes have reached him there; and one or two of his poems hint, what I have learnt from some of his countrymen, that he has been obliged to form the resolution of leaving his native land, to seek under a West-Indian clime° that shelter and support which Scotland has denied him. But I trust means may be found to prevent this resolution from taking place; and that I do my country no more than justice, when I suppose her ready to stretch out her hand to cherish and retain this native Poet, whose 'wood-notes wild'° possess so much excellence. To repair the wrongs of suffering or neglected merit; to call forth genius from the obscurity in which it had pined indignant, and place it where it may profit or delight the world; these are exertions which give to wealth an enviable superiority, to greatness and to patronage a laudable pride.

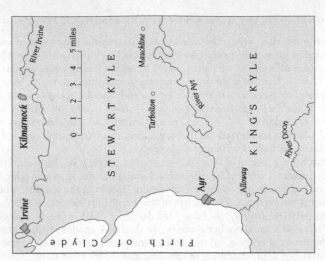

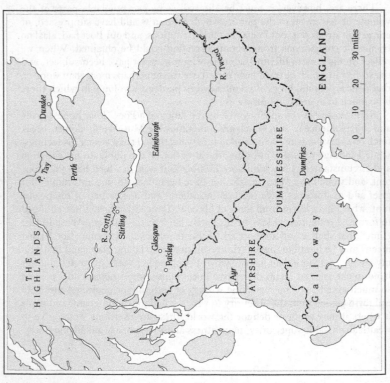

Southern Scotland, with (enlarged) Kyle District, Ayrshire

NOTES

THE notes are intended to indicate, as appropriate in each instance, the context in which each poem or song was produced and read, both material (the sorts of texts in which they appeared, and how they changed over time); literary (the forms they adopt from, and allusions they make to, previous literature); social (their role in the poet's correspondence, their relation to other social practices); and political (their stake in the conflicts of the time). They are not primarily intended to elucidate Scots vocabulary: in case of difficulty the reader should first consult the Glossary, and only if it fails to provide satisfaction should the notes be consulted instead.

Each note begins with a number preceded by the capital 'K'. This is the number of the text in James Kinsley's standard scholarly edition. As the present volume generally uses the titles under which these texts were first published, it was thought advisable to retain the reference to Kinsley's numbering in case of confusion; as Kinsley arranged his texts in likely order of composition, these numbers also give some sense of the relative priority of the texts. The debt of these notes to Kinsley in the matter of Burns's allusions to other eighteenth-century poets is enormous and I hope consistently acknowledged. Where a number is preceded by a capital 'L', this is a reference to a letter in G. Ross Roy's edition also listed below; again, by the number of the letter, not the page number of Roy's two-volume set.

EDITIONS OF BURNS REFERRED TO IN THE NOTES

Cunningham	*The Works of Robert Burns; with his life*, ed. Alan Cunningham. Eight volumes. London, 1834.
Douglas	*The Complete Poetical Works of Robert Burns*, ed. William Scott Douglas. Two volumes. Kilmarnock, 1876.
Henley and Henderson	*The Poetry of Robert Burns*, ed. William Ernest Henley and Thomas F. Henderson. Four volumes. London, 1896.
Kinsley	*The Poems and Songs of Robert Burns*, ed. James Kinsley. Oxford, 1968.
McGuirk	*Robert Burns: Selected Poems*, ed. Carol McGuirk. London, 1993.
Wallace	*The Life and Works of Robert Burns*, ed. Robert Chambers, revised William Wallace. Four volumes. Edinburgh and London, 1896.

OTHER ABBREVIATIONS

BE	*Burns Encyclopedia Online*: www.robertburns.org/encyclopedia
DNB	*Oxford Dictionary of National Biography*: www.oxforddnb.com

DSL   *Dictionary of the Scots Language*: www.dsl.ac.uk
Fergusson   Robert Fergusson, *The Poems of Robert Fergusson*, Vol. II,
                   ed. Matthew P. McDiarmid (Edinburgh, 1956).
HPO   *History of Parliament Online*:
                   www.historyofparliamentonline.org
Letters   *The Letters of Robert Burns*, ed. J. De Lancey Ferguson,
                   2nd edn. ed. G. Ross Roy (Oxford, 1985).
Lonsdale   Roger Lonsdale, ed., *The Poems of Thomas Gray, William*
                   Collins, Oliver Goldsmith (London, 1969).
Macpherson   James Macpherson, *The Poems of Ossian and related works*,
                   ed. Howard Gaskill (Edinburgh, 1996).
OED   *Oxford English Dictionary*: www.oed.co.uk
Pope   *The Poems of Alexander Pope*, ed. John Butt (London, 1989).
Ramsay   *The Works of Allan Ramsay*, Vols. I and II, ed. Burns Martin
                   and John W. Oliver; Vols. III–V ed. Alexander M. Kinghorn
                   and Alexander Law (Edinburgh, 1945–74).
SC   *A Select Collection of Original Scotish Airs, for the Voice*, ed.
                   George Thomson, in six volumes (London, 1798–1841).
Shenstone   William Shenstone, *The Works in Verse and Prose, of*
                   William Shenstone Esq, in two volumes (London 1764).
SMM   *The Scots Musical Museum*, ed. James Johnson, in six
                   volumes (Edinburgh, 1787–1803).
Thomson   James Thomson, *The Seasons and The Castle of Indolence*,
                   ed. James Sambrook (Oxford, 1987).
Young   Edward Young, *The Complaint: or, night thoughts on life,*
                   death, and immortality. A new edition, corrected by the author
                   (London, 1755).

Poems, Chiefly in the Scottish Dialect (Kilmarnock, 1786)

This volume, Burns's first, is usually referred to as the 'Kilmarnock edition':
later, enlarged editions of the *Poems* were published in Edinburgh in 1787,
1793, and 1794. For the circumstances of its publication see the Introduction.

   1 *Epigraph.* These are Burns's own words, but they are clearly informed by
   the following lines:

> *Nature!* informer of the poet's art,
> Whose force alone can raise or melt the heart,
> Thou art his guide; each passion, every line,
> Whate'er he draws to please, must all be thine.

These are ll. 27–30 of the 'Prologue' to James Thomson's tragedy
Sophonisba (1730) by Alexander Pope; but as John Butt notes, they are
probably by David Mallet, born Malloch (1701–65), another Scottish poet
in Pope's circle (Pope 807).

   3 *Preface*

   Theocrites or Virgil. Theocritus, Greek pastoral poet who lived *c*.300–*c*.260
   BC; Roman poet Publius Vergilius Maro (70–19 BC), author of the pastoral

Eclogues, and whose poems describing the routines of rural life, the *Georgics*, were an important model and source of authority for descriptive poetry in the eighteenth century.

'A fountain shut up, and a book sealed'. Burns conflates the Song of Songs 4: 12, 'A garden inclosed is my sister, my spouse; a spring shut up, a fountain sealed', with the more obviously relevant Isaiah 29: 11, 'And the vision of all is become unto you as the words of a book that is sealed, which men deliver to one that is learned, saying, Read this, I pray thee: and he saith, I cannot; for it is sealed'.

Shenstone. William Shenstone (1714–63), English nature-poet and essayist. The lines quoted are the closing advice to poets from Shenstone's essay 'On allowing Merit in Others': 'Banish the self-debasing principle, and scorn the disingenuity of readers. Humility has depressed many a genius into a hermit; but never yet raised one into a poet of eminence' (Shenstone Vol. II, 15).

Ramsay. Allan Ramsay (1684–1758), influential post-Union revivalist of poetry in Scots.

4 *Ferguson.* Robert Fergusson (1750–74), vivid chronicler of the Edinburgh scene who died in poverty. Burns arranged and paid for a stone to mark Fergusson's grave on his first visit to Edinburgh in 1786–7.

Subscribers. For publication by subscription see the Introduction to this volume.

5 *The Twa Dogs, a Tale.* K71. The first poem of the Kilmarnock edition is Burns's earliest composition in iambic tetrameter couplets, a form to which he will return, not often, but with great success, for example in 'Tam o' Shanter'. It had been used by Robert Fergusson for an earlier dialogue, 'Mutual Complaint of Plainstanes and Causey' in *Poems on Various Subjects* (1779; Fergusson 122–6).

l. 2. *auld king COIL.* 'Coilus, King of the Picts, from whom the district of Kyle is said to take its name', as Burns will explain in a footnote to 'The Vision' (see p. 302). For Kyle, see Map.

l. 12. *Where sailors gang to fish for Cod.* That is, Newfoundland, whose Grand Banks had been fished by Europeans for centuries.

l. 27 and footnote. *Cuchullin's dog in Ossian's Fingal. Fingal* is an epic prose-poem published by James Macpherson (1736–96) in 1761–2. Macpherson claimed that it was a translation of a poem composed and sung to the harp by Ossian, a third-century Gaelic bard, but was widely suspected of forgery: Burns alludes to the controversy in l. 28. Cuchullin is one of the heroic warriors of the tale.

6 l. 44. *arse.* The next two editions of *Poems*, published in Edinburgh in 1787 and 1793, gesture towards politeness with 'They sat them down upon their a—,'; then in the fourth edition of 1794 Burns replaces ll. 43–4 altogether with 'Until, wi' daffin weary grown, | Upon a knowe they sat them down'.

6 l. 51. *racked rents*. That is, excessive rents. Specifically, 'rack-rent' meant a rent approaching the total income that the rented land could generate for the tenant, leaving them little to live on. Rent inflation was a serious problem in Burns's Scotland.

l. 58. *Geordie*. The guinea, a gold coin displaying the monarch's head worth 21*s*.

l. 63. *ragouts*. French-style stews.

l. 65. *Whipper-in*. The Huntsman's assistant in managing a pack of foxhounds, responsible for keeping them together as a pack.

7 l. 69. *Cot-folk*. For cottars see headnote to 'The Cotter's Saturday night', p. 306.

l. 70. *I own it's past my comprehension*. The line, as Kinsley notes, is borrowed from Shenstone's 'The Price of an Equipage', where the bafflement is produced by a small farmer maintaining a coach and footmen. The next line explains: 'Yes, Sir, but DAMON has a pension—', that is, a government salary (Shenstone Vol. I, 219).

l. 71. *they're*. From the 1793 *Poems*, correcting Kilmarnock's 'their'.

l. 74. *Bairan*. In the context this clearly means 'digging', but neither Burns's glossaries nor *DSL* offer this as a possible sense.

l. 93. *court-day*. Usually refers to the day on which a court of justice meets, but here applied, perhaps ironically, to the quarter-days on which rents are due.

l. 98. *He'll apprehend them, poind their gear*. Ramsay had evoked the same fear in Act I scene ii of *The Gentle Shepherd*: 'With glooman Brow the Laird seeks in his Rent: | 'Tis no to gi'e . . . | *His Honour* mauna want, he poinds your Gear' (ll. 138–40; Ramsay Vol. II, 222).

8 l. 119. *patronage an' priests*. The Church of Scotland had been settled with a Presbyterian constitution, whereby the appointment of a parish minister requires the consent of the congregation, in 1690. But in 1711 the British parliament passed an act restoring 'lay patronage': that is, the inherited right of certain landowners, including the crown, to appoint ministers. This contradiction was a source of popular anger throughout the eighteenth century, especially in staunchly Presbyterian western counties such as Ayrshire, to the point where '[l]arge numbers of the rural lower orders left the Established Church in the 1760s and 1770s as a result of often violent patronage disputes which rent parishes asunder' (Brown, *Religion and Society*, 19).

l. 123. *Hallowmass*. The Feast of All Saints, 1 November.

9 l. 144. *Some rascal*. That is, a factor of the type mentioned at ll. 96f. In the biographical letter to John Moore of 2 August 1787 reproduced in Appendix 1, Burns says he had in mind the factor who harried his father at Mount Oliphant (p. 261).

l. 148. *For Britain's guid his saul indentin*. That politicians seeking election might 'indent' (contract, sell into servitude) their souls is an idea, Kinsley

observes, that Burns gets from Fergusson's *The Election* ll. 120–1: 'their
saul is lent, | For the town's gude indent' (Fergusson 190).

l. 151. *as PREMIERS lead him*. The ability of eighteenth-century
administrations to secure the assent of parliament by offering MPs sine-
cures and other benefits was identified as 'corruption' in 'Patriot' or
'Country-Party' rhetoric, of which these lines are an example.

ll. 157–8. *To make a tour an' tak a whirl, | To learn bon ton an' see the
worl'*. The 'Grand Tour' of France and Italy was typically the culmination
of a young British gentleman's education, to encounter (among other
things) elevated manners and the latest fashions, or 'bon-ton': as the
phrase suggests, defined as French.

l. 160. *He rives his father's auld entails*. An 'entail' was a legal mechanism
for maintaining the integrity of a landed estate in its passage from one
generation to the next by preventing the current owner from selling or
mortgaging it, in part or as a whole. But lawyers had long since found ways
to get round these clauses in order to raise the ready cash of which pleas-
ure-seeking young gentlemen were so often in short supply.

l. 164. *groves o' myrtles*. The myrtle is an evergreen shrub sacred to Venus
in the pagan mythology.

l. 165. *German-water*. Mineral water from a German spa-town.

l. 168. *b—res an' ch—ncres*. Presumably bores, with bore in the sense of
'small hole' and meaning here the female sex (see headnote to 'Green
Grow the Rashes', p. 340, for an instance of this metaphor); and chancres,
the infectious lesions which are the first symptom of syphilis. In the 1787
Edinburgh edition and subsequently ll. 167–8 are replaced with 'An' clear
the consequential sorrows, | Love-gifts of Carnival Signioras'.

10 ll. 181, 183. *breakin o' their timmer . . . Or shootin of a hare or moor-
cock*. Eighteenth-century landowners were often aggressive in asserting
their legal property rights in the face of the traditional claims of the poor
to e.g. timber or game.

11 l. 204. *Her dizzen's done*. 'Dizzen' here means her 'hank or dozen cuts of
yarn, the standard quantity allotted to a woman for a day's spinning'
(*DSL*).

l. 215. *party-matches*. Perhaps gatherings of a local political faction or
'interest', or perhaps just social visits: not a phrase in *OED*.

l. 226. *the devil's pictur'd beuks*. Playing-cards, in the language in which
gambling was denounced from the pulpit.

12 *Scotch Drink*. K77. In a letter of 20 March 1786 to Robert Muir of
Kilmarnock Burns wrote, 'I am heartily sorry I had not the pleasure of
seeing you as you returned thro Machline [Mauchline] . . . I here enclose
you my SCOTCH DRINK, and "may the —— follow with a blessing
for your edification."—I hope, sometime before we hear the Gowk, to
have the pleasure of seeing you, at Kilm^k; when, I intend we shall have a
gill between us, in a Mutchkin-stoup' (L23). The blank should be filled up
with 'Deil'; the Gowk is the cuckoo, which first arrives in southern

Scotland in the second half of April. The verse form used here is the Standard Habbie stanza: see headnote to 'Poor Mailie's Elegy', p. 295, for its origins.

12 *Epigraph.* This is an extrapolation from King Lemuel's advice to his son in Proverbs 31: 6–7: 'Give strong drink unto him that is ready to perish, and wine unto those that be of heavy hearts. | Let him drink, and forget his poverty, and remember his misery no more.'

l. 2. *Bacchus.* The Roman god of wine.

l. 8. *wimplin worms.* McGuirk suggests this refers to 'the network of tubes at the top of a still' (McGuirk 232).

l. 20. *souple scones.* Thin barley scones were a treat compared to the staple oatcake.

13 ll. 28–9. *oil'd by thee, | The wheels o' life.* Kinsley notes the borrowing from Ramsay's 'Epistle to Robert Yarde': 'A cheerfu' Bottle' 'brawly oyls the Wheels of Life' (ll. 105, 108; Ramsay Vol. II, 60).

l. 45. *the saunts.* The orthodox in religion.

l. 47. *the tents.* A 'tent' in this sense is 'a moveable wooden pulpit, with steps and a canopy, erected in the open air, esp. at the half-yearly communion services when the congregation is too large for the church to contain', and metonymically the preacher himself (*DSL*). For the communion events alluded to here, see headnote to 'The Holy Fair', p. 291.

l. 53. *a wee drap sp'ritual burn.* Burn is 'the water used in brewing' (*DSL*).

l. 55. *Vulcan.* The Roman god of fire and smithying.

14 l. 68. *gossips.* The women of the neighbourhood, enjoying the traditional party with the howdie (midwife) at a birth.

l. 69. *fumbling.* Sexually impotent (*OED*).

ll. 70–2. In the 1787 Edinburgh edition and subsequently these lines are replaced with 'Wae worth the name! | Nae Howdie gets a social night, | Or plack frae them'.

l. 95. *dearthfu' wines.* This is a conjunction, Kinsley observes, borrowed from Ramsay's 'Last Speech of a Wretched Miser', l. 42 (Ramsay Vol. II, 63).

15 ll. 97–8. *Gravels . . . An' Gouts.* Gout is an arthritic condition of the joints, to which heavy drinking can contribute: the 'gravel' is a related condition in which crystals form in the urine, making its passage painful.

l. 109. *Ferintosh.* A famous whisky distilled on the Black Isle, north of Inverness.

l. 113. *loyal Forbes' Charter'd boast.* The Ferintosh distilleries belonged to Forbes of Culloden. At the Revolution in 1689, the then laird, Duncan Forbes, was an active and influential supporter of the new king, William; supporters of the deposed James VII ravaged the Ferintosh and Culloden estates in retaliation. In compensation the Scottish parliament granted

Forbes, in perpetuity, the privilege of distilling whisky at Ferintosh free of duty. This privilege disappeared under new (British) legislation in 1784 (see headnote to the following poem), leading to the closure of the Ferintosh distilleries shortly after.

l. 115. *Thae curst horse-leeches o' th' Excise.* That is, the customs officers responsible for enforcing payment of duty and destroying illicit stills. Burns would himself become an exciseman in 1788.

16 *The Author's earnest cry and prayer, to the right honorable and honorable, the Scotch representatives in the House of Commons.* K81. In the 1787 Edinburgh edition and subsequently Burns provides a footnote to the title: 'This was wrote before the Act anent the Scotch Distilleries, of session 1786; for which Scotland and the Author return their most grateful thanks'. An earlier act, in 1784, had tried to rationalize the excise laws, but ended up producing new restrictions that increased the rewards for illicit production and drove many legitimate distilleries out of business. This is the situation against which Burns's poem protests. The tax regime introduced in 1786 instead tended to reward more efficient production (though this in turn would end up causing a new set of problems).

Epigraph. Burns parodies Adam's response to Eve's account of her fall in Book VIII of John Milton's *Paradise Lost* (1667): 'O fairest of Creation, last and best | Of all Gods works . . . | How art thou lost, how on a sudden lost, | Defac't, defloured, and now to Death devote?' (ll. 896–7, 900–1).

l. 1. *Irish lords.* Under the terms of the Treaty of Union of 1707, Scottish peers elected from among themselves sixteen 'representative peers' to sit in the British House of Lords, the number limited in this way to reflect the much smaller population of Scotland; but the remaining Scottish peers, as peers, remained excluded from election to the House of Commons. Irish peers *could* be elected to the Commons for Scottish (as for English) constituencies.

l. 16. *AQUAVITÆ.* 'Water of life', Latin equivalent to the Gaelic *uisge beatha* from which the word 'whisky' is derived.

l. 19. *PREMIER YOUTH.* William Pitt the younger (b. 1759, the same year as Burns), backed by George III, had been confirmed as First Lord of the Treasury (and thus 'Premier' or 'Prime Minister') by the general election of 1784, and would remain in that office until 1801.

l. 25. *great man.* Since its use to describe prime minister Robert Walpole earlier in the century, this phrase had evoked ministerial power dominating the Commons through its distribution of offices and other rewards (the '*posts* an' *pensions*' of l. 27).

17 l. 39. *Excise-men.* See note to p. 15, l. 115.

l. 44. *A blackguard Smuggler.* The eighteenth-century British state's use of import duties to raise revenue created a thriving black economy along its coasts. Tea, brandy, rum, and tobacco were the main contraband involved. Burns mentions his personal encounter with this trade in the biographical letter to John Moore of 2 August 1787 reproduced in Appendix 1, p. 263.

17 l. 52. *dung in staves*. That is, staved in.

l. 57. *could I like MONGOMERIES fight*. A leading Ayrshire aristocratic family, distinguished on the royalist side in the seventeenth-century civil wars, and whose current head, Archibald, 11th Earl of Eglinton, had led a regiment in North America in the Seven Years War (1756–63).

l. 58. *BOSWELL*. James Boswell (1740–95), advocate; famous as friend of Samuel Johnson in London, but now back on the family's Ayrshire estate at Auchinleck and active in local politics.

18 l. 71. *Saint Stephen's wa's*. Until the old Palace of Westminster burnt down in 1834, its St Stephen's Chapel served as the debating chamber of the House of Commons.

l. 73. *Dempster*. George Dempster of Dunnichen (1732–1818), MP for the Perth district of burghs (Perth, Dundee, St Andrews, Forfar, and Cupar) 1761–90. 'From the start a frequent and passionate speaker' (*DNB*), and, in a period when Scottish MPs typically backed the government of the day, famous for speaking and voting independently (for example on the American War), earning him the nickname 'honest George'.

l. 74. *Kilkerran*. Sir Adam Fergusson of Kilkerran (1733–1813), MP for Ayrshire for ten years before his replacement by one of Pitt's people in 1784: he would regain the seat in the next election in 1790. 'An old woman who as a child had once seen Sir Adam in a temper described . . . how "Sir Adam cam out and he chappit on the ground wi' his stick, and says he, 'Dinna think that because I'm no swearin I'm no angry'"', hence 'aith-detesting' (Fergusson, *Lowland Lairds*, 94).

l. 76. *The Laird o' Graham*. James Graham (1755–1836). Barred as the eldest son of a Scottish peer from standing in Scotland, Graham was an MP for English seats until he succeeded his father as Duke of Montrose in 1790. He was active in promoting Scottish interests, and had a reputation for independence until joining the government as a Lord of the Treasury in 1783. The Graham estates are around Loch Lomond in the southern Highlands, hence 'Highland Baron'.

l. 78. *Dundas*. Henry Dundas (1742–1811), MP for Midlothian 1774–90. As Lord Advocate 1775–84 Dundas gained powers of patronage across the Scottish political scene; on joining Pitt's new administration in 1784 he also became the government's all-powerful political manager in Scotland.

l. 79. *Erskine*. Thomas Erskine (1750–1823), brother of the Earl of Buchan (in north-east Scotland, hence a 'norland billie'): a London lawyer and talented courtroom speaker, but only very briefly an MP (for Portsmouth) in 1783–4.

l. 80. *True Campbells, Frederick and Ilay*. Frederick Campbell, brother of the Duke of Argyll, MP for the Glasgow district of burghs (Glasgow, Rutherglen, Dumbarton, and Renfrew) 1761–80, and then for Argyll

1781–99; Sir Ilay Campbell (1734–1823), no direct relation to Frederick, but a successor as MP for the Glasgow burghs in 1784: Dundas made him Lord Advocate in the same year and thus a principal agent of his power. Both Campbells were Pitt's men; neither seems to have been distinguished for eloquence.

l. 81. *Livistone, the bauld Sir Willie.* Sir William Augustus Cunynghame, proprietor of Milncraig in Ayrshire and Livingstone in Linlithgow, for which latter county he was MP 1774–90.

l. 83. *Demosthenes or Tully.* Famous classical orators: Demosthenes of Athens (384–322 BC); and the Roman Marcus Tullius Cicero (106–43 BC). Both died trying to defend their republics against, respectively, Alexander of Macedon and Mark Antony and his allies.

l. 92. *Her lost Militia fir'd her bluid.* When, two years into the Seven Years War in 1759, invasion by France had looked likely, the British government had revived the moribund local militias of England in response. A section of the Scottish elite, centred on literary and legal figures, campaigned for a militia to be established in Scotland as well, as a means of reviving the 'national spirit' and countering the alienating and feminizing effects of commercial society, as well as for defence. Acts were prepared for parliament in 1760 and 1762; the campaign was revived, during the American Revolutionary War, in 1776 and 1782. It came to nothing, due as much to hostility or indifference in Scotland as to the opposition of government: Scotland's militia was 'lost' only in the sense that it had not been won. James Graham had put forward the most recent bill, and most of the MPs Burns mentions in this poem had been active in the campaign at some point. See Robertson, *The Scottish Enlightenment and the Militia Issue*, chs. 4 and 5.

19 l. 99. *durk.* That is, dirk, the Highland dagger.

l. 100. *She'll tak the streets.* This poem's contrast between two modes of political agency—the parliamentary eloquence of land-owning gentlemen, and riot—reminds us that the MPs whom Burns addresses were elected by a tiny proportion of the population, and that street disorder was the only way in which ordinary people brought pressure to bear on their rulers. '[T]he tetchy sensibilities of a libertarian crowd defined, in the largest sense, the limits of what was politically possible,' writes E. P. Thompson of the period; 'the price which aristocracy and gentry paid for a limited monarchy and weak state was, perforce, the licence of the crowd'. Such licence did not threaten the existence of the social hierarchy itself: it 'bred riots but not rebellions: direct action but not democratic organizations' ('Patrician Society, Plebian Culture', 396, 403, 397).

l. 105. *the muckle house.* That is, parliament.

l. 109. *Charlie Fox.* Charles James Fox (1749–1806), populist leader of the opposition to Pitt's government; despite his current reforming agenda he had tasted power in 1783 as part of a coalition with Lord North, prime minister 1770–82 and a much more conservative figure than Pitt (see notes to p. 139, ll. 39ff.).

19 l. 112. *cadie*. Burns's glossary translates this as 'person' merely, but *DSL* notes that it can mean specifically a 'ragamuffin or rough fellow' (Fox had a reputation for scruffiness).

ll. 113–14. *his dicing box,* | *An' sportin lady*. *DNB* notes that Fox was 'the doyen of the gambling craze that disturbed so many family fortunes' in the period. 'Sporting lady', Kinsley notes, also means whore: Fox was notorious for a string of mistresses, but by this time had settled down with the experienced courtesan Elizabeth Armitstead.

l. 115. *yon guid blood o' auld Boconnock's*. Pitt again: his great-grandfather had been Governor of Madras, and used the fortune he made in India to buy the estate of Boconnoc in Cornwall. This gave him control of a seat in parliament and began the family's political rise.

l. 117 and footnote. *Nanse Tinnock's*. Nanse Tonnock kept a respectable tavern in Mauchline: on reading this poem, she denied that Burns had ever been a regular in her establishment.

l. 119. *tea and winnocks*. One of Pitt's priorities on coming to power was to pay off the United Kingdom's huge national debt, incurred in a long series of expensive wars with France. Reorganizing the tax system was part of his strategy. The 1784 Commutation Act slashed duty on tea to reduce the incentive for smuggling, and recouped the revenue with a tax on houses, calculated by the number of windows; hence '*commutation*' in l. 121.

l. 126. *The Coalition*. That is, the Fox–North coalition (see note to l. 109 above), the heavily defeated party of the 1784 election.

20 l. 133. *ye chosen FIVE AND FORTY*. By the terms of the Treaty of Union, the number of Scottish seats sending MPs to the Commons. Scotsmen could sit for English constituencies, as did James Graham (l. 76) and Thomas Erskine (l. 79).

ll. 135–6. *though a Minister grow dorty,* | *An' kick your place*. 'Place' here refers to any lucrative office or sinecure an MP might have been given by the executive in exchange for his vote, and 'kick' something like 'kick away from under you'; as well as suggesting a physical kick in a bodily place.

l. 142. *St. Jamie's*. That is, the Court: St James's Palace was the official London residence of the monarch.

l. 145. *half-starv'd slaves in warmer skies*. *Not* a reference to the chattel slaves of Britain's Caribbean colonies, or elsewhere in the Americas, but to southern Europeans: 'slaves', in the political idiom of eighteenth-century Britain, because subject to absolutist rulers (pre-eminently the kings of France and Spain) without the liberties supposedly guaranteed by the British constitution; and because Catholic, and thus subject to the Pope. The Postscript's association of liberty with a capacity for military service was a commonplace of early-modern political thought which had informed the mid-century militia debate (see note to l. 92 above).

21 l. 163. *bring a SCOTCHMAN frae his hill*. Scottish regiments, and in particular Highlanders (long suspected of disloyalty to the Hanoverian

regime because of their prominence in the Jacobite rebellions of 1715 and 1745–6), had proven valuable in two campaigns in North America: against France in the Seven Years War, and more recently against the United States in the Revolutionary War.

l. 173. *latest*. That is, last.

ll. 177–8. *physically causes seek,* | *In clime an' season.* The idea that cultural differences could be traced to differences of climate was much discussed by Enlightenment philosophers. As Kinsley notes, Burns could have come across it in Henry Mackenzie's essay in the *Mirror* no. 18 (27 March 1779) where he quotes its most famous formulation in Montesquieu's *De L'esprit des Lois* (1748); in its rejection by David Hume in his essay 'Of National Characters' (1741); or its discussion by Adam Ferguson in Part III, section i of *An Essay on the History of Civil Society* (1766).

l. 184. *dam*. A 'quantity of urine discharged at once' (*DSL*); to 'tine your dam' is to wet yourself.

ll. 183–6. In the fourth edition of 1794, Burns substituted a less shocking form of incontinence: 'Till when ye speak, ye aiblins blether; | Yet deil mak matter! | *Freedom* and *Whisky* gang thegither, | Tak aff your whitter'.

The Holy Fair. K70. In the 1787 Edinburgh edition and subsequently Burns provides a footnote to the title: '*Holy Fair* is a common phrase in the West of Scotland for a sacramental occasion'. The sacrament in question is Holy Communion, rarely celebrated more than two or three times a year in the Church of Scotland. In summer, a parish might hold a 'Communion Season' over several days, which other congregations were invited to attend and at which their ministers were invited to preach. Because a parish church could not hold so many people, this was an open-air occasion, and 'a highly popular event in seventeenth- and eighteenth-century Scotland, but it was more often an annual holiday than a holy event; thus, rarely more than 20 per cent of parishioners came forward to receive the sacrament' (Brown, *Religion and Society*, 73).

The verse form here is a version of the 'Christ's Kirk on the Green' stanza, named after a poem attributed to James I of Scotland, 'Chrystis Kirk of the Greene'. Burns would have come across this poem in Allan Ramsay's anthology *The Ever-Green: being a collection of Scots Poems, wrote by the ingenious before 1600* (1724), but also Ramsay's adaptation of it, with the addition of two further cantos, in his 1721 *Poems* (Ramsay Vol. I, 57–82). The form was also adopted by Robert Fergusson for 'Hallow-Fair', 'Leith Races', and 'The Election'. All of these poems celebrate communal holiday high-jinks of one kind or another. The ending of the final, short, line with 'that day' or 'that night' is conventional.

Epigraph. Kinsley ascribes these lines to Thomas Brown's 1704 comedy *The stage-Beaux toss'd in a blanket: or, hypocrisie alamode*, but they appear nowhere in Brown's play and are probably Burns's own. *A-LA-MODE*: in the current fashion.

22 l. 5. *owre GALSTON Muirs.* Galston is a village on the River Irvine, about seven miles north of Burns's farm at Mossgiel. The 1787 Edinburgh edition's 'owre', used here, corrects the Kilmarnock edition's 'our'.

23 l. 37. *My name is FUN.* The six introductory stanzas of this poem take their cue from the first five of 'Leith Races': the girl encountered by the speaker of Fergusson's poem similarly announces 'They ca' me MIRTH' (l. 32; Fergusson 161), and his agreement with her plan is equally enthusiastic.

l. 41. *I'm gaun to ********* holy fair.* The asterisks fit the name of Mauchline, the village just a mile from Mossgiel.

l. 66. *black-bonnet.* The officiating elder, responsible for gathering money in the collection-plate.

24 l. 75. *racer Jess.* According to Kinsley, the half-witted daughter of the 'Poosie Nansie' in whose Mauchline tavern the 'Jolly Beggars' gather in Burns's poem.

l. 80. *Blackguarding frae K*******ck.* To blackguard is 'to loaf, play the vagabond' (*OED*, though this line is its only example of the verb in this sense, so probably Burns's coinage). Kilmarnock, the nearest town, is about ten miles from Mauchline (see Map).

l. 86. *an Elect swatch.* In the 1787 Edinburgh edition and subsequently this becomes 'a Chosen swatch'. In either case, the reference is to those enjoying the inner conviction that they have been chosen or elected for salvation by God's grace (hence 'grace-proud' in l. 87) in accordance with the Kirk's Calvinist theology, as summarized in *The Westminster Confession of Faith* (1647): 'By the decree of God, for the manifestation of His glory, some men and angels are predestinated unto everlasting life; and others foreordained to everlasting death' (ch. III, para. iii).

25 l. 102. *For ****** speels the holy door.* The name elided here is that of (Alexander) Moodie, the orthodox minister of Riccarton parish in Kilmarnock (Kinsley), whom Burns had lampooned in an earlier satire, 'The Holy Tulzie' (K52).

l. 103. *tidings o' s—lv—t—n.* In the 1787 Edinburgh edition and subsequently Burns changes this (salvation) to d—mn—t—n (damnation). The change accords with the advice Burns was given by Revd Hugh Blair, Professor of Rhetoric and Belles Lettres at Edinburgh University; but Burns ignored almost all of Blair's other advice, and 'damnation' in any case better reflects the emphasis of orthodox preaching.

l. 104. *Hornie.* The Devil.

l. 116. *cantharidian plaisters.* The glossary to the 1787 Edinburgh edition helpfully explains 'cantharidian' as meaning 'made of cantharides': that is, Spanish Fly, the famous aphrodisiac. In the old medicine remedies were often applied by spreading them inside a bandage as a 'plaster'.

l. 118. *the tent.* See note to p. 13, l. 47.

l. 122. ***** *opens out his cauld harangues.* The name elided here is that of (George) Smith, minister at Galston (Kinsley). A modernizing 'moderate', whose preaching attended to living a moral life, rather than the state of the listener's soul; orthodox Calvinism rejected mere 'good works' as a means to salvation (see note to p. 95, l. 50).

ll. 128–9. *Of moral pow'rs and reason?* | *His English style.* Smith's sermon draws on the terminology of the Enlightenment, and adopts the more genteel, less impassioned manner of the Anglican church. For the importance of *'reason'* in 'moderate' attitudes, see note to p. 109, l. 112.

l. 131. *SOCRATES or ANTONINE.* Respectively the Athenian philosopher (d. 399 BC) and hero of Plato's dialogues; and Marcus Aurelius Antoninus (AD 121–80), Roman Emperor and Stoic moralist.

26 l. 138. *For *******, frae the water-fit.* The name elided here is that of (William) Peebles, orthodox minister of the Newton parish in Ayr (Kinsley), on the right bank of the river where it enters the sea (hence 'water-fit').

l. 142. *COMMON-SENSE.* This stanza opens by adopting the rhetoric of the orthodox party, for whom Smith's worldly morals are 'poosion'd nostrum'; so 'common-sense' here could name Smith's moderate party in the church, as well as reasonableness in the abstract.

l. 143. *the Cowgate.* In the 1787 Edinburgh edition and subsequently Burns provides a footnote: 'A street so called, which faces the *tent* in ⸺', i.e. in Mauchline.

l. 145. *Wee ****** neist, the Guard relieves.* The name elided here is that of (Alexander) Miller, assistant minister at St Michael's parish church in Mauchline (Kinsley). More strictly orthodox ministers, including William Peebles (see note to l. 138 above) often claimed (it seems with some justification) that 'moderate' clergy publicly subscribed to the Westminster Confession only because subscription was a condition of a career in the established church, while regarding its doctrines with scepticism in private: Miller, Burns suggests, is one of these. See Kidd, 'Scotland's Invisible Enlightenment', 35, 41f.

l. 154. *Change-house.* 'A small inn or alehouse'; 'perhaps with reference to the changing of horses' for long-distance travellers (*DSL*).

27 l. 181. *the L⸺'s ain trumpet touts.* Among the many trumpets in the Bible, perhaps the most relevant is that of Revelation 1: 10–11: 'I was in the Spirit on the Lord's day, and heard behind me a great voice, as of a trumpet, Saying, I am Alpha and Omega, the first and the last'. Or, given the way in which this stanza proceeds, Ezekiel 33: 4: 'Then whosoever heareth the sound of the trumpet, and taketh not warning; if the sword come, and take him away, his blood shall be upon his own head'.

l. 184. *Black ****** is na spairan.* The name elided here is that of 'Black' John Russel (Kinsley). Russel was minister at the Old High Kirk in Kilmarnock, a terrifying disciplinarian, and the other target of Burns's 'Holy Tulzie'.

l. 185. *His piercin words, like Highlan swords,* | *Divide the joints an' marrow.* This alludes to Paul's Epistle to the Hebrews 4: 12: 'For the word of God is quick, and powerful, and sharper than any twoedged sword, piercing even to the dividing asunder of soul and spirit, and of the joints and marrow, and is a discerner of the thoughts and intents of the heart'.

27 l. 188 and footnote. *Our vera 'Sauls does harrow'*. In Shakespeare's tragedy, the ghost of Hamlet's father warns him: 'I could a tale unfold whose lightest word | Would harrow up thy soul, freeze thy young blood' (I. 5. 19–20).

29 *Address to the Deil.* K76.

Epigraph. Beelzebub's address to Satan in Book I, ll. 128–9 of *Paradise Lost* (1667).

ll. 1–2. *O Thou, whatever title suit thee!* | *Auld Hornie, Satan, Nick, or Clootie*. As Kinsley observes, this echoes the address to Jonathan Swift which Alexander Pope (1688–1744) added to *The Dunciad* in the 1729 Variorum edition, listing his friend's various personae: 'O thou! whatever Title please thine ear, | Dean, Drapier, Bickerstaff, or Gulliver!' (Book I, ll. 17–18; Pope 351).

30 l. 19. *like a roaran lion*. The image is from the First Epistle of Peter 5: 8: 'Be sober, be vigilant; because your adversary the Devil, as a roaring lion, walketh about, seeking whom he may devour'.

l. 49. *Let Warlocks grim, an' wither'd Hags*. Witchcraft had long since ceased to be recognized in official legal and religious practice: the Witchcraft Act had been repealed in 1736, and its last victim had been executed in 1727. But it had survived as the object of popular belief, or half-belief. The disruption of dairy production, and male impotence, as described in the following stanzas, were typical of the everyday frustrations ascribed to the malice of neighbours in league with the devil.

31 l. 79. *MASONS' mystic word an' grip*. Freemasonry had been established in Scotland at least since the formation of the Grand Lodge in 1736: Burns joined in 1781 (see also notes to 'The Farewell', below). Aside from its mystical mumbo-jumbo, it functioned as an organization for mutual assistance operating outside but parallel to the systems of family and political patronage that structured eighteenth-century British society, and therefore potentially useful for poorer brothers such as Burns. On first joining a Lodge as an Apprentice, brothers are given secret words and 'grips' (handshakes) in order to identify themselves as such to fellow masons. Although Freemasonry had a somewhat tangential relation to orthodox Christianity, and some rituals may have invoked a figure named 'Lucifer', in this stanza Burns is having fun with the accusation that Freemasons engaged in Devil-worship, not revealing any secrets of the Lodge.

32 l. 101. the *man of Uzz*. Job, 'perfect and upright', and very rich: the Book of Job begins when God puts everything of Job's in Satan's power to prove that His servant does not only obey Him because he is rewarded for it. Satan proceeds to visit every kind of devastation on Job's household, family, and body.

l. 111. *that day MICHAEL did you pierce.* Satan 'first knew pain' when the Archangel Michael cuts him with a sword during the War in Heaven in *Paradise Lost*, Book VI, ll. 325–8.

33 l. 113. *Wad ding a Lallan tongue, or Erse.* That is, would defeat both Scots and Gaelic to express.

The death and dying words of Poor Mailie, the Author's only Pet Yowe. An unco mournfu' Tale. K24. Based on a true incident, though readers will be relieved to know that Mailie in fact survived her fall into a ditch. The precedent for this sort of poem was 'The Last Dying Words of Bonny Heck, a Famous Grey-Hound in the Shire of Fife' by William Hamilton of Gilbertfield (d. 1751), published in the important collection *A Choice Collection of Comic and Serious Scots Poems both ancient and modern. By several hands* (Edinburgh, 1706). According to Kinsley, 'The death and dying words of Poor Mailie' was 'Burns's first significant essay in Scots'. 'Pet' here means quite specifically 'a lamb or sheep which has been hand-reared and kept separate from the flock' (*DSL*).

l. 20. *wicked strings o' hemp or hair.* Mailie is tethered, not because she is a 'pet', but to stop her wandering onto arable ground, an indication that this is an old-style, unenclosed, rural setting: see Leask, *Robert Burns and Pastoral*, 151.

l. 24. *packs of woo'.* A pack is 'a measure of wool, gen. 12 stones Scots weight' (*DSL*).

34 l. 27. *gie.* From the 1793 *Poems*, correcting Kilmarnock's 'gae'.

l. 47. *ridin time.* That is, 'the mating time of animals, esp. sheep' (*DSL*). In the 1787 Edinburgh edition and subsequently Burns substitutes for this line: 'An' warn him, what I winna name'.

35 l. 64. *thou'se get my blather.* Hughoc, useless in Mailie's crisis, is rewarded with almost the only part of a sheep not eaten in eighteenth-century Scotland. 'The bequest of the bladder, a thing of no worth, is a medieval death-bed joke . . . which probably survived in popular tradition' (Kinsley).

Poor Mailie's Elegy. K25. Here, Burns uses the 'Standard Habbie' stanza in its original, elegiac, form, with the last line always ending in 'dead': the stanzas of Robert Sempill's 'The Life and Death of the Piper of Kilbarchan, or the Epitaph of Habbie Simpson' (1690), from which it takes its name, end with the lines '*Hab Simpson's* dead', 'Sen *Habbi's* dead', 'But now he's dead', and so on. Ramsay and Fergusson had also used the stanza for elegies (comic and otherwise) in this form, but, like Burns, for other purposes too.

36 l. 34. *Frae 'yont the TWEED.* That is, Mailie belongs to one of the new breeds, such as the Cheviot, starting to be imported into Scotland from England (the river Tweed marks the border) to improve the wool-yield of the rougher native stock.

l. 43. *DOON.* The river Doon flows past Burns's birthplace, Alloway: see Map.

36 l. 44. *wha on AIRE your chanters tune.* The river Ayr flows past
Mauchline, near Burns's farm at Mossgiel: see Map. A chanter is 'that
pipe of a bagpipe, with finger-holes on which the melody is played'
(*OED*).

To J. S****. K79. The addressee is James Smith (b. 1765), a draper in
Mauchline, and one of Burns's best friends there: he collected 41 sub-
scriptions for the Kilmarnock edition. This is Standard Habbie used for
the other main purpose to which Ramsay and Fergusson had adapted it,
the familiar verse epistle.

Epigraph. From Robert Blair's 1743 poem *The Grave*, ll. 88–90 (slightly
altered).

37 l. 19. *fit o' rhyme.* McGuirk notes that Burns may have known Ben
Jonson's 'A Fit of Rhyme against Rhyme', poem XXIX in *Underwoods*
(1640).

l. 32. *the russet coat.* Russet is 'a coarse homespun woollen cloth of a red-
dish-brown, grey or neutral colour, formerly used for the dress of peasants
and country-folk' (*OED*).

l. 33. *damn'd my fortune to the groat.* *DSL* notes that 'groat-man' was
used, in 1795, to mean 'day-labourer, one who originally worked for a
groat a day', though Burns was never in this situation.

l. 38. *guid, black prent.* Kinsley notes that the phrase is borrowed from
Robert Fergusson, in 'Answer to Mr. J. S.'s Epistle': 'For whan in gude
black print I saw thee | Wi' souple gab, | I skirl'd fou loud, "Oh wae befa'
thee! | "But thou'rt a daub"' (ll. 3–6; Fergusson 71).

38 l. 59. *th' inglorious dead.* This recalls Thomas Gray's meditation on the
graves of the poor in *Elegy Written in a Country Churchyard* (1751): 'Some
mute inglorious Milton here may rest, | Some Cromwell guiltless of his
Country's Blood' (ll. 59–60; Lonsdale 128).

39 l. 102. *high disdain.* McGuirk suggests this continues the echoes of
Gray's *Elegy*, where the rich are requested not to hear 'The short and
simple annals of the poor' with 'a disdainful smile' (ll. 32, 31; Lonsdale
123); lines that Burns uses in the epigraph to 'The Cotter's Saturday
night'.

40 l. 117. *Luna.* The moon, representing change.

l. 122. *And kneel, ye Pow'rs.* The Kilmarnock edition, and all three subse-
quent editions published by Creech, open the quotation marks here:

And kneel, 'Ye *Pow'rs*, and warm implore,

I follow Kinsley in adopting the present reading from Burns's manuscript.

l. 133. *DEMPSTER.* See note to p. 18, l. 73.

l. 134. *A Garter gie to WILLIE PIT.* That is, accession to the elite order
of knighthood in the United Kingdom, the Order of the Garter. For
'Willie Pit', see note to p. 16, l. 19.

l. 135. *Cit.* In the eighteenth century, 'cit' (from 'citizen') was 'usually applied, more or less contemptuously, to a townsman as distinguished from a countryman, or to a tradesman or shopkeeper as distinguished from a gentleman' (*OED*).

41   l. 157. *sentimental traces.* 'Trace' is a word just coming into use to mean 'A mark or impression left on the face, the mind etc.': *OED*'s earliest example is from 1809 (6b). It had however been used by John Locke in something like this sense, to mean 'A change in the brain as the result of some mental experience' (*OED* 6d) in his *Essay Concerning Human Understanding* of 1690: 'The memory of Thoughts, is retained by the impressions that are made on the Brain, and the traces there left after such thinking' (Book II, ch. i, §15). Burns uses the phrase again in 'The Vision' l. 55, in describing Coila, his muse.

l. 159. *arioso.* Melodious (as a musical direction; Italian).

l. 161. *gravissimo.* Solemn (as a musical direction; Italian).

l. 165. *hairum-scairum.* 'Reckless, careless, heedless in action' (*OED*).

l. 166. *rambling.* This is changed to 'rattling' in the 1787 and 1793 editions, and then to 'rattlin' in 1794.

A Dream. K113. The monarch's birthday was a major event in the courtly calendar, and was marked by, among other things, a levee (a formal reception), and a birthday ode from the poet laureate (George III's current laureate was Thomas Warton). Burns's poem uses the 'Christ's Kirk on the Green' stanza typically used to describe more boisterous and plebeian occasions: see headnote to 'The Holy Fair', p. 291 above. A tighter rhyme-scheme is used here than in that poem, with only two rhymes (though often rough and ready) in all eight long lines.

42   l. 4. *Bardie.* In the 1793 and 1794 editions, the narrator becomes a slightly less humble-sounding 'Poet', both here and again in l. 76.

l. 23. *YOUR GRACE.* An older mode of address to a monarch, this had only been replaced by 'your Majesty' in Scottish usage at the Act of Union in 1707. Burns thus adopts a style never officially used to address a king of the House of Hanover, which acceded to the British throne in 1714.

ll. 25–6. *There's monie waur been o' the Race, | And aiblins ane been better.* Burns retained a sentimental loyalty to the long-lost cause of the House of Stuart (see notes to 'There'll never be peace till Jamie comes hame' and 'Written on a window in Stirling', pp. 344 and 349). Accordingly, this is usually taken as a reference to Charles Edward Stuart, the 'Bonnie Prince Charlie' who had attempted to win back the throne for his father James, from George's grandfather, in the Jacobite Rebellion of 1745–6. In this case, l. 26 has to mean 'perhaps one *would have* been better', since Charles was never king (at this point, he was living in exile in Rome: he died in early 1788).

43   ll. 34–5. *And now the third part o' the string, | An' less, will gang about it.* This is a reference to the British Empire's massive loss of territory, actual and potential, by the secession of the United States. The Treaty of

Paris which ended the Revolutionary War in 1783 had recognized the new republic's claim to all land east of the Mississippi and south of the Great Lakes.

43   l. 54. *I' the craft some day*. 'Craft', or croft, means the piece of cultivated land attached to the cottage, sometimes called the 'infield'.

l. 57. *Will's a true guid fallow's get*. Pitt was the offspring ('get') of William Pitt the elder, prime minister 1757–61 and again 1766–8. The elder Pitt was generally credited with Britain's successes in the Seven Years War, and respected for refusing ennoblement as reward for his services.

l. 59. *he intends to pay your debt*. See note to p. 19, l. 119.

44   l. 67. *dissection*. The bodies of the hanged were made available to surgeons for dissection in anatomy lessons.

l. 70. *your QUEEN*. George had married Charlotte of Mecklenburg-Strelitz (1744–1818), daughter of a German ducal family, the year after his accession to the throne in 1760.

l. 77. *Thae bonie Bairntime*. In her first 22 years of marriage Charlotte bore 15 children.

l. 82. *young Potentate o' W—*. George, Prince of Wales (1762–1830). As this stanza suggests, the heir to the throne was famously dedicated to dissipation.

l. 88. *brak Diana's pales*. Diana was the Roman goddess of chastity, so breaking into her sanctuary is a figure for sexual licence.

l. 89. *rattl'd dice wi' Charlie*. That is, with Charles James Fox MP, leader of the Opposition, for whom see notes to p. 19, ll. 109 and 113–14. His friendship with opposition politicians was another reason for the profound alienation between the Prince of Wales and his father.

l. 97 and footnote. *funny, queer Sir John*. As the footnote indicates, a reference to the loose-living Sir John Falstaff, companion to the young Prince Hal in Shakespeare's *Henry IV* plays. On acceding to the throne at the end of *Henry IV Part II*, Hal rejects his old companion, and goes on to become the hero-king who defeats the French at the battle of Agincourt in *Henry V*. Queer: here, 'amusing, funny, entertaining' (*DSL*).

45   l. 100. *right rev'rend O—*. The second son, Prince Frederick, Duke of York (1763–1827). The Hanoverian kings remained rulers of their native principality in Germany, retaining their historic rights and privileges there: George exercised one of these when he had Frederick, at six months old, 'elected' Prince-Bishop of Osnaburg (Osnabrück) to secure the substantial revenues attached to this position.

l. 101. *the lawn-sleeve*. Lawn was a type of fine linen used for the sleeves of a bishop's dress.

l. 102. *a ribban at your lug*. That is, the black cockade worn in the hats of officers in the Hanoverian army, in which Frederick was a Major-General.

ll. 104–5. *As ye disown yon paughty dog,* | *That bears the Keys of Peter.* That is, the Pope. The Bishopric of Osnaburg alternated between Protestant and Catholic incumbents, and Frederick of course was the former, and thus free to marry. His religious title did not inhibit him from adopting the same debauched lifestyle as his elder brother, and Burns's concern in the following lines is ironic. Frederick made the expected marriage with a German princess in 1791.

l. 109. *Young, royal TARRY-BREEKS.* Prince William Henry (1765–1837), the third son, who had been sent into the navy in 1779 (hence 'tarry-breeks': wooden ships were sealed with tar), 'chiefly to prevent him from falling under the influence of his eldest brother' (*DNB*). In the winter of 1785–6, William, at this point a lieutenant, was staying in Portsmouth with Sir Henry Martin, Commissioner to the Navy there, and fell in love with his host's daughter, Sarah: this is the 'Amour' referred to in Burns's footnote. William was keen to marry but the distance in rank made this impossible and they were quickly separated.

l. 113. *hang out.* 'To suspend (a sign, colours, or the like) . . . to display as a sign or signal' (*OED*): in this context, like a signal-flag from the mast of a ship.

l. 119. *Ye royal Lasses dainty.* There were six princesses in the royal brood.

ll. 123–4. *Kings are unco scant ay,* | *An' German-Gentles are but sma'.* In the event, Princess Charlotte married the King of Württemberg, and Princess Elizabeth married the Duke of Hesse-Homburg; Princess Mary married her cousin the Duke of Gloucester, and the other three never married.

46 *The Vision.* K62. This poem is divided into two 'duans': as Burns's footnote explains, a term taken from James Macpherson (see note to p. 5, l. 27). 'Cath-Loda', a poem in Macpherson's 1765 *Works of Ossian* Vol. II (Macpherson 305–20), is divided into three.

Duan First

l. 2. *roaring.* The sound of curling stones on ice.

ll. 3–4. *hunger'd Maukin taen her way* | *To kail-yards green.* As Kinsley notes, an image borrowed from James Thomson's 'Winter' (1726): 'The hare, | Though timorous of heart . . . the garden seeks, | Urged on by fearless want' (ll. 257–8, 260–1; Thomson 135–6).

l. 16. *The auld, clay biggin.* The houses of the poor were often at least partly built of clay plastered on a timber base. The cottage in which Burns was born was of this type; by 1786 Burns was living in the more substantial stone farmhouse at Mossgiel.

47 l. 37. *the string the snick did draw.* From outside, the latch was typically lifted by a string passing through a hole in the door.

l. 49. *Holly-boughs.* Coila will crown the speaker with holly as her parting gesture at l. 224. 'The Vision' borrows its title, though little else, from a poem by Allan Ramsay, which masquerades as a sixteenth-century Scottish poem among the genuine sixteenth-century Scottish poems he collected in *The Ever Green* (1724). Coila's holly may be an allusion to the title of Ramsay's collection.

47 l. 55. *A 'hare-brain'd, sentimental trace'*. Burns is quoting from his own verse, namely 'To J. Smith', l. 157 (p. 41). 'Trace' is used again in something like the same sense in l. 147 of the present poem.

48 l. 61. *a tartan sheen*. The wearing of tartan in the Highlands had been proscribed by law after the defeat of the Jacobites in 1746, because of its association with the rebel clans; a proscription only recently repealed, in 1782. But tartan had been appropriated as a signifier of Scottishness generally in the aftermath of the Union of 1707, for example in Allan Ramsay's poem 'Tartana, or the Plaid' (in the *Poems* of 1721; Ramsay Vol. I, 27–37).

l. 63. *BESS*. Usually identified with Elizabeth Paton, a servant at Burns's father's farm at Lochlie, and the mother of Burns's first child, also Elizabeth, born in May 1785 (see also note to p. 113, ll. 37–72). By then Burns was already in love with Jean Armour, who would be his lover by the end of the year, and would bear him twins little more than a month after the publication of the Kilmarnock *Poems* in July 1786. In the Edinburgh edition of 1787, and subsequently, 'my BESS, I ween' is replaced by 'my bonny JEAN'.

ll. 79–80. *DOON . . . IRWINE*. The Doon and Irvine are rivers in Ayrshire, and form the borders of Kyle, Burns's district: see Maps.

l. 81. *Auld, hermit AIRE staw thro' his woods*. In its reaches above and below Mauchline the river Ayr flows through a winding, thickly-wooded ravine.

l. 86. *An ancient BOROUGH*. Ayr, a Royal Burgh since 1205.

ll. 88–90. *a Race, | To ev'ry nobler virtue bred, | And polish'd grace*. These lines seem to anticipate the seven stanzas that continue Duan First in the Edinburgh edition of 1787 and subsequently, which offer examples of this noble 'Race'; suggesting that Kinsley is right to say that these stanzas were not a later composition, but a deleted section of the original draft.

> By stately tow'r, or palace fair,
> Or ruins pendent in the air,
> Bold stems of Heroes, here and there,
>   I could discern;
> Some seem'd to muse, some seem'd to dare,
>   With feature stern.
>
> My heart did glowing transport feel,
> To see a Race heroic wheel,
> And brandish round the deep-dy'd steel
>   In sturdy blows;
> While back-recoiling seem'd to reel
>   Their Suthron foes.

His COUNTRY'S SAVIOUR, mark him well!
Bold *Richardton's* heroic swell;
The chief on *Sark* who glorious fell,
              In high command;
And *He* whom ruthless Fates expel
              His native land.

There, where a sceptr'd *Pictish* shade
Stalk'd round his ashes lowly laid,
I mark'd a martial Race, pourtray'd
              In colours strong;
Bold, soldier-featur'd, undismay'd
              They strode along.

Thro' many a wild, romantic grove,
Near many a hermit-fancy'd cove,
(Fit haunts for Friendship or for Love,
              In musing mood)
An *aged Judge*, I saw him rove,
              Dispensing good.

With deep-struck, reverential awe,
The learned Sire and Son I saw,
To Nature's God and Nature's law
              They gave their lore,
This, all its source and end to draw,
              That, to adore.

Brydon's brave Ward I well could spy,
Beneath old *Scotia's* smiling eye;
Who call'd on Fame, low standing by,
              To hand him on,
Where many a Patriot-name on high
              And Hero shone.

In a series of footnotes, Burns identifies the 'Race heroic' with the Wallace family; 'His COUNTRY'S SAVIOUR' with William Wallace (d. 1305), a leader in Scotland's Wars of Independence from England (the 'Suthron'); Richardton with Adam Wallace of Richardton, 'cousin to the immortal preserver of Scottish independence'; and 'The chief on *Sark* who glorious fell' with 'Wallace, Laird of Craigie, who was second in command, under Douglas Earl of Ormond, at the famous battle on the banks of Sark, fought *anno* 1448. That glorious victory was principally owing to the judicious conduct and intrepid valour of the gallant Laird of Craigie, who died of his wounds after the action.' The earliest records of the Wallaces as a landed family relate to Ayrshire estates (Riccarton—'Richardton'—and Craigie are both near Kilmarnock), though the hero William held land further north, in Renfrewshire. The Sark is a stream on the border, and Craigie's battle was with an invading English army. On Burns's Wallace-worship see the letter of 2 August 1787 to

John Moore in Appendix 1, p. 260. A direct descendant of Craigie, Mrs Frances Dunlop (neé Wallace) was to become an important patron and correspondent of Burns. '*He* whom ruthless Fates expel | His native land' does not get a footnote: Kinsley suggests this refers to Mrs Dunlop's eldest son, in 'exile' in England after selling the Craigie estate to pay off his debts.

The 'sceptr'd Pictish shade', another footnote explains, is 'Coilus King of the Picts, from whom the district of Kyle is said to take its name' and who 'lies buried, as tradition says, near the family-seat of the Montgomeries of Coilsfield, where his burial-place is still shown' (for the Montgomeries see note to p. 17, l. 57). The 'wild, romantic grove' is the Ayr gorge at 'Barskimming, the seat of the Lord Justice Clerk': that is, Sir Thomas Miller, an improving landlord as well as a judge. The 'learned *Sire* and *Son*' are 'the late Doctor and present Professor Stewart': Dugald Stewart (1753–1828) attended to his father Matthew's duties as Professor of Mathematics at the University of Edinburgh in the years leading to the latter's death in 1785, when the son took up the chair of Moral Philosophy there. Their country house was at Catrine, a couple of miles outside Mauchline. Finally, '*Brydon's* brave Ward' is named as 'Colonel Fullarton': another improving local landlord, William Fullarton (1754–1808) had been conducted on the Grand Tour by Patrick Brydone (1741–1818), author of *A Tour through Sicily and Malta*. Fullarton had distinguished himself in the war with Mysore in India in 1782–3, leading a regiment raised on his Ayrshire estate.

Duan Second

49 l. 104. *many a light, aerial band.* As McGuirk suggests, this may be based on the 'machinery' of spirits deployed by Pope in 'The Rape of the Lock', including 'The light Militia of the lower Sky' (canto I, l. 42; Pope 219).

l. 111. *the Patriot.* In the rhetoric of eighteenth-century British politics, this means the representative who refuses the personal advantages offered by the executive in return for his support (cf. note to p. 16, l. 25) and holds ministers to account in the name of the nation.

l. 120. *And grace the hand.* In the Edinburgh edition of 1787, and subsequently, another extra stanza is added here:

> 'And when the Bard, or hoary Sage,
> 'Charm or instruct the future age,
> 'They bind the wild, Poetic rage
>   'In energy,
> 'Or point the inconclusive page
>   'Full on the eye.

l. 121. *FULLARTON.* Colonel William Fullarton (see note to ll. 88–90 above).

l. 122. *DEMPSTER.* See note to p. 18, l. 73.

ll. 123–4. *BEATTIE sung | His 'Minstrel lays'.* James Beattie (1735–1803), Professor of Moral Philosophy and Logic at Marischal College, Aberdeen. Beattie was highly influential on British Romantic culture, starting with Burns, as author of *The Minstrel: or, The Progress of Genius*, a poem in two books (1771, 1774) on the education of a poet.

l. 126. *The Sceptic's bays.* The sceptic is David Hume (1711–76). Beattie was also celebrated for his *Essay on the Nature and Immutability of Truth* (1770), a scathing (and unconvincing) rebuttal of the scepticism of Hume's *Treatise of Human Nature* (1739–40).

l. 129. *Hind.* 'A farm servant, an agricultural labourer' (*OED*).

50   ll. 135–6. *to meliorate the plain, | With tillage-skill.* The introduction of modern agricultural techniques, ongoing in Burns's Scotland, gets its own muse.

l. 151. *COILA.* In the stanzas added to Duan First in the Edinburgh edition of 1787, Burns will cite the legendary origins of the name of the district of Kyle in a Pictish king, Coilus (see note to ll. 88–90 above); the name of Burns's muse also recalls the Water of Coyle, a tributary of the Ayr.

l. 153. *the Campbell's, chiefs of fame.* Since the fourteenth century, a branch of the Campbell family had owned the extensive Loudon estate in Ayrshire, which included Mossgiel, the farm Burns was working with his brother in 1786. As 'chiefs of fame' Burns may be thinking of the Dukes of Argyll, chiefs of the Clan Campbell and decisive agents of government power in the West Highlands. Loudon was an Earldom in its own right, and the fourth Earl had fought both against the Jacobites and in North America in the Seven Years War; but the fifth Earl got himself into financial difficulties, and shot himself in April 1786, so that Burns's ultimate feudal superior at the time of the Kilmarnock edition was 6-year-old Flora Campbell, the fifth Earl's daughter.

51   l. 200. *Thomson's landscape-glow.* James Thomson (1700–48), Scottish-born, London-based author of the nature-descriptive *The Seasons* (1726–46).

l. 202. *Shenstone's art.* For Shenstone see note to Preface, p. 283.

l. 203. *Gray.* Thomas Gray (1716–71), author of elegies, odes, and bardic verse.

52   l. 213. *Potosi's mine.* The silver mine in what is now Bolivia, a source of massive wealth for the Spanish Empire.

53   *Halloween.* K73. Another adaptation of the 'Christ's Kirk on the Green' stanza used in 'The Holy Fair' and 'A Dream'. In the first stanza, and in the first four lines of stanzas III and VI, Burns does not rhyme the long lines in the usual way, but gives them each an internal rhyme of their own.

Epigraph. From Oliver Goldsmith (d. 1774), *The Deserted Village* (1770), ll. 251–4 (Lonsdale 686). Burns has capitalized the initials of 'rich' and 'proud', and changed Goldsmith's 'blessings' to more Burnsian 'pleasures'.

53 l. 2 and footnote. *Cassilis Downans*. Cassillis House, seat of the Kennedy family, stands at the sharp bend in the river Doon near Maybole. Nearby Dowan's Hill is topped by the remains of an ancient hill-fort, which attracted associations with supernatural activity.

l. 5 and footnote. *Colean*. In 1786 Culzean Castle (pronounced more or less as Burns spells it), another Kennedy property, on the coastal cliff-top west of Maybole, was in the process of being transformed to designs by Robert Adam on the orders of the tenth Earl of Cassillis. The caves below the castle referred to in the footnote had been extensively used by the ninth Earl for storing contraband, landed on the adjacent beaches.

l. 12. *Where BRUCE ance rul'd*. Robert de Brus became Earl of Carrick (that part of Ayrshire south of the river Doon) by marriage in 1271; his son Robert was crowned King of Scots in 1306, and went on to (eventually) defeat the English and re-establish Scotland's independence.

54 l. 20. *fine*. That is, in their finery.

l. 32. *fell aff the drift*. That is, fell off the herd, got left behind.

56 l. 96. *kiln*. A structure for drying grain, consisting of 'a lattice-work of beams supporting a bed of straw with the grain strewed upon it, and a lower chamber containing the fire' (*DSL*). Merran drops her ball of blue thread from the upper chamber into the fire chamber or 'kiln-pot' below (the '*pat*' of l. 102).

57 l. 127. *the Sherra-moor*. The battle of Sheriffmuir, near Stirling, between a government army under the Duke of Argyle and Jacobite rebels led by the Earl of Mar, in 1715. Inconclusive on the day, that was a bad enough result for the Jacobites to ensure the collapse of the rebellion a few months later.

58 l. 139. *Achmacalla*. As Kinsley comments, 'a place-name concocted to make the rhyme'.

59 l. 163. *lord Lenox' march*. A regimental march of the 25th Regiment of Foot, eventually to become the King's Own Scottish Borderers, and since 1762 under the command of Lord George Henry Lennox. The tune is in Sir Herbert Maxwell, ed., *The Lowland Scots Regiments* (Glasgow, 1918), 338.

60 l. 201. *the Stack he faddom't thrice*. For 'faddom't' Burns's 1787 glossary gives only 'fathomed', but *DSL* confirms that faddom means 'to encircle with the outstretched arms' as a means of measuring a quantity of e.g. peat, but also 'specif. of corn-stacks at *Halloween* to call up the apparition of one's future spouse'.

l. 202. *timmer-propt for thrawin*. Kinsley suggests 'propped with lengths of timber to prevent warping'.

62 l. 240. *Mar's-year*. 1715: see note to l. 127 above.

The auld Farmer's new-year-morning Salutation to his auld Mare, Maggie, on giving her the accustomed ripp of Corn to hansel in the new-year. K75. A hansel or handsel is 'a gift bestowed to commemorate an inaugural occasion, event, or season, e.g. the beginning of the year' (*DSL*); to hansel in the New Year is to give such a gift. Nigel Leask points out that Burns's title alludes to *The Farmer's New-Year Gift to his Countrymen, Heritors, and Farmers, for the Year 1757* by landowner Sir Archibald Grant of Monymusk, a work embodying a paternalistic relation between landowner and tenant which Burns transfers to that between master and horse (Leask, *Robert Burns and Pastoral*, 158).

63 l. 22. *fifty mark*. A mark was a unit of currency equivalent to 13*s*. 4*d*.; so 50 mark was £33 6*s*. 8*d*.

l. 35. *KYLE-STEWART*. Kyle district is historically divided by the river Ayr into Kyle Stewart to its north, and Kyle Regis or King's Kyle to its south: see Map.

l. 44. *Fairs*. That is, country fairs, market days.

64 l. 49. *mellow*. That is, tipsy.

l. 53. *pay't them hollow*. In the modern idiom, beat them hollow.

l. 55. *droop-rumpl't, hunter cattle*. This reading is from the 1787 Edinburgh edition, correcting the Kilmarnock text's 'droot-'. Hunters are horses bred for the recreational purposes of the gentry, not working horses like Maggie.

l. 57. *Scotch mile*. Its abolition as a standard measure by the Scottish parliament in 1685 meant that this had no statutory definition, but *OED* suggests 1976 yards, as opposed to the 1760 yards of the English mile.

l. 65. *sax rood*. A rood is a quarter-acre, so Maggie could plough an acre and a half in her eight-hour day.

ll. 75–6. *I gied thy cog a wee-bit heap | Aboon the timmer*. That is, heaped the grain in your (wooden) tub above the level of the rim.

65 l. 85. *My Pleugh*. That is, my plough *team*. These lines reflect the transitional stage reached by agricultural 'improvement' in Burns's Ayrshire. Horses, the faster, more specialized beast of burden, have replaced oxen; but the plough is still the old, heavy, wooden one, requiring four horses to pull it (l. 86), not the new lightweight iron one, which required only two.

l. 106. *To some hain'd rig*. The Kilmarnock edition glosses 'hain' as 'to save, to spare', but here it is used in a more specific sense: 'to enclose or protect a field or wood by a hedge or fence; to preserve grassland from cattle for hay or winter pasture' (*DSL*).

The Cotter's Saturday night. K72. For this poem Burns adopts the verse form invented by Edmund Spenser for his allegorical epic *The Faerie Queene* (1590, 1596). The Spenserian stanza had been revived in the eighteenth century, and used for widely varying purposes by many of the poets admired by Burns: by William Shenstone in 'The School-Mistress' (1737, enlarged 1742); by James Thomson in *The Castle of Indolence* (1748); and by James Beattie in *The Minstrel* (1770, 1774). The most important precedent for 'The Cotter's Saturday night', however, was Robert Fergusson's 'The Farmer's Ingle' (published posthumously in 1779), which used a simplified Spenserian stanza for a sympathetic description, in Scots, of evening in a rural cottage (Fergusson 136–40).

A 'cotter' or cottar rented a few acres of land on which to grow food for himself and his family; he paid rent in the form of labour for the landowner. This class was rapidly vanishing from lowland Scotland in 1786, as such patches of land were incorporated into larger units farmed commercially by tenants employing waged labour where they could afford to do so. The domestic piety depicted in the poem certainly reflects the household in which Burns grew up, but the family were always tenants, working substantial farms of between 70 and 120 acres.

The poem is inscribed to Robert Aiken (1739–1807), the prosperous Ayr solicitor who gathered almost a quarter (145) of the subscriptions that made the Kilmarnock edition possible. In a letter of early 1786 to John Kennedy, factor to the Earl of Dumfries at Cumnock (and brother-in-law of Burns's Mauchline friend Gavin Hamilton), Burns describes Aiken as now '[m]y chief Patron'; and enclosed with his next letter, at Kennedy's request, a copy of this poem (L21, 17 February; and L22, 3 March).

65 *Epigraph.* Thomas Gray, *Elegy Written in a Country Churchyard* (1751) ll. 29–32 (Lonsdale 122–3).

66 l. 18. *weary, o'er the moor, his course does hameward bend.* Echoes ll. 3–4 of Gray's *Elegy*: 'The plowman homeward plods his weary way, | And leaves the world to darkness and to me' (Lonsdale 117).

l. 26. *Does a' his weary kiaugh and care beguile.* In the later Edinburgh editions of 1793 and 1794 Burns changed this line to 'Does a' his weary carking cares beguile'. *DSL* suggests 'kiaugh' or 'kauch' is a specifically south-western word, from Dumfries and Galloway: its use here is the only example offered from an Ayrshire context.

l. 29. *At Service out, amang the Farmers roun'.* The older children are in full-time paid employment on neighbouring farms. Especially in areas like Ayrshire, farm-servants '[o]ften came of cottar families . . . [T]hrough life, the child of a cottar bound to give service for some days in the year, yet with that precious if insecure title to land, would move into full-time service for a period before marrying and returning finally to the cottar position' (Gray, 'The Social Impact of Agrarian Change', 54). Burns avoided this kind of service as a child: see the biographical letter to John Moore of 2 August 1787 reproduced in Appendix 1, p. 260.

67 l. 63. *Rake.* That is, 'a fashionable or stylish man of dissolute or promiscuous habits' (*OED*), which habits usually require ready cash, though the young Burns laughingly uses 'rakish' of himself in his song 'O leave novels, ye Mauchline belles' (included in this volume).

69 l. 106. *Those strains that once did sweet in ZION glide.* The Psalms of David.

ll. 111–13. *Dundee . . . Or plaintive Martyrs . . . Or noble Elgin.* The Church of Scotland published its authorized metrical translation of the Psalms in 1650, using a restricted number of verse-forms to facilitate setting them to music. 'Common Metre' verses have lines of eight syllables, then six, then eight, then six. 'Dundee', 'Martyrs', and 'Elgin' are three of the many tunes to which Common Metre psalms could be sung.

l. 115. *Italian trills.* The displacement of native styles of singing and music generally by fashionable Italian modes provoked great displeasure in eighteenth-century Scotland and England alike. See, for example, Robert Fergusson's 1773 'Elegy, on the Death of Scots Music': 'Now foreign sonnets bear the gree, | And crabbit queer variety | Of sound fresh sprung frae *Italy*, | A bastard breed!' (ll. 49–54; Fergusson 39).

l. 121. *Amalek's ungracious progeny.* Amalek, a Duke of Edom, is defeated by Joshua in Exodus 17; but his descendants keep coming back for more, on and off, throughout the first half of the Old Testament.

ll. 122–3. *the royal Bard . . . Beneath the stroke of Heaven's avenging ire.* When King David, putative author of the Psalms, gets another man's wife pregnant, and arranges for her husband to die in battle, God punishes him by having the child die (2 Samuel 11–12).

l. 124. *Job's pathetic plaint.* For Job see note to p. 32, l. 101.

l. 126. *other Holy Seers.* That is, one of the other sixteen books of the Prophets in the Protestant Bible.

l. 127. *the Christian Volume.* The New Testament.

l. 130. *whereon to lay His head.* Echoes Matthew 8: 20 and Luke 9: 58: 'And Jesus saith unto him, The foxes have holes, and the birds of the air have nests; but the Son of man hath not where to lay his head'. These first four lines evoke the 'theme' of the four gospels (Matthew, Mark, Luke, John).

l. 131. *How His first followers and servants sped.* As recorded in Acts.

l. 132. *The Precepts sage they wrote to many a land.* The Epistles of Paul, James, Peter, John, and Jude.

l. 133. *he, who lone in Patmos.* It was on the island of Patmos that St John the Divine had the visions recorded in the Book of Revelation, the last book of the New Testament. John sees 'an angel standing in the sun' (l. 134) at 19: 17; the fate of Babylon (l. 135) is the theme of the preceding chapter.

70 l. 138 and footnote. *Hope 'springs exulting on triumphant wing'.* As Burns notes, from Alexander Pope, *Windsor-Forest* (1713): 'See! from the Brake the whirring Pheasant springs, | And mounts exulting on triumphant Wings' (ll. 111–12). The pheasant is shot in the following couplet (Pope 199).

l. 140. *uncreated rays.* Kinsley notes an echo of Thomson's God in 'Summer' (1727): 'How shall I then attempt to sing of Him | Who, Light Himself, in uncreated light | Invested deep, dwells awfully retired | From mortal eye' (ll. 175–8; Thomson 42); and that Thomson is himself echoing the more convoluted formulation of the same idea at the start of *Paradise Lost*, Book III.

70 l. 142. *hymning their CREATOR'S praise.* Kinsley suggests that this echoes the celestial choir's celebration of the creation in *Paradise Lost* (1667): 'And touch't thir Golden Harps, & hymning prais'd | God and his works, Creatour him they sung' (Book VII, ll. 258–9).

l. 153. *His Book of Life.* See Paul's Epistle to the Philippians 4: 3: 'And I entreat thee also, true yokefellow, help those women which laboured with me in the gospel . . . and with other my fellowlabourers, whose names are in the book of life'.

ll. 158–9. *HE who stills the raven's clam'rous nest,* | *And decks the lily fair in flow'ry pride.* The conjunction suggests that Burns has in mind Luke's account of the Sermon on the Mount: 'Consider the ravens: for they neither sow nor reap; which neither have storehouse nor barn; and God feedeth them: how much more are ye better than the fowls?' (12: 24); 'Consider the lilies how they grow; they toil not, they spin not; and yet I say unto you, that Solomon in all his glory was not arrayed like one of these' (12: 27). Matthew's version (6: 26–9) doesn't mention ravens. Luke, and Burns, may also be remembering Job 38: 41: 'Who provideth for the raven his food? when his young ones cry unto God, they wander for lack of meat.'

l. 163. *From scenes like these, old SCOTIA'S grandeur springs.* Kinsley notes another echo of Thomson's 'Summer', this time of lines added in the 1744 edition of *The Seasons*: 'A simple scene! yet hence Britannia sees | Her solid grandeur rise' (ll. 423–4; Thomson 48). But the grandeur Thomson celebrates is political and economic, not moral, and the 'simple scene' is one of sheep-shearing, not prayer; his point being that wool exports were still, in 1744, the basis of Britain's material prosperity, as they had been since the Middle Ages.

l. 165. *Princes and lords are but the breath of kings.* Kinsley notes the echo of Goldsmith's *Deserted Village*: 'Princes and lords may flourish or may fade; | A breath can make them, as a breath has made; | But a bold peasantry, their country's pride, | When once destroy'd, can never be supply'd' (ll. 51–6; Lonsdale 678).

l. 166. *'An honest man's the noble work of GOD.'* Kinsley notes that Burns is quoting, and altering, Pope's *Essay on Man* Epistle IV here: 'A Wit's a feather, and a Chief a rod; | An honest Man's the noblest work of God' (ll. 246–7; Pope 543).

71 ll. 176–8. *Luxury's contagion . . . A virtuous Populace.* Burns here articulates an opposition at the core of the eighteenth-century critique of modern commercial society, inherited ultimately from Italian Renaissance political thinking. Commerce and empire enrich a nation, but their very material wealth ('luxury') morally weakens citizens by withdrawing them from the exercise of public duties ('virtue') into the enjoyment of merely personal pleasures. This ultimately allows political power to be gathered up by a single person (a 'tyrant'), so that citizens lose their liberties altogether. But the 'citizens' with which this theory is typically concerned are the land-owning and thus enfranchised elite who have public duties to neglect in the first place. Burns's lines here ascribe 'virtue' to the

unenfranchised poor instead, who, since *they* are not being enriched by commerce and empire, are not in danger of being corrupted either.

l. 181. *the patriotic tide*. 'Patriotic' names something more specific than 'loving one's country' here: in the rhetoric described in the previous note, the 'patriot' is one who stands up to the 'tyrant'. See l. 111 of 'The Vision' and note (p. 302), and the equation of Wallace and George Washington in the 'Ode on General Washington's Birthday': the American rebels understood themselves as 'patriots' in just this sense.

l. 182. *unhappy WALLACE' heart*. For William Wallace, see note to p. 48, ll. 88–90. 'Unhappy' in the old sense of 'unfortunate, unlucky, ill-fated; miserable in lot or circumstances' (*OED*): Wallace was betrayed, captured by the English king Edward I, then hanged, drawn, and quartered as a traitor. Kinsley points out that Thomson uses 'unhappy' of the 'Great patriot-hero' Wallace in a pair of lines (ll. 900–1) added to 'Autumn' in 1744 (Thomson 113).

l. 189. *her Ornament and Guard!*. Kinsley finds an echo of lines added to Thomson's 'Winter' in *The Seasons* of 1744: 'O thou, whose wisdom, solid yet refined, | Whose patriot virtues . . . Give thee with pleasing dignity to shine | At once the guardian, ornament, and joy | Of polished life' (ll. 656–7, 661–3; Thomson 146). The addressee is Lord Chesterfield; the speaker is 'the Rural Muse'.

To a Mouse. K69.

72 ll. 7–8. *Man's dominion | Has broken Nature's social union*. Kinsley finds the latter phrase in a related context in Pope's *Essay on Man*, Epistle III, where the speaker advises learning from the building skills of ants and bees: 'Here too all forms of social union find, | And hence let Reason, late, instruct Mankind: | Here subterranean works and cities see; | There towns aerial on the waving tree' (ll. 179–82; Pope 531). But perhaps more relevant is William Warburton's note to just this section of Pope's poem in his 1751 edition, which denounces the misinterpretation of the Bible which has allowed man to regard 'the whole animal creation . . . as being created for no use of their own, but for his only; and therefore treated them with the utmost barbarity. . . . It became one [i.e. Pope] who adhered to the Scripture account of Man's dominion to reprove this abuse of it' (59–60). See also notes to p. 116, ll. 19 and 22.

l. 29. *coulter*. The blade at the front of the plough, making the first, vertical, cut into the ground.

ll. 39–40. *The best laid schemes o' Mice an' Men, | Gang aft agley*. As Kinsley points out, the famous moral of this poem echoes a (rather more specific) sentiment in *The Grave* (1743), a widely read poem of the 'grave-yard' school by Scottish minister Robert Blair (1699–1746): 'The best concerted Schemes Men lay for Fame | Die fast away' (ll. 185–6).

73 ll. 47–8. *forward, tho' I canna see, | I guess an' fear*. Kinsley notes that the contrast of the final stanza is borrowed from Samuel Johnson's philosophical tale *The History of Rasselas, Prince of Abyssinia* (1759), where the hero

asks, 'What . . . makes the difference between man and all the rest of the animal creation?' and finds the source of humanity's distinguishing unhappiness in the fact that 'I sometimes shrink at evils recollected, and sometimes start at evils anticipated' (ch. II). But as Carol McGuirk has observed, this conclusion is contradicted by what has been said of the mouse in the rest of the poem: it *has* been looking forward, it *has* been 'anticipating evil', in the shape of 'weary *Winter* comin fast' (l. 26); this is precisely why it was building a nest (*Robert Burns and the Sentimental Era*, 9).

73 *Epistle to Davie, a Brother Poet*. K51. David Siller (1760–1830) had been a teacher at Tarbolton, the nearest village to Burns's father's last farm at Lochlie; by 1786 he was a grocer in Irvine. A poet and a fiddler, he had been like Burns a member of the Tarbolton Batchelor's Club (see Introduction to this volume).

This poem uses the complex 'Cherrie and the Slae' stanza, so named after a poem in this form published in 1597 by Alexander Montgomerie (d. 1598), one of a circle of poets at the court of James VI. Burns would have found this poem in Volume II of Ramsay's anthology *The Ever-Green: being a collection of Scots Poems, wrote by the ingenious before 1600* (1724). He would also have come across Ramsay's own use of this form for half-serious verse epistle (e.g. 'To the Right Honourable, the Town-Council of Edinburgh'; 'To the Whin-Bush Club') in his 1721 *Poems* (Ramsay Vol. I, 208–9, 211–12).

l. 1. *BEN-LOMOND*. The southernmost high summit of the Scottish Highlands, due north of Ayrshire, across the Firth of Clyde.

l. 19. *countless thousands*. That is, on an income of many thousands of pounds per annum.

74 l. 25. *'Mair spier na, nor fear na'*. Burns quotes from the last four short lines (the 'wheel' of a 'Cherrie and the Slae' stanza) that close Ramsay's 'A Poet's Wish: An Ode' (in the 1721 *Poems*). The wish is for life and health to continue composing verse, expressed to the Oracle of Apollo, and the stanza quoted is the Oracle's reply: 'Mair speer na, and fear na, | But set thy Mind to rest, | Aspire ay still high'r ay, | And always hope the best' (ll. 53–6; Ramsay Vol. I, 244).

l. 29. *kilns*. Structures for drying grain: see note to p. 56, l. 96.

l. 55. *we'll time till't*. The Kilmarnock edition has no apostrophe in 'we'll': it is inserted in one of the two printings of the 1787 editions, disappears in 1793, and reappears in 1794. 'Well *timed* till't' (of the rhyme to the tune) would make good sense; but 'time' here is the verb in an old intransitive usage meaning 'to keep time to' (*OED* 3c), so I adopt 'we'll' here.

75 ll. 58–9. *It's no in wealth like Lon'on Bank, | To purchase peace and rest*. This perhaps recalls, to make a rather different point, Adam Smith's distinction between the rewards appropriate for industry, and for benevolence: 'What reward is most proper for promoting the practice of truth, justice, and humanity? The confidence, the esteem, and love of those we live with.

Humanity does not desire to be great, but to be beloved. It is not in being rich that truth and justice would rejoice, but in being trusted and believed, recompenses which those virtues must almost always acquire' (Smith, *Theory of Moral Sentiments*, 166–7).

76 l. 107. *Ye hae your MEG*. Siller's sweetheart was Margaret Orr, a servant at Stair House, twelve miles south-east of Irvine.

l. 121. *Her dear idea brings relief,* | *And solace to my breast*. Kinsley notes the echo of Shenstone's pastoral 'Elegy IX': 'But come, my friend, with taste, with science blest, | Restore thy dear idea to my breast' (ll. 45, 47). Shenstone's poem, like Burns's, praises love and friendship over the pursuit of wealth, though Shenstone's 'dear idea' is of the friend, not the lover (Shenstone Vol. I, 36).

77 l. 131. *Had number'd out my weary days*. Kinsley observes that the phrase recalls Laurence Sterne's *Sentimental Journey* (1768): 'Sweet pliability of man's spirit, that can at once surrender itself to illusions, which cheat expectation and sorrow of their weary moments!—long—long since had ye number'd out my days, had I not trod so great a part of them upon this enchanted ground' (87). The illusions Yorick celebrates are those of the imagination, not love.

l. 138. *tenebrific*. That is, 'dark, gloomy' (*OED*), but this seems to be Burns's coinage (from the older 'tenebrificous').

l. 145. *Phœbus and the famous Nine*. That is, Phoebus Apollo, Roman god of (among other things), music and poetry, and in this role leader of the nine Muses, goddesses who inspire the various arts.

l. 147. *My spavet Pegasus*. The winged horse of Greek mythology had become an image of poetry itself.

The Lament. Occasioned by the unfortunate issue of a friend's amour. K93. The subtitle's disclaimer notwithstanding, this poem has for its biographical context Burns's own enforced separation from a pregnant Jean Armour in early 1786; a situation unresolved when the Kilmarnock edition went to press (see Introduction to this volume, and the biographical letter to John Moore of 2 August 1787 reproduced in Appendix 1, p. 266).

The stanza form here is a version of the medieval 'ballade' stanza used by Chaucer and, in Scotland, Robert Henryson and William Dunbar. James VI, in his *Essayes of A Prentise in the Divine Art of Poesie* (1584), had described this stanza as suitable for 'any heich & graue subiectis, specially drawin out of learnit authoruis' and named it 'Ballat Royal'. Burns would have come across many poems using this rhyme scheme in Ramsay's *Ever-Green*, which made available to a modern readership a wide selection of fifteenth- and sixteenth-century Scottish poetry that had been preserved in the Bannatyne Manuscript (compiled in 1568), but most of these abandon the ten-syllable line of Chaucer and Henryson (cited by James) for an eight-syllable line (sometimes used by Dunbar). This is the model that Burns adopts: the *Ever-Green* poems often adopt it for a similar 'lover's complaint' theme.

77 *Epigraph.* Lady Randolph in John Home's 1757 play *Douglas: A Tragedy*
Act I.

79 l. 54. *Keen Recollection's direful train.* Kinsley notes the echo of Goldsmith's
The Deserted Village, when the speaker sees the 'ruined ground' where the
cottage once stood: 'Remembrance wakes with all her busy train, | Swells
at my breast and turns the past to pain' (ll. 80–1; Lonsdale 679).

80 *Despondency, an Ode.* K94. Another example of the 'Cherrie and the Slae'
stanza: see headnote to 'Epistle to Davie', p. 310.

81 l. 22. *Unfitted with an aim.* Compare the biographical letter to John Moore
of 2 August 1787 reproduced in Appendix 1, p. 263.

l. 30. *How blest the Solitary's lot,* | *Who, all-forgetting, all-forgot.* Kinsley
points out the echo of Alexander Pope, 'Eloisa to Abelard' (1717): 'How
happy is the blameless Vestal's lot! | The world forgetting, by the world
forgot' (ll. 207–8; Pope 257).

ll. 31, 33–4. *Within his humble cell,* | | *Sits o'er his newly-gathered fruits,* |
Beside his crystal well. Kinsley spots that the phrasing here echoes ll. 3–4
of Thomas Parnell's poem 'The Hermit': 'the Cave his humble Cell, | His
Food the Fruits, his Drink the chrystal Well': *Poems on Several Occasions*
(Dublin, 1722), 123.

l. 54. *Or human love or hate.* The first 'or' means 'either'. See *OED*, 'or
(*conj.* 1)' 3: a poetic, but not specifically Scottish, usage.

82 *Man was made to Mourn, a Dirge.* K64. In the earliest manuscript copy of
this poem Burns names a tune for which it was composed, 'Peggy Bawn'.

A little slow

This score is adapted from the version of this Irish song in *The Scots
Musical Museum* (509). A tune is not mentioned in any of the published
editions of the present poem, but the stanza, with its alteration of tetram-
eter and trimeter lines, is typical of popular song, with the second quatrain
of each stanza being sung to the second section of the tune.

l. 7. *furrow'd o'er with years.* Kinsley observes that Burns takes this phrase
from Robert Blair's *The Grave*: 'Shatter'd with Age, and furrow'd o'er

with Years' (l. 195: see note to p. 72, ll. 39–40). Blair is describing the pyramids.

l. 11. *Does thirst of wealth thy step constrain.* Kinsley notes the echo of a similar encounter between youth and experience in Shenstene's 'Elegy VII': 'Stranger, he said, amid this pealing rain, | Benighted, lonesome, whither wouldst thou stray? | Does wealth or pow'r thy weary step constrain? | Reveal thy wish, and let me point the way' (ll. 20–3). Shenstone's interlocutor knows whereof he speaks, being the ghost of Cardinal Wolsey, lord chancellor to Henry VIII, no less (Shenstone Vol. I, 28).

83   l. 34. *Manhood's active might.* Kinsley spots another phrase borrowed from Shenstone, this time 'Elegy XI', though Shenstone *contrasts* the imaginative joys of youth with the power of adulthood: 'Not all the force of manhood's active might, | Not all the craft to subtle age assign'd, | Not science shall extort that dear delight, | Which gay delusion gave the tender mind' (ll. 45–8; Shenstone Vol. I, 42).

ll. 37–8. *But see him on the edge of life, | With Cares and Sorrows worn.* As Kinsley points out, another echo of Blair's *The Grave,* describing the erosion of a memorial a few lines later: 'Worn on the Edge of Days, the Brass consumes, | The Busto moulders, and the deep-cut Marble, | . . . gives up its Charge' (ll. 203–5).

l. 39. *Then Age and Want, Oh! ill-match'd pair.* Kinsley suggests an echo of Edward Young's *Night Thoughts,* Night First: '*Want,* and incurable *Disease* (fell Pair!) | On hopeless Multitudes remorseless seize | At once; and make a Refuge of the Grave' (Young 8).

84   ll. 49–50: *the num'rous Ills | Inwoven with our frame.* This last phrase Kinsley finds in Young's *Night Thoughts,* Night Seventh, but there it is not ills but 'delicate Moralities of *Sense*', supplementing reason, which are 'By Skill Divine inwoven in our Frame' (Young 152).

ll. 53–4. *Man, whose heav'n-erected face, | The smiles of love adorn.* Kinsley observes the phrasing borrowed from Thomson's version of 'man', 'Who wears sweet smiles, and looks erect on Heaven'; Thomson contrasts this with man's inhumanity to *animals,* though, giving a different point to the word 'erect': 'Spring' (1728), l. 355 (Thomson 12).

ll. 55. *Man's inhumanity to Man.* Kinsley points to two parallels in *Night Thoughts:* 'And *Inhumanity* is caught from Man, | From smiling Man' (Young, Night Fifth, 82); 'Turn the World's History; what find we there, | But *Fortune*'s Sports, or *Nature*'s cruel Claims, | Or *Woman*'s Artifice, or *Man*'s Revenge, | And endless Inhumanities on Man?' (Young, Night Eighth, 186).

ll. 65–8. *If I'm designed yon lordling's slave . . . E'er planted in my mind?.* Kinsley identifies this with 'the stock complaint of the Restoration stage hero', giving as an example Arimant in John Dryden's heroic drama *Aureng-Zebe* (1675): 'Why am I thus to slavery design'd | And yet am cheated with a free-born mind?' (Act 3, ll. 43–4). But Arimant's 'slavery' is that of love for an imperious mistress, not a matter of low birth.

85 l. 87. *relief for those*. Changed to 'relief to those' in later copies of the 1787 edition and subsequently. These final lines again recall *Night Thoughts*: see note to l. 39 above.

Winter, a Dirge. K10. Like two other poems at this point in the Kilmarnock edition, 'A Prayer, in the Prospect of Death' and 'To Ruin', this is a very early composition, written in English, before Burns turned to Scots: in the biographical letter to John Moore of 2 August 1787 reproduced in Appendix 1, Burns refers to 'Winter' as 'the earliest of my printed pieces' (p. 264). Like its fellow 'dirge' 'Man was made to Mourn', manuscript versions, but no published version, set this poem to a tune, and it takes the same song-type stanza.

This is 'McPherson's Farewell', the tune of a ballad 'properly so called' (L586), published in *The Scots Musical Museum* as song 114, from which this score is adapted.

l. 9 and footnote. *'The sweeping blast, the sky o'ercast'*. Burns offers this as another borrowing from Edward Young, but it does not seem to correspond to anything in Young with the exactness suggested by the quotation marks. Kinsley suggests it is a general 'recollection' of the dimeter lines of *Ocean: An Ode* (1728): 'As from the North, | Now rushes forth | A Blast, that thunders in my lay' ('To the King', XIV); 'When rushes forth | The frowning *North* | On blackning billows, with what dread | My shudering soul | Beholds them rowl' (XIII), and so on. But the words might come from Young's 'The Force of Religion: or, Vanquished Love' (1714), a verse-narrative of the martyrdom of Lady Jane Grey. Jane's husband approaches with news of her father's execution 'like a gloomy Storm, at once to sweep, | And plunge her to the Bottom of the Deep'; a few lines later a new verse paragraph begins, 'Thus the fair Lily, when the Sky's o'ercast, | At first but shudders in the feeble Blast' (end of Book I).

86 *A Prayer, in the Prospect of Death.* K13. The stanza form here is also the Common Metre of the Scottish Metrical Psalms: see note to p. 69, ll. 111–13.

ll. 1, 19. *O THOU unknown, Almighty cause; But, Thou art good.* Kinsley notes that the poem begins and ends with echoes of the second stanza of Pope's 'The Universal Prayer' (1738), which is written in the same form: 'Thou Great First Cause, least Understood! | Who all my Sense confin'd | To know but this,—that Thou art Good, | And that my self am blind' (ll. 5–8; Pope 247).

87 *To a Mountain-Daisy.* K92. The Standard Habbie stanza is used here for sentimental apostrophe, as in 'To a Mouse'. This was another poem sent by Burns to John Kennedy, factor to the Earl of Dumfries (see headnote to 'The Cotter's Saturday night', p. 306): in the accompanying letter, he calls it 'the very latest of my productions.—I am a good deal pleas'd with some sentiments in it myself; as they are just the native, querulous feelings of a heart, which, as the elegantly melting Gray says, "Melancholy has marked for her own" ' (L28, 20 April 1786; the allusion is to Gray's 'Elegy' l. 120).

ll. 11–12. *to greet | The purpling East.* McGuirk suggests an echo of Milton's 'L'Allegro', where the lark sings 'From his watch-tower in the skies, | Till the dappled dawn doth rise' (ll. 43–4).

l. 26. *Thy snawie bosom sun-ward spread.* Kinsley detects an echo of Book II of James Beattie's *The Minstrel* (1774): 'One cultivated spot there was, that spread | Its flowery bosom to the noonday beam' (ll. 73–4).

l. 29. *share.* That is, the ploughshare, the blade that cuts the ground horizontally at the bottom of the furrow.

88 l. 47. *Till wrench'd of ev'ry stay but HEAV'N.* Kinsley spots the borrowing from Thomson's depiction in 'Autumn' of Lavinia who is 'deprived of all, | Of every stay save innocence and Heaven' (ll. 179–80; Thomson 94).

l. 51. *Stern Ruin's plough-share drives, elate.* Kinsley points out the borrowing from Young's vision of the Apocalypse in *Night Thoughts*: 'Stars rush; and final *Ruin* fiercely drives | Her Ploughshare o'er Creation!' (Young, Night Ninth, 230).

To Ruin. K12. The 'Cherrie and the Slae' stanza once again: see headnote to 'Epistle to Davie', p. 310.

89 *Epistle to a young Friend.* K105. The addressee is Andrew Aiken, son of Robert Aiken: see headnote to 'The Cotter's Saturday night', p. 306. The stanza form here, odd lines being tetrameters, rhyming in pairs, and even lines trimeters but with an additional syllable to give a feminine rhyme, is the stanza form of songs like 'Corn Rigs' and 'From thee Eliza I must go'.

90 l. 15. *views.* Here, 'view' is in the old sense of 'an aim or intention; a design or plan; an object or purpose' (*OED* II.12).

l. 43. *th' illicit rove.* Clearly, 'wandering' in a sexual sense.

92 ll. 87–8. *may ye better reck the rede, | Than ever did th' Adviser.* Kinsley points out the echo of Ophelia's objection to her brother's advice to guard her chastity 'Whiles like a puffed and reckless libertine | Himself the primrose path of dalliance treads | And recks not his own rede' in Shakespeare's *Hamlet* (1. 3. 49–51).

92 *On a Scotch Bard gone to the West Indies.* K100. For the whole of the year in which the Kilmarnock edition was published, 1786, Burns planned to take up a position as an overseer of slaves on a sugar plantation in Jamaica: see Introduction to this volume (his best friend in Mauchline, James Smith, *did* eventually go to Jamaica).

l. 14. *petitions.* Here in the sense of 'a solemn and humble prayer to God' (*OED*).

l. 20. *taen aff.* 'Take off' in the sense of 'lead away summarily' (*OED*).

l. 20. *bummle.* A bumble-bee, but also a traditional figure for the sexually incompetent: Kinsley quotes William Dunbar's 'The tua mariit Wemen and the Wedo', where one wife complains that her husband is 'ane bumbart, ane dron bee' (l. 91; *The Poems of William Dunbar*, ed. John Small, Vol. II, Edinburgh, 1893).

l. 21. *fumble.* Here with the specific connotation of sexual inadequacy: see note to p. 14, l. 69.

93 l. 23. *wumble.* That is, wimble. As a tool for piercing holes, this was a traditional metaphor for the penis: see headnote to 'Green Grow the Rashes', p. 340, for a related use.

l. 25. *KYLE.* Burns's district of Ayrshire, between the rivers Irvine and Doon: see Map.

l. 28. *In flinders flee.* 'An old alliterative phrase' found in ballads, notes Kinsley.

94 *A Dedication to G**** H*******, Esq;* K103. Gavin Hamilton (1751–1805) was Mauchline's solicitor, with James Smith one of Burns's best friends there, and frequently at odds with its Kirk Session (the governing body of a parish, consisting of minister and elders): see the headnote to 'Holy Willie's Prayer', p. 378, for an instance of this. Along with Smith and Robert Aiken, he was instrumental in getting the Kilmarnock *Poems* published, collecting 40 subscriptions. In placing a 'Dedication' to a 'patron' so late in the volume, instead of at its head, Burns may be alluding to Laurence Sterne's dedication in Volume I of *Tristram Shandy* (1759), which does not appear until chapter 8 (and does not name an individual, but offers itself for sale).

l. 5. *sirnam'd like His Grace.* That is, like the Duke of Hamilton, a powerful nobleman in the region.

ll. 11–16. *This may do—maun do, Sir . . . I can beg.* Burns quotes these lines in a letter to a local laird, John Arnot of Dalquhatswood, in an April 1786 letter inviting him to subscribe to the Kilmarnock *Poems*. Arnot declined, but was a subscriber to the Edinburgh edition of the following year.

95 l. 35. *Landlord.* Hamilton was in one sense Burns's landlord: he had subleased the farm at Mossgiel to Burns and his brother Gilbert since 1783.

ll. 39–40. *a milder feature, | Of our poor, sinfu', corrupt Nature.* Burns refuses the Calvinist insistence that *no* good can proceed from human nature, but only from the grace of God; and adopts instead the secular moral theory of the Enlightenment, which considers benevolence and compassion as natural to human beings (though perhaps placed in us by God). Compare the founding statement of the Church of Scotland's official doctrine, *The Westminster Confession of Faith* (1647) with the first sentence of Adam Smith's *The Theory of Moral Sentiments* (1759): 'From this original corruption [of Adam and Eve], whereby we are utterly indisposed, disabled, and made opposite to all good, and wholly inclined to all evil, do proceed all actual transgressions' (ch. VI, para. iv); 'How selfish soever man may be supposed, there are evidently some principles in his nature, which interest him in the fortune of others, and render their happiness necessary to him, though he derives nothing from it except the pleasure of seeing it' (Smith, *Theory of Moral Sentiments*, 9).

l. 42. *Gentoos.* 'Hindus, as opposed to Moslems. (Anglo-Indian, f. Portugese *gentio*, "gentile")' (Kinsley).

l. 43. *Ponotaxi.* A generic South American location.

l. 44. *Orth–d–xy.* That is, the orthodox Calvinism of the Kirk.

l. 49. *And Och! That's nae r–g–n–r–t–n.* Regeneration, that which distinguishes the elect whom God has chosen to save. *The Westminster Confession* continues: 'This corruption of nature, during this life, does remain in those that are regenerated; and although it be, through Christ, pardoned, and mortified; yet both itself, and all the motions thereof, are truly and properly sin' (ch. VI, para. v). This line was omitted in the 1787 Edinburgh and subsequent editions.

l. 50. *Morality, thou deadly bane.* This paragraph voices the Calvinist rejection of 'good works' (that is, moral living) as a means to salvation: 'Works done by unregenerate men, although for the matter of them they may be things which God commands; and of good use both to themselves and others: yet, because they proceed not from a heart purified by faith; nor are done in a right manner, according to the Word; not to a right end, the glory of God, they are therefore sinful and cannot please God, nor make a man meet to receive grace from God' (*Westminster Confession*, ch. XVI, para. vii). This and the next 28 lines constitute a 'digression' (l. 79) in which Burns ironically gives voice to the attitudes and practices which he thought Calvinist doctrine encouraged.

l. 54. *stretch a point to catch a plack.* Bend the truth to make a profit.

l. 57. *point.* That is, point out, or point at in accusation.

96 l. 65. *damn a' Parties but your own.* A glance at the divisions within the Kirk, between the 'moderate' party and the orthodox one.

l. 68. *C–lv–n.* Jean Calvin (1509–64), French Protestant reformer whose theology was the basis of Scottish Church doctrine.

l. 72. *When Vengeance draws the sword in wrath.* The 'day' of the previous line is clearly the Day of Judgement, but the imagery here comes from Ezekiel's prophesy of the destruction of Israel: 'That all flesh may know that I the LORD have drawn forth my sword out of its sheath: it shall not return any more' (21: 5).

96 l. 74. *Ruin, with his sweeping besom.* Another prophecy of apocalypse, visiting Babylon this time: 'I will also make it a possession for the bittern, and pools of water; and I will sweep it with the besom of destruction, saith the LORD of hosts' (Isaiah 14: 23).

ll. 76–8. *While o'er the Harp . . . and heavier groans.* Perhaps a dig at the quality of psalm-singing in the kirk (the Psalms often refer to accompaniment on this instrument, though singing in church was unaccompanied).

l. 82 *My readers then are sure to lose me.* 'Then' is changed to 'still' in the 1787 and subsequent editions. For the specific context of the anti-clericalism shared by Burns and Hamilton, see headnote to 'Holy Willie's Prayer', p. 378.

l. 98. *the CLERK.* That is, the lawyer. 'Clerk' could mean simply 'a man (or woman) of book learning, one able to read and write'; similarly, 'an ordinary legal practitioner in country towns' like Hamilton was referred to as a 'writer' (*OED*).

97 l. 101. *K******'s far-honor'd name.* Hamilton's wife, Helen Kennedy.

98 *To a Louse.* K83.

l. 14. *sprawl.* 'To crawl from one place to another in a struggling or ungraceful manner' (*OED*).

l. 17. *horn nor bane.* Combs were made of horn or bone.

l. 21. *Na faith ye yet!.* 'Na faith!' is an expression of surprise; 'yet', here, is 'a cheer or rallying cry' (*DSL*).

l. 28. *red smeddum.* Powdered mercury, used as an insecticide.

99 l. 35. *Miss's fine Lunardi.* A fashionable type of bonnet, named after a recent Italian pioneer of balloon-flight: see note to p. 111, l. 171.

ll. 41–2. *Thae winks and finger-ends, I dread, | Are notice takin.* Others in the church have noticed the louse, not only the speaker.

ll. 43–4. *O wad some Pow'r the giftie gie us | To see oursels as others see us.* Burns's moral comes from Adam Smith: 'If we saw ourselves in the light in which others see us, or in which they would see us if they knew all, a reformation would generally be unavoidable. We could not otherwise endure the sight' (Smith, *Theory of Moral Sentiments*, 158–9).

*Epistle to J. L*****k, an old Scotch Bard.* K57. Usually referred to as the 'First Epistle to Lapraik'. John Lapraik (1727–1807) had lost his farm in 1772 as a result of the closure of the Ayr Bank (see Introduction to this volume), had been imprisoned for debt in 1785, and was now leasing a farm near the village of Muirkirk, about twelve miles up the valley of the Ayr from Mauchline. He went on to publish *Poems, on Several Occasions* in 1788.

l. 7. *On Fasteneen we had a rockin.* Fasteneen is Shrove Tuesday. Burns's glossary explains that a 'rockin' is 'a meeting on a winter evening': the name derives from 'rock' meaning distaff, the tool which held the unspun flax or wool during spinning. As the next line suggests, these could be work parties as well as social occasions.

l. 13. *ae sang*. The theme of married love identifies the song as Lapraik's 'When I upon thy bosom lean', published in his 1788 *Poems*. This is an adaptation to fit the tune 'Johnny's Grey Breeks' (see headnote to 'My Father was a Farmer', p. 391) of a poem published in *The Weekly Magazine, or Edinburgh Amusement* in October 1773, which begins 'When on thy bosom I recline': Kinsley suggests Lapraik may have been the author of this also. Burns in turn adapted Lapraik's lyric as song 205 in *The Scots Musical Museum*, set to a different tune.

100 l. 17. *It thirl'd the heart-strings thro' the breast*. As Kinsley notes, this echoes Peggy's praise of Patie, the titular *Gentle Shepherd* of Allan Ramsay's 1725 pastoral comedy: 'And then he speaks with sic a taking Art | His Words they thirle like Musick thro' my Heart' (1. 2. 96–7; Ramsay Vol. II, 221).

ll. 21–2. *Pope, or Steele, | Or Beattie's wark*. Alexander Pope (1688–1744), the greatest English poet of his time; Richard Steele (1672–1729), poet, playwright, and essayist. For Beattie see note to p. 49, l. 123. These comparisons reflect the fact that Lapraik's song is in English; Burns's adaptation will translate it into Scots.

l. 35. *'Tween Inverness and Tiviotdale*. Inverness is the Highland capital; the river Teviot is a tributary of the Tweed, in the Borders.

101 l. 61. *What's a' your jargon o' your Schools*. Kinsley observes that this borrows from John Pomfret, *Reason: A Poem* (1700): 'What's all the noisy Jargon of the Schools | But idle Nonsense of laborious Fools, | Who fetter *Reason* with perplexing Rules' (ll. 57–9). Pomfret is denouncing medieval scholastic philosophy.

l. 71. *Parnassus*. The mountain which, in Greek mythology, is the home of the Muses.

l. 73. *Gie me ae spark o' Nature's fire*. Kinsley notes the similarity with Tristram's prayer for authorial autonomy from regulation in Volume III (1761) of Laurence Sterne's *Tristram Shandy*: 'Great *Apollo!* If thou art in a giving humour,—give me,—I ask no more, but one stroke of native humour, with a single spark of thy own fire along with it,—and send *Mercury*, with the *rules* and *compasses*, if he can be spared, with my compliments to—no matter' (144). Burns's line also echoes Pope's 'Essay on Criticism' (1711) which argues exactly the opposite case. Having discussed Homer and Virgil, Pope's poem exclaims, 'Oh may some Spark of *your* Cœlestial Fire | The last, the meanest of your Sons inspire' (ll. 195–6; Pope 150). Homer and Virgil are indeed great because they follow '*Unerring Nature*, still divinely bright, | One *clear, unchang'd*, and *Universal* Light' (ll. 70–1); but Pope's Nature is not set in opposition to classical rules of composition, as in Burns and Sterne, but produces them: 'Those RULES of old *discover'd*, not *devis'd*, | Are *Nature* still, but *Nature Methodiz'd*' (ll. 88–9; Pope 146).

l. 79. *ALLAN'S glee*. That is, Allan Ramsay's: see note to Preface, p. 283.

101   l. 80. *FERGUSON'S*. That is, Robert Fergusson's: see note to Preface, p. 283.

102   l. 103. *MAUCHLINE*. The nearest village to Burns's farm at Mossgiel: see Maps.

l. 107. *rhymin-ware*. The phrase is borrowed from William Hamilton's third epistle to Ramsay, where he imagines himself as a pedlar of poetry: 'Sae little worth's my rhyming Ware, | My Pack I scarce dare apen mair' (ll. 49–50; Ramsay Vol. I, 129).

ll. 115–18. *Awa ye selfish, warly race . . . To catch-the-plack!*. The opposition of this and the following stanza recalls, as McGuirk points out, Shenstone's 'Elegy IX': 'Scorn'd be the wretch that quits his genial bowl, | His loves, his friendships, ev'n his self, resigns; | Perverts the sacred instinct of his soul, | And to a ducate's dirty sphere confines' (Shenstone Vol. I, 35).

103   *To the same*. K58. Usually known as the 'Second Epistle to Lapraik'.

l. 1. *at the stake*. The cows are 'tethered for milking' (Kinsley).

l. 11. *awkart*. Burns glosses this as simply 'awkward', but Kinsley goes further: 'cantankerous, perverse' (nothing like this in *DSL*).

104   ll. 27–30. '*Roose you sae weel for your deserts . . . An' thank him kindly?*'. Kinsley notes that this echoes a stanza in an earlier exchange of Standard Habbie 'Familiar Epistles', between Allan Ramsay and William Hamilton of Gilbertfield: 'Thy blyth and cheerfu' merry Muse, | Of Compliments is sae profuse; | For my good Haivins dis me roose | Sae very finely | It were ill Breeding to refuse | To thank her kindly' (Hamilton's Epistle III, ll. 25–30, in Ramsay's 1721 *Poems*; Ramsay Vol. II, 129).

l. 32. *stumpie*. 'The stump of a quill-pen, esp. one that has been much sharpened' (*DSL*).

l. 45. *your moorlan harp*. As its name suggests, Muirkirk is an upland district.

l. 47. *how Fortune waft an' warp*. On a loom, the warp threads are fixed vertically in the frame, and the waft thread woven through it horizontally. The point of the image perhaps lies in the sudden shifts involved in weaving on a hand-loom: the shooting of the shuttle to-and-fro, the movement of the frame back and forth.

105   l. 65. *Brugh*. That is, a burgh, a market-town.

l. 66. *A Baillie's name*. A baillie is a magistrate in a burgh.

l. 67. *feudal Thane*. 'Thane' is an ancient level of nobility which in fact vanished with the advent of feudalism properly so-called: Burns has found it in Shakespeare's *Macbeth*.

l. 77. *cits*. See note to p. 40, l. 135.

106   l. 92. *the ragged Nine*. Kinsley finds a precedent for describing the Muses as 'ragged' in William Congreve's comedy *Love for Love* (1710): 'as ragged as one of the Muses' (1. 1).

l. 99. *May in some future carcase howl*. The transfer of souls into new bodies after death (metempsychosis) is associated in the West with the beliefs ascribed to Pythagoras (d. *c*.495 BC); Plato (*c*.427–*c*.348 BC) describes a version of it at the end of the *Republic*.

To W. S*****n, Ochiltree. K59. William Simson (1758–1815) was educated at Glasgow University and in 1786 was schoolmaster at Ochiltree, about five miles south of Mauchline on the Lugar water.

l. 13. *My senses wad be in a creel*. That is, 'in confusion, in a state of perplexity' (*DSL*).

107 l. 15. *Wi' Allan, or wi' Gilbertfield*. 'Allan' is Allan Ramsay (see note to Preface, p. 283), 'Gilbertfield' is Ramsay's close friend and collaborator, William Hamilton of Gilbertfield (d. 1759), most celebrated for his abridged and modernized version of Blind Harry's *Wallace*, making available to a modern audience this long fifteenth-century poem narrating the exploits of the hero of the Wars of Independence. These two are particularly relevant to this poem as the authors of 'Familiar Epistles between Lieutenant William Hamilton and Allan Ramsay', written in the same Standard Habbie stanza, published in Ramsay's 1721 *Poems* (Ramsay Vol. I, 115–34).

l. 17. *Ferguson, the writer-chiel*. Robert Fergusson (see note to Preface, p. 283): 'writer-chiel' refers to Fergusson's job in 1769–73 as a lawyer's clerk, 'copying legal documents at the rate of a penny a page' (*DNB*).

l. 31. *COILA*. Burns's muse, with responsibility for Kyle poets generally: see note to p. 50, l. 151.

l. 33. *chanters*. A chanter is 'that pipe of a bagpipe, with finger-holes on which the melody is played' (*OED*).

l. 40. *New Holland*. That is, Australia. The Dutch were the first Europeans to reach Australia: our current name for the continent was just coming into use in English in Burns's lifetime.

l. 42. *Magellan*. The Strait of Magellan is the passage between the southern tip of South America and the island of Tierra del Fuego. The Atlantic and Pacific oceans meet south of the latter, at the notoriously stormy Cape Horn.

ll. 44–5. *Forth an' Tay . . . Yarrow an' Tweed*. Eastward-flowing Scottish rivers: see Map (the Yarrow is a tributary of the Tweed). Ramsay praises '*Tay* and *Tweed's* smooth Streams' in 'A Poet's Wish' in the 1721 *Poems* (l. 10; Ramsay Vol. I, 243). Fergusson hymns Forth, Tweed, and Tay in 'The Rivers of Scotland. An Ode', and both the Tweed and the Yarrow in ll. 25–30 of 'Elegy on the Death of Scots Music', both in his 1773 *Poems* (Fergusson 40–6, 38).

ll. 47–8. *While Irwin, Lugar, Aire an' Doon, | Naebody sings*. These are all Ayrshire rivers. The Lugar flows into the Ayr just south of Mauchline; for the others, see Map. Kinsley points out that Burns's complaint about their poetic neglect relative to the bigger east-flowing rivers named in ll. 44–5 takes its turn after Fergusson's about the poetic neglect of the latter in comparison to the classical rivers of Italy, in 'Hame content. A satire' of 1779: 'The ARNO and the TIBUR lang | Hae run fell clear in Roman sang; | But, save the reverence of Schools! | They're baith but lifeless dowy pools. | Dought they compare wi' bonny Tweed, | As clear as ony lammer-bead? | Or are their shores more sweet and gay | Than Fortha's haughs or banks o' Tay?' (ll. 75–82; Fergusson 159).

108 l. 49. *Th' Illissus, Tiber, Thames, an' Seine.* The river Ilissos skirted the walls of classical Athens; the Tiber runs through Rome. For parallels with Burns's comparisons here, see the lines from Fergusson above, and also a poem in Ramsay's 1728 *Poems*, 'Epistle from Mr. William Starrat': 'Give me the Muse that calls past Ages back, | And shaws proud Southren Sangsters their Mistake, | That frae their *Thames* can fetch the Laurel North, | And big *Parnassus* on the Frith of *Forth*' (ll. 19–22; Ramsay Vol. II, 70).

l. 52. *cock your crest.* Cf. the phrase '*to set up one's crest,* to assume an air of importance or self-confidence' (*DSL*): Kinsley suggests the image is of two pipers setting up their pipes and playing together.

l. 58. *WALLACE.* See note to p. 48, ll. 88–90.

l. 73. *Ev'n winter bleak has charms to me.* Kinsley hears an echo of Thomson's 'Autumn', describing the man of rural retirement, 'from all the stormy passions free': 'Even winter wild to him is full of bliss' (l. 1327; Thomson 125).

109 l. 97. *Fareweel, 'my rhyme-composing brither!'.* The Kilmarnock edition closes the quotation marks after 'composing'; the present text follows the 1793 and 1794 editions where this is sorted out.

ll. 109–86. *POSTSCRIPT.* In this section of Burns's epistle he gets round to replying to Simson's own, which had asked about the context of 'The Holy Tulzie' (K52), a poem satirizing the conflict between two clergymen in Kilmarnock, both of the orthodox party in the church, Alexander Moodie and John Russel (see notes to p. 25, l. 102, p. 27, l. 184). The 'Postscript' here is a straightforward allegory of orthodoxy's conflict with theological revisionism, and nothing to do with the intra-party conflict in Kilmarnock ridiculed in the earlier poem.

l. 112 and footnote. *new-light; Dr. TAYLOR of Norwich.* John Taylor (1694–1761), minister of a Presbyterian congregation in Norwich in the east of England, 'a profound influence on Scottish theology' and a 'totem to the liberal wing of the Kirk' (Kidd, 'Scotland's Invisible Enlightenment', 48) through his work *The Scripture-Doctrine of Original Sin proposed to free and candid Examination*, published in 1740 (Burns mentions reading this book in the biographical letter to John Moore of 2 August 1787 reproduced in Appendix 1, p. 262). English Presbyterians, like their Scottish co-religionists, held to the Calvinist theology summarized in the Westminster Confession of Faith (see note to p. 95, ll. 39–40 and *passim*), which placed great emphasis on the inherent sinfulness of human nature unless redeemed by the grace of God. Taylor's book rejected this by confirming common-sense notions of innocence and guilt: 'And therefore if we understand, that it is *unjust*, that the Innocent should be under Displeasure, or a Curse . . . then God understands it to be so too. And pray, consider seriously what a God he must be, who can be displeased with, and curse his innocent Creatures, even before they have a Being' (p. 151). This move of course involves assessing God's intentions by the standards of human justice and rationality, and for orthodox Calvinism such faculties were as fallen, and thus as inadequate, as every other aspect of human nature. Taylor argues, on the contrary, that while the Genesis account of the Fall speaks of God punishing Adam and Eve with mortality, there is 'Not one Word of a Curse upon their Souls, upon the Powers of their Minds, their Understanding and Reason. Not one Word of darkening or weakening their rational Powers; not one Word of clogging those with any additional Difficulties' (19). Burns adopts one use of 'New Light' current in the period, to name the illumination that human reason can shed on God's purposes in the eyes of the Kirk's modernizing, 'moderate' faction; 'New Light' or 'New Licht' can mean other things in other contexts.

110 l. 133. *Some herds*. Burns picks up the traditional figure of clergymen as shepherds, their congregations as flocks, also deployed in 'The Holy Tulzie'. The particular 'herds' referred to in this line are the moderate ministers.

l. 145. *it gaed to sticks*. It went to cudgels; that is, it got violent.

111 l. 153. *took the sands*. To 'take the sands' is 'to make for the sea, to flee the country, to "clear out"' (*DSL*).

l. 168. *By word an' write*. By word of mouth, and in writing: as Kinsley notes, 'an old conjunction'.

l. 171. *things they ca' balloons*. A very recent invention. James Tytler had made the first balloon flight in Britain in Edinburgh in 1784, and the Italian pioneer Vincenzo Lunardi made several flights in Scotland in 1785.

l. 182. *moonshine*. Here, 'vain, empty, foolish; worthless' (*OED*).

112 *Epistle to J. R*******, *enclosing some Poems*. K47. John Rankine (d. 1810) was tenant of Adamhill farm, Tarbolton. His friendship with Burns dates from the period of the family's tenure of nearby Lochlie (Rankine was, like Burns, a member of the Tarbolton Masonic Lodge: see notes to 'The Farewell', below), though this poem, Burns's first verse epistle, dates from after Burns and his family moved to Mossgiel. It is not known which poems originally accompanied the present text to Rankine. It was however the third poem sent by Burns to John Kennedy, factor to the Earl of Dumfries (after 'The Cotter's Saturday night' and 'To a Mountain-Daisy) in May 1786: the accompanying letter announces that 'In about three or four weeks I shall probably set the Press agoing' with his first printed work (L30 [3], 16 May).

l. 2. *cocks*. 'Cock' here in the sense of 'one who fights with pluck and spirit. Hence a familiar term of appreciation among the vulgar' (*OED*).

112 l. 4 footnote. *A certain humorous dream of his was then making a noise in the world.* The 1787 Edinburgh and subsequent editions change 'world' for the more modest 'country-side'. In explanation of the dream, Cunningham passes on the story of Rankine and his landlord, named only as 'Lord K—', who 'was in the practice of calling all his familiar acquaintances "brutes," and sometimes "damned brutes."—... Once, in company, his lordship having indulged in this rudeness more than his wont, turned to Rankine and exclaimed, "Brute, are ye dumb? have ye no queer, sly story to tell us?"—"I have nae story," said Rankine, "but last night I had an odd dream."—"Out with it, by all means," said the other. "Aweel, ye see," said Rankine, "I dreamed I was dead, and that for keeping other than good company on earth I was damned. When I knocked at hell-door, wha should open it but the deil; he was in a rough humour, and said, 'Wha may ye be, and what's your name?'—'My name,' quoth I, 'is John Rankine, and my dwelling-place was Adam-Hill.'—'Gae wa' wi',' quoth Satan, 'ye canna be here; ye're ane of Lord K—'s damned brutes—hell's fou o' them already!' " This sharp rebuke, it is said, polished for the future his lordship's speech' (Cunningham Vol. II, 283–4).

l. 5. *Korah-like.* In Numbers, Korah leads the rebellious sons of Levi against the authority of Moses. Moses announces that the Lord will make an example of them: 'And the earth opened her mouth, and swallowed them up, and their houses, and all the men that appertained unto Korah, and all their goods. They, and all that appertained to them, went down alive into the pit, and the earth closed upon them; and they perished from among the congregation' (16: 32–3).

l. 9. *mak a devil o' the Saunts.* The 'saunts' are the orthodox in religion. Kinsley connects this to another story of Rankine's humour, apparently passed on by his youngest daughter, and related by Robert Chambers: 'Rankine amused the fancy of Burns by a trick which he played upon a "sanctimonious professor" [i.e. one professing a religious life] whom he invited to a jorum of toddy in his farm-house. "The hot-water kettle had, by pre-arrangement, been primed with proof-whisky, so that the more water Rankine's guest added to his purpose of diluting it, the more potent the liquor became" ' (Wallace Vol. I, 120).

l. 23. *unregenerate.* Applies to those not redeemed by the grace of God: see note to p. 95, l. 50.

113 l. 36. *Bunker's hill.* That is, at the Battle of Bunker Hill near Boston in 1775, early in the American Revolutionary War. A victory on the field for the British army, but at such cost that it served as a victory for the rebels in terms of propaganda and morale.

ll. 37–72. *'Twas ae night lately, in my fun . . . An' thole their blethers.* What follows is an allegory of Burns's affair with Elizabeth Paton, a servant-girl, in 1784; her pregnancy; its discovery by the church authorities; and Burns's punishment by them for 'fornication': sex out of wedlock.

l. 47. *the Poacher-Court.* That is, the Kirk Session: the minister and the elders of a parish, responsible for supervising the morals of the congregation.

l. 54. *An' pay't the fee.* As a punishment for fornication, both parties had to take their place in the 'stool of repentance', seats raised or in a gallery in front of the pulpit, there to be publicly admonished by the minister on three successive Sundays; the man also had to pay a fine. See Burns's account of this experience in 'The Fornicater' (included in this volume).

l. 61. *As soon's the clockin-time is by.* That is, as soon as Elizabeth has had the child. Burns will celebrate this event in 'A Poet's welcome to his love-begotten Daughter' (included in this volume).

l. 65. *the buckskin kye.* 'Buckskin' is a term used of Americans. Kinsley suggests that the 'kye' (cattle) 'are probably plantation slaves'.

114   l. 71. *a yellow George.* A guinea, a gold coin displaying the monarch's head, worth 21*s*.

l. 75. *pennyworths.* That is, 'money's worth, value for money, return for one's payment or trouble' (*OED*).

Song [It was upon a Lammas night]. K8. The three songs included at this point in the Kilmarnock edition are among Burns's earliest compositions: see the biographical letter to John Moore of 2 August 1787 reproduced in Appendix 1, p. 264.

Tune: Corn Rigs are bonie.

On the account of James Dick, the origins of this tune seem to lie in London, where it appears in a 1680 play by Thomas D'Urfey with a song called 'Sawney was tall and of noble race'; as 'A Northern Song' in a 1681 collection; as 'Sawney will never be my love again' in 1685; and the tune alone is titled 'Sawney' in 1687 (*Songs of Robert Burns*, ed. Dick, 353). 'There was, in London in the 1680s, a flourishing genre called

"Scotch songs"; these were somewhat debased popular songs of allegedly Scottish origin, some with fake tunes, all with fake words, and Londoners liked them because they were refreshingly different from the classical productions of Purcell and Lully.' The male character in these songs is usually called 'Sawney', the name for a stage-Scotsman (Johnson, *Music and Society*, 130–1). The tune became popular in Scotland under the present title as the setting for the closing song of Allan Ramsay's 1725 pastoral comedy *The Gentle Shepherd*, 'My Patie is a lover gay', included in the first volume of *The Scots Musical Museum* as song 93 (from which the score above is adapted). Burns could have found the score in several of the collections, including James Oswald's *Caledonian Pocket Companion*, Vol. II (1745), 22.

114 l. 4. *I held awa to Annie*. *DSL*'s meanings for 'haud awa' are 'to keep away, keep out or off' and 'to continue on one's way, go away' (though these are listed as east-coast usages).

l. 5. *tentless heed*. Reading 'heed' as the English word, it has been suggested (e.g. in Wallace Vol. I, 97) that this is an oxymoron, 'tentless' meaning, precisely, 'heedless'. The Kilmarnock edition of 1786, and the first Edinburgh edition of 1787, give the final word as 'head', and Wallace suggests that the intended word is the Scots 'heid', meaning 'head', but pronounced like 'heed'. Against this is the use in both editions of 'tentless heed' in 'To J. Smith', l. 55. Following this precedent; because 'head' invites a mistaken pronunciation from the modern reader; and in the absence of any textual authority for 'heid', I take the present reading from the 1793 and 1794 editions.

115 l. 23. *That shone that hour so clearly*. This reading is from the 1787 Edinburgh and subsequent editions, which change the Kilmarnock edition's 'night' to 'hour' to avoid a repetition of 'night' in the following line.

Song, composed in August. K2.

Tune: I had a horse, I had nae mair.

Very slow

The tune was published, with its traditional words, as song 185 in *The Scots Musical Museum*, and the score above is adapted from this version. The present song was republished as song 351 in *The Scots Musical Museum* set to a different tune, 'When the King comes o'er the water', and re-titled with its first line. For the *SMM* version Burns altered some of the vocabulary in the ways listed below, mostly by substituting Scots words for English ones. George Thomson substituted 'sportsmen's' for 'slaught'ring' and added three lines to the end of each stanza to make it fit a third tune, 'Ally Croaker', to produce song 93 in the *Select Collection* (1799).

ll. 1–2. *slaught'ring guns | Bring Autumn's pleasant weather.* The open season for red grouse ('muir-fowl') began, then as now, on 12 August; for partridge, on 1 September. Kinsley observes that Burns is remembering two lines from Alexander Pope's description of Autumn in *Windsor-Forest* (1713): 'When milder Autumn Summer's Heat succeeds' (l. 97; Pope 198) and 'With slaught'ring Guns th'unweary'd Fowler roves' (l. 125; Pope 199).

l. 3. *And.* Deleted in the 1787 and subsequent editions of *Poems*.

l. 9. *The Partridge loves the fruitful fells.* 'The Paitrick lo'es the fruitfu' fells' in *SMM*.

l. 10. *The Plover loves.* 'The Plover lo'es' in *SMM*.

116 l. 11. *The Woodcock haunts the lonely dells.* These are 'lanely dells' in *SMM*. Another echo of *Windsor-Forest*, as Kinsley notes: 'And lonely Woodcocks haunt the watry Glade' (l. 128; Pope 199).

l. 14. *The path of man.* 'The path o' man' in *SMM*.

ll. 19–23. *Some social join . . . Tyrannic man's dominion; | The Sportsman's joy.* For the contrast of 'social' nature and 'man's dominion' see note to p. 72, ll. 7–8. Kinsley notes that this opposition also occurs in Thomson, where 'the rude clamour of the sportsman's joy' is rejected as a subject for poetry: his muse is instead 'most delighted when she social sees | The whole mixed animal creation round | Alive and happy', unlike 'the steady tyrant, man' ('Autumn', ll. 360, 381–3, 390; Thomson 98–9).

l. 24. *The flutt'ring, gory pinion.* Another image adapted from Pope's 'Windsor-Forest', as Kinsley observes: the shot pheasant 'Flutters in Blood, and panting beats the Ground' (l. 114; Pope 199).

l. 30. *the charms of Nature.* The 'charms o' Nature' in *SMM*.

l. 32. *ev'ry happy creature.* Becomes 'ilka happy creature' in *SMM*.

l. 34. *Till the silent moon.* 'While the silent moon' in *SMM*.

l. 35. *I'll grasp thy waist.* 'I'll clasp thy waist' in *SMM*.

l. 36. *how I love thee.* Becomes 'how I lo'e thee' in *SMM*.

Song [From thee, Eliza, I must go]. K9.

Tune: Gilderoy.

The tune takes its name from a seventeenth-century English ballad about a Highland outlaw: this tune seems to become attached to it in Scotland a bit later (*Songs of Robert Burns*, ed. Dick, 359–60). Burns could have found the score in several of the collections, including James Oswald's *Caledonian Pocket Companion*, Vol. V (1753), 20; the score given here is adapted from song 66 of *The Scots Musical Museum*. Burns's lyric was set to another tune and republished in George Thomson's *Select Collection of Original Scotish Airs* for 1793 (song 15).

117 l. 13. *latest*. That is, last.

The Farewell. To the Brethren of St. James's Lodge, Tarbolton. K115.

Tune: Good night and joy be wi' you a'.

The tune is that of the Scottish traditional song of parting (until it was replaced, largely thanks to Burns, by 'Auld Lang Syne'). Burns would have found the score in James Oswald's *Caledonian Pocket Companion*, Vol. IV (1752), 32: the score given here is adapted from

The Scots Musical Museum. At Burns's request, Johnson ended the *Museum* with this as song no. 600, giving the traditional words as part of the score, followed by Burns's verses. The traditional words are as follows:

> The night is my departing night,
>   The morn's the day I maun awa:
> There's no a friend or fae o' mine
>   But wishes that I were awa.—
> What I hae done, for lake o' wit,
>   I never, never can reca':
> I trust ye're a' my friends as yet,
>   Gude night and joy be wi' you a'!

But instead of following this rhyme scheme, with every second line rhyming, Burns uses the B rhyme of the first quatrain as the A rhyme of the second quatrain to produce the ballade stanza already used in 'The Lament'.

On Freemasonry, see note to p. 31, l. 79. Burns joined the Tarbolton Lodge in 1781, and was elected Depute Master in 1784. The occasion of the poem is Burns's prospective departure for Jamaica, also anticipated in 'On a Scotch Bard gone to the West Indies'.

l. 3. *Ye favored, ye enlighten'd Few.* The second 'ye' appears in neither the 1786 Kilmarnock nor 1787 Edinburgh editions. I take this reading from the 1793 version: necessary for the metre, unless 'favored' is given three syllables.

118 l. 11. *honour'd with supreme command.* As Depute Master Burns would have chaired meetings in the absence of the Grand Master.

l. 13. *that Hieroglyphic bright.* Freemasonry is very fond of symbols and diagrams, interpreted allegorically.

l. 20. *ARCHITECT Divine.* Freemasonry imagines God in terms consistent with the craft from which it claims descent and borrows its symbols (such as, in the following two lines, the plumb-line used by builders to establish a true vertical).

l. 25. *YOU.* The person wearing the '*highest badge*' of Grand Master of the Tarbolton Lodge was Captain James Montgomerie of Coilsfield, local landowner and one of the Montgomerie family mentioned in l. 57 of 'The Author's earnest cry and prayer' (see note to this line on p. 288). One of the major attractions of Freemasonry was that it could bring a member of an influential noble family like Montgomerie, and a struggling tenant farmer like Burns, into mutually respectful social contact.

EPITAPHS AND EPIGRAMS. This title does not appear at this point in the Kilmarnock or Edinburgh editions; it is inserted to correspond with the heading in the Contents.

Epitaph on a henpecked Country Squire; Epigram on said occasion; Another. K96, K97, K98. These are the only verses in the Kilmarnock edition of 1786 to be omitted in the Edinburgh edition of 1787 and subsequently. The 'henpecked' squire was, according to a note Burns made in a copy of these poems, William Campbell of Netherplace (the 'N**********' of the third of these verses), near Mauchline (Kinsley).

The first stanza of the third poem repeats a story told of Artemisia II of Caria in western Anatolia (d. 350 BC).

119 On a *celebrated ruling Elder*. K32.

l. 1. *Sowter ****.* A sowter or souter is a cobbler. The missing name is presumably 'John'.

On a noisy Polemic. K33. 'Polemic' here is in the now very unusual sense of polemicist: 'a person who argues or writes in opposition to another, or who takes up a controversial position; a controversialist' (*OED*). 'Jamie' is James Humphrey (d. 1844), a stonemason in the Mauchline-Tarbolton area, and a theological sparring-partner of the poet's.

On Wee Johnie. K34. Probably, suggests Kinsley, John Wilson, schoolmaster and clerk to the Kirk Session in Tarbolton.

120 *For the Author's Father.* K35. On the death of William Burnes, see Introduction to this volume.

l. 8 and footnote. *'For ev'n his failings lean'd to Virtue's side'.* 'Thus to relieve the wretched was his pride, | And even his failings leaned to virtue's side': the village parson from Oliver Goldsmith's *The Deserted Village*, ll. 163–4 (Lonsdale 683).

For R.A. Esq. K36. For Robert Aiken, see headnote to 'The Cotter's Saturday night', p. 306.

For G.H. Esq. K37. For Gavin Hamilton, see headnote to 'A Dedication to Gavin Hamilton', p. 316.

l. 2. *canting wretches.* Specifically, Mauchline Kirk Session, with whom Hamilton had 'a long-running feud' (Crawford, *The Bard*, 170). See headnote to 'Holy Willie's Prayer', p. 378.

A Bard's Epitaph. K104. Thomas Gray ends 'An Elegy Written in a Country Churchyard' (1751) with an 'Epitaph' which seems to be for the poet (Lonsdale 138–40); Alexander Pope ends 'Elegy to the Memory of an Unfortunate Lady' (1717) by imagining his own eventual death (Pope 264).

121 l. 8. *Who, noteless, steals the crouds among.* The image of the poet is borrowed from Shenstone, who contrasts him with the self-advertising 'fool': 'But ill-star'd sense, nor gay nor loud, | Steals soft, on tip-toe, through the crowd'. 'The Progress of Taste; or, the Fate of Delicacy. A Poem on the Temper and Studies of the Author; and how great a Misfortune it is for a Man of small Estate to have much Taste', ll. 41–2 (Shenstone Vol. I, 264).

l. 11. *frater.* Brother (Latin), comrade (*OED*).

From *Poems, Chiefly in the Scottish Dialect* (Edinburgh, 1787)

For the circumstances of this volume's publication, see Introduction. It included all the poems of the Kilmarnock edition except the epitaph and epigrams on a hen-pecked country squire, plus 19 additional poems, of which five are included here. It also included a new dedication, a list of 1,527 subscribers,

a greatly expanded glossary (on which the present volume's is based), and a fron-
tispiece with an engraving of the poet, reproduced here. There were two print-
ings: during the printing of the second batch of sheets, after the type for the first
batch had been broken up, it was decided to extend the print-run; the type for
the first batch was re-set, and discrepancies inevitably crept in. The two print-
ings are known by one of these discrepancies, at l. 45 of 'To a Haggis', where
'skinking' became 'stinking'. The present texts follow the 'skinking' copy.

122 *Frontispiece.* The publisher of the Edinburgh edition, William Creech,
commissioned a half-length portrait of Burns in oils by Alexander
Nasmyth (1758–1840), which is now the best-known image of the poet.
This engraving was based on Nasmyth's painting, but Burns also sat for
the engraver, John Beugo, and it may be the better likeness. For the vast
majority of Burns's early readers, the engraving, not the painting, pro-
vided their only idea of the poet's appearance.

123 *Dedication. To the Noblemen and Gentlemen of the Caledonian Hunt.* The
Caledonian Hunt was a sporting and social association for the Scottish
aristocracy and gentry, organizing (for example) balls and race meetings.
At the instigation of the Earl of Glencairn (see headnote to 'Lament for
James, Earl of Glencairn', p. 359) the Hunt subscribed collectively to a
second edition of Burns's poems: it is allocated 100 copies at the top of the
list of subscribers.

*as the prophetic bard Elijah did Elisha . . . and threw her inspiring mantle over
me.* The Lord tells the aged prophet Elijah to anoint Elisha as his succes-
sor, and he finds him 'plowing with twelve yoke of oxen before him, and he
with the twelfth: and Elijah passed by him, and cast his mantle upon him'
(1 Kings 19: 19).

125 *The Brigs of Ayr.* K120. Work began in May 1786 on a new bridge across
the river at Ayr to carry the ever-increasing traffic of this expanding
commercial centre. This poem is dedicated to merchant and banker
John Ballantine (1743–1812), the town's Dean of Guild, the burgh magis-
trate responsible for the regulation of trade, and an initiator of civic
improvements such as this. Ballantine had offered to help Burns when it
looked possible that a second edition of the *Poems* might be published at
Kilmarnock.

The most obvious model for a dialogue between parts of the public
highway is Robert Fergusson's 'Mutual Complaint of Plainstanes and
Causey'. Here Burns's couplets pair iambic pentameter lines rather than
the tetrameters used in that poem (and familiar in Burns's work from 'The
Twa Dogs'); following instead the model of other dialogues from
Fergusson's *Poems on Various Subjects* (1779), 'The Ghaists' and 'A Drink
Eclogue'. But Burns also uses a twelve-syllable line (an alexandrine) in
this poem, often to end his paragraphs.

l. 12. *mercenary Swiss.* Switzerland, like some other poor, mountainous
countries, had a history of exporting soldiers for hire, and had long been a
by-word in this way.

125 l. 13. *close.* 'The closing passage of a speech, argument etc.' (*OED* 1b).

l. 18. *honest Fame.* Kinsley notes precedents in the last line of Pope's 'Temple of Fame' (1715): 'Oh grant an honest Fame, or grant me none!' (l. 524; Pope 188); and towards the end of Goldsmith's 'Deserted Village' (1770), where poetry is 'Unfit, in these degenerate times of shame, | To catch the heart, or strike for honest fame' (ll. 409-10; Lonsdale 694).

l. 33. *The death o' devils, smoor'd wi' brimstone reek.* Burns's language, suggests Kinsley, recalls the end of William Dunbar's 'Dance of the Sevin Deidly Synnis' (*c.*1507), where the Gaelic damned so deafen the Devil 'That in the deipest Pot of Hell | He smorit them all with Smuke' (Ramsay's version in *The Ever Green* [1724], Vol. II, 246).

126 l. 57. *Dungeon-clock.* The 'New' or 'High' Tolbooth in the Sandgate combined, as was usual, meeting-space for the council above, the town jail below, and a belfry; a steeple had been added in 1726. No longer standing.

l. 58 and footnote. *Wallace-Tow'r.* Also known as the 'Auld Tower', an old fortified house on the High Street to which a belfry had been added in 1731. There seems to be no historical basis for its association with William Wallace. Not the building of this name on the same site today. Burns's footnote refers to 'Dungeon-clock' as well as 'Wallace Tow'r'.

l. 62. *The silent moon shone high o'er tow'r and tree.* Echoes the opening verse of 'Mary's Dream' by John (a.k.a. Alexander) Lowe (1750-98), later collected as song 37 of *The Scots Musical Museum*: 'The moon had climb'd the highest hill | which rises o'er the source of Dee, | And from the eastern summit shed | her silver light on tow'r and tree'.

l. 66. *The clanging sugh of whistling wings.* As Kinsley observes, Pope's translation of Homer's *Odyssey* has Jove's eagles 'clang their wings, and hovering beat the sky' (II, l. 176).

127 l. 71. *warlock.* Apparently in *OED*'s weaker Scottish sense of 'magician, conjurer': see following note.

l. 74. *the sp'ritual folk.* In a letter of 18 November 1786 Burns mentions 'those visionary Bards . . . who hold commerce with aerial beings' (L56).

l. 75. *Fays, Spunkies.* Fairies and will-o'-the-wisps.

ll. 77-8. *of ancient Pictish race,* | *The vera wrinkles Gothic.* 'Gothic' here might mean, as later at l. 107, 'medieval, pre-modern' in a general sense. The Auld Brig was built in 1470, but its style is not specifically Gothic in the architectural meaning of the term. Some early eighteenth-century accounts describe the Picts (the 'Caledonians' encountered by the Romans) as 'Gothic' in an ethnic sense, speaking a Germanic language and originating from Northern Europe: for example, Robert Sibbald in *The History, Ancient and Modern, of the Sheriffdoms of Fife and Kinross* (1710) argues that 'the *Picts* . . . were of a *Gothish* Extract' (p. 18). Burns picks up on this at l. 97. The more obvious assumption, that they were of the same Celtic stock as the other inhabitants of ancient Britain, was also current.

l. 82. *ane Adams.* Robert Adam (1728–92), the great Scottish architect, based in London since 1758, although his plan for the bridge had not been taken up, and it was being constructed instead to a design by its builder, Alexander Steven.

l. 83. *five taper staves.* This is obscure. The New Bridge had five arches, and this line may imagine them, or the scaffolding holding them up during construction, in terms of the staves of a barrel.

l. 84. *virls an' whirlygigums.* Presumably the neo-classical decoration gracing the upper part of the bridge.

l. 97. *Vandal.* That is, barbarian: the Vandals were the Germanic tribe who sacked Rome in 455.

128 ll. 115–18. *Coil . . . Lugar . . . Greenock . . . Garpal.* Tributaries of the Ayr.

l. 134. *Supporting roofs, fantastic, stony groves.* A manuscript copy has a dash in place of the first comma, making it clear that fantastic, stony groves are supporting roofs, rather than stony groves supporting roofs fantastic.

129 l. 140. *the second dread command.* 'Thou shalt not make unto thee any graven image, or any likeness of any thing that is in heaven above, or that is in the earth beneath, or that is in the water under the earth' (Exodus 20: 4).

ll. 146–9. *Cuifs of later times . . . unblest with resurrection!.* Even while mocking medieval monasticism, the enlightened New Brig gets in a dig at the manners fostered by the orthodox Calvinist clergy, and praises Ayr for choosing moderate ministers instead.

l. 150. *yealings.* Contemporaries by age (*OED*).

l. 152. *Proveses . . . Bailie.* That is, Priors (of monastic houses); and a magistrate in a Scottish town.

l. 154. *Deacons . . . Conveeners.* Deacon was one of many ecclesiastical ranks that disappeared under Presbyterian church government; a Convener is chairman of council meetings.

l. 159. *Writers.* That is, lawyers, perhaps specialists in canon law, before the Reformation; to be contrasted with the scepticism towards the modern church shown by Burns's lawyer friends like Robert Aiken and Gavin Hamilton.

l. 173. *Harbours.* Improving the quays at the mouth of the Ayr, especially to facilitate the export of coal to Ireland, was an ongoing concern.

130 l. 175. *mak to through.* 'make good, prove' (*OED*). The present instance is *OED*'s only example of this usage, which does not appear in *DSL*.

l. 177. *a shot right kittle.* A tricky target.

l. 183. *'A Citizen'.* See note to p. 40, l. 135.

l. 187. *Seisins.* In Scots Law, a seisin is 'the instrument by which the possession of feudal property is proved' (*OED*).

l. 196. *featly.* 'Nimbly' (*OED*), an archaism used, Kinsley notes, by Dryden and Pope in similar contexts, e.g. 'So featly tripp'd the light-foot Ladies round' (Pope, 'January and May' l. 620; Pope 93).

130   l. 202. *M'Lauchlan*. James McLauchlan, Highland fiddler and composer much in demand among the Ayrshire gentry.

131   l. 213. *The Genius of the Stream*. Recalls the appearance of the river-gods in Milton's *Lycidas* of 1638 ('Camus', for the river Cam in Cambridge, at l. 103), and Pope's 'Windsor Forest' of 1713 ('Old Father *Thames*' at ll. 329–33; Pope 206–7).

l. 216. *tangle*. i.e. seaweed.

ll. 217–24. *Next came the loveliest pair . . . Hospitality with cloudless brow*. Kinsley suggests that this conventional procession of the seasons especially recalls the unfinished Book VII of Spenser's *The Faerie Queene*, canto vii, verses 28–31.

ll. 225–6. *Courage . . . the Feal*. The Water of Fail is a stream running past Tarbolton into the river Ayr, through the Coilsfield estate of Hugh Montgomerie, one of the military family noted at l. 57 of 'The Author's earnest cry and prayer' above. Hugh had served in the American Revolutionary War and was currently M P for Ayrshire.

ll. 227–8. *Benevolence . . . tow'rs of Stair*. Stair House, close to the Ayr a few miles downstream from Coilsfield, was owned by Major-General Alexander Stewart and his wife Catherine; it is the latter, the recipient of two of Burns's manuscript collections, who is figured here.

ll. 229–30. *Learning and Worth . . . Catrine*. Catrine, on the Ayr upstream from Mauchline, was the home of Professor Dugald Stewart; see note to p. 48, l. 90, and headnote to 'Extempore Verses on Dining with Lord Daer', p. 382.

ll. 232–3. *To rustic Agriculture did bequeath | The broken, iron instruments of Death*. 'And he shall judge among the nations, and shall rebuke many people: and they shall beat their swords into plowshares, and their spears into pruninghooks: nation shall not lift up sword against nation, neither shall they learn war any more' (Isaiah 2: 4).

Address to the Unco Guid, or the Rigidly Righteous. K39. The verse form here is the song stanza used in the Kilmarnock volume for another poem of moral advice, 'Epistle to a Young Friend'.

132   *Epigraph*. 'All things have I seen in the days of my vanity: there is a just man that perisheth in his righteousness, and there is a wicked man that prolongeth his life in his wickedness. Be not righteous over much; neither make thyself over wise: why shouldest thou destroy thyself?' (The son of David in Ecclesiastes 7: 15–16). Burns's verse paraphrase of verse 16 makes a rather different point. As McGuirk suggests, the New Testament offers a better gloss on Burns's poem, when the Pharisees bring to Jesus a woman condemned to be stoned to death for adultery, and he says, 'He that is without sin among you, let him first cast a stone at her' (John 8: 7).

l. 8. *still the clap plays clatter*. The clapper of a mill shakes or knocks the hopper to feed grain down to the mill-stones.

133   l. 49. *scan*. In *OED*'s sense 2: 'to judge by a certain rule or standard'; or sense 3, 'examine'. This word is used in a similar context in Goldsmith's

Deserted Village, describing the parson who offers hospitality to vagrants: 'Pleased with his guests, the good man learned to glow, | And quite forgot their vices in their woe; | Careless their merits or their faults to scan, | His pity gave ere charity began' (ll. 159–62; Lonsdale 683). *OED* observes that sense 2 sometimes alludes to its first sense of 'scan', 'To analyse (verse) by determining the nature and number of the component feet or the number and prosodic value of the syllables'.

134 *To a Haggis.* K136. This poem is unique among those added to the *Poems* for the edition of 1787 in having been previously published, in the *Caledonian Mercury* newspaper for 19 December 1786, and the *Scots Magazine* for the following January. A haggis is chopped offal mixed with oatmeal, suet, and onion, seasoned and stuffed in a sheep's stomach, and boiled. A dish native to all of northern Britain in Burns's time, but already thought of as distinctively Scottish.

l. 4. *Painch, tripe, or thairm.* All refer to the stomach or intestines of an animal.

l. 9. *Your pin.* Such a thing as a 'pudding-pin' existed, perhaps used in sealing and serving the haggis. 'Mrs Haliburton . . . sat bolt upright, her lips skewered up and twisted, as if by a pudding-pin' (Christian Isobel Johnstone, *Elizabeth de Bruce* [1827], 226). The term was also used to signify something trivial, perhaps informing the pin's mock-heroic transformation in these lines.

ll. 11–12. *distil* | *Like amber bead.* Oil of amber was distilled from the raw material for medical uses.

l. 19. *horn for horn.* That is, spoon for spoon (spoons were carved from horn).

l. 24. *Bethankit.* A blessing: here, the grace after the meal.

ll. 25–7. *ragout . . . olio . . . fricassee.* All of these are highly seasoned stews of meat and vegetables: olio is of Spanish or Portuguese origin, the other two are French.

135 ll. 39–42. *Clap in his walie nieve a blade . . . Like taps o' thrissle.* Kinsley notes that Fergusson makes a similar case for Scottish fare, in this case kail and bannocks, in 'The Farmer's Ingle': 'On sickan food has mony a doughty deed | By Caledonia's ancestors been done' in defending the country from the Romans and the Danes (ll. 37–8; Fergusson 138). It is also the case made by Burns for whisky in the 'Postscript' to 'The Author's earnest cry and prayer', ll. 163–74.

ll. 43–8. The *Caledonian Mercury* and *Scots Magazine* versions have an alternative last stanza:

> Ye Powers wha gie us a' that's gude,
> Still bless auld Caledonia's brood
> Wi' great John Barleycorn's heart's blude
>   In stowps or luggies;
> And on our board that king o' food
>   A glorious Haggice.

135 *John Barleycorn. A Ballad.* K23. The tradition on which Burns draws in this poem is very old. The personification of barley as Allan-a-Maut, and the allegory of his being fostered, murdered, and his blood invigorating his murderers, appears in a poem in the sixteenth-century Bannatyne manuscript; the fertility myth underlying it is immeasurably older (see Kinsley). Burns expands on his source material by paying more attention to the actual processing of the grain. The malting process described is the first stage of making both whisky and beer, before distillation (for whisky) or the addition of hops (for beer).

136 l. 30. *cudgell'd.* Threshing, to beat the grain from the stalks.

l. 32. *turn'd him o'er and o'er.* Winnowing, to remove the chaff from the grain.

ll. 33–4. *a darksome pit | With water.* Soaking in a tub.

137 ll. 39–40. *as signs of life appeared, | They toss'd him to and fro.* The wet grain is allowed to germinate on the malting floor, and raked to ensure this happens evenly.

l. 41. *wasted o'er a scorching flame.* The germinating grain is then dried in a kiln, completing the malting process.

l. 44. *crush'd him between two stones.* The malt is then ground into 'grist' (to which water and yeast will be added to begin fermentation).

138 *A Fragment.* K38. Also known as 'Ballad on the American War' and by its first line.

Tune: Gillicrankie (better known as Killiekrankie).

Burns transcribed a version of this old Jacobite song (see headnote to 'There'll never be peace', p. 344) for *The Scots Musical Museum* as song 292. As well as the tune, Burns adopts for this poem the internal rhyme used in the first and third lines of its chorus and third verse ('Or I had fed an Athole Gled | On th' braes o' Killiecrankie, O') and makes it a consistent structuring principle in his stanzas.

l. 1. *Guilford.* Frederick North, second Earl of Guilford (1732–92), usually referred to as Lord North, prime minister 1770–82.

l. 2. *hellim.* Simply 'a common Sc. pronunciation of Eng. *helm*, tiller' (*DSL*): this line is the only instance that *DSL* cites.

ll. 3–6. *Ae night, at tea . . . And in the sea did jaw.* To assist the East India Company North allowed it to export its tea direct to the American colonies to be sold by authorized merchants there, without passing through a British port or paying the duty this would incur; instead, a tax would be levied on the tea in America to pay for colonial administration. This programme was imposed without consultation with the colonies themselves; threatened to make colonial government financially independent of the governed; and undercut other traders in tea, both legitimate and illegitimate. On 16 December 1773 protesters in Boston seized the cheap tea from three Company ships and dumped it overboard: the 'Boston Tea Party'.

l. 7. *full Congress.* In September 1774 twelve of the thirteen colonies sent delegates to a Continental Congress in Philadelphia to demand the repeal of punitive legislation passed by North's government in response to events in Boston, and agreed to work for the repeal of all British colonial legislation passed since the end of the war with France in 1763. The Second Continental Congress assembled in May the following year, by which time fighting had already broken out between colonial militias and the British army. It was this Congress which declared the independence of the United States from Britain on 4 July 1776.

l. 9. *Montgomery.* Richard Montgomery was the Irish-born leader of the first campaign by the Continental Army in the Revolutionary War, an invasion of Quebec from Lake Champlain in late 1775.

l. 12. *C–rl–t–n.* General Guy Carlton (1724–1808), the Governor of Quebec, narrowly escaped capture after evacuating Montreal, and Montgomery's forces continued down the St Lawrence ('*Lowrie's burn*').

ll. 13–16. *he, at Quebec . . . Amang his en'mies a', man.* Montgomery was killed in a failed attempt to storm Quebec city on 31 December: 'Montgomery-like . . . Wi' sword in hand' connects him to the militarily-inclined Montgomeries (no relation) of Burns's own county (see note to p. 17, l. 57).

l. 17. *Tammy G–ge.* General Thomas Gage (1721–87), commander-in-chief of the British army in America and Governor of Massachusetts, sent his soldiers out of Boston in April 1775 to capture rebel arms. The skirmishes this provoked at Lexington and Concord began the war, and drove the British force back into Boston, where Gage then found himself penned in by the New England militias.

l. 19. *Willie H––e.* General Sir William Howe (1729–1814), who succeeded Gage as commander-in-chief in October 1775. With 'a deep affection for American colonists' (*DNB*) he pulled his punches in the months after the Declaration of Independence and pursued the possibility of a negotiated settlement from his base at New York. Even when this failed he avoided any strategy likely to crush the rebellion outright, instead mounting an expedition to Philadelphia in the summer of 1777 (Burns's verse obscures this chronology).

138 l. 24. *Sir Loin*. That sirloin of beef is so called because this cut was knighted by an epicure monarch is a 'fictitious etymology' dating back at least to the seventeenth century, says *OED*.

l. 25. *B–rg—ne*. General John Burgoyne (1723–92), commander of the British army in Canada. In the autumn of 1777 he led his forces south via Lake Champlain, planning to link up with Howe's army advancing from New York. But Howe had ignored this plan in favour of his Philadelphia expedition, and Burgoyne instead found American forces under General Gates blocking his way. An attempt to break through was defeated at the battle of Bemis Heights: Burns mentions Simon Fraser, a career soldier from Inverness and one of Burgoyne's brigade commanders, killed in this action. At Saratoga, surrounded and short of supplies, Burgoyne was forced to surrender his entire army to the Americans.

l. 29. *C–rnw–ll–s*. General Charles Cornwallis (1738–1805) led successful operations in the southern colonies in the summer of 1780, but in the autumn of 1781 became trapped in his base at Yorktown on the Virginia coast by a Franco-American army on land and a large French naval force at sea.

139 l. 30. *Buckskins*. The rebel troops (and Americans in general, as at l. 65 of 'Epistle to J. Rankine').

l. 31. *Cl–nt–n's glaive*. General Sir Henry Clinton (1730–95) succeeded Howe as commander-in-chief on the latter's resignation in 1778. He was slow to send forces from New York to relieve Cornwallis at Yorktown: Cornwallis surrendered on 19 October 1781, effectively ending the war. Clinton's ships then turned back without engaging the superior French fleet. 'Glaive' means sword: a poetic archaism.

l. 33. *M–nt–gue*. John Montagu (1718–92), fourth Earl of Sandwich. First Lord of the Admiralty under North; he took the blame for the naval situation which led to the disaster at Yorktown.

l. 35. *S–ckv–lle*. George Sackville Germain (1716–85), Secretary of State for the American Colonies in North's government and 'the driving force in the execution of global strategy' during the war (*DNB*).

ll. 35–6. *wha stood the stoure,* | *The German Chief to thraw*. Sackville's strategy was often frustrated by his generals in America: Wallace glosses 'stoure' as 'brunt of the struggle' and suggests that the 'German Chief' refers to the 'commander of the Hessian auxiliaries' deployed there (Wallace Vol. II, 64). Kinsley instead reads these lines as a reference back to the event that almost finished Sackville's career two decades earlier, his alleged disobedience of a (very imprecise) order from his commanding officer, Prince Ferdinand of Brunswick, at the battle of Minden in 1759; an incident used against him for the rest of his life.

l. 37. *Paddy B–rke*. Edmund Burke (1729–97), MP for Malton: only 'Paddy' because he was Irish.

l. 39. *Charlie F–x*. Charles James Fox: see note to p. 19, l. 109 and *passim*. As country gentlemen lost faith in the North government over its handling of the American war, the opposition scented blood: in the House of Commons, the angry eloquence of Burke and Fox linked this crisis to the ability of the King's ministers to corrupt the independence of parliament through Treasury money and powers of patronage.

l. 41. *R–ck–ngh–m*. Charles Watson-Wentworth (1730–82), second Marquess of Rockingham, who had been prime minister in 1765–6 and then led the anti-North faction that included Fox and Burke in the Commons. When North resigned in March 1782, Rockingham took his place, but died in July of that year.

l. 43. *Sh–lb–rne meek held up his cheek*. William Petty (1737–1805), second Earl of Shelburne, was the leader of the other faction in opposition to North. He entered government in alliance with Rockingham in 1782, and replaced the latter as prime minister on his death, inheriting the thankless task of concluding a peace treaty with the United States and France. His policy in the negotiations was to concede everything demanded by the Americans, to ensure that France, the real enemy, gained next to nothing from their very expensive war. Burns jokingly explains this policy as an example of Christian charity ('resist not evil: but whosoever shall smite thee on thy right cheek, turn to him the other also', Matthew 5: 39). Later events proved its wisdom, but it caused outrage among MPs ('Saint Stephen's Boys': see note to p. 18, l. 71). In the words of one historian, 'The country would accept peace because it needed it, but then condemn the man who had made it' (Watson, *Reign of George III*, 257).

l. 47. *N–rth an' F–x united stocks*. Shelburne resigned in February 1783; Fox then formed a coalition government with the man who had been until recently their common enemy, Lord North, under the nominal premiership of the Duke of Portland.

l. 49. *Clubs an' Hearts were Charlie's cartes*. Perhaps representing Fox's combination of ruthless political manoeuvring and personal charm. For Fox's gambling, see note to p. 19, ll. 113–14.

ll. 51–2. *Till the Diamond's Ace, of Indian race, | Led him a sair faux pas*. Burke and Fox prepared a bill reforming the relationship of the East India Company to the Crown, to prevent governments from using its influence over appointments to Company jobs as a means of controlling MPs. But Fox and Burke were by now widely seen as 'factious': that is, serving only the interest of their own political friends and allies, rather than that of the nation as a whole. In this light, Fox's India Bill looked like an attempt to put Indian patronage permanently in the hands of Foxites, replacing a tyranny of the Crown with a tyranny of party, and the Commons began to turn against them.

l. 53. *placads*. 'Placad' is the Scots equivalent of 'placard', but here with the specific meaning of 'summons, call. Rare. Appar. orig. in some 18th c. Jacobite song adapted by Burns and Scott' (*DSL*).

l. 54. *Chatham's Boy*. William Pitt the younger (see note to p. 16, l. 19) was the second son of William Pitt the elder (see note to p. 43, l. 57), who was made Earl of Chatham in 1766. Pitt had been first brought into government by Shelburne, and resigned with him; now those opposed to the India Bill, including the King, began to line up Pitt as an alternative prime minister.

139   l. 56. *'Up, Willie, waur them a', man!'*. 'Up an' waur them a', Willie' was a Jacobite song on the Battle of Sheriffmuir (see note to p. 57, l. 127), a version of which Burns adapted as song 188 for *The Scots Musical Museum*.

l. 57. *Behind the throne then Gr–nv–lle's gone.* George Grenville, third Earl Temple (1753–1813) communicated to the House of Lords the King's view 'that he should consider all who voted for it [Fox's India Bill] as his enemies'. The Lords duly rejected it on 17 December 1783, allowing the King to dismiss Fox and North and appoint Pitt as First Lord of the Treasury.

l. 59. *slee D–nd–s.* For Henry Dundas see note to p. 18, l. 78. A key ally of Pitt's, working to secure him support among Scottish MPs; the 'Roman wa'' is Hadrian's, running across England to the south of the border with Scotland.

140   ll. 65–6. *N–rth, F–x, and Co. | Gowff'd Willie like a ba'.* Although Pitt was now prime minister, Fox retained control of the Commons, and Pitt's measures were repeatedly voted down there in the following months.

ll. 67–8. *and coost their claise | Behind him in a raw.* The image seems to be of men stripping for a fight. Pitt came to convince as a 'Patriot' politician, governing independently of factional interests, and Fox's majorities in the Commons were steadily whittled away even before the general election in the spring of 1784.

l. 72. *To mak it guid in law.* Established by the constitutionally dubious tactics described in the note to l. 57, Pitt's government was made 'guid in law' by the 1784 election to the extent that it gave him a majority in the Commons of around 120; Dundas's efforts made the Pittite victory particularly convincing in Scotland ('*Caledon*').

Songs from *The Scots Musical Museum*

For a description of this publication, and Burns's role in it, see the Introduction to this volume.

142   *Green grow the Rashes.* K45; song 77 in *SMM* Vol. I (1787), with the attribution 'The words by Mr R. Burns'.

The tune is traditional, recorded as early as 1627, as are the first two lines of the chorus. In Burns's time this seems mostly to have been used for bawdy lyrics: there are two such sets in *The Merry Muses of Caledonia* (see headnote to 'The Fornicater', p. 383), one collected by Burns, and another probably by him, where the chorus continues 'The lasses they hae wimble bores, | The widows they hae gashes, O' (K124). In the present version, sexual pleasure provides a perspective from which the priorities of commercial society can be criticized. These words were also published in the second, Edinburgh, edition of *Poems Chiefly in the Scottish Dialect* in the same year under the title 'Green grow the Rashes. A Fragment' (hence, presumably, the exception to Burns's usual rule of anonymity in *SMM*). The title above the song in *SMM* is the name of the tune (as that above 'Ae Fond Kiss' is 'Rory Dall's Port'), as derived from the chorus of the traditional lyric, which, following a Scottish usage, has 'grows', not 'grow'; the index in *SMM*, like the Edinburgh *Poems*, changes this to 'grow' after Burns's chorus.

143 l. 19. *The wisest Man the warl' saw.* Solomon, the Old Testament king proverbial for wisdom, granted by God 'a wise and an understanding heart' in 1 Kings 3: 12; and who 'loved many strange women' and had 'seven hundred wives, princesses, and three hundred concubines' (1 Kings 11: 1, 3).

144 *The Birks of Aberfeldy.* K170; song 113 in *SMM* Vol. I (1787), with no attribution, but signed 'B'.

The tune is that of an older song, 'The Birks of Abergeldie', recorded in the late seventeenth century and common in the eighteenth-century collections: Johnson also prints its chorus and three, much simpler, stanzas, in which the seducer's promises are more material ('Ye shall get a gown of silk, | And coat of calinmancoe') and the bonny lassie answers back ('Na, kind Sir, I dare nae gang, | My Minnie she'll be angry'). Abergeldie is on Deeside in the north-east; Aberfeldy is on the upper Tay, where Burns wrote this song on his Highland tour earlier in 1787.

146 *The Ploughman.* K205; song 165 in *SMM* Vol. II (1788), with no attribution.

The tune is in several of the eighteenth-century collections. Burns borrows stanzas 2 and 3 from the lyric in David Herd, *Ancient and Modern Scots Songs* (1769), 317–18; like Herd before him he also has an eye on the bawdy version later published in *The Merry Muses of Caledonia* (1799), where ploughing is an extended metaphor for sex.

l. 4. *His bonnet it is blue.* The flat round cap of blue wool was the traditional headgear of Scottish farmers and farm labourers.

147 l. 18. *Saint Johnston.* An old name for Perth.

l. 26. *Corn-mou.* 'A pile of unthreshed grain stored in a barn' (*DSL*).

148 *Rattlin, roarin Willie.* K216; song 194 in *SMM* Vol. II (1788), with no attribution.

Another tune dating from at least the late seventeenth century. The first two stanzas are traditional: Burns adds a third to turn it into a celebration of his own convivial circle.

149 l. 6. *The saut tear blin't his e'e.* A mock-heroic moment. As Kinsley notes, this is a phrase typical of tragic ballads, e.g. *Mary Hamilton*: 'But when she cam to the gallows-foot, | The saut tear blinded her ee' (Child, *English and Scottish Popular Ballads* no. 173, version M, ll. 23–4).

149   l. 17. *Crochallan.* The Crochallan Fencibles was a drinking club founded in Edinburgh by William Smellie, a printer, which met in a tavern in Anchor Close owned by Daunie Douglas. Douglas was famous for singing the Gaelic song 'Crodh Chailein' (Colin's Cattle), which gave the club the first part of its name. The second is the designation for the militias raised for home defence since the American Revolutionary War, members of the club adopting mock-military rank. Mention of the Crochallan here turns 'Willie' into a specific figure, its president 'Colonel' William Dunbar, a lawyer.

150   *Tibbie, I hae seen the day.* K6; song 196 in *SMM* Vol. II (1788), with no attribution, but signed 'X'.

The tune, named in *SMM*, is 'Invercauld's Reel', found in several eighteenth-century collections of Strathspeys. As Kinsley's number indicates, this is one of Burns's earliest pieces, composed when he was 17 or 18.

152   *Ay waukin, O.* K287; song 213 in *SMM* Vol. III (1790), with no attribution.

An old tune, and words that also draw on traditional materials. The second and third verses, with only five syllables in the first line, are scored with an alternative first bar in the text:

154   *My love she's but a Lassie yet.* K293; song 225 in *SMM* Vol. III (1790), with no attribution.

The first stanza is traditional, and had been attached to this tune, 'Miss Farquarson's Reel', before Burns; he turns it into a drinking song, with the last stanza borrowed from another version of 'Green grows the Rashes'.

156   *I Love my Jean.* K227; song 235 in *SMM* Vol. III (1790), with no attribution, but signed 'R'.

The first line is sometimes used as the title. The index in *SMM* comments 'Music by Marshall', but William Marshall's 'Miss Admiral Gordon's Strathspey' is in turn based on an older tune. Written for Burns's wife, Jean (née Armour); George Thomson emphasized this autobiographical context in renaming the tune 'The Poet's ain Jean' for publication in the *Select Collection* in 1805.

158   *John Anderson my Jo.* K302; song 260 in *SMM* Vol. III (1790), with no attribution, but signed 'B'.

A very old tune, long attached to this title; but the version circulating in eighteenth-century Scotland was a wife's brisk complaint about her ageing husband's impotence, as reflected in the lyric included in *The Merry Muses of Caledonia*: 'John Anderson, my jo, John, | When first that ye began, | Ye had as good a tail-tree, | As ony other man', and so on.

Burns slows down the tune, and, as with 'Green grows the Rashes', turns a bawdy song into something very different. Republished in Thomson's *Select Collection* in 1799.

160 *Ca' the ewes to the knowes.* K185; song 264 in *SMM* Vol. III (1790), with no attribution. 'Ewes' must be pronounced as it is usually spelt in Scots, 'yowes'.

Kinsley designates this version the 'A' text. This is a rare instance of Burns 'collecting' a traditional song from an oral source, rather than writing new lyrics, or adapting old ones, for already-published tunes. His source was Revd John Clunie, at the time of his meeting Burns in 1787 a schoolmaster in Fife; writing to Thomson in 1794, Burns says that Clunie 'sung it charmingly; & at my request, Mr Clarke took it down from his singing.—When I gave it to Johnson, I added some Stanzas to the song and mended others, but still it will not do for you' (L636). Right enough, a 'B' text (K456), revised further for Thomson, never appeared in the *Select Collection*. The verse needs to fit in five syllables before the second bar, where the chorus has only three, so the score offers separate notation for this:

162 *The rantin dog the Daddie o't.* K80; song 277 in *SMM* Vol. III (1790), with no attribution, but signed 'Z', which the Index tells us designates 'old verses, with corrections or additions' rather than a particular author: Burns is trying to distance himself from what are clearly his words.

The tune is named in *SMM* as 'East nook o' Fife'. The words follow the pattern of a lyric by Allan Ramsay, 'The Cordial' (Ramsay Vol. III, 40–1), whose tune is known by the first line of Ramsay's song, 'Where will bonny Annie lie', and sometimes proposed as an alternative setting for the present song. I have made consistent the random capitalization of 'wha' in the score. Included, as it stands, in *The Merry Muses of Caledonia*.

163 l. 6. *groanin maut.* 'Ale brewed to celebrate a birth' (*DSL*).

l. 9. *Creepie-chair.* The stool of repentance, in church, where those guilty of 'fornication' stood to be publicly rebuked: see note to p. 133, l. 54. Compare also the same experience narrated from the male point of view in 'The Fornicater' from *The Merry Muses of Caledonia* (in this volume).

164 *Tam Glen.* K236; song 296 in *SMM* Vol. III (1790), with no attribution.

The tune is 'The Merry Beggars', an English tune from the opera *The Jovial Crew* (1731) which had found its way into Oswald's *Caledonian Pocket Companion*. The lyric was republished in the *Select Collection* in 1799 set to 'The Muckin' o' Geordie's Byre': one of Thomson's favourite tunes, but a setting never suggested by Burns.

165 l. 18. *hunder marks ten.* The mark or merk was an old unit of Scottish currency, equivalent to 13s. 4d.

165   l. 21. *the Valentines' dealing.* 'A custom observed on St.Valentine's eve whereby the names of the members of a company of both sexes are written on slips of paper and then chosen by lot by the opposite sex, the person whose name was drawn supposedly becoming the drawer's sweetheart for the year' (*DSL*).

l. 26. *My droukit sark-sleeve.* Another way of discovering your destined partner: 'You go out . . . to a south-running spring or rivulet . . . and dip your left shirt sleeve. Go to bed in sight of a fire, and hang your wet sleeve before it to dry. Ly awake; and sometime near midnight, an apparition, having the exact figure of the grand object in question, will come and turn the sleeve, as if to dry the other side of it' (Burns's note to 'Halloween' in the Kilmarnock *Poems*, p. 61).

166   *My Tochers the Jewel.* K345; song 312 in *SMM* Vol. IV (1792), with no attribution, but signed 'B'.

The tune is 'The Muckin' o' Geordie's Byre', which dates from the early eighteenth century, and is found in many of the song collections of the period. The last four lines of the lyric, and possibly others, are borrowed from traditional materials. Thomson republished this song in the *Select Collection*, 1799.

167   l. 9. *airle-penny.* 'Payment as a token of engagement of services, or as the preliminary to the striking of a bargain' (*DSL*).

168   *There'll never be peace till Jamie comes hame.* K326; song 315 in *SMM* Vol. IV (1792), with no attribution.

The tune is in Oswald's *Caledonian Pocket Companion* Vol. I, 20. Sending this song to his friend Alexander Cunningham, an Edinburgh lawyer, in March 1791, Burns introduces it thus: 'You must know a beautiful Jacobite Air, There'll never be peace till Jamie comes hame.—When Political combustion ceases to be the object of Princes and Patriots, it then, you know, becomes the lawful prey of Historians & Poets.—' He continues, 'If you like the air, & if the stanzas hit your fancy, you cannot imagine, my dear Friend, how much you would oblige me if by the charms of your delightful voice you would give my honest effusion to "The memory of joys that are past," to the few friends whom you indulge in that pleasure.—' (L442).

'Jacobites' were loyalists of the exiled King James, VII of Scotland and II of England (deposed by William and Mary in 1688); and after his death in 1701 of his son, also James (d. 1766). Jacobite sentiment remained widespread in Scottish song even as political commitment to a Stuart restoration shrivelled.

169   l. 5. *The Church is in ruins.* James was driven out in 1688 for being a Catholic, and for having a son and heir whom he could raise a Catholic. But many Jacobites were adherents of the 'national' church as they understood it: high-church Anglicans in England, opposed to tolerance for dissenting Protestant denominations; and Episcopalians in Scotland, opposed to the Presbyterian constitution confirmed for the Church of Scotland in 1690.

l. 7. *we ken wha's to blame.* Either William, or the House of Hanover, the German Protestant princely family on whom the British crown was settled on the death of James VII's childless, but Protestant, daughters Mary and Anne. George of Hanover acceded to the throne on Anne's death in 1714 as George I.

l. 9. *for Jamie drew sword.* John Graham of Claverhouse raised forces for the elder James that defeated government forces at Killiecrankie in 1689; and there were two significant uprisings in Scotland in support of the younger James, in 1715 and in 1745–6.

170 *Rory Dall's Port [Ae fond kiss].* K337; song 347 in *SMM* Vol. IV (1792), with no attribution, but signed 'X'.

SMM gives as the title the name of the tune, which is in Oswald's *Caledonian Pocket Companion,* Vol. VIII, 24: 'port' is Gaelic for 'tune', and Rory Dall is the traditional name of the harper of the MacLeods at Dunvegan on Skye. This tune is very different to the one to which Burns's words are usually sung today.

The song is associated with Burns's relationship with Mrs Agnes McLehose, whom he met in Edinburgh in 1787 when she had been separated from her lawyer husband for many years. Herself a poet, they entered into an intense sentimental relationship conducted mostly through the exchange of letters and verse. Burns adapted two of McLehose's poems for publication as lyrics in *SMM* Vol. II (186, 'Talk not of love' and 190, 'To a Blackbird', both 'By a Lady'), a volume which also included his own song (198) 'Clarinda' sung by 'Sylvander': pseudonyms the pair used in their letters. McLehose broke with Burns on learning of his marriage to Jean Armour later in 1788; but contact was renewed in late 1791, just before McLehose made the dangerous crossing to Jamaica in a failed attempt at reconciliation with her husband. Anticipation of this journey clearly prompted the three poems of farewell to 'Nancy' of which this is one. Yet the letter in which Burns sent them to McLehose frames them in a quite different way: 'I have yours, my ever dearest Nancy, this moment.—I have just ten minutes before the Post goes, & these I shall employ in sending you some Songs I have just been composing to different tunes for the Collection of Songs, of which you have three volumes—& of which you *shall* have the fourth.—' (L486).

172 *Bess and her Spinning Wheel.* K365; song 360 in *SMM* Vol. IV (1792), with no attribution.

The tune is called 'Sweet's the lass that loves me' in the *Caledonian Pocket Companion,* Vol. V, 10 but dates from around 1700.

l. 2. *rock and reel.* The distaff, the tool which held the unspun flax or wool during spinning, and the reel onto which it was spun.

173 l. 9. *the burnies trot.* In the sense of 'to flow rapidly and noisily, to purl, ripple' (*DSL*).

l. 21. *craik.* Corncrake.

174 *Ye Jacobites by Name.* K371; song 371 in *SMM* Vol. IV (1792), with no attribution.

The tune had been published in an English collection of 1719-20: in the list of songs for inclusion in *SMM* drawn up by Burns and Johnson, its title is given as 'Up, Black-nebs by Name, alias Ye Jacobites by Name'. 'Black-neb' is a (usually derogatory) name for a democrat, sympathetic to the aims of the French Revolution (for 'Jacobites' see headnote to 'There'll never be peace till Jamie comes hame', p. 344). Both titles promise a song inciting political action from those content with the mere name of a party: the song delivers something much more ambivalent.

176 *The Banks o' Doon.* K328; song 374 in *SMM* Vol. IV (1792), with no attribution, but signed 'B'.

This, Kinsley's 'B' text, is the song now known under this title, and was published again in Thomson's *Select Collection* in 1798; the earlier 'A' text was written for a different tune. The present tune is 'The Caledonian Hunt's Delight', first published in Niel Gow's second volume of *Strathspey Reels* (1788). For the river Doon, see Map.

177 ll. 7–8. *departed joys,* | *Departed never to return.* Kinsley suggests an echo of Robert Blair's *The Grave* (1743): 'Of Joys departed | Not to return, how painful the Remembrance!' (ll. 109–10).

178 *Such a parcel of rogues in a nation.* K375; song 378 in *SMM* Vol. IV (1792), with no attribution.

The specific 'rogues' accused here are the 31 Scottish Commissioners who negotiated a Treaty of Union between the English and Scottish parliaments in 1706. Headed by the Duke of Queensberry, they included two directors of the Bank of Scotland and the Provost of Edinburgh as well as noblemen. Most stood to gain financially from the terms of the Treaty, which included compensation for the losses incurred by investors in Scotland's calamitous colonial venture in Central America the previous decade. Securing the assent of the Scottish parliament to its own abolition in 1707 also required considerable bribery, so this song's targets can be understood to include a large part of Scotland's politically enfranchised class, as well as the Commissioners. The Union was deeply unpopular with ordinary Scots, and Burns has adapted a song, both words and music, from around that time: the tune is in the *Caledonian Pocket Companion*, Vol. IV, 26.

179 ll. 5–6. *Now Sark runs o'er the Solway sands,* | *And Tweed rins to the ocean.* The river Sark marks the western end of the border between England and Scotland, and runs into the Solway Firth; the river Tweed, as it approaches the North Sea, forms its eastern end.

l. 20. *Bruce and loyal Wallace.* Robert Bruce, King of Scots 1306–29, and William Wallace (d. 1305), leaders of Scotland's Wars of Independence from England.

180 *Afton Water.* K257; song 386 in *SMM* Vol. IV (1792), with no attribution, but signed 'B'.

Burns sent this lyric to his friend and patron Mrs Dunlop in February 1789, with these words: 'There is a small river, Afton, that falls into Nith, near New-Cumnock, which has some charming, wild, romantic scenery on its banks.—I have a particular pleasure in those little pieces of poetry such as our Scots songs, &c. where the names and landskip-features of rivers, lakes, or woodlands, that one knows, are introduced.—I attempted a compliment of that kind, to Afton, as follows: I mean it for Johnson's Musical Museum.—' (L310).

181 ll. 5–6: *Thou stock dove . . . Ye wild whistling blackbirds in yon thorny den.* Kinsley suggests that the birds are borrowed from James Thomson's 'Spring': 'The blackbird whistles from the thorny brake' at l. 604, and 'the stock-dove breathes | A melancholy murmur through the whole' at l. 613; the stock-dove first appears in the second edition of 1730 (Thomson 19).

182 *The Deil's awa wi' th' Exciseman.* K386; song 399 in *SMM* Vol. IV (1792), with no attribution.

In early 1792 Burns sent this song to John Leven, a General Supervisor in the Excise Office at Edinburgh, and thus one of Burns's superiors. The letter is mostly Excise business, but ends, 'Mʳ Mitchell mentioned to you a ballad which I composed & sung at one of his Excise-court dinners: here it is.—' (L500). The tune is in the *Caledonian Pocket Companion*, Vol. VIII, 21, though it also appears in an earlier, English collection: in his letter Burns gives its name as 'Madam Cassey'.

183 l. 3. *Mahoun.* The devil.

l. 15. *the ae best dance.* 'Before a superlative, ae adds emphasis' explains *DSL*.

184 *A red red Rose.* K453; song 402 in *SMM* Vol. V (1796), with no attribution, but the 'Old Set' (see below) is signed 'R'.

The tune is 'Major Graham', from Niel Gow's first volume of *Strathspey Reels* (1784). This three-part tune requested by Burns creates a problem for setting the words: in performance, one of those parts has to be repeated to accommodate all four stanzas. The full lyric, as reproduced here, appears in song 403, an 'Old Set' of these words to a different (but, as Kinsley notes, no more traditional) tune. The lyric borrows from traditional materials but reorganized by Burns. In a letter to Alexander Cunningham with the song in late 1793, Burns describes giving it to Pietro Urbani, the Milanese-born composer and teacher who was himself publishing a collection of Scottish songs in Edinburgh: '—I likewise gave him a simple old Scots song which I had pickt up in this country [i.e. Dumfriesshire], which he promised to set in a suitable manner.—I would not even have given him this, had there been any of Mʳ Thomson's airs, *suitable to it*, unoccupied' (L593A). Thomson republished the song to the same tune in the *Select Collection* in 1799.

186 *Auld lang syne.* K240; song 413 in *SMM* Vol. V (1796), with no attribution, but signed 'Z' (signifying 'old verses, with corrections or additions').

The tune is in the *Caledonian Pocket Companion*, Vol. III, 21, and dates from at least 1700. How much of that lyric is Burns's invention has been debated: the title, and a version of the chorus, had certainly long been in circulation. In his own comments Burns consistently attributes the song to an earlier source. In a letter to Mrs Dunlop in 1788, Burns describes it as 'an old song & tune which has often thrilled thro' my soul'; and at the end of the transcription he adds, 'Light be the turf on the breast of the heaven-inspired Poet who composed this glorious Fragment! There is more of the fire of native genius in it, than in half a dozen of modern English Bacchanalians' (L290). Writing to Thomson five years later he comments, 'The air is but mediocre; but the following song, the old Song of the olden times, & which has never been in print, nor even in manuscript, untill I took it down from an old man's singing; is enough to recommend any air—' (L586). However, McGuirk suggests this may be a deliberate policy of self-effacement on Burns's part, rather than an accurate reflection of how this lyric came into being (McGuirk, p. 251). Thomson published it in the *Select Collection* in 1799 with the tune 'O can ye labour lea' to which it is now usually sung.

188 *Comin thro' the rye.* K560; song 417 in *SMM* Vol. V (1796), with no attribution, but signed 'B'.

Johnson calls this the '1ˢᵗ Sett.' of this song; song 418 gives a second song under this title with variant words and different music. Burns's song is a variation on a widely circulating sexually suggestive *topos*: there is an explicitly bawdy version in *The Merry Muses of Caledonia*. In a manuscript list Burns names the tune as 'Miller's Wedding—a Strathspey'.

190 *O leave novels &c.* K43; song 573 in *SMM* Vol. VI (1803), with the attribution 'By Burns'.

A song from early in Burns's career, as suggested by his reference to himself as 'Rob Mossgiel': Mossgiel was the farm Burns shared with his brother Gilbert in 1783–6, and Scottish farmers were routinely known by the names of their farms in this way. The tune has not been traced.

191 l. 5. *Tom Jones and Grandisons. The History of Tom Jones, a Foundling* (1749) by Henry Fielding; *The History of Sir Charles Grandison* (1753–4) by Samuel Richardson. Tom is a spontaneous and warm-hearted hero whose sexual adventures land him in trouble; Sir Charles is a model of masculine chastity. But the particularities of these texts are less relevant here than Burns's play with the idea, often expressed throughout the century, that reading novels warped young women's expectations of their lives in ways that left them vulnerable to seduction by more knowing men; a possibility often acted out in the plots of novels themselves. In Burns's favourite, Henry Mackenzie's *The Man of Feeling*, for example, prostitute Emily Atkins recounts her original seduction and betrayal by a young gentleman whose figure, address, and conversation 'were not unlike those warm ideas of an accomplished man which my favourite novels had taught me to form' (p. 43).

Songs from *A Select Collection of Original Scotish Airs, for the Voice*

For a description of this publication, and Burns's relationship to it, see the Introduction to this volume.

192 *Duncan Gray came here to woo.* K394; song 48 in *SC* Vol. I (1798). Attribution under the title, 'Written for this work by Mr Robert Burns'.

The tune is traditional, and traditionally used for sexual comedy. There is an explicitly bawdy version in *The Merry Muses of Caledonia*, possibly 'mended' by Burns; Burns also wrote a cleverly suggestive lyric for *The Scots Musical Museum*, Vol. II (1788) song 160, keeping the repeated line of the bawdy version, 'Ha, ha the girdin o't'. This song differs from both earlier versions in replacing premarital sex with 'wooing'; but like Burns's earlier version for *SMM*, and unlike the bawdy version, the story ends with a happy marriage.

196   *O whistle, and I'll come to you, my lad.* K420; song 94 in *SC* Vol. II (1799). Attribution under the title, 'Written for this work by Mr Robert Burns'.
      The first four lines of each stanza, and the tune, are traditional. Burns had already published a very basic version of this song in *The Scots Musical Museum*, Vol. II (1788) as song 106, adding to the first four lines only another repeating four ('Come down the back stairs when ye come to court me; | | And come as ye were na' coming to me').

Other poems and songs published in Burns's lifetime

199   *Written on a window in Stirling.* K166A. These lines were first 'published' by Burns on the window of his room in an inn at Stirling, etched with a diamond-tipped stylus, in August 1787, on his way north to tour the Highlands. But they were copied by other hands and circulated in manuscript, and first printed the following year, as evidence for the prosecution in a 24-page pamphlet, *Animadversions on some Poets and Poetasters of the present age, especially R—T B—S, and J—N L—K. By James Maxwell, Poet in Paisley.* Maxwell (1720–1800) was best known for a metrical version of the Psalms (1773), and attacks Burns for impiety in, for example, 'The Cotter's Saturday night' and 'The Holy Fair'. The present text is then offered on page 8 as 'Another Specimen of the same Author, said to be written on a Window in Stirling'. It is followed by three verse 'answers' to Burns's denunciation of the reigning dynasty. The first, by Revd George Hamilton, begins, 'Thus wretches rail, whom sordid gain | Has dragg'd in faction's gilded chain'; and ends, 'These few rash lines shall damn thy name, | And blast thy hopes of future fame' (ll. 13–14). The other two, 'By another hand', both end by bidding Burns back to his master in hell, and the second contains an outright threat: 'For this thy life in danger stands, | If thou art found within his lands', that is, the King's (ll. 13–14). Burns's poem was already being held against him by potential sponsors in his quest for a job in the Excise (see Introduction). He wrote to Mrs McLehose: 'I have almost given up on the excise idea. . . . I have been question'd like a child about my matters, and blamed and schooled for my Inscription on Stirling window' (L189, 27 January 1788). William Scott Douglas tells the story that, on a return visit two months after the first, Burns went back to the inn 'and dashed out the pane with the butt-end of his riding-switch' (Douglas Vol. II, 309). In the Glenriddell manuscript (see Introduction) Burns's title for 'these imprudent lines' is 'Written by Somebody in the window of an inn at Stirling on seeing the Royal Palace in ruins'.

199 l. 1. *STEWARTS*. The royal family of Scotland from Robert II (r. 1371–90), and of England from the accession of James VI as James I of England in 1603, to Anne (d. 1714). Stirling Castle was the principal base for the Stewart court until the departure of James for London.

l. 2. *for Scotia well*. The version in the Glenriddell manuscript has 'for Scotland's weal': Maxwell may have worked from a corrupted copy, or Burns may have amended the line in the later version (see note to l. 4).

l. 3. *unroof'd*. Burns is referring to the collapse ten years earlier, from natural causes, of the ceiling in the King's Inner Hall, the royal presence chamber (the castle was garrisoned, and not otherwise a ruin).

l. 4. *other's hands*. The manuscript version has 'other hands' and then inserts two additional lines: 'Fallen indeed, and to the earth, | Whence grovelling reptiles take their birth.—' Kinsley suggests that these 'appear to be Burns's addition for the Glenriddell MS'.

l. 6. *A Race, outlandish*. The House of Hanover. With no children surviving the ageing Anne, a 1701 act of the English parliament settled the succession on this German princely family as the nearest Protestants in line, to preclude the restoration of Anne's father, the Catholic James II and VII, deposed in 1688, or his Catholic son. George of Hanover accordingly became George I of Great Britain and Ireland on Anne's death in 1714; his great-grandson, George III, was the reigning monarch in Burns's lifetime.

l. 7. *ideot*. This spelling was still current.

ll. 7–8. *An ideot Race to honour lost, | Who know them best despise them most*. Two major editions, published in 1834 while the throne was still filled by this outlandish race, confessedly omit these lines, condemning their 'severe and improper remarks' (*The Works of Robert Burns*, ed. James Hogg and William Motherwell, Vol. II, 71); 'What was improper in the days of Burns is not proper now' (Cunningham Vol. III, 294). Allan Cunningham does however add Burns's 'Reply' to the Revd Hamilton's 'Answer', and his mocking 'Reproof' to his own poem (K166C), appealing to the legal authority of the great (Scottish-born) English judge, William Murray (1704–93), Earl of Mansfield:

> RASH mortal, and slanderous Poet, thy name
> Shall no longer appear in the records of fame;
> Dost not know that old Mansfield, who writes like the Bible,
> Says the more 'tis a truth, Sir, the more 'tis a libel?

Here Lies Robert Fergusson Poet. K142. Fergusson, Burns's most important inspiration for poetry in Scots, had died penniless in the Edinburgh insane asylum (probably on 17, not 16, October 1774) and been buried in an unmarked grave at Canongate Church. On his first visit to Edinburgh Burns wrote to the Bailies of the Canongate 'for your permission to lay a simple stone over his revered ashes, to remain an unalienable property to his deathless fame' (L81, 6 February 1787). The stone was eventually erected, at Burns's expense, in August 1789, and the present text is taken from the inscription. On the back of the letter to the Bailies Burns wrote a version with two additional stanzas:

> She mourns, sweet, tuneful youth, thy hapless fate,
> Tho' all the pow'rs of song thy fancy fired;
> Yet Luxury and Wealth lay by in state,
> And thankless starv'd what they so much admir'd.

> This humble tribute with a tear he gives,
> A brother Bard, he can no more bestow;
> But dear to fame thy Song immortal lives,
> A nobler monument than Art can show.

These were eventually published in Alexander Smith, *The Poetical Works of Robert Burns* (1865), Vol. I, 348. See also the posthumously published 'Verses, Written under the Portrait of Fergusson the Poet' and 'Ill-fated genius!'

l. 1. *No sculptur'd Marble here.* Still the case, but a bronze Fergusson now strolls out of the gates of the kirkyard: David Annand's statue was unveiled in 2004.

l. 2. *No storied Urn nor animated Bust.* In the manuscript version this is in quotation marks, adapted as it is from Gray's 'Elegy Written in a Country Churchyard': 'Can storied urn or animated bust | Back to its mansion call the fleeting breath?' (ll. 41–2; Lonsdale 125).

Elegy, On the departed Year 1788. K250. Published in the *Edinburgh Evening Courant* for Saturday, 10 January 1789. The *Courant* was a newspaper published three times a week, selling for 3*d.*, in the usual format of a single sheet folded once with text carried in four columns on each page: the outside pages carried mostly advertisements and commercial news, the inside spread mostly foreign and domestic politics and social notices. This poem appeared on page 3 in column 3 and was signed 'Thomas A Linn' (a 'linn' is a waterfall, hence an appropriate pen-name for 'Burns').

200 l. 9. *The Spanish empire's tint a head.* Charles III, King of Spain (b. 1716), had died on 14 December after a 29-year reign.

l. 10. *Bautie.* 'A name given to a dog' (*DSL*).

l. 11. *The tulzie's teugh 'tween PITT and FOX.* William Pitt the younger, the prime minister; and Charles James Fox, the leader of the opposition (see notes to p. 16, l. 19, p. 19, l. 109 and *passim*); on the cause of the 'tulzie' see note to l. 35 below.

l. 14. *to the hen birds unco civil.* Referring to Fox's mistresses.

l. 21. *mony a plack and mony a peck.* Church of Scotland clergy were paid in a combination of money and agricultural produce, mostly oats.

l. 28. *dowielie.* When this poem was republished in Thomas Stewart's *Poems Ascribed to Robert Burns* (1801) this was replaced by 'dowie now'; in R. H. Cromek's *Reliques of Robert Burns* (1808), with 'daviely'. Right enough, 'dowielie' does not appear in the *Dictionary of the Scots Language*, while the two alternatives do; and 'dowf and dowie' is a common pairing. But Burns might be coining a new word, taking the adjective 'dowie' and adding 'lie' to make it an adverb.

200 l. 30. *Embrugh wells are grutten dry*. A hard winter had frozen much of Edinburgh's water supply.

l. 35. *Nae hand-cuff'd, mizzl'd, half-shackl'd Regent*. George III had become mentally incapacitated the previous November. The issue of the *Courant* in which this poem appeared carried, on the facing page, a report of the ongoing 'tulzie' in the House of Commons over the terms on which George's eldest son might be appointed Prince Regent. Fox wanted the younger George granted full monarchical powers; Pitt wanted him 'half-shackl'd' to prevent the prince dismissing Pitt and asking his friend Fox to form a new government (which, the prince assumed, would then pay off his considerable debts). The King recovered before any legislation was passed: Burns wrote an 'Ode to the departed Regency Bill' in March.

201 *On Captain Grose's present Peregrinations through Scotland*. K275. Published in the *Edinburgh Evening Courant* for Thursday, 27 August 1789; once again on page 3 in column 3, and again signed 'Thomas A Linn'.

Francis Grose (1731–91) had published *The Antiquities of England and Wales* in 1772–87, a set of engravings of mostly medieval buildings with accompanying explanatory text. Burns met him on his second trip to Scotland to make sketches and collect information for *The Antiquities of Scotland*, of which the first volume appeared in 1789. They became firm friends and collaborators (see headnote to 'Tam o' Shanter', below). When this poem was included in the two-volume edition of the *Poems* in 1793, the title was amended to 'On the Late Captain Grose's Peregrinations . . .' (Vol. II, 219).

201 l. 1. *Land o' Cakes*. That is, of oatcakes or bannocks.

l. 2. *Frae Maiden-kirk to Johnie Groat's*. Maidenkirk in Wigtownshire is the most southerly of Scottish parishes; John o'Groats in Caithness is traditionally taken as its most northerly community.

ll. 11–12. *an unco slight | O' cawk and keel*. Unusual skill with chalk and pencil, i.e. drawing.

l. 20. *glamor*. Magic. 'When Devil, Wizards, or Juglers deceive the Sight, they are said to cast *Glamour* o'er the Eyes of the Spectator' (glossary to Ramsay's 1721 *Poems*; Ramsay Vol. I, 254).

l. 25. *a sodger bred*. Grose served in the British Army 1747–51, and remained a Captain in the Surrey Militia.

l. 27. *the spurtle blade*. A 'spurtle' can be a flat implement for turning oatcakes, a spatula; but by extension 'a (broad) sword, used jocularly or in disparagement' (*DSL*).

202 l. 32. *gingling jackets*. Mail coats, medieval armour.

l. 38. *Tubalcain*. Zillah's son, 'an instructor of every artificer in brass and iron' (Genesis 4: 22).

l. 40. *Balaam's ass*. Shying away from an armed angel that Balaam can't see, the Lord lets his ass talk back to Balaam when he beats it for this disobedience (Numbers 22: 21–30).

l. 41. *the Witch of Endor*. When Saul gets no supernatural guidance from the Lord, he sends instead for 'a woman that hath a familiar spirit' from Endor (1 Samuel 28).

l. 44. *philibeg*. The *fèileadh beag* (Gaelic) is the kilt, an early eighteenth-century invention.

l. 45. *Abel*. The younger son of Adam and Eve, murdered by his brother Cain in Genesis 4: 8.

203 *Tam o' Shanter*. K321. This poem first appeared in three publications in the Spring of 1791. It was commissioned by Francis Grose (see headnote to 'On Captain Grose's present Peregrinations', p. 352) for the second volume of *The Antiquities of Scotland*, to accompany the etching (included here) and description (see below) for Alloway Church in the Ayrshire section (pp. 199–201); but it was also published in *The Edinburgh Magazine, or, Literary Miscellany*, for March; and in the *Edinburgh Herald* newspaper for 18 March, where it takes up more than two whole columns out of four on the front page. In both periodicals the title is 'Aloway Kirk; or, Tam o'Shanter. A Tale'. The present text is based on Grose's book, this being the context for which the poem was originally written.

Grose's account of Alloway Church is as follows:

> This church stands by the river, a small distance from the bridge of Doon, on the road leading from Maybole to Ayr. About a century ago it was united to the parish of Ayr; since which time it has fallen to ruins. It is one of the eldest parishes in Scotland, and still retains these privileges: the minister of Ayr is obliged to marry and baptise in it, and also here to hold his parochial catechisings. The magistrates attempted, some time ago, to take away the bell; but were repulsed by the Alloites, *vi & armis*.

There is a footnote to the chapter heading which introduces the poem thus:

> This church is also famous for being the place wherein the witches and warlocks used to hold their infernal meetings, or sabbaths, and prepare their magical unctions; here too they used to amuse themselves with dancing to the pipes of the muckle-horned Deel. Diverse stories of these horrid rites are still current; one of which my worthy friend Mr. Burns has here favoured me with in verse.

The poem is contained in this footnote, in two columns; but it is a footnote that takes over almost all of the three pages devoted to Alloway Kirk, with Grose's text only occupying two or three lines along the top of each.

When this poem was included in the two-volume edition of the *Poems* in 1793, Burns added an epigraph: *'Of Brownyis and of Bogillis full is this buke.'* This is l. 18 from the Prologue to Book VI of Gavin Douglas's *Eneados*, his translation of Virgil's *Aeneid* into Scots (completed 1513; a modern edition had appeared in 1710). For Burns's attitude to 'brownies and bogles' see his letter to Dr Moore in Appendix 1, p. 260.

203 l. 1. *chapmen billies.* Pedlars, as in Fergusson's 'Hallow Fair', ll. 28–9: 'Here chapmen billies tak their stand, | An' shaw their *bonny wallies*' (Fergusson 90).

l. 7. *long Scots miles.* See note to p. 64, l. 57.

204 l. 23. *melder.* 'The grinding of one customer's load of corn at a mill' (*DSL*).

l. 28. *the L—d's house.* The name of a pub. This seems to refer to the village inn at Kirkoswald in Carrick (south of the Doon, Tam's part of Ayrshire) run by Jean Kennedy (hence 'Kirkton Jean') and her sister, and known as 'the Leddies' House' after them. But Burns needs a monosyllable here, so we are left to imagine a pub called 'The Lord's House'.

l. 40. *reamin swats.* A conjunction spotted by Kinsley in Ramsay's 'Elegy on Lucky Wood', l. 34 (Ramsay Vol. I, 19).

205 l. 63. *the borealis race.* The aurora borealis, or northern lights.

l. 66. *Evanishing.* A self-consciously 'literary' word, as Kinsley observes, which Burns could have found in the mouth of Sir William in Ramsay's *Gentle Shepherd*, 3. 4. 117: 'Cares evanish like a Morning Dream' (Ramsay Vol. II, 251).

l. 83. *his gude blue bonnet.* The flat round cap of blue wool was the traditional headgear of Scottish tenant farmers and farm labourers.

l. 84. *sonnet.* Here clearly just meaning 'song'. *DSL* suspects that this becomes a Scottish usage only because of its appearance in this line. On the other hand, the English word derives from the Italian *sonetto*, which means 'little song'.

l. 88. *nightly.* As Kinsley notes, in its now-obsolete sense of 'at or by night; during the night' (*OED* 2) rather than 'every night'.

206 ll. 90–6. *Where in the snaw . . . Mungo's mither hang'd hersel.* 'These calamities are to be attributed to witchcraft', observes Kinsley (III, 1358), referring to the (not quite so terrible) misfortunes blamed on Mause in Ramsay's *The Gentle Shepherd*, 2. 3. 31–50, e.g. 'When *Watie* wander'd ae Night thro' the Shaw, | And tint himsell amaist amang the Snaw; | When *Mungo*'s Mear stood still, and swat with Fright, | When he brought East the *Howdy* under Night' (Ramsay Vol. II, 231).

l. 98. *The doubling storm.* In the now-defunct sense of 'resounding, echoing'. Kinsley, and *OED*, offer the precedent of Pope's 'Temple of Fame' (1715), 1. 333: 'Thro' the big Dome the doubling Thunder bounds' (Pope 183).

ll. 99–100. *The light'nings flash from pole to pole; | Near, and more near, the thunders roll.* This is a neo-classical formula borrowed, Kinsley notes, from Dryden and Pope, for example in the latter's translation of the *Odyssey*: 'Then Jove in anger bids his thunder roll, | And forky lightnings flash from pole to pole' (XII, ll. 485–6).

l. 110. *Fair-play.* 'In justice to him' (Kinsley).

l. 116. *cotillon.* Cotillion could name several types of fashionable dance.

l. 119. *A winnock-bunker.* (In) a window-seat (*DSL*).

l. 123. *He screw'd the pipes.* The drones of a bagpipe are tuned by turning them.

l. 131. *gibbet-airns.* The bodies of hanged criminals were hung up in chains on gibbets as a warning to others.

207 l. 132. *Twa span-lang . . . bairns.* Kinsley suggests that this phrase, followed as it is a few lines later by a reference to a 'strangled' child (l. 137), suggests an echo of *The Grave* (1743) by Robert Blair, where the inmates of the churchyard include 'the *Child* | Of a Span long, that never saw the Sun, | Nor press'd the Nipple, strangled in Life's Porch' (ll. 517–19).

ll. 141–2. *awefu' . . . unlawfu'.* Kinsley points out that this rhyme is borrowed from Ramsay, 'A Tale of Three Bonnets', canto I, ll. 173–4: 'Sae tho the Aith we took was awfu', | To keep it now appears unlawfu'' (Ramsay Vol. III, 13).

ll. 143–6. *Three lawyers' tongues . . . in every neuk.* When this poem was included in the two-volume edition of the *Poems* in 1793 these lines were cut, on the advice of Alexander Fraser Tytler, an Edinburgh lawyer and historian, who argued that the shift into social satire distracted from the effect of pure horror.

l. 158. *seventeen-hunder.* 'Hunder' just means hundred, but in weaving more specifically 'a unit for denoting the fineness of a web . . . and hence the fineness of the cloth itself' (*DSL*). The other examples cited by *DSL* are between six and twelve, so seventeen must be very fine indeed.

l. 164. *spean.* Wean, but 'in transferred use, of creating an aversion to food through disgust, fear or the like' (*DSL*).

l. 168. *There was a winsome wench and walie.* Almost quoting, as Kinsley notes, Ramsay's 'A Tale of Three Bonnets', canto I, l. 83: 'She was a winsome Wench and waly' (Ramsay Vol. III, 10).

208 ll. 171–4. *For mony a beast to dead she shot . . . And kept the country-side in fear.* Another of the calamities laid at Mause's door in Ramsay's *The Gentle Shepherd*, 2. 3, is '*Bawsy* shot to dead upon the Green' (Ramsay Vol. II, 231), 'bawsy' being a name for 'a horse or a cow having a white stripe or patch on the face' (*DSL*).

l. 175. *Paisley harn.* Harn is 'coarse linen cloth made from the refuse of flax or hemp' which 'labouring people use for shirts' (*DSL*, quoting a 1795 account). Paisley was a major centre of Scottish textile production: as we learn from ll. 178–9, Nannie's sark has been bought, not home-made.

208 l. 81. *twa pund Scots.* There had been no separate Scottish currency since the union of 1707, at which point the Scottish pound was worth 1s. 8d. in English currency. But the term 'pund Scots' survived to mean this amount: so Nannie's sark has cost 3s. 4d.

ll. 197–202. *As bees bizz out . . . When 'catch the thief!' resounds aloud.* The similes here follow the 'As . . . When . . .' form of the Homeric or epic simile, and, as Kinsley points out, Burns may be borrowing the first two from Pope's translation of the *Iliad* (1715–20): 'As Wasps, provok'd by Children in their Play, | Pour from their Mansions', describing the Greeks pouring from their tents (XVI. 314–15); and 'As when two skilful Hounds the Lev'ret winde', describing the Greek pursuit of a Trojan spy (X. 427).

l. 199. *open.* 'Of a hound: to bay or cry loudly when on a scent or in sight of the quarry' (*OED*).

209 l. 210. *the key-stane o' the brig.* 'It is a well known fact that witches, or any evil spirits, have no power to follow a poor wight any farther than the middle of the next running stream.—It may be proper likewise to mention to the benighted traveller, that when he falls in with *bogles*, whatever danger may be in his going forward, there is much more hazard in turning back' (Burns's footnote in the 1793 edition: Vol. II, 61).

Extempore on some late commemorations of the poet Thomson. K332. First published in *The Edinburgh Gazetteer* newspaper for Friday, 23 November 1792, in the first column on the back page, signed 'Thomas à Rhymer'. This issue of the *Gazetteer* was only its second: bi-weekly publication was planned but at this stage it appeared every Friday, price 3½d. It had been launched by Captain William Johnston (d. 1817), who had helped found the Scottish Friends of the People the previous July, an association, mostly of lawyers and landowners, dedicated to 'restoring our constitution to its original purity' through reforms aimed at preventing the 'corruption' of parliamentarians by governments (Brims, 'From Reformers to "Jacobins"', 35). Since then, a French Republic had been declared, and its army had unexpectedly triumphed over the Prussian and Austrian forces intent on destroying it (the present poem is followed by another, not by Burns, 'On the retreat of the Duke of Brunswick': see note to p. 237, l. 11). This had inspired an explosion of political activity among ordinary people too (see also headnote to 'The Tree of Liberty', p. 403). The many political pamphlets circulating in this period included, in the west of Scotland, some purporting to reproduce thirteenth-century prophecies by Thomas the Rhymer of a time when 'after terrible convulsions in church and state, military, civil and religious despots would be forced to flee in shame' (Brims, 'From Reformers to "Jacobins"', 37): this may inform Burns's choice of pseudonym. Johnson's paper quickly became a crucial 'vehicle for the circulation of radical addresses and motions . . . as well as the dissemination of information about radical activities throughout the British Isles' (*DNB*), and unusually balanced coverage of events of France. Burns was enthusiastic from the start: see his letter to Johnston of 13 November in Appendix 1, p. 267f. The number for 23 November covered, under the headline 'TRIAL OF THE KING', the ongoing debate in the National Convention in Paris regarding the fate of the imprisoned Louis XVI; the establishment of a 'Society of Friends to Liberty and Equality' in Flanders, after the French had driven out its Austrian overlords; and, sharing the back page with this poem, a list of the toasts made at the Revolution Society in Sheffield on the anniversary of the 1688 Revolution in Britain. Although Johnston's paper consistently advocated the reform, not the overthrow, of the British constitution, by February he had been sentenced to three months in prison for reporting a sedition trial. By the end of the year his successor as editor had been charged with seditious libel, and the last issue appeared in January 1794. Burns's connection to the paper threatened to cause him problems, too: see the letter to Fintry dated 5 January 1793 in Appendix 1, p. 271f.

The commemorations to which the poem refers were for James Thomson (1700–48), author of *The Seasons*, at Ednam, his birthplace, in Roxburghshire, in September 1791. They were the idea of David Erskine, Earl of Buchan (1742–1829), who had erected a monument to the poet: Burns wrote a poem for the occasion, as requested, but did not attend.

210   ll. 11–12. *th' unfading garland there,* | *Thy sair-won rightful spoil.* Buchan's event was to culminate in crowning a bust of Thomson with a laurel-wreath. Burns's 'Address, to the Shade of Thomson, on crowning his Bust . . . with Bays' ends with a reference to 'that wreath thou well hast won' (K 331, l. 18).

l. 17. *'To wham hae routh, shall yet be given'.* Matthew, Mark, and Luke all report Jesus's explanation for talking in parables that only some can understand: 'For whosoever hath, to him shall be given, and he shall have more abundance: but whosoever hath not, from him shall be taken away even that he hath' (Matthew 13: 12).

The Rights of Woman. K390. First published in the third issue of *The Edinburgh Gazetteer* (see headnote to 'Extempore on some late commemorations of the poet Thomson', p. 356), Friday, 30 November 1792. The news pages of this number are dominated by coverage of the continuing French campaign in Flanders, speeches in the National Convention in Paris, and the Russian invasion of Poland; the editorial on page 3 begins publication of the 'Scotch Pension list', revealing the incomes paid by the government to various prominent Scots. Burns's poem appears in the first column on the back page, unsigned. This column continues with a letter from his friend and former neighbour Robert Riddell of Glenriddell, signed 'Cato', urging the Scottish landed class to press for constitutional reform, and sent with Burns's poem as explained in the letter to Fintry of 5 January 1793 in Appendix 1, p. 272. Burns also sent a copy of this poem to his friend and patron Mrs Dunlop in a letter of 6 December (see Appendix 1, p. 269); early editors reproduced it in that context, starting with Currie in 1800 (Vol. II, 418–19).

Title. The Rights of Woman by Mary Wollstonecraft (1759–97) had appeared at the start of the year. Wollstonecraft argues against the education for subordination typically given to girls, one that prevents the full development of their talents and virtues.

210 *Subtitle*. Louisa Fontenelle (1773–99) was a well-known actress, at this point working with George Sutherland's company at the theatre which had opened in Dumfries the previous September. A 'benefit night' was a performance from which a share of the box-office takings went to a specified performer; benefit nights were built into the schedules of eighteenth-century theatres. Burns wrote several occasional pieces for the theatre at Dumfries.

l. 2. *the fall of kings*. Louis XVI had been deposed by a popular uprising in Paris on 10 August; a French Republic was declared on 22 September.

l. 3. *While quacks of state must each produce his plan*. Since September, France had been governed by a National Convention elected to debate and decide on a new constitution for the country. The *Edinburgh Gazetteer* pressed for constitutional reform in Britain, but the editorial of the previous issue had warned that, 'Whilst we cease not to remind the people of this country, of the utility, and even absolute necessity, of a Reform in the representation of the Commons, they will not forget that it is only a rational measure we are engaged in indicating. Schemes, splendid and captivating in theory, but impracticable or destructive in execution, may indeed please the imagination whilst reviewing the gay vision, but can have no tendency to serve the real interests of the community' (pp. 2–3).

l. 4. *The Rights of Man*. The title of a book published in two parts (1791, 1792) by Thomas Paine (1737–1809), defending the rational critique of inherited power against Edmund Burke's reactionary polemic, *Reflections on the Revolution in France* (1790). Paine argued for a transformation of the British state far beyond the reforms campaigned for by Johnston, Riddell, and their friends. His book had achieved an unprecedentedly wide readership, with cheap editions selling for 6*d*., and abridgements for 1½*d*., since the government had issued a proclamation against seditious writings in May with the intention of suppressing it. As this issue of the *Gazetteer* reported, Paine was now in Paris, having been elected to the National Convention.

l. 19. *kick up a riot*. Currie's note to l. 24 identifies this with the aristocratic 'roar of Folly and Dissipation' (Burns's words in L645, 29 October 1794) which accompanied the Caledonian Hunt's balls and races: the Hunt had met in Dumfries in the autumn of 1792. But at the same time, elsewhere in Scotland, street disorder had been coming from the other end of the social scale, prompted by the triumph of the French Republic's army in Flanders: see headnote to 'The Tree of Liberty', p. 403. The constitutional reformers of the *Gazetteer*, while also enthused by events on the Continent, were anxious to distance themselves from popular law-breaking. This issue of the paper reports the meeting of 'The Convention of Delegates from the Societies of the Friends of the People in and around Edinburgh' on 28 November which elected as vice-president Thomas Muir of Hunters Hill, one of the founders of the Scottish organization (for which see headnote to 'Extempore on some late commemorations of the poet Thomson', p. 356). This meeting also resolved to publish its decision 'That the name or names of any person or persons belonging to the Associated Friends of the People, who may be found guilty of rioting, of creating or aiding sedition or tumult, shall be expunged from the books of the Society' (p. 3, col. 4).

211 l. 21. *Gothic.* Here, 'barbarous, rude, uncouth, unpolished, in bad taste' (*OED*).

l. 24. *Such conduct neither spirit, wit, nor manners.* In Currie's edition there is a footnote to this line: 'Ironical allusion to the saturnalia of the *Caledonian Hunt*' (see note to Dedication to the Edinburgh *Poems*, p. 331).

l. 38. *Ah! cà ira!.* The title of the French revolutionary anthem is 'Ça ira' ('So it will be'): the *Gazetteer* presumably lacked cedillas in its type. In the letter to Mrs Dunlop with this poem, Burns notes that there had been calls for this song in place of 'God Save the King' in the Dumfries theatre (see Appendix 1, p. 269).

Lament for James, Earl of Glencairn. K334. First published in the third edition of *Poems, Chiefly in the Scottish Dialect*, an expanded version of the Edinburgh edition published in two volumes by Creech in 1793; this poem appears in Vol. II, pp. 188–93.

James Cunningham, fourteenth Earl of Glencairn (1749–91), was Burns's most important early patron. When he first travelled to Edinburgh in November 1786 Burns was given a letter of introduction to Glencairn by an Ayrshire landowner and fellow mason who was married to Glencairn's sister. The nobleman had already read and been impressed by the Kilmarnock *Poems*. He in turn introduced Burns to many useful connections, including William Creech, the bookseller who would produce the Edinburgh editions of the *Poems*, and arranged for the Caledonian Hunt to subscribe *en masse* to the new volume (see note to Dedication to the Edinburgh *Poems*, p. 331). On leaving the city Burns wrote to him: 'I came to this town without friend or acquaintance, but I met with your Lordship; and to YOU, Your good family I owe in a great measure all that at present I am and have' (L103, 4 May 1787). Glencairn had been one of the Representative Scottish Peers (see note to p. 16, l. 1) in the House of Lords in 1780–4, where he aligned himself with Charles James Fox. He died on 30 January 1791; Burns first sent this poem to a friend on 10 March.

l. 1. *THE wind blew hollow.* Kinsley observes that 'hollow winds' blow through scenes of loss in Pope: 'The hollow Winds thro' naked Temples roar' ('Windsor Forest', l. 68; Pope 197); 'The darksom pines . . . Wave high, and murmur to the hollow wind' ('Eloisa to Abelard' ll. 155–6; Pope 256).

l. 4. *Lugar's winding stream.* A tributary of the river Ayr.

l. 9. *He lean'd him to an ancient aik.* The association of an aged, friendless bard, mourning the loss of his friends, with an aged oak, comes from Ossian in Macpherson's poems: 'I, like an ancient oak on Morven,

I moulder alone in my place. The blast hath lopped my branches away; and I tremble at the wings of the north' (*Fragments of Ancient Poetry* [1760], VII; Macpherson 16).

212 ll. 19–20. *Ye woods that shed . . . The honours of the aged year.* Kinsley notes the borrowing from Thomson's 'Winter': 'Low waves the rooted forest, vexed, and sheds | What of its tarnished honours yet remain—' (ll. 181–2; Thomson 134).

l. 36. *Alike unknowing and unknown.* The structure mirrors another line from Pope's 'Eloisa to Abelard': 'The world forgetting, by the world forgot' (l. 208; Pope 257).

ll. 39–40. *silent, low, on beds of dust | Lie a' that would my sorrows share.* As Kinsley spots, an echo of Cuchullin's words in 'Fingal' (1761–2), Book III: 'Pale, silent, low on bloody beds, are they who were my friends!' (Macpherson 76).

l. 46. *all the life of life is dead.* Kinsley notes that this borrows from James Thomson's song, 'For ever Fortune wilt thou prove', l. 8: 'And all the life of life is gone?' (*Poems on Several Occasions* [1750], 16).

213 ll. 61–2. *the morning sun | That melts the fogs in limpid air.* As Kinsley observes, this condenses Thomson's lines in 'Summer': 'the potent sun | Melts into limpid air the high-raised clouds | And morning fogs' (ll. 199–201; Thomson 42).

ll. 77–9: *The mother may forget the child . . . But I'll remember thee, Glencairn.* 'Can a woman forget her sucking child, that she should not have compassion on the son of her womb? yea, they may forget, yet will I not forget thee' (Isaiah 49: 15).

Bruce's Address to his Troops. K425. First published in the London daily *Morning Chronicle* for 8 May 1794, on page 3. Under the owner-editorship of James Perry (born Pirie, in Aberdeen) this was the widely read national journal of the opposition, now reduced in parliament to a core of loyalists around Charles James Fox after it split over Fox's sympathy for the French Revolution: Burns's poem appears alongside reports of the second reading in parliament of a bill to lend £2.5 million to the King of Prussia, since February 1793 Britain's ally in the war with France, and of initial French success in their offensive against the allies in the Low Countries. Charges of seditious libel eventually earned Perry a prison sentence. In March Burns had turned down an offer of regular work for Perry's paper, mindful that his political alignment had once before (see letters of December 1792 and January 1793 in Appendix 1, p. 270f) threatened his government job: 'My prospect in the Excise is something; at least, it is, encumbered as I am with the welfare, the very existence, of near half-a-score of helpless individuals, what I dare not sport with.' Accordingly, while the paper could publish the song, 'let them insert it as a thing they have met with by accident, & unknown to me' (L620B). It appeared anonymously, with the following introduction: 'If the following warm and animating Ode was not written near the time to which it applies, it is one of the most faithful imitations of the simple and beautiful style of the Scottish Bards we ever read, and we know but of one *living* Poet to whom to ascribe it.'

Burns sent the first version of this song to George Thomson at the end of August 1793, to be set to the tune 'Hey tutti taiti'. This was best known as a drinking song, included as song 170 in *SMM* from which the score below is adapted:

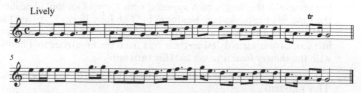

'There is a tradition, which I have met with in many parts of Scotland', Burns told Thomson, that this tune 'was Robert Bruce's March at the battle of Bannock-burn', the 1314 victory that secured Bruce the Scottish throne independent of Edward II of England (L582). Burns explains in the same letter that he had been inspired by 'the accidental recollection of that glorious struggle for Freedom, associated with the glowing ideas of some other struggles of the same nature, *not quite so ancient*' (the French Republic had just introduced mass conscription, the *levée en masse*, in response to the new coalition ranged against it). However, Thomson preferred an old Jacobite tune, 'Lewis Gordon', already published in *SMM* as song 86 in Vol. I, from which the score below is adapted.

This tune, however, required an extra two syllables in the final line of the stanza. Burns obliged (I have noted the additional words in the notes below), and when Thomson suggested further alterations, Burns replied, 'My Ode pleases me so much that I cannot alter it. . . . I am exceedingly obliged to you for putting me on reconsidering it: as I think I have much improved it' (L587).

This version of the text, with the longer final line in each stanza, was the song that Burns sent to Mrs Dunlop in December (L605), and that Burns agreed could be published in the *Morning Chronicle* in the spring of the following year (the London paper clearly did not know what to make of the name that appeared below the title on the manuscript they had been sent, so that a subheading reads '*Scene*—LEWIS GARDEN'). This is also the version of the song which appears, with 'Lewis Gordon' identified as the tune, in chapbooks (see headnote to 'The Jolly Beggars', p. 371) later in the decade. But collections of Burns's work, starting with James Currie's in 1800, have invariably taken their text from the first letter to Thomson, with the shorter final line, set to 'Hey tutti taiti'.

214   l. 4. *glorious*. Should be omitted to make this line fit the original tune, 'Hey tutti taiti'.

l. 8. *EDWARD*. Should be omitted to make this line fit the original tune.

l. 12. *Traitor, coward, turn and flie*. The line for 'Hey tutti taiti' is 'Let him turn and flee'.

l. 14. *FREEDOM's sword*. On the page facing this poem appears a letter to the editor from 'A Friend of Mankind' which concludes, 'Whatever be the ultimate fate of the French revolutionists, the friends of freedom must ever consider them as the authors of the greatest attempt that has hitherto been made in the cause of man' (2).

l. 16. *CALEDONIAN! on wi' me*. The line for 'Hey tutti taiti' is 'Let him follow me'.

l. 20. *But they shall—they* SHALL *be free!*. Omit a 'they shall' to make this line fit the original tune.

ll. 21–3. *Lay the proud usurpers low . . . LIBERTY's in every blow!*. In a manuscript note Burns observes that these lines borrow 'a Couplet worthy of Homer' from William Hamilton's 1722 modernization of Blind Harry's fifteenth-century epic poem *Wallace*: 'A false Usurper sinks in every Foe, | And Liberty returns with ev'ry blow' at the battle of Biggar in Book VI, ch. II (*A New Edition of the Life and Heroick Actions of the renoun'd Sir William Wallace*, 122).

l. 24. *Forward*. Should be omitted to make this line fit the original tune.

The Election: a new song. K492. This is one of three songs that Burns wrote to support Patrick Heron of Kerroughtrie (d. 1803) in his successful campaign for the parliamentary seat of the Stewartry of Kirkcudbright in Spring 1795. Burns wrote a fourth 'Heron ballad' (as they are known) for the General Election the following year, when Heron was re-elected. They were published, anonymously, as 'broadsides': single sheets of cheap paper, in this case printed on one side only. This text follows the copy in the Abbotsford Library. The Heron ballads were first republished in two 1834 *Works of Robert Burns*, the one edited by James Hogg and William Motherwell (in Vol. I), the other by Cunningham (in Vol. III).

Tune: Fy, let us a' to the Bridal.

This score has been adapted from song 58 in *The Scots Musical Museum*, 'The Blithsome Bridal'. Burns's lyric follows the form of this traditional song: 'And there will be Saundy the sutor, | And Will wi' the meikle mou, | And there will be Tam the blutter, | With Andrew the tinkler, I trow' (stanza 2), and so on.

The member of parliament for a county was elected by its 'freeholders' of land over a certain extent (nothing prevented a landowner voting in more than one county on this basis). At the previous election in 1790 there were 154 qualified freeholders in Kirkcudbrightshire. They were obliged to attend a meeting in the county town between 12 and 2 on the designated day in order to cast their votes, and it is this assembly that Burns is anticipating in the present ballad. The election followed the death of the previous MP, Major-General Alexander Stewart of Cairn (see note to p. 131, ll. 227–8), grandson of an Earl of Galloway. It was not a contest between national political parties, but between rival local 'interests' (networks of patronage, influence, and family alliance). Heron headed one such interest; John Stewart, seventh Earl of Galloway (d. 1806), headed another, and through his brother-in-law James Murray of Broughton was backing Thomas Gordon of Balmaghie, Murray's nephew, for the seat. Heron too was a wealthy landowner, with family estates in England and other business interests (he was co-founder in 1769 of the Ayr Bank which collapsed four years later); but he also enjoyed the support of Secretary of State Henry Dundas, who managed the election of Scottish MPs for the government. The *History of Parliament* records Heron being returned unopposed, which suggests that Balmaghie must have withdrawn from the contest when his defeat looked inevitable.

l. 1. *K*————. Kirkcudbright (pronounced 'kirk*oo*brie'). The county town of one of the two shires making up the historic region of Galloway (the other being Wigtownshire, to the west).

214   l. 3. *M*————. Murray. James Murray of Cally and Broughton (d. 1799), a grandson of the fifth Earl of Galloway, was one of the wealthiest land-owners in south-west Scotland.

l. 6. *G*————. Gordon. Thomas Gordon of Balmaghie (d. 1806), nephew of Murray, and Heron's opponent.

l. 8. *Sae knit in alliance and kin.* Ten years before Murray had deserted his wife Catherine, sister of the Earl of Galloway, for his mistress, Grace Johnston, who was his nephew Gordon's sister's daughter, and thus his own great-niece. Remarkably, this did not destroy his political alliance with Galloway, nor dent the two men's confidence in being able to impose their candidate on the county. When sending Heron two of his election ballads (probably including this one) in March, Burns comments:

> To pillory on Parnassus the rank reprobation of character, the utter dere-liction of all principle, in a profligate junto which has not only outraged virtue, but violated common decency; which, spurning even hypocrisy as paltry iniquity below their daring;—to unmask their flagitiousness to the broadest day—to deliver such over to their merited fate, is surely not merely innocent, but laudable; is not only propriety, but virtue.—You have already, as your auxiliary, the sober detestation of mankind on all your opponents; and I swear by the lyre of Thalia to muster on your side all the votaries of honest laughter, and fair, candid ridicule! (L660)

215   l. 9. *black-nebbit Johnie.* John Bushby (d. 1802), banker and sheriff clerk of Dumfries, factor on the Galloway and Broughton estates, and manager of their political interest. 'Black-nebbit' is ironic: a black-neb was a democrat.

l. 13. *K*————'*s birkie.* Kempleton. William Bushby of Kempleton (d. 1813), John's brother, had been ruined by the fall of Heron's bank, gone to India, and returned with a fortune. A 'nabob' (l. 15) was just such a wealthy returnee: the wealth was usually assumed to be the product of oppression and corruption in India, which its deployment in parliamen-tary politics threatened to reproduce in Britain.

l. 17. *W*——'*s new Sh*——*ff.* Wigtown's new sheriff was another Bushby, John's son John Bushby Maitland of Eccles (b. 1767).

l. 21. *C*————. Cardonness. David Maxwell of Cardoness (d. 1825) was a very wealthy Kirkcudbrightshire landowner.

l. 25. ————*ses doughty.* Douglases. 'Doughty' traditionally attached to this surname, from the old ballad 'The Battle of Otterburn': 'The doughty earl of Douglas rode | Into England, to catch a prey'. But Sir William Douglas and James Douglas of Orchardton, referred to here, were not descended from medieval warlords, but, from humble beginnings, had made a fortune in trade and manufacturing.

l. 26. *New-christening towns far and near.* Having extended the town of Carlinwark around his cotton mills Sir William had it renamed 'Castle Douglas'; he also built mills in Newton Stewart in Wigtownshire which then became 'Newton Douglas'.

l. 28. *kissin the a— of a Peer.* Arse. The peer is Galloway, to whom the Douglases paid court; what their previous 'democrat doings' might have been is not clear.

l. 29. *K———, sae gen'rous.* Kenmure. John Gordon of Kenmure (1750–1840) had been MP for the constituency: Burns and a friend had stayed with the family on a tour.

l. 33. *R———stle.* Redcastle. Walter Sloan Lawrie of Redcastle, near Castle Douglas.

l. 37. *L— L———t.* Lord Lieutenant, the King's representative in the county; in this case George Stewart, styled Lord Garlies, the eldest son of the Earl of Galloway.

l. 38. *Sae fam'd for his gratefu' return.* This might refer to the controversy over the writ (see following note).

ll. 39–40. *getting his questions | To say in S–nt St–ph–n's the morn.* St Stephen's Chapel was the old debating chamber of the House of Commons. Galloway managed to delay the Sheriff's execution of the writ calling the election to gain time for his campaign; Garlies was called to account for this by parliament. To 'get one's questions' is 'to memorise the Catechism' (*DSL*): that is, Garlies is preparing his *answers*.

l. 42. *M———.* Muirhead. Revd James Muirhead, minister of Urr, but also freeholder of the Logan estate.

l. 43. *B———'s Apostle.* Buittle. Revd George Maxwell, minister of Buittle.

l. 44. *mair o' the black than the blue.* 'Not true blue' suggests Wallace (Vol. IV, 199).

l. 45. *Folk frae Saint MARY's.* Saint Mary's Isle is a peninsula just south of Kirkcudbright town, and seat of the Earl of Selkirk, a man of reformist instincts whose eldest son Burns greatly admired (see headnote to 'Extempore Verses on Dining with Lord Daer', p. 382). Scottish peers and their eldest sons could not vote in Scottish elections; but Selkirk's younger sons John, Dunbar, and Thomas were freeholders of the county and could.

216 l. 48. *Tho' deil ane will gie them his vote.* A survey of Scottish county politics in 1788 reported that Selkirk 'has never interested himself in politicks, or affected to be at the head of any interest in the County' (Elphinstone, ed., *View of the Political State of Scotland*, 194).

l. 49. *young RICHARD.* Richard Alexander Oswald of Auchencruive (b. 1771), nephew to Lord Methven and heir to a fortune built by his father in the Atlantic slave-trade. The names from this point on are those of Heron's supporters.

l. 53. *rich brother Nabobs.* David Anderson of St Germains in East Lothian and his brother James of Lincluden, who returned to Scotland in 1785–6 after successful careers in the East India Company.

l. 55. *C–ll–st–n's whiskers.* Collieston. William Copeland of Collieston and Mollins: 'remarkable for large whiskers', says a contemporary commentary.

216 l. 56. *Quintin.* Quintin McAdam of Waterside (b. 1763), nephew of John McAdam of Craigengillan near Mauchline, an early friend to Burns.

l. 57. *Stamp-office Johnie.* John Syme (1755–1831), a close friend of Burns's. Another victim of the collapse of Heron's bank, he held the sinecure position of 'distributor of stamps' in Dumfries: these were the stamps confirming that duty had been paid on taxable stuffs, hence the warning in the following line.

l. 59. *C–ss–nc–ry.* Cassencary. Colonel Alexander Muir Mackenzie of Cassencarry.

l. 60. *gleg Colonel Tam.* Lieutenant-Colonel Thomas Goldie of Goldielea.

l. 61. *trusty KIROCHTREE.* Patrick Heron of Kerroughtrie, the candidate: see headnote.

l. 65. *the auld MAJOR.* The candidate's brother, Major Basil Heron of Drumnaught.

l. 66. *the Greys.* The Greys were the Royal North British Dragoons, Major Heron's cavalry regiment.

l. 69. *maiden K–lk–rr–n.* Kilkerran. Sir Adam Fergusson of Kilkerran, MP for Ayrshire. 'Maiden' because he never married, but see also note to p. 18, l. 74.

l. 70. *B–rsk–m–n's gude Knight.* Barskimming. Sir William Miller of Glenlee (in Kirkcudbrightshire), Barskimming (in Ayrshire), and the legal dynasty.

l. 71. *roaring B–rtwh–stle.* Alexander Birtwhistle, merchant, part-owner of cotton mills in Gatehouse of Fleet, and Provost of Kirkcudbright town.

l. 73. *N–ddisd–le border.* Niddisdale or Nithsdale is the western division of Dumfriesshire: the lowest part of the river Nith, at Dumfries town, forms the border with Kirkcudbrightshire, and the estates mentioned below are on the Stewartry side.

ll. 74–5. *M–xw–lls . . . Teuch Jockie, staunch Geordie, and Walie.* John Maxwell of Terraughty, 'the Maxwels' veteran Chief' of an earlier Burns poem ('To Terraughty', K325); George Maxwell of Carruchan; and Wellwood Maxwell of Barncleugh, son-in-law to John (these men were not otherwise related).

l. 76. *griens.* This is 'greens' in the broadside text (corrected by hand in the Abbotsford copy).

l. 77. *L–g–n M—d–w–l.* Lieutenant-Colonel Andrew McDouall (or McDowall) of Logan (b. 1758), MP for Wigtownshire.

l. 78. *Sculdudry.* 'fornication' (*DSL*). McDouall was notorious for the consequences of a ten-year affair with Margaret Kennedy, a niece of Burns's friend Gavin Hamilton (and for whom Burns wrote the song 'Young Peggy', K65). Margaret was just 16 when McDouall seduced her, but when she bore him a surviving child he denied promising her marriage in that event. Her relatives had taken him to court in 1794; the case was concluded in 1801, with £3,000 damages awarded to the daughter (Margaret having died in the meantime).

l. 80. *Sogering, gunpowder Bl—r.* Presumably Lieutenant John Blair, younger of Borgue.

217 l. 81. *the chaste Int'rest o' B——.* Broughton.

l. 83. *send B—— to the C————ns.* Balmaghie; Commons.

l. 84. *S–d–m.* Sodom.

l. 85. *the sanctified M——.* Murray.

l. 86. *Ch–p–ls.* Chapels. Perhaps a reference to the facilities of Murray's planned village at Gatehouse of Fleet, in ironic contrast to his bad moral example.

The Dumfries Volunteers. K484. First published in the *Edinburgh Evening Courant* (see headnote to 'Elegy, On the departed Year 1788', p. 351) for 4 May 1795, 'By Mr. Burns', on page 3, column 4, which it shares with descriptions of army deserters. Elsewhere in this issue we find a debate in the House of Lords on the Prince of Wales's debts, and an editorial on the war:

> Peace continues still to be generally talked of. It is indeed so desirable an event, and the very sound carries with it such a charm, that it operates on men's minds as a reality, when we fear in the present instance, it will prove only a shadow. If we reflect for a moment on the kind of language always held out by his MAJESTY's Ministers in regard to the necessity of prosecuting the war, so long as the Revolutionary Government in France continues to exist, and on the measures now pursued to carry it on with redoubled vigour, we shall find no cause to believe that a peace is at all in agitation. (3)

Tune: Push about the jorum.

With Spirit

Burns's lyric was republished posthumously as song 546 in *The Scots Musical Museum*, from which this score is adapted. In *SMM*, the last two lines of each stanza are repeated as a chorus ('We'll ne'er permit . . .' etc.) to accompany the last four bars of the present score. The poem was published in many other newspapers, including the *Dumfries Journal* (5 May) and the *Caledonian Mercury* (7 May).

The withdrawal of Prussia from the coalition in April 1795 had allowed the French unchallenged occupation of the whole of the Low Countries, their fleets and harbours, exposing the long coastline of Britain to assault as never before; but there was no immediate threat of invasion by France at this time. The government had called for counties to organize their own forces in May of the previous year, more to suppress internal disorder and rebellion than to repel any external threat, thus freeing the regular army for service elsewhere. The offer to constitute the Royal Dumfries Volunteers, signed by 90 men, including Burns, on 3 February 1795 and sent to the King's representative in Dumfriesshire, the Lord Lieutenant, makes no mention of an anti-invasion role:

> We the subscribers, all inhabitants of the burgh and neighbourhood of Dumfries, within the County of Dumfries, do hereby declare our sincere attachment to the person and government of His Majesty King George the Third; our respect for the happy Constitution of Great Britain; and our firm resolution on every occasion to protect the lives and properties of ourselves and our fellow-subjects from every attempt of the ambitious and turbulent who threaten to overturn the laws of our country, and who, by anarchy, sedition, and bloodshed may endeavour to destroy the sacred bonds of society; and, as we are of opinion that the only way we can obtain a speedy and honourable peace is by the Government vigorously carrying on the present war, humbly submit the following proposals to His Majesty for the purpose of forming ourselves into a Volunteer Corps, in order to support the internal peace and good order of the town, as well as to give energy to the measures of Government . . . (reproduced in Will, *Robert Burns as a Volunteer*, 43–4)

As an employee of the Crown Burns could not avoid joining; given his detestation of the government of William Pitt, he cannot have relished the idea of becoming its policeman. In practice, on the other hand, the Volunteers were a self-organizing body of men such as Burns had always enjoyed participating in: they determined the conditions of their service (e.g. 'the Corps shall not be obliged to march more than five miles from the town of Dumfries', Will 45); they elected their own officers; and discipline and other matters were administered by a committee, of which Burns was elected a member in August. This very independence caused misgivings in government, and Volunteer units were eventually replaced by a drafted Militia firmly under the authority of country gentlemen. The Royal Dumfries Volunteers gave Burns a military funeral in July 1796, it seems against his dying wishes.

217   l. 3. *WOODEN WALLS.* A conventional metonym for the Royal Navy. This issue of the *Courant* includes a report to the French National Convention,

putting a brave face on the narrow British naval victory at Genoa in March.

l. 5. *Nith.* The river Nith runs through Dumfries.

l. 21. *Our FATHERS BLUDE the kettle bought.* See the mention of 'our ancestors' in the Perth loyal address extracted below.

218 ll. 25, 27. *that would a tyrant own,* | | *Who'd set the mob above the throne.* For another example of the equivalence of these dangers, see Burns's closing wish for the nobility and gentry of Scotland in the Dedication to the Edinburgh *Poems*: 'may tyranny in the Ruler and licentiousness in the People equally find you an inexorable foe!' (p. 124).

ll. 31–2. *while we sing, GOD SAVE THE KING,* | *We'll ne'er forget THE PEOPLE.* It has been suggested that Burns here echoes the words of 'a most elegant and forcible speech' by Thomas Muir, co-founder in Scotland of the Association of the Friends of the People (see headnote to 'Extempore on some late commemorations of the poet Thomson', p. 356), as Scottish delegate to a meeting of the Friends of the Liberty of the Press in London the previous year, when he said

> That with respect to Loyalty, he was not exceeded by any one, if by Loyalty, Affection to the Constitution was intended; but if the word meant, (as he feared it did at present) an inclination to perpetuate abuse, or to rivet still more tightly the yoke of oppression about the necks of his countrymen, he feared he had but little of it; he honoured, he loved his Sovereign, but he could not on that account forget the People. (*Morning Post*, 16 January 1793, 3)

The same qualification was frequently, if less eloquently, expressed in the declarations of loyalty published by the more reform-minded public bodies in the same period. For example, on 18 December 1792 a town meeting in Perth had resolved to 'express and make public our loyalty and attachment to his Majesty' and to

> a Constitution which we love and revere as a monument of political wisdom, equally glorious to our ancestors, by whom it was framed, and happy for us who enjoy the enviable advantages of it; but, in our opinion, its stability would be rendered more permanent, and liberty better secured, if the House of Commons were a more general as well as a truer Representation of the People. (*Morning Chronicle*, 28 December 1792, 2)

Song [A man's a man for a' that]. K482. First published, anonymously, in the *Glasgow Magazine* for August 1795, p. 115. This was only the third issue of the radical monthly. As well as Burns's song it included a second instalment of a biography of Thomas Muir (see note above), now serving a 14-year sentence in Botany Bay for sedition; the act passed by the legislature of Virginia in 1785 guaranteeing freedom of religion; and a third instalment of a retrospect of recent history, covering Britain's 'scandalous' (p. 117) support for Continental absolutism against the French Republic. This ends with the consequences of Britain's campaign against the French West Indies: complaints had been made in parliament about the disruption to Britain's own Caribbean trade. This issue of the *Glasgow Magazine* concludes:

> The arms of Great Britain, when carried into distant countries, have seldom been celebrated for justice or humanity. The desolated regions of the East [i.e. British-controlled India] confirm this deplorable truth; and it appears, that the same system of rapacity and cruelty had been adopted in the West. . . . Legislators, as such, should have no private interest, but should feel an equal concern for every portion of the people subject to their authority, however distant, and in whatever capacity: And of what consequence are the present disappointments of the West India merchants, compared with the miseries of millions of Africans, whom their infamous trafic has reduced to slavery, or of those millions in the East, who have perished without their assistance or sympathy? (119)

Manuscript versions, including the one which Burns sent to George Thomson for the *Select Collection* in January 1795, begin with an additional stanza:

> Is there, for honest poverty
> That hangs his head, and a' that;
> The coward-slave, we pass him by,
> We dare be poor for a' that!
> For a' that, and a' that.
> Our toils obscure, and a' that,
> The rank is but the guinea's stamp,
> The man's the gowd for a' that.

This is the version printed in all the nineteenth-century collections which reproduce the letters to Thomson, starting with Currie's in 1800 (Vol. IV, 216–17); and also in the 1799 Stewart and Meikle chapbook that includes *Holy Willie's Prayer*. The present version was republished in *The Oracle* newspaper for 2 June 1796 and *The Scots Magazine* for August 1797, in both cases attributed to Burns.

Tune: For a' that and a' that.

Burns had already set a lyric to this tune for his 'cantata' 'Love and Liberty', later published as 'The Jolly Beggars'; part of which had already appeared as song 290 of *The Scots Musical Museum*, from which this score is adapted.

218 l. 2. *hodden grey.* 'Coarse homespun, undyed woollen cloth, of a greyish colour, due to a mixture of white and black wool . . . Freq. used . . . to describe one dressed in simple rustic fashion, or a homely unaffected individual' (*DSL*).

l. 14. *His ribband, star, and a' that.* The sash and chest insignia of an order of nobility. Compare this stanza to Thomas Paine, *The Rights of Man,* Vol. I (1791):

> Titles are but nick-names, and every nick-name is a title. The thing is perfectly harmless in itself; but it marks a sort of foppery in the human character, which degrades it. It reduces man into the diminutive of man in things which are great, and the counterfeit of woman in things which are little. It talks about its fine *blue ribbon* like a girl, and shows its new *garter* like a child. A certain writer, of some antiquity, says, 'When I was a child, I thought as a child; but when I became a man, I put away childish things'. (*Rights of Man, Common Sense, and Other Political Writings,* 131)

The blue riband and the garter are insignia of the Order of the Garter, the highest order of chivalry in Britain. The 'writer of some antiquity' is Paul: 1 Corinthians 13: 11.

l. 17. *The king.* The five-stanza version substitutes 'A prince'.

219 l. 22. *His.* The five-stanza version substitutes 'Their'.

Other poems and songs published posthumously

220 *The Jolly Beggars.* K84. This, and the following two texts, were first published in 1799 by Stewart and Meikle of Glasgow in 'chapbooks': small-format pamphlets of, in this case, 16 pages, often containing works by more than one author, and sold for 2d. each. In each of them the title-page attributes these works to 'Robert Burns, The Ayrshire Poet' (a version of 'A Poet's welcome to his love-begotten daughter' also appeared in these pamphlets: see headnote to that poem, p. 407). In the printing used here, 'The Jolly Beggars; or, Tatterdemallions. A Cantata' takes up 14 pages, the other two containing poems by other writers. This title is the publishers' invention: it seems that the only title in the manuscript from which they worked was 'A Cantata', but the other extant manuscript is entitled 'Love and Liberty: A Cantata', and this is generally adopted in modern editions. Burns's title borrows from Pope's celebration of extra-marital love in 'Eloisa to Abelard' (1717): 'Oh happy state! when souls each other draw, | When love is liberty, and nature, law' (ll. 91–2; Pope 254). The publishers' title evokes the many traditional songs about beggars, and the multi-character songs *The Happy Beggars* and *The Merry Beggars* in the later editions of Allan Ramsay's *Tea-Table Miscellany,* Vol. IV (10th edition of 1740, pp. 348–9 and 374–5); in constructing a more extended sequence on this theme, Burns clearly also had in mind the ballad-opera form of John Gay's *The Beggar's Opera* (1728), the songs of which enter Ramsay's collection in the same edition. From the start the *Tea-Table Miscellany*

included a short 'Scots Cantata' consisting of two recitatives and two airs (Ramsay Vol. III, 36–7).

'Love and Liberty' was written in 1785–6. It seems that an early draft or drafts included several more songs, and characters to sing them, than in the version published in 1799. One of these, sung by a 'merry-andrew' or clown and introduced by its own recitative, later came into the hands of the publisher Thomas Stewart, and he inserted it into the existing text at l. 80, after the camp follower's song, in his 1802 *Stewart's Edition of Burns's Poems*.

220 RECITATIVO. *Recitative* is the type of delivery, between speaking and singing, used to fill in the dialogue and narration between songs in eighteenth-century opera. This one takes the 'Cherrie and the Slae' stanza already used by Burns for e.g. the 'Epistle to Davie' in the Kilmarnock *Poems* (see headnote to that poem, p. 310).

l. 2. *wavering*. 'Waver' can mean 'flutter' (*OED* sense 3).

l. 3. *Boreas*. The North Wind.

l. 9. *Poosie-Nansie's*. 'The Hostess of a noted Caravansary in M——, well known to and much frequented by the lowest orders of Travellers and Pilgrims' (Burns's note in the manuscripts): i.e. an inn in Mauchline.

l. 15. *red rags*. The remains of a British army uniform.

l. 16. *brac'd*. 'Surrounded, encompassed' (*OED*); possibly also 'burdened': the old soldier has been carrying bags of meal as well as his knapsack. Kinsley points out that 'oatmeal was the common alms', so the implication may be that the soldier has been very successful in attracting charity.

l. 24. *aumos dish*. 'Alms-dish' explains Burns in a manuscript note. Robert Chambers notes in his editions that 'The Scottish beggars used to carry a large wooden dish for the reception of any alms which took the shape of food' (1838, p. 30).

l. 27. *Then staggering and swaggering*. Kinsley spots that this line is borrowed from this section, the 'wheel', of another 'Cherrie and the Slae' stanza, in Ramsay's 'The Vision', stanza xix: 'Quhen staggirand and swaggirand | They stoyter Hame to sleip' (ll. 263–4; Ramsay Vol. III, 90).

221 ll. 29–48. *Tune—Soldier's Joy.*

This score is adapted from Alexander McGlashan's *A Collection of Scots Measures* (1781), 32; it appears in a couple of other eighteenth-century collections. I follow *Low* (pp. 128–9) in putting the high strain first, for the verse; the last eight bars are for 'lal de daudle' etc.

l. 34. *the heights of Abram.* General James Wolfe's 1759 victory over the French on the Plains of Abraham, a plateau above the St Lawrence outside Quebec, established British control of Canada, but Wolfe himself was killed.

l. 35. *I served out my trade.* Completed my apprenticeship (*OED* 'serve' 2a).

l. 36. *the Moro low was laid.* At the other end of the American theatre of the Seven Years War, the storming of El Morro, the Spanish fortress on Cuba, secured Havana for British troops in 1762.

ll. 37, 39. *with Curtis, among the floating batt'ries . . . with Elliot to head me.* During the war with France and Spain that accompanied the American Revolutionary War, General George Eliot's British garrison held Gibraltar against a three-year Spanish siege, aided by naval forces under Roger Curtis, who led a marine brigade during the destruction of the naval batteries bombarding the peninsula in 1782.

l. 43. *my wallet, my bottle and my callet.* A wallet is 'a bag for holding provisions . . . a pedlar's pack, or the like'; a callet is 'a lewd woman, trull, strumpet, drab' (both *OED*).

l. 47. *tell.* In something like *OED*'s sense 21a, 'To count out (pieces of money) in payment; hence, to pay (money)'; except this has to mean 'pay *for*'. The soldier sells a spare bag of meal he has been given as alms to pay for an extra bottle of whisky.

222 l. 53. *fairy.* Here just meaning 'delicate, finely formed' (*OED*).

ll. 57–80. *Tune—Soldier Laddie.*

Lively

This is a seventeenth-century tune which Burns could have found in a number of the collections, including *Orpheus Caledonius*, Vol. II (1733), 27.

The present score is adapted from song 323 in *The Scots Musical Museum*, where the singer does *not* follow the camp: 'And when he comes hame, he'll make me a Lady, | My blessings gang wi' my soger laddie'. Burns's version was included in *The Merry Muses of Caledonia* (1799). The last eight bars are for 'lal de lal' etc.

222 l. 71. *spontoon to the fife*. A spontoon was 'a species of half-pike or halberd carried by infantry officers' (*OED*); the fife would have been played by a boy.

l. 73. *the peace*. The Peace of Paris, in 1783, that ended the American Revolutionary War and the war with France and Spain that accompanied it.

l. 74. *Cunningham*. The district of Ayrshire north of the River Irvine: see Map.

223 l. 80. At this point Stewart's 1802 edition inserted the following, from a manuscript fragment (a 'merry-andrew' is a clown):

> Recitative
> Poor Merry-Andrew, in a neuk,
>   Sat guzzling wi' a Tinkler-hizzie;
> They mind't na wha the chorus teuk
>   Between themsels they were sae busy:
> At length wi' drink an' courting dizzy,
>   He stoiter'd up an' made a face;
> Then turn'd, an' laid a smack on Grizzie,
>   Syne tun'd his pipes wi' grave grimace.
>
> Air. Tune, Auld Sir Symon.
>
> Sir Wisdom's a fool when he's fou;
>   Sir Knave is a fool in a Session;
> He's there but a 'prentice, I trow,
>   But I am a fool by profession.
>
> My Grannie she bought me a beuk,
>   And I held awa' to the school;
> I fear I my talent misteuk,
>   But what will ye hae of a fool.
>
> For drink I would venture my neck;
>   A hizzie's the half o' my Craft:
> But what could ye other expect
>   Of ane that's avowedly daft.
>
> I, ance, was ty'd up like a stirk,
>   For civilly swearing and quaffing;
> I, ance, was abus'd i' the kirk
>   For towsing a lass i' my daffin.
>
> Poor Andrew that tumbles for sport,
>   Let nae body name wi' a jeer;
> There's even, I'm tauld, i' the Court
>   A Tumbler ca'd the Premier.

Observ'd ye yon reverend lad
  Mak faces to tickle the Mob;
He rails at our mountebank squad,
  It's rivalship just i' the job.

And now my conclusion I'll tell,
  For faith I'm confoundedly dry:
The chiel that's a fool for himsel,
  Gude L—d, he's far dafter than I.

l. 84. *douked.* From the manuscript; 'ducked' in the 1799 text, but clearly pronounced as the Scots word.

l. 85. *love.* This is 'dove' in the 1799 text, but this is a misreading (easily made) of the poet's handwriting in the manuscript.

ll. 89–116. *Tune—O an ye were dead gudeman.*

Burns could have found the tune in James Oswald's *Caledonian Pocket Companion*, Vol. IV (1752), 24. This score is adapted from song 409 of *The Scots Musical Museum*, where, the gudeman being dead, 'I wad bestow my widowhood | upon a ranton Highlandman'; Burns's lyric has more in common with songs celebrating the Highland Jacobite rebels of 1715 and 1745.

l. 97. *his philibeg an' tartan plaid.* The *fèileadh beag* (Gaelic) is the kilt, developed earlier in the century to dress the legs, leaving the plaid, originally used to cover the whole body, to be carried instead as cloak and bedding.

l. 98. *claymore. Claidheamh mòr* (Gaelic): broadsword.

l. 99. *trepan.* 'to catch in a trap; to entrap, ensnare, beguile' (*OED*).

224 l. 101. *Tweed to Spey.* The river Tweed flows through south-east Scotland, one stage forming the border with England; the river Spey runs north-east through the central Highlands.

225 l. 125. *Arioso*. Melodious; 'Used of instrumental music, it describes a sustained, vocal style' (*OED*).

l. 126. *Apollo*. Here in his capacity as god of music.

l. 127. *Allegretto*. Italian musical term meaning 'somewhat brisk' (*OED*).

l. 128. *giga*. Italian musical term for 'piece of music, of a lively character, in two strains or sections, each of which is repeated' (*OED*); but the fiddler is probably just playing a jig. Kinsley notes the echo of Ramsay's 'The Life and Acts of, or, An Elegy on Patie Burnie, The Famous Fidler of Kinghorn' in his 1721 *Poems*, where a standard Habbie stanza describes the first fiddle, 'On which *Apollo*, | With meikle Pleasure play'd himself | Baith Jig and Solo' (ll. 52 –4; Ramsay Vol. I, 188).

ll. 129–48. *Tune—Whistle owre the lave o't.*

The tune is in several of the eighteenth-century collections, and, Burns told Thomson, 'said to be by a John Bruce, a celebrated violin-player, in Dumfries about the beginning of this century' (L644, 19 October 1794). In Burns's version for *The Scots Musical Museum* song 249 (on which the score above is based), the title phrase comes in place of what cannot be said ('Now we're married, spier nae mair, | But Whistle o'er . . .') and to express an acceptance of fate ('Wiser men than me's beguil'd | So Whistle o'er . . .'). The present song was included in *The Merry Muses of Caledonia* (1799).

l. 146. *thairms*. Burns explains in a manuscript note, 'small guts = fiddle strings'.

226 l. 158. *hunkers*. Burns explains in a manuscript note, 'the position of one going to sit down on the floor'; a squat.

ll. 165–80. *Tune—Clout the caudron.*

Burns could have found this tune in *Orpheus Caledonius*, Vol. II (1733), 25; as the title suggests, it was used for songs about the services offered by tinkers, usually with a layer of sexual innuendo. The score above is adapted from song 23 in *The Scots Musical Museum*.

l. 169. *I've ta'en the gold.* That is, accepted the bounty for joining the army.

227 l. 178. *Kilbaigie.* 'Keilbaigie' in the 1799 text: another simple misreading of the poet's handwriting. The distillery in question was at Kilbagie in Clackmannanshire.

ll. 182–207. *RECITATIVO.* This recitative takes the 'Christ's Kirk' stanza used by Burns in 'The Holy Fair', 'A Dream', and 'Halloween' in the Kilmarnock *Poems.*

ll. 197–8. *An' shor'd them Dainty Davie | O boot.* 'Shore' means 'offer, present with as a mark of favour' (*DSL*). 'Dainty Davie' seems to be functioning here as a euphemism for sex; the poet is in effect wishing the couple all the best in their encounter (although the 'lord' of the 'dame' involved, he has two others in reserve, as we learn in l. 214).

l. 200. *listed.* That is, enlisted.

228 ll. 208–35. *Tune—For a' that an' a' that.* For a score, see notes to 'A man's a man for a' that', p. 370. Burns used the last three verses of the present lyric in another version published as song 290 of *The Scots Musical Museum,* from which this score is adapted. The 'Jolly Beggars' version was included in *The Merry Muses of Caledonia* (1799) under the title 'I am a Bard'.

ll. 216–17. *I never drank the Muses' stank, | Castalia's burn.* Castalia is a spring in Greek mythology that could inspire the gift of poetry in those who heard its sound or drank its waters: it is placed on either Mount Parnassus or on Mount Helicon (l. 220). The wording here suggests a renaissance convention to Kinsley, with examples from Sir David Lindsay's *Ane dialoge* of 1554 ('I did never sleep on Pernasso . . . Nor drank I never | Off Hylicon', ll. 226, 230–1), and Sir Philip Sidney's sonnet 74 in *Astrophil and Stella* of 1591 ('I never drank of Aganippe well', l. 1).

l. 218. *But there it streams, and richly reams.* More immediately, Fergusson also substitutes drink as the fount of poetic inspiration: 'O *Muse*, be kind, and dinna fash us | To flee awa' beyont Parnassus, | Nor seek for *Helicon* to wash us, | That heath'nish spring; | Wi' Highland whisky scour our hawses, | And gar us sing' ('The King's Birth-Day in Edinburgh', ll. 13–18; Fergusson 52).

l. 222. *will.* In *OED*'s sense 2, 'carnal desire or appetite'.

l. 230. *clear your decks.* In preparation for a toast.

229 l. 241. *To quench their lowan drouth.* The 1799 text has a space after this line, corresponding to a page-break in the manuscript, turning the first six lines into a stanza in their own right. In fact the final recitative has returned to the 'Cherrie and the Slae' stanza of the opening one.

229 l. 247. *his twa Deborahs.* Deborah is a prophetess in the Book of Judges. Kinsley points to Judges 5: 12, 'Awake, awake, Deborah: awake, awake, utter a song'; but also relevant to the bard's companions might be Deborah's answer to Barak: 'I will surely go with thee: notwithstanding the journey that thou takest shall not be for thine honour' (Judges 4: 9).

ll. 250-81. *Tune—Jolly Mortals fill your glasses.*

Burns would have known a song of this title in Joseph Ritson's *Select Collection of English Songs* (1783), Vol. II, song xvii: the score above is adapted from this source.

230 l. 270. *variorum.* A Scottish usage, says *OED*, meaning 'a varying or changing scene'.

l. 273. *character.* From the manuscript: 'characters' in the 1799 text. 'The estimate formed of a person's qualities; reputation . . . favourable estimate, good repute' (*OED*).

Holy Willie's Prayer. K53. Stewart and Meikle's chapbook follows this poem with more works by Burns, namely 'Letter to John Goudie' (usually known as 'Epistle to John Goldie') and six song-lyrics (all but the second and last included in the present volume): 'Duncan Gray', 'The lass that made the bed to me', 'A man's a man for a' that', 'Of a' the airts', 'Now westlin' winds', and 'I gaed a waefu' gate yestreen'. This text follows the version 'Printed by Chapman and Lang' (on the title page).

The manuscript versions add an epigraph from Pope ('And send the Godly in a pet to pray—', *The Rape of the Lock*, canto IV, l. 64; Pope 234); some also add a prologue explaining the background to the poem, for example the 'Argument' in the Glenriddell copy:

> Holy Willie was a rather oldish batchelor Elder in the parish of Mauchline, & much & justly famed for that polemical chattering which ends in tippling Orthodoxy, & for that Spiritualized Bawdry which refines to Liquorish Devotion.—In a Sessional process with a gentleman in Mauchline, a M[r]. Gavin Hamilton, Holy Willie, and his priest, father Auld, after full hearing of the Presbytry of Ayr, came off but second best; owing partly to the oratorical powers of M[r]. Robt. Aiken, M[r]. Hamilton's Counsel; but chiefly to M[r]. Hamilton's being one of the most irreproachable & truly respectable characters in the country.— On losing his Process, the Muse overheard him at his devotions as follows—

For Hamilton see the headnote to 'A Dedication to Gavin Hamilton', p. 316; for Aiken, the headnote to 'The Cotter's Saturday night', p. 306). The charges brought against Hamilton by the Session of his church in August 1784 included missing attendance at church, travelling on a Sunday, and neglecting family worship. The Presbytery of Ayr, the next level up in the government of the church, was in the control of its 'moderate' faction, perhaps predisposed to find in favour of the 'respectable' 'gentleman' Hamilton, and in January 1785 it duly did so. On the Mauchline Session's reaction to this poem, see the letter to John Moore of 2 August 1787 in Appendix 1, p. 266.

231   l. 4. *A' for thy glory.* This is the orthodox Calvinism of the Church of Scotland, as set out in *The Westminster Confession of Faith* (1647): 'By the decree of God, for the manifestation of His glory, some men and angels are predestinated unto everlasting life; and others foreordained to everlasting death' (ch. III, para. iii).

ll. 5–6. *And no for ony guid or ill | They've done afore thee!.* 'Those of mankind that are predestinated unto life, God . . . hath chosen in Christ unto everlasting glory, out of His mere free grace and love, without any foresight of faith or good works, or perseverance in either of them' (*Westminster Confession*, ch. III, para. v).

l. 10. *For gifts an' grace.* For Paul, 'Having then gifts differing according to the grace that is given to us' explains why different individuals have different roles in the church (Romans 12: 6).

l. 11. *A burnin' an' a shinin' light.* The words of Jesus, describing John the Baptist; 'He was a burning and a shining light' (John 5: 35).

l. 13. *generation.* Here, 'ancestry, lineage, descent' (*OED*).

l. 17. *Five thousand years.* The manuscript versions have 'Sax thousand': the date of the creation of the world, including Adam and Eve, had been dated to 4004 BC, so 6,000 is a closer approximation to the age of humanity in 1784.

l. 22. *burnin' lake.* John sees the devil 'cast into the lake of fire and brimstone' in Revelation 20: 10; the chains and stake of l. 24 are the sort of additional details beloved of orthodox preachers.

l. 25. *Yet I am here a chosen sample.* '. . . men, attending the will of God revealed in His Word, and yielding obedience thereunto, may, from the certainty of their effectual vocation, be assured of their eternal election' (*Westminster Confession*, ch. III, para. viii). Willie may be taken as an example of this assurance.

l. 27. *a pillar in thy temple.* Another echo of Revelation: 'Him that overcometh will I make a pillar in the temple of my God, and he shall go no more out: and I will write upon him the name of my God, and the name of the city of my God, which is new Jerusalem' (3: 12).

231 l. 29. *buckler*. In the Old Testament, the Lord, or his truth, is a buck-ler (shield) to the faithful (e.g. 2 Samuel 22: 31; Psalms 18 and 91; Proverbs 2: 7).

l. 30. *To a' thy flock*. When this poem was reprinted in *Stewart's Edition of Burns's Poems* (1802), an additional stanza appeared after this line:

> O L—d thou kens what zeal I bear,
> When drinkers drink, and swearers swear,
> And singin' there, and dancin' here,
>   Wi' great an' sma';
> For I am keepet by thy fear,
>   Free frae them a'.—

As with the 'merry andrew' section added to 'The Jolly Beggars' in the same volume, Stewart seems to have got hold of a discarded manuscript fragment, though in this case the fragment has not survived.

l. 32. *fleshly lust*. 'The Lord knoweth how to deliver the godly out of temptations, and to reserve the unjust unto the day of judgment to be punished: But chiefly them that walk after the flesh in the lust of unclean-ness, and despise government' (2 Peter 2: 9–10).

l. 33. *trust*. 'a duty or office . . . entrusted to one' (*OED*).

l. 35. *thou remembers we are dust*. In Genesis 2: 7, God 'formed man of the dust of the ground'; and in Psalm 103, 'Like as a father pitieth his chil-dren, so the Lord pitieth them that fear him. For he knoweth our frame; he remembereth that we are dust'.

232 ll. 37–48. *O L—d! yestreen . . . Wad ne'er hae steer'd her*. In Robert Chambers's editions of 1838, 1851, and 1856 these two stanzas are omitted and replaced by a row of asterisks, without explanation.

ll. 39–40. *a livin' plague, | To my dishonour*. That is, a child.

l. 41. *l–g*. Leg.

l. 49. *this fleshly thorn*. Willie in this stanza takes Paul as his type, who explains in the second Epistle to the Corinthians that 'lest I should be exalted above measure through the abundance of the revelations, there was given to me a thorn in the flesh, the messenger of Satan to buffet me, lest I should be exalted above measure' (12: 7). Manuscript versions have Paul's 'buffet' in place of 'beset' in l. 50.

l. 51. *o'er*. From the manuscripts; the 1799 text used here has 'our' (another printing has 'owre').

l. 53. *borne*. From the manuscripts; the 1799 text has 'born'.

l. 56. *a chosen race*. The doctrine of predestination made Israel's status as a 'chosen people' in the Old Testament a paradigm for Calvinists.

l. 58. *blast*. Here, 'to bring infamy upon', or 'to strike or visit with the wrath and curse of heaven' (*OED*).

l. 61. *G——n H————n.* Gavin Hamilton (see headnote above); but the line scans better if the first name is abbreviated to the familiar 'Gaun', as in the manuscripts.

l. 62. *cartes.* From the manuscripts; the 1799 text has 'carts'.

l. 63. *takin' arts.* For this usage, cf. Peggy's praise of Patie, in Allan Ramsay's 1725 pastoral comedy *The Gentle Shepherd*: 'And then he speaks with sic a taking Art | His Words they thirle like Musick thro' my Heart' (1. 2. 96–7; Ramsay Vol. II, 221).

l. 65. *ain.* From the manuscripts; the 1799 text has 'an'.

l. 71. *Curse thou his basket and his store.* In Deuteronomy 28, 'thy basket and thy store', along with many other things, shall be either 'blessed' (28: 5), or 'cursed' (28: 17), depending on whether thou wilt or wilt not 'hearken unto the voice of the Lord thy God' (28: 15).

233 l. 75. *Thy strong right hand.* 'Thy right hand, O Lord, is become glorious in power: thy right hand, O Lord, hath dashed in pieces the enemy' (Exodus 15: 6).

l. 79. *A——n.* Aiken (see headnote above), Hamilton's lawyer.

l. 81. *we.* That is, Willie and his minister, Revd Auld.

l. 83–4: *While he wi' hingin' lips and snakin'* | *Held up his head.* At this point the manuscripts describe Auld, Willie's ally, rather than Aiken, his enemy: 'While Auld wi' hingin lip gaed sneaking | And hid his head!' In 1876 William Scott Douglas, with access to the Glenriddell manuscript and taking the present text as the earlier version, comments

> It seems to me that the Bard had latterly been induced to alter—and in our humble opinion, to spoil—this stanza, by the importunity of Dumfriesshire friends who could not form an intelligible idea of the word 'snakin' as used in the original Ayrshire copies . . . where [it] has the very opposite meaning [from the English 'sneaking'], namely *exulting*. The picture in the early version is truly grand. The orator observes the effect of his eloquence on his client's persecutors, and rears his head like a leopard after hitting a damaging blow with his forepaw; the under jaw firmly lowers itself, while the nostrils distend, and from the palate of the speaker escapes a sound of defiance and contempt for his opponent. This is what Burns calls 'snakin'.' It may not be found in any Scotch Dictionary; but every Ayrshire man, and hundreds in other lowland and even highland counties of Scotland, understand the word so, when read in the connection referred to. (Douglas Vol. II, 437–8)

DSL has no record of 'snaking' in this sense other than Scott Douglas's claim; in the entry for 'snaik' ('to prowl, snuff about looking for food') it suggests Burns perhaps meant to use *this* word in a figurative sense to mean 'snuffling, sniffing contemptuously'.

l. 85. *day of vengeance.* The Old Testament prophets mention this, for example Jeremiah: 'For this is the day of the Lord God of hosts, a day of vengeance, that he may avenge him of his adversaries: and the sword shall devour, and it shall be satiate and made drunk with their blood' (46: 10).

233 l. 86. *visit them.* That is, punish them. A biblical usage, as in Jeremiah again: 'the Lord doth not accept them; he will now remember their iniquity, and visit their sins' (14: 10).

l. 87. *pass not in thy mercy by 'em.* A usage from the minor prophet Amos, where the Lord warns, 'The end is come upon my people of Israel; I will not again pass by them any more' (8: 2).

Extempore verses on dining with Lord Daer. K127. Accompanied in the 1799 Stewart and Meikle chapbook by 'The Dominie Depos'd; or, some reflections on his Intrigue with a young lass. By William Forbes, A.M. Late School-master at Petercoulter'. The Burns text comes from a letter to Dr John Mackenzie, the surgeon in Mauchline and a close friend, and the chapbook follows the poem with the letter:

DEAR SIR

I NEVER spent an afternoon among great folks, with half that pleasure, as when in company with you I had the honour of paying my devoirs to that plain, honest, worthy man, the Professor. I would be delighted to see him perform acts of kindness and friendship, though I were not the object, he does it with such a grace.—I think his character, divided into ten parts, stands thus—four parts Socrates—four parts Nathaniel—and two parts Shakespeare's Brutus.

The foregoing verses were really extempore, but a little corrected since. They may entertain you a little, with the help of that partiality with which you are so good as favour [*sic*] the performances of,

DEAR SIR,
Your very humble servant
ROBERT BURNS.

'The Professor' was Dugald Stewart (1753–1828), Professor of Moral Philosophy at the University of Edinburgh. Impressed by the Kilmarnock edition, Stewart invited Burns to dinner at Catrine House, his country home near Mauchline, on 23 October 1786, where his former student Basil William Douglas, styled Lord Daer (1763–94), was also a guest. Daer, eldest surviving son of the Earl of Selkirk, was an improving landlord and proponent of political reform; he went on to be active in the radical circles of the early 1790s.

The poem is written in a 'tail-rhyme' stanza: Burns could have found forms in Chaucer and Dunbar, but just this type, where a trimeter 'tail' follows a rhyming couplet of tetrameter lines in a six-line stanza, had been used by William Collins for some of his *Odes on Several Descriptive and Allegoric Subjects* (1746) and by Thomas Gray for 'Ode on the Death of a Favourite Cat' (1753).

234 l. 7. *Writers.* That is, lawyers.

l. 11. *Quorum*. Justices of the Peace as a body, in contexts where a certain number have to be present for their decision to be binding.

l. 13. *stand out my shin!*. *DSL* offers 'to *set* or *turn out the brunt side o one's shin*: to be proud of oneself, to hold one's head high, be quite uplifted'; 'to set out the shin' means 'to walk proudly' in *OED*.

l. 16. *lang Scotch ell*. The Scotch ell, a measure of length, at 37 inches, was actually shorter than the English one, at 45.

l. 18. *sonnet*. Song: see note to p. 205, l. 84.

l. 19. *Hogarth*. William Hogarth (1697–1764), painter and engraver of 'modern moral subjects' such as *The Rake's Progress* and *Marriage à-la-mode*.

l. 25. *good Stuart*. Dugald Stewart: see headnote above. The editions of Currie and Cunningham omit this stanza.

l. 26. *Scotia's sacred Demosthenes*. Demosthenes (d. 322 BC), the great Athenian orator; Henley and Henderson suggest (Vol. II, 342) that this refers to Hugh Blair, who seems to have attended this dinner as well. Blair was Professor of Rhetoric and Belles Lettres at Edinburgh University.

l. 37. *I watch'd*. That is, watched *for* (something expected): *OED* 4d.

235 *The Fornicater*. K61. This and the following two songs appear in a volume entitled *The Merry Muses of Caledonia; a collection of favourite Scots songs, Ancient and Modern; selected for use of the Crochallan Fencibles*. Printed for private distribution, the title-page names no publisher; one of the extant copies gives the date as 1799, but was probably produced the following year. The title page has an epigraph:

> Say, Puritan, can it be wrong,
> To dress plain truth in witty song?
> What honest Nature says, we should do;
> What every lady does,—or would do.

Burns was a member of the Crochallan Fencibles (see note to p. 149, l. 17), collected bawdy songs and shared them with like-minded friends, and is certainly the author, in whole or in part, of many of the 85 songs in *Merry Muses*. It is impossible to say if his involvement in the production of this volume went any further, but his name remained associated with it even as other material was added in the following century-and-a-half of its unofficial circulation, until a more liberal age permitted its open publication (in the United States in 1964, and in Great Britain in 1965).

This song, the first in the volume (pp. 3–4), is certainly by Burns: a manuscript in his hand exists (in which 'fornicator' is spelt correctly), and the lyric describes the experience of public penance for 'fornication' allegorized in 'Epistle to J. Rankine' in the Kilmarnock edition. An avowedly bowdlerized version was published in 1876 by Scott Douglas.

Tune: Clout the Cauldron. For a score, see notes to p. 226, ll. 165–80.

235 l. 3. *daintless*. The manuscript has 'dauntless'. The present version per-
haps reflects a vernacular pronunciation, although it does not appear in
DSL.

l. 4. *Whate'er the lass discovers*. The verb in the sense of 'divulge, reveal,
disclose to knowledge (anything secret or unknown)' or 'reveal the identity of
(a person)' (*OED* 4, 6): for example, to the Church Session. The manuscript
has 'When the bonny lass discovers', which Kinsley glosses as 'reveals her
pregnancy', although this is not a usage listed in *OED* or *DSL*.

l. 6. *frater*. Brother (Latin).

l. 9. *Before the congregation wide*. For punishment in the 'stool of repent-
ance', see note to p. 113, ll. 37–72; and see the experience narrated in the
woman's voice in 'The rantin dog the daddie o't' from *SMM*.

l. 12. *ditty*. 'The matter of charge, or ground of indictment, against a
person accused of a crime' (*DSL*).

l. 15. *limbs*. This reading is from the manuscript. The *Merry Muses* text
has 'lambs': probably a mistake.

l. 18. *buttock hire*. 'A fine exacted by the church in cases of fornication'
(*DSL*).

l. 20. *convoy*. The manuscript has 'convey'.

ll. 25–32. *But, by the sun an' moon I swear...A harden'd Fornicater*. Compare
the sentiments expressed towards the real 'Betsey', Elizabeth Paton, and
her daughter in 'A poet's welcome to his love-begotten daughter' in this
volume.

236 l. 30. *pater*. Father (Latin).

l. 32. *A harden'd Fornicater*. The manuscript has two more stanzas, not
included in *Merry Muses*. 'Tipt you off blue-boram' means 'given you
syphilis'; 'esse Mater' means 'to become a mother'.

> Ye wenching blades whose hireling jades
>   Have tipt you off blue-boram,
> I tell ye plain, I do disdain
>   To rank you in the Quorum;
> But a bony lass upon the grass
>   To teach her esse Mater,
> And no reward but for regard,
>   O that's a Fornicator.
>
> Your warlike Kings and Heros bold,
>   Great Captains and Commanders;
> Your mighty Cèsars fam'd of old,
>   And Conquering Alexanders;
> In fields they fought and laurels bought

>   And bulwarks strong did batter,
>   But still they grac'd our noble list
>   And ranked Fornicator!!!

Nine inch will please a lady. K252. Probably by Burns (ll. 5–7 survive in his handwriting), starting from a traditional scenario; *Merry Muses*, 32–4.

Tune: The Quaker's wife.

In L567 (June 1793) Burns recommends this tune to Thomson for his song 'Blythe hae I been on yon hill'; but the version Thomson uses has an altered second part. The present score reflects the traditional tune, and is adapted from 'Merrily dance the Quaker' in *A Collection of Scots Reels or Country Dances* published by Robert Bremner (1759).

l. 3. *graith.* Here, tackle.

l. 7. *Annandale.* The eastern district of Dumfriesshire.

l. 12. *p——e.* Pintle, i.e. cock.

l. 15. *and a daud.* 'Daud' can mean 'a lump of any solid matter' (*DSL*); or this phrase might just mean 'and then some'.

l. 16. *He nidg't it in. DSL* has 'press, squeeze' among its meanings for 'knidge'.

l. 17. *laithron.* 'Lazy, loitering' (*DSL*). This reading is from the manuscript: *Merry Muses* has 'laithern'.

l. 22. *nyvle.* Navel.

l. 24. *gyvel.* Gable-end, used figuratively here, suggests *DSL*, for the pudendum.

237 *Poor bodies do naething but m—w.* K395. Also known as 'Why shouldna poor folk mowe?' and by its first line. For 'mow' or 'mowe' *DSL* offers 'copulate'; the British-English 'shag' might be a closer equivalent, except a 'mow' can also be enjoyed by livestock. *Merry Muses*, 80–3.

Tune: The Campbells are coming.

Burns made a version of the old Jacobite song for *The Scots Musical Museum*, song 299, from which this score is adapted. The chorus is traditionally sung to the lower part of the tune; *Low* sets it to the higher in this instance.

Most of this is certainly by Burns. Several manuscript versions exist in his hand: one sent to his Edinburgh friend Robert Cleghorn in a letter of 12 December 1792 ('a song, just finished this moment'), L527; another in L632 of July 1794 to George Thomson, editor of the *Select Collection*, who marked in the margin, 'What a pity this is not publishable'. But stanzas 4 and 6 of the present text appear in none of them, and have been added by others; the stanzas by Burns also reveal many changes which cannot be attributed to him, only a few of which I have noted below.

237 l. 1. *WHEN*. 'While' in the manuscripts: see note to l. 46 below.

l. 3. *had*. This is 'hae' in the manuscripts: see note to l. 46 below.

l. 11. *B—s—k's great prince*. Brunswick (Braunschweig, in Germany). Charles William Ferdinand, Duke of Brunswick and brother-in-law to George III, invaded France with a mostly Prussian and Austrian army in August 1792, intending to reverse the revolution and restore Louis XVI to his full powers. The invasion was halted by the French at Valmy on 20 September.

l. 12. *Gade*. 'Cam' in the manuscripts: see note to l. 46 below.

l. 17. *The E—p—r swore*. 'Emperor' may refer to Francis II, Holy Roman (that is, German) Emperor, another leader of the anti-revolutionary coalition; or his father Leopold II, who in August 1791 had, with the King of Prussia, made a joint declaration of their readiness to punish France for any harm visited on Louis XVI and his family (though Leopold died before the war began).

l. 23. *the brave duke of Y—k*. York. Britain joined the coalition in February 1793. Frederick, Duke of York and Albany, second son of George III, commanded the British contingent in the coalition armies in the spring and summer of that year.

l. 24. *The Rhine first did pass.* In the copy of *Merry Muses* in the National Library of Scotland, Victorian editor William Scott Douglas has annotated this terrible line with an alternative: 'At the Rhine fell to work'. Douglas included a few heavily bowdlerized stanzas from this song in his 1876 *Complete Poetical Works*.

l. 27. *his P—ss—n dame.* Prussian. In 1791 Frederick had married Princess Frederica Charlotte, daughter of the King of Prussia.

238   l. 30. *Proud P—ss–a.* Prussia.

l. 32. *F—d——k.* King Frederick-William II, one of the leaders of the Coalition.

l. 35. *The black-headed eagle.* A black double-headed eagle was the emblem of the Empire.

l. 38. *the braes of Gemap.* French forces, invading the Austrian Netherlands, defeated the Imperial army at Jemappes on 6 November 1792.

ll. 41–2. *Kate laid her claws,* | *On poor St——l—s.* Stanislaus. Stanisław August Poniatowski, last King of the Polish-Lithuanian Commonwealth, had sided with his reformist parliament to produce a modernizing Constitution for Poland, partly inspired by events in France, in 1791. The Polish nobility rebelled, and the following year Catherine the Great, Empress of Russia ('Kate'), sent in her troops to reassert Russian hegemony and aristocratic privilege; Stanisław then went over to the reactionary side. Decades earlier, Catherine and Stanisław had been lovers.

l. 43. *was.* This is 'has' in the manuscript: see following note.

l. 46. *An' why, &c.* The manuscript versions end with an additional stanza (I have added line-breaks to replicate the form of the stanza in *Merry Muses*):

> But truce with commotions
> And new-fangled notions,
> A bumper I trust you'll allow:
> Here's George our gude king
> And Charlotte his queen,
> And lang may they tak a gude mowe!

Burns wrote this song during the attempts to destroy the new regimes in France and Poland that it describes. If the preceding stanzas implicitly explain the belligerence of Charles, Francis, and Frederick-William as a substitute for sex, this last stanza reassures the British reader that the United Kingdom will remain at peace, given the famous attention of 'Farmer George' to his connubial duties (in her first 22 years of marriage Charlotte had borne 15 children). Although Burns retains this stanza in the song he sends to Thomson in 1794, this meaning had been lost, because Britain had by then entered the war. The *Merry Muses* text updates the song for wartime, omitting this closing reassurance, adding the reference to the Duke of York's campaign in stanza 4, and making the changes noted in ll. 1, 3, 12, and 43 to more consistently place these events in the past (Poland, for example, had not merely 'bent like a bow' by 1799, but had vanished from the map entirely, in the Third Partition of 1795).

Poem on Pastoral Poetry. K82. This, and the following two texts, were first published in *The Works of Robert Burns; with an account of his life, and a criticism on his writings. In four volumes* (London and Edinburgh, 1800), Vol. IV. Researched and edited by Dr James Currie, this was the first major collection not only of Burns's poetry and songs but also of his correspondence. This poem appears at pp. 359–61. This title is Currie's invention: a manuscript version gives the title only as 'Sketch'. Burns had used the Standard Habbie stanza to talk *about* poetry before, for example in the Epistles to John Lapraik.

238 l. 9. *sock or buskin.* Originally, the low shoe (*soccus*) worn by comic actors, in contrast to the high thick-soled boot (*buskin* in renaissance English) worn by the actors in ancient Athenian tragedy; metonyms for comic and tragic theatre respectively.

239 l. 13. *Homer's craft.* Epic poetry, its greatest modern instance being Milton's *Paradise Lost* (1667).

l. 14. *Eschylus.* Athenian playwright (d. *c.*456 BC), author of tragedies including the series known as the *Oresteia*.

ll. 15–16. *Wee Pope . . . Horatian fame.* Disease left Alexander Pope (1688–1744) with restricted growth and a hunchback. He appears here as the pre-eminent satirist of the modern age, in the tradition of the Roman poet Quintus Horatius Flaccus (65–8 BC), known in English as Horace.

ll. 17–18. *Barbauld . . . E'en Sappho's flame.* Anna Lætitia Barbauld, née Aiken (1743–1825), at this point probably the best-known female poet writing in English; Sappho, d. *c.*570 BC, Greek poet hugely admired in antiquity, though only fragments of her work now survive.

l. 19. *Theocritus.* Currie's 1800 text has 'Theopocritus', a mistake corrected in the second edition of the following year. A third-century BC Greek poet, his *Bucolics* are credited with initiating the pastoral tradition in European poetry. Living in Sicily, Theocritus wrote in the Doric version of Greek rather than the language of Athens. In his Preface to his 1721 *Poems*, Allan Ramsay appeals to this as a precedent for writing in Scots: 'The *Scotticisms*, which perhaps may offend some over-nice Ear, give new Life and Grace to the Poetry, and become their Place as well as the *Doric* Dialect of *Theocritus*, so much admired by the best Judges' (Ramsay Vol. I, xix).

l. 20. *herd's ballats, Maro's catches.* This makes perfect sense as it stands: the sort of ballads composed or sung by a shepherd or cattleherd, contrasted with the work of the Roman poet Publius Vergilius Maro (70–19 BC), known as Virgil in English, whose pastoral *Eclogues* are modelled on Theocritus. But the manuscript has 'Herd's', which has suggested to some that Burns means the songs collected in *Ancient and Modern Scottish Songs* (1769) by David Herd (d. 1810).

ll. 21–2. *skinklin patches | O' heathen tatters.* Pope's *Pastorals* are teenage works, modelled on and frequently borrowing from Virgil's *Eclogues.*

l. 32. *Allan.* Allan Ramsay (1686–1758), author of the verse drama *The Gentle Shepherd* (1725; later turned into a ballad-opera) which naturalizes pastoral conventions in Scots.

l. 35. *Tamtallan.* The impressive ruins of Tantallon castle stand on an East-Lothian clifftop.

l. 40. *Philomel.* A pastoral-conventional name for the nightingale: in Greek myth, Philomela is raped and her tongue cut out to prevent her accusing her rapist: she is eventually turned into a nightingale by the gods. The nightingale is not a species native to Scotland.

240 ll. 43–54. *In gowany glens thy burnie strays . . . The sternest move.* The manuscript version has these two stanzas in reverse order.

Poetical Inscription for an Altar to Independence. K505. First published in Currie's *Works of Robert Burns* (1800), Vol. IV, p. 369. For Patrick Heron of Heron and Kerroughtrie, see headnote to 'The Election', p. 363; this poem was written around the same time.

Address to a Lady. K524. First published in Currie's *Works of Robert Burns* (1800), Vol. IV, p. 381. The title is again Currie's invention: universally known by its first line. It took another seventy years before these words were matched to the air for which they were written, at least in print. Currie does not mention a tune; Cunningham (Vol. V) assigns them to 'Lass o' Livingstone'. Eventually, in the 1850s, Robert Chambers tracked down Jessy Lewars, who as a girl had helped out in the Burns household during the poet's final illness. She told him that Burns had offered to write words for any tune she cared to play for him on the piano, and these lines were the result. But in Volume IV of his 1856 edition, Chambers identified this tune as 'The Wren's Nest' in *The Scots Musical Museum*, Vol. V, song 406. It was in fact another tune included in that volume, 'Lennox love to Blantyre', paired there with a lyric called 'The Wren' as song 483. This is the source of the score below.

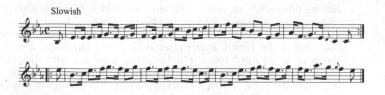

Chambers's mistake was rectified by William Scott Douglas in his *Complete Poetical Works of Robert Burns* (1871), Vol. II.

241 *Lines written extempore in a lady's pocket-book.* K412. Written in June 1793; first published by Thomas Stewart in *Poems Ascribed to Robert Burns, the Ayrshire Bard* (Glasgow, 1801), 74. This volume collected most of the poems Stewart and Meikle had published in their chapbook series and added many others. See also headnote to 'The Tree of Liberty', p. 402. The form is that strongly associated with Pope: iambic pentameter ('heroic') couplets.

Verses, Written under the Portrait of Fergusson the Poet. K143. First published in *The Scots Magazine*, LXV (November 1803). An up-market but unchallenging monthly, this issue includes a biographical essay on the seventeenth-century physician Sir Andrew Balfour, and a series of extracts from recent books about the East Indies, including an account of the fall of Seringapatam to British forces in 1799. The present poem appears on p. 798 without any more comment than appears in the subtitle; it is followed by another piece inscribed by Burns in the same source, the very early 'Tragic Fragment' (K5). The *Scots Magazine* text has been mangled in transcription. A facsimile of the holograph inscription can be found in Henley and Henderson Vol. II, between pages 408 and 409. The poem is a rare excursion for Burns into blank verse.

l. 2. *pleasure!*. The exclamation mark is from the holograph: the text published in 1803 has only a comma.

l. 4. *muse.* From the holograph: the 1803 text has 'Muses'.

l. 6. *unfitted for.* This is taken from the holograph. The 1803 text has 'unpitied for', which makes no sense; nineteenth-century editions change this to 'unpitied by', until the correct reading appears in 1896.

Song [My father was a farmer]. K21. This, and following two texts, were first published in *Reliques of Robert Burns; consisting chiefly of original letters, poems and critical observations on Scottish songs, collected and published by R. H. Cromek* (London, 1808). All three texts come from the notebooks, now known as the First and Second Commonplace Books, in which Burns jotted ideas and drafts beginning in April 1783. Cromek combined material from these two manuscript volumes, and claimed to reproduce the resulting text in its entirety, explaining that 'It has been the chief object in making this collection, not to omit any thing which might illustrate the character and feelings of the bard at different periods of his life' (p. 315). 'My father was a farmer' appears on pp. 330–1. It is a very early production, and in the First Commonplace Book Burns introduces it with a comment dated April 1784: 'The Following Song is a wild Rhapsody, miserably deficient in Versification, but as the sentiments are the genuine feelings of my heart, for that reason I have a particular pleasure in conning it over' (p. 329). The long lines of this poem can be thought of as pairs of shorter iambic tetrameter lines conjoined, the first often structured with an internal rhyme, the second ending on a feminine rhyme with 'O' completing the measure.

Tune: The Weaver and his shuttle O, also known as Jockey's (or Johnny's) grey breeks.

Slow

This score is adapted from *The Scots Musical Museum* song 27, 'The Gentle Swain'. It allows for the repetition of the last two lines of verse in the last eight bars: we have no indication that this is what Burns expected in setting these words to this tune.

l. 1. *My father was a farmer upon the Carrick border.* Cromek has 'Father' and 'Farmer': the present text follows his manuscript source which uses lower case for both initials. Carrick is the southernmost district of Ayrshire, across the river Doon from Burns's native Kyle: see Map.

242 l. 18. *moil.* 'To make oneself wet and muddy' (*OED*). This reading is from the manuscript: Cromek has 'broil'.

l. 35. *Potosi.* The silver mine in present-day Bolivia, the source of great wealth to the Spanish Empire.

243 *Fragment [There was a lad was born in Kyle].* K140. Also known as 'Rantin rovin Robin'. This song and the following 'Elegy' come from a section of Cromek's version of the Commonplace Book headed 'EGOTISMS from my own Sensations'. It begins, 'I don't well know what is the reason of it, but some how or other though I am, when I have a mind, pretty generally beloved; yet, I never could get the art of commanding respect.—I imagine it is owing to my being deficient in what Sterne calls "that understrapping virtue of discretion."—I am so apt to a *lapsus linguæ*, that I sometimes think the character of a certain great man, I have read of somewhere, is

very much *apropos* to myself—that he was a compound of great talents and great folly. N.B. To try if I can discover the causes of this wretched infirmity, and, if possible, to mend it' (Cromek, pp. 339–40; Burns quotes *Tristram Shandy*, Vol. VI, p. 351). The song appears on pp. 341–2, and comes from the Second Commonplace Book, begun in Edinburgh in 1787 at the height of Burns's celebrity there.

The tune, 'Dainty Davie', dates from the seventeenth century. It is used for song 34 of *The Scots Musical Museum*, from whence the score below is adapted:

In 1871 William Scott Douglas (in *Complete Poetical Works*, Vol. II) observed that it was 'almost universally' sung to a different tune, 'O an ye were dead gudeman' (see note to p. 223, ll. 89–116).

243 l. 2. *what na day o' what na style*. 'what na' means 'which, of two or more' (*DSL*). Britain had switched from the Julian to the Gregorian calendars in 1752; dates calculated in the old and new 'styles' differ by 11 days in consequence.

l. 4. *nice*. In the now obsolete sense of 'particular, strict, or careful with regard to a specific point or thing' (*OED*).

l. 9. *Our monarch's hindmost year but ane*. George III ascended the throne in 1760.

l. 11. *Janwar Win'*. A note in Cromek's source text, the Second Commonplace Book, but not included by him, explains: 'January 25, 1759, the date of my bardship's vital existence.—R.B'.

l. 12. *hansel*. 'A gift bestowed to commemorate an inaugural occasion, event or season, e.g. the beginning of the year . . . with the idea of bringing good-luck to the recipient' (*DSL*).

l. 13. *keekit*. Cromek has 'keckit': clearly a compositor's mistake.

l. 26. *Ye'll gar the lasses lie aspar*. That is, 'aspread, with legs apart' (*DSL*). This is from the Second Commonplace Book: Cromek has 'Ye gar the lasses ****'.

244 *Elegy on the Death of Robert Ruisseaux.* K141. First published in Cromek, p. 343, from the Second Commonplace Book. 'Ruisseaux' is French for 'streams' and hence an equivalent for 'burns'. The Standard Habbie stanza again used for its original purpose, humorous elegy.

l. 1. *lair.* 'The resting place of a corpse; a grave, tomb' (*OED*).

Sketch of an Epistle to R. Graham, Esq. of Fintray. K318. Written in 1790, and sent in a letter to its addressee on 10 June; first published in *The Edinburgh Magazine, and Literary Miscellany* for April 1811. This journal had merged with the very similar *Scots Magazine* in 1804 (it was also known by this older name) and was published by the prestigious Archibald Constable and Co., responsible for the mighty *Edinburgh Review*, the *Encyclopaedia Britannica*, and Walter Scott. The April issue includes extracts from travellers' accounts of China and Nepal; 'Memoirs of the Progress of Manufactures, Chemistry, Science, and the Fine Arts'; an 'Account of the Establishment of the present System of Public Education in Scotland', extracted from a new history of the Reformation; a letter describing 'Recent Improvements in Glasgow'; and a review of 'A Sketch of the State of British India, with a view of pointing out the best means of civilizing its Inhabitants, and diffusing the knowledge of Christianity throughout the Eastern World'. Burns's poem appears on pp. 294–5. Beneath the title we are told that 'The following poem, from the pen of the celebrated Robert Burns, has never before been published.' The poem is written in the same type of tail-rhyme stanza as the 'Extempore verses on dining with Lord Daer': see headnote to that poem, p. 382.

In two of the manuscripts the title is 'Epistle to Robt. Graham of Fintry on the close of the disputed Election between Sir J. Johnston and Captn. Miller, for the Dumfries district of Boroughs' of 1790; this poem is sometimes (for example in Hogg and Motherwell's 1834 edition) grouped with the 1795 Heron poems as an 'Election ballad'. Those towns that had political rights as 'Royal Burghs' were grouped in fours or fives to elect MPs: in this case Dumfries, Kirkcudbright, Annan, Lochmaben, and Sanquhar ('The Five Carlins' of Burns's ballad on this election, K269). In contested elections, each town council first voted on which candidate to support; then a delegate from each town would cast their vote at the election itself. County elections (see headnote to 'The Election', p. 363) were vulnerable to the ability of great landowners to create votes by parcelling out their lands to their allies; but burgh elections, like the administration of the burghs themselves, were simply and openly corrupt, with bribery routine and violence unremarkable, and the Dumfries Burghs contest of 1790 was notorious even by these low standards. Miller's patron, the Duke of Queensberry, doled out £8,000; Johnstone's people spent £12,000, secured the vote of Lochmaben by kidnapping a hostile member of its finely hung council, and still lost the election 2–3 (for details see *HPO*).

Title. Robert Graham (1749–1815) was factor on some large estates in Perthshire and Forfarshire. He had sold the family's Fintry estate in Forfarshire in 1780 to pay off personal debts, but retained the designation.

He became a Commissioner of the Scottish Board of Excise in 1787, and in this capacity was in a position to help Burns in his career when he became an exciseman the following year: in his letters Burns often refers to Fintry as his 'patron'. It was to Fintry that Burns turned when his political alignments threatened his job: see Appendix 1, p. 270f. Burns wrote several poems addressed to him: the present text is sometimes known as the 'Second Epistle to Fintry'.

245 l. 7. *Drumlanrig*. The Dumfriesshire seat of William Douglas, fourth Duke of Queensberry (1724-1810), at the head of the most powerful 'interest' in the county, though rarely there in person.

l. 9. *Of fiddles, whores and hunters*. Queensberry was a generous patron of both musicians and prostitutes; he also owned a famous racing stud ('hunters' are a type of horse). The *Edinburgh Magazine* was using a manuscript that Burns had sent to his friends the McMurdos, where this line reads 'Of Princes and their darlings'. The four other surviving manuscripts have the present reading: John McMurdo was Chamberlain to Queensberry at Drumlanrig, so Burns clearly chose to pull his punches in that particular version.

l. 10. *buying*. This becomes 'winning' in the *Edinburgh Magazine* text, for the same reason.

l. 11. *wabster louns*. Weavers, an important demographic in town life, self-employed artisans working at home.

l. 12. *bunters*. This becomes 'carlins' in the *Edinburgh Magazine* text, to rhyme with 'darlings'; 'bunter' in Samuel Johnson's sense, being roughly synonymous with 'carlin': 'used, by way of contempt, for any low vulgar woman' (*OED*). The present version of this stanza was first published in Cunningham Vol. III, 161, in a note after the poem.

ll. 7-12. *I'll sing the zeal Drumlanrig bears . . . And kissing barefit bunters*. Burns drafted an alternative beginning for this poem, incorporating the present second stanza, which continues after the first stanza thus:

> But where shall I gae rin a ride,
> That I may splatter nane beside?
>   I wad na be uncivil:
> In manhood's various paths and ways
> There's aye some doytan body strays,
>   And I ride like the devil.—
>
> Say, I break off wi' a' my birr,
> And down yon dark, deep alley spur,
>   Where Theologics dander:
> Alas! curst wi' eternal fogs,
> And damn'd in everlasting bogs,
>   As sure's the creed I'll blunder!

I'll stain a Band, or jaup a gown,
Or rin my reckless, guilty crown
   Against the haly door:
Sair do I rue my luckless fate,
When, as the Muse an' Deil would hae't,
   I rade that road before.——

Suppose I take a spurt, and mix
Amang the wilds o' Politicks
   Electors and Elected,
Where dogs at Court (sad sons of bitches!)
Septennially a madness touches
   Till all the Land's infected.——

I'll sing the zeal Drumlanrig bears,
Who left the all-important cares
   Of fiddles, whores and hunters;
And bent on buying borough towns,
Came shaking hands wi' wabster louns,
   And kissing barefit bunters.

All-hail! Drumlanrig's haughty Grace,
Discarded remnant of a Race,
   Once godlike great in story:
Thy fathers' virtues all contrasted;
The very name of D—— blasted;
   Thine that inverted glory.——

Hate, Envy, oft the Douglas bore,
But thou hast superadded more,
   And sunk them in Contempt:
Follies and Crimes have stained the name,
But Queensberry thine the virgin claim,
   From aught of Good exempt.——

Great was the drinking, dancing, singing,
Bonfireing, racketing and ringing,

The manuscript ends with those two lines. This fragment was first published in Douglas Vol. II, pp. 418–19, separately from the rest of the poem.

l. 13. *Combustion.* A word used in Burns's letter to Mrs Dunlop: see note to l. 117 below.

l. 16. *buff and blue.* The colours of the opposition to William Pitt's government. Charles James Fox and his supporters began wearing blue coats with buff waistcoats in imitation of Washington's army, to signal their sympathy with the rebels, during the American war. Queensberry had been a 'mentor' to the young Fox, at least at the card-table and the race-track. But Queensbury had been extending his influence in the burghs with the backing of Henry Dundas, Pitt's right-hand man and manager of Scottish elections; and once in parliament, Queensberry's candidate, Patrick Miller (d. 1845), seems to have voted against the government only twice. On the other hand, Miller was well enough connected in opposition circles to communicate to Burns the prospect of a job with the *Morning Chronicle* in 1794: see headnote to 'Bruce's Address to his Troops', p. 360.

245 l. 17. *Westerha' and Hopeton.* Sir James Johnstone of Westerhall (1726–94), the sitting member for the constituency, head of a rival interest to Queensberry's. Johnstone's political career had been founded on the fortune he had made in India. As an MP he seems to have been a model of 'independence', the political virtue most highly regarded by Burns; only in his opposition to reform of the burghs themselves was he resolutely with the government (see *HPO*). John Hope, fourth Earl of Hopetoun (d. 1823), backed Johnstone.

l. 18. *Whig.* See note to ll. 82–3 below for the inheritance evoked by this name.

l. 20. *his star.* The insignia of his rank as a duke.

ll. 23–4. *Cesarean fight, | Or Ciceronian pleading.* Contrasting the Roman general and conqueror of Gaul, Gaius Julius Caesar (d. 44 BC), and the great orator and defender of the Republic, Marcus Tullius Cicero (d. 43 BC).

l. 25. *Monsmeg.* Mons Meg, the 20-inch-calibre fifteenth-century cannon, built in Mons, Flanders, but long resident at Edinburgh Castle where it was fired to mark ceremonial occasions; in 1790 it was languishing in London.

l. 26. *muster.* The grammar here suggests this verb must be in the sense of 'talk volubly and incessantly' (*DSL*), but there is clearly also a play on 'come together . . . in preparation for battle' (of an army: *OED*).

l. 31. *McM—rdo and his lovely spouse.* Burns's friends John and Jean McMurdo: see note to l. 9 above. They were on the winning, Queensberry, side, as the victor's 'laurels' of the next line reminds us.

l. 34. *Burgess.* A freeman of the town.

l. 35. *sub rosa.* That is, ' "under the rose", in secret, secretly' (*OED*). This reading is from most of the manuscripts: the *Edinburgh Magazine* text has 'all-conquering' here, removing the innuendo in deference to the McMurdos for whom its version was written (see notes to ll. 9 and 10 above).

l. 37. *Craigendarroch.* Alexander Fergusson of Craigendarroch (d. 1796), Dumfriesshire landowner and lawyer; allied to the Queensberry interest.

l. 39. *Hecla.* The Icelandic volcano. A major eruption had continued from April 1766 till May 1768.

246 l. 40. *Glenriddel, skill'd in rusty coins*. Burns's friend and neighbour the antiquarian Captain Robert Riddell of Glenriddell (see headnote to 'On Glenriddel's Fox breaking his chain', p. 404).

l. 41. *each Tory's dark designs*. Here, and at l. 45, the term 'Tory' is introduced in the context of the agency of Miller's supporters, Glenriddell and Staig. For the political lineage evoked by this term, see note to l. 86 below; but no serious politician called themselves a Tory in this period, when the name was 'a term of political abuse' (Kidd, 'Burns and Politics', 64). Glenriddell and Staig see themselves as opposing 'Tories' because that is what self-defined Whigs call their enemies, and the poem ironically adopts this usage (for another example of Burns's ironic take on 'Whigs', see 'On Glenriddel's Fox breaking his chain').

l. 44. *Redoubted Staig*. David Staig (1740–1824), Provost of Dumfries for twenty years, on and off. 'A popular and energetic public figure' (*BE*).

l. 46. *Walsh*. John Walsh, Sheriff Substitute for the County.

ll. 47–8. *his magnum-bonum round | With Cyclopean fury*. A magnum-bonum is 'a bottle containing two quarts of wine or spirits' says *DSL* (Latin, 'a great good'). The reference is to the enraged Polyphemos after Odysseus and his men have blinded him in his single eye to secure their escape in Homer's *Odyssey* Book IX.

l. 49. *Miller*. A footnote in one of the manuscripts, and the reference to banks in the next line, identify this as Patrick Miller, senior of Dalswinton, father of the Queensberry candidate, a banker, and Burns's landlord at Ellisland.

l. 52. *Maxwelton, that baron bold*. Sir Robert Laurie, fifth baronet of Maxwelton, MP for the county of Dumfries 1774–1804. In the Queensberry interest, and so on Miller's side, but also a supporter of the government.

l. 53. *Lawson*. 'A famous wine merchant' (Burns's manuscript footnote).

ll. 70–2: *As flames amang a hundred woods . . . Such is the rage of battle*. Kinsley spots the echo of Macpherson's 'Fingal', ii: 'As a hundred winds in Lochlin's groves, as fire in the firs of a hundred hills; so loud, so ruinous and vast the ranks of men are hewn down' (Macpherson 67–8).

247 l. 78. *the Buchan bullers*. A collapsed cave in the sea-cliffs near Peterhead in the north-east, where a heavy swell can produce violent breakers.

ll. 82–3. *The muffled murtherer of Charles | The Magna Charta flag unfurls*. Eighteenth-century 'Whigs' could define themselves as the descendants of the parliamentary resistance to the Stuart monarchs of the seventeenth century, which often justified itself with reference to the rights extracted from King John in the Magna Carta (the Great Charter) of 1215. The expulsion of James II and VII in the 'Revolution' of 1688–9, and the transfer of the throne to the House of Hanover in 1714, were seen as the culmination of this struggle; this triumphalist history usually skated over parliament's execution of Charles I in 1649 during the civil war. The executioner was masked.

247 l. 86. *Bold Scrimgeour follows gallant Graham*. John Scrymgeour, first Earl of Dundee (d. 1668), joined Charles's army in 1648; James Graham, first Marquis of Montrose (d. 1650), raised an army for Charles in Scotland in 1644. But the figure who might make 'Auld Covenanters shiver' (l. 87) was a different Graham, John, first Viscount Dundee (d. 1689), notorious in south-west Scotland as the ruthless enemy of those who defended their presbyterian church against the Stuart regime in the 1670s and 1680s. Burns's footnotes to one of the manuscripts confirm that he has conflated the two Dundees. These were 'Tories' in the original sense, for whom loyalty to the monarch was the paramount political virtue.

l. 88. *much-wrong'd Montrose*. Captured by Scottish parliamentary forces, Montrose was hanged in Edinburgh in 1650, his head displayed there and his limbs sent to other Scottish towns.

l. 106. *Not Pulteney's wealth can Pulteney save*. Sir James's brother William had become one of the richest commoners in Britain in 1767: an improbable series of deaths in her family had made his wife Frances heir to the fortune of her uncle, William Pulteney, Earl of Bath, if the couple changed their name to his.

l. 108. *Stewart*. 'William Stewart of Hillside' says Burns in a manuscript note.

248 l. 109. *Pitt*. William Pitt the younger (1759–1806), prime minister.

l. 110. *Thurlow*. Edward, first Baron Thurlow (1731–1806), lord chancellor: 'the ferocity of his demeanour could inspire respect, and sometimes fear' (*DNB*).

l. 111. *Melville*. Henry Dundas of Melville castle (1742–1811), treasurer of the navy, commissioner of the board of control, Pitt's right-hand man and his manager of Scotland.

l. 112. *Fox and Sheridan*. Charles James Fox (1749–1806), leader of the opposition; Richard Brinsley Sheridan (1751–1816), an MP as well as a playwright and a close friend and ally of Fox.

l. 113. *Burke shall sing, 'O Prince arise!'*. Edmund Burke MP (1729–97) had been a close ally of Fox and Sheridan since the American war, including their attempts the previous year to have the Prince of Wales made Regent when his father George III became mentally ill: see note to p. 200, l. 35. But Burke had since split with his friends over the French Revolution.

l. 116. *He only hears and sees the war*. The *Edinburgh Magazine* has 'He hears, and only hears the war' which has no manuscript authority; then prints a row of '&c's and stops. From this point the present text follows Cunningham's version (see note to l. 12 above), which completes this stanza, and supplies the final stanza in the endnote to the poem.

l. 117. *A cool spectator purely*. Burns wrote to Mrs Dunlop from Ellisland:

I have just got a summons to attend with my men-servants armed as well as we can, on Monday at one o'clock in the *morning* to escort

Capt[n] Miller from Dalswinton in to Dumfries to be a Candidate for our Boroughs which chuse their Member that day.—The Duke of Queensberry & the Nithsdale Gentlemen who are almost all friends to the Duke's Candidate, the said Capt[n], are to raise all Nithsdale on the same errand.—The Duke of Buccleugh's, Earl of Hopeton's people, in short, the Johnstons, Jardines, and all the Clans of Annandale, are to attend Sir James Johnston who is the other Candidate, on the same account.—This is no exaggeration.— . . . What will be the event, I know not.—I shall go to please my Landlord, & to see the Combustion; but instead of trusting to the strength of Man, I shall trust to the heels of my horse, which are among the best in Nithsdale. (L403, 9 July 1790)

John Bushby (see note to p. 215, l. 9), managing the final election as sheriff-clerk, kept the three delegates for Miller in the courthouse overnight before the vote, to protect them from a mob of (he claimed) four thousand, 'one half at least armed with bludgeons', and called in the army to maintain order (*HPO*).

l. 122. *land o' cakes.* That is, oatcakes: meaning Scotland.

Epistle to the President of the Highland Society. K108. Written in 1786; first published in *The Edinburgh Magazine, and Literary Miscellany* for February 1818 under the present title, but usually known as the 'Address of Beelzebub'. This issue also includes an essay 'On whether Pope was a poet'; letters on popular superstitions and proposing a philharmonic society for Edinburgh; a continuation of a review of Walter Scott's novel *Rob Roy*; and some natural history. Burns's poem appears on pp. 130–1, between a continuation of an essay on the life and writings of James Hogg and a discussion of the original ballad of 'Rob Roy'. It is introduced with a long letter to the editor:

I was happy to observe in your last Number, a complete copy of a song by Burns ['Here's a Health to them that's awa',' K391] which the public had hitherto only seen in an imperfect state [in Cromek's *Reliques*, 1808]. It is well to preserve in some secure and accessible repository all such reliques and memorials of remarkable men, as are either interesting on account of their intrinsic merit, or that serve in any degree to illustrate the state of our national literature and manners,—though perhaps unworthy of a place in more classical collections. With this view, I enclose for your Magazine another production of our great Scottish poet, which has not yet appeared in print. You will find several indifferent enough lines in it, and one or two rather rough expressions, but nothing, I think, that can offend any true old-fashioned unsophisticated Scotchman, or even the more fastidious *Southron*, who has not lost all remembrance of Fielding, or who has learned to estimate the irresistible naïveté of the author of Waverley. In one word, while I deprecate as much as any one can the injudicious zeal of such editors as

Cromek . . . yet I consider it a duty to preserve from oblivion every production which the public has a claim to inherit as the legacy of departed genius, unless its publication be offensive to right feeling, or derogatory to the talents and character of the author. These remarks may perhaps appear disproportioned to the importance of the following careless effusion, but you will at least recognize in it something of the unpruned vigour of Burns' genius,—the rustic but keen severity of his sarcasm,—and the manly detestation of oppression (real or supposed) which so strongly characterized him. The internal evidences of its authenticity are sufficiently obvious; but for your more complete satisfaction, I enclose the original in his own handwriting. It was given to me by a friend who got it many years ago from the well known 'ready-witted Rankin,' the poet's early and intimate acquaintance. I am, &c.   R.W.
Ayr, Jan. 30, 1818.

The Highland Society, an organization of Highland landowners, met in London on 23 May 1786 to discuss

the encouragement of the fisheries in the Highlands, &c. Three thousand pounds were immediately subscribed by eleven gentlemen present for this particular purpose. The Earl of Breadalbane informed the meeting that five hundred persons had agreed to emigrate from the estates of Mr McDonald of Glengarry; that they had subscribed money, purchased ships, &c., to carry their design into effect. The noblemen and gentlemen agreed to co-operate with government to frustrate their design; and to recommend to the principal noblemen and gentlemen in the Highlands to endeavour to prevent emigration, by improving the fisheries, agriculture, and manufactures, and particularly to enter into a subscription for that purpose.

This is the account of the meeting that Burns read in the *Edinburgh Advertiser* of 30 May. John Campbell, Earl of Breadalbane (1762–1834), was currently one of the Scottish representative peers in the House of Lords; Thomas Mackenzie of Highfield had been laird of Applecross since 1774; and Duncan Macdonell of Glengarry (d. 1788) was 'chief' of clan Macdonell. Within ten years one of the 'improvements' proposed was requiring the mass eviction of tenants to make way for sheep runs, a process that was reaching a climax by the time this poem was published in the *Edinburgh Magazine*; and emigration, far from being prevented, was sometimes forced on the evicted.

249 l. 7. *A* **** *s.* Applecross.

l. 13. *Hancocke, or a Franklin.* John Hancock (1737–93), President of the Continental Congress at the signing of the Declaration of Independence in 1776; Benjamin Franklin (1706–90), scientist, inventor, and writer who helped draft the Declaration.

l. 15. *Washington.* George Washington (1732–99), commander in the war with Britain and first President of the new state.

l. 16. *Montgomery.* Richard Montgomery (1738–75), a retired British soldier who led a rebel unit to capture Montreal but was killed attacking Quebec in the opening of the war.

l. 21. *North.* Frederick, Lord North (1713–92), prime minister 1770–82 and thus responsible for the failure in America; *Sackville*: George, first Viscount Sackville (1716–85), Secretary of State for American Affairs during the war.

l. 23. *Howes and Clintons.* William, fifth Viscount Howe (1729–1814), the general in charge of British forces; Sir Henry Clinton (1738–95), general whose inability to relieve the siege of General Cornwallis's army at Yorktown led to its surrender and the final British collapse in 1781. These references are of course ironic: Howe and Clinton had failed to bring the American rebels 'to a right repentance'.

l. 31. *G ****.* Glengarry.

250 l. 44. *Drury Lane.* At one end of Covent Garden (where the Highland Society had met); both names were synonymous with prostitution.

l. 47. *Flaffan wi' duds.* Kinsley notes the echo of Fergusson's 'The Ghaists', where the ghost of George Heriot, wealthy merchant and philanthropist in the reign of James VI, mourns the effect of the union with England on the finances of his hospital: 'Hale interest for my fund can scantly now | Cleed a' my callants backs, and stap their mou'. | How maun their weyms wi' sairest hunger slack, | Their duds in targets flaff upo' their back' (ll. 73–6; Fergusson 143).

l. 58. *'Tween Herod's hip an' Polycrate.* Herod was king of Judea under Rome at the time of Christ's birth; Polycrates was king of Samos in the Aegean in the mid sixth century BC.

l. 60. *Almagro an' Pizarro.* Diego D'Almargo (1475–1538) and Francisco Pizarro (1478–1541), leaders of the brutal Spanish conquest of Peru.

Beelzebub. 'The prince of the devils' (Matthew 12: 24) in the New Testament, and Satan's lieutenant in *Paradise Lost.*

Anno Mundi 5790. That is, 1786, plus the 4004 years traditionally calculated to have elapsed between the creation of the world and the birth of Christ: Beelzebub of course does not count years from the latter.

The Selkirk Grace. K531. First published in *The Works of Robert Burns; with his life. In eight volumes*, ed. Alan Cunningham (1834), Vol. III, p. 311. Cunningham's note claims: 'On a visit to St. Mary's Isle, the Earl of Selkirk requested Burns to say grace at dinner. These were the words he uttered—they were applauded then, and have since been known in Galloway by the name of "The Selkirk Grace."' An almost identical version appeared the same year in *The Works of Robert Burns*, ed. The Ettrick Shepherd [James Hogg] and William Motherwell, Vol. II p. 78, entitled 'A Grace, spoken at the table of the Earl of Selkirk', and in Chambers's edition of 1838. The earliest written version of the grace to have survived is in the papers of James Grierson of Dalgoner (1753–1843), who knew the poet at Ellisland, though he only began collecting Burns material in 1805. Grierson's version is in English, apart from the last line; his is the text used by Kinsley. See the article by J. A. Mackay in *Burns Chronicle*, 98 (1989), 24–8.

250 *The Tree of Liberty.* K625. First published in *The Poetical Works of Robert Burns*, ed. Robert Chambers (1838), 86–7: 'Here printed for the first time, from a MS. in the possession of Mr James Duncan, Mosesfield, near Glasgow'. Only 148 pages long with the text in two columns on each page, Chambers's first edition aimed to be 'the cheapest, so that it may be expected to find its way where hitherto none but the most inferior editions, or none at all, have been introduced' ('Preface', 3): he would later refer to it as the 'People's Edition'.

Many have doubted that this poem is by Burns: the manuscript on which Chambers based it, in Burns's handwriting, has been lost. But some of the doubts seem grounded in political distaste, and there is no obvious reason to doubt Chambers's account of his source. He included it in both his subsequent editions. In his 1856–7 *Life and Works of Robert Burns* he introduces it with a discussion of Burns's anger at the war with France: 'Being . . . little apt to think his words of great consequence, it is to be feared that he was much less cautious in the expression of his opinions than was necessary for his escaping censure. We have already had some of these escapes of political sentiment before us. Some others have survived till these times on the breath of tradition and otherwise' (p. 77). Chambers then offers the poem included in the present volume as 'Lines written extempore in a lady's pocket-book' as one of two examples, and continues,

> It is far from likely that the whole of the democratic effusions of Burns have come down to us. For many years, that kind of authorship was attended with so much reproach, that men of humanity studied to conceal rather than to expose the evidence by which it could be proved against him. And even after the poor bard's death, the interests of his young family demanded of all the admirers of his name, that nothing should be brought forward which was calculated to excite a political jealousy regarding him. Hence, for many years there was a mystery observed on this subject. During that time, of course, many manuscripts might perish. As things now stand—the whole matter being looked on as only a curious piece of literary history—there can be no great objection to the publication of any piece of the kind which may have chanced to be preserved. There is one which, but for the manner in which it introduces the name of the unfortunate Louis XVI., might have now been read without any pain, as containing only the feelings of a man who looked too sanguinely upon the popular cause in France:— (p. 78)

The following poem is 'The Tree of Liberty'. Although Chambers's text does not name a tune, the stanza form, with the repetition of 'man' in every second line, is that of Burns's 'Fragment' on the American war from the Edinburgh *Poems*, which is written to fit the tune 'Killiecrankie'.

Title. Thomas Paine had published a poem called 'Liberty Tree' in the *Pennsylvania Magazine* in 1775. There, the tree is planted by the first colonists, and 'The fame of its fruit drew the nations around, | To seek out this peacable shore'; but now 'all the tyrranical pow'rs, | King, commons, and lords, are uniting amain, | To cut down this guardian of ours' (ll. 11–12, 26–8; *Works of Thomas Paine*, ed. Carey, 385–6). The practice of planting a young tree as part of a ritual declaring a community's liberation was formalized during the revolution in France: it seems to have developed from the use of maypoles in rural areas as gestures of collective defiance of landlords (see Ozouf 1988). In the autumn of 1792, the new republic's army defeated a Prussian invasion at Valmy (20 September) and then turned north to overwhelm the Austrians at Jemappes (6 November) and seize what had been the Austrian Netherlands (present-day Belgium). The news of General Dumouriez's arrival in Brussels triggered popular celebration and protest in many Scottish towns, often accompanied by street disorder. This sometimes involved, for example, burning an effigy of Henry Dundas, the government's hated manager of Scottish politics. In Fife and the north-east (Dundee, Stonehaven, Aberdeen, Fochabers) it included the erection of liberty trees. The one in Dundee carried a sign saying 'Liberty and Equality, no sinecures' (Harris, 'Political Protests', 66).

l. 3. *patriots*. That is, partisans of the 'country' or the 'nation' as opposed to the king.

251 l. 5. *It stands where ance the Bastile stood*. Symbolically, at least. The Bastille prison in Paris was stormed on 14 July 1789: King Louis XVI having lost control of his capital city to its people, the revolution at this point became irreversible. The Bastille was quickly demolished: I can find no record of a liberty tree being planted on the site.

l. 7. *Superstition's hellish brood*. The French Catholic church, closely integrated in the pre-revolutionary absolutist state.

l. 26. *Gallia*. France, 'Gaul' in Roman times.

l. 28. *Frae yont the western waves*. The poem understands the American Revolution as an inspiration for the French one.

l. 37. *King Loui' thought to cut it down*. Louis XVI went along with the reforms imposed on him by the new government, even as his Austrian in-laws prepared to reverse the revolution by force of arms. But on 21–2 June 1791, he fled with his queen in the direction of Austrian territory; was recognized, stopped at Varennes, and brought back to Paris, deeply suspected as an enemy of the state of which he remained, for another year, head.

l. 40. *Cut aff his head*. Louis was sent to the guillotine on 21 January 1793; his queen followed in October. At a time of European war, 'What is there in the delivering over a perjured Blockhead & an unprincipled Prostitute into the hands of the hangman, that it should arrest for a moment, attention [?]' Burns asked Mrs Dunlop on 12 January 1795 (L649); at which point she stopped answering his letters.

252 l. 41. *A wicked crew*. The Coalition of European monarchies ranged against the French republic, with Austria and Prussia at its core, but after the execution of Louis including Britain as well.

ll. 49–50. *Freedom . . . Her sons did loudly ca'*. Perhaps referring to the mass mobilization with which the French republic countered the expanded coalition against it in 1793.

l. 55. *The hirelings ran*. The Prussian and Austrian armies included many mercenaries. In fact important victories were thin on the ground in the year following Louis's execution; but the republic survived.

l. 64. *Tweed*. The river that marks the border between England and Scotland.

253 *'Ill-fated genius' [on Robert Fergusson]*. K144. First published in *The Life and Works of Robert Burns*, ed. Robert Chambers, in four volumes, Vol. III (1852), on p. 221, where Chambers tells us it was 'inscribed . . . in a copy of *The World*', a literary journal which ran 1753–6 and was frequently reprinted in book form.

l. 1. *Heaven-taught Fergusson*. The epithet is borrowed from Henry Mackenzie's description of Burns in *The Lounger*: see Appendix 2, p. 279. Fergusson in fact spent four years at the University of St Andrews.

A Fragment—On Glenriddel's Fox breaking his chain. K527. Only known from the Glenriddell manuscripts (see Introduction to this volume). First published in an account of those manuscripts by Henry A. Bright in 1874, and in an edition of Burns's poetry by William Scott Douglas in his *Complete Poetical Works of Robert Burns* (1876), Vol. II, pp. 441–3. The absence of any other surviving source for this poem, probably written in 1790, suggests that Burns thought of it as to some extent private between himself and Glenriddell. The present text is taken from the Glenriddell manuscript itself: the Scott Douglas text follows it very accurately, only tidying up some punctuation, capitalization and so on.

Title. Burns's farm at Ellisland in Dumfriesshire, to which he moved in 1788, was less than a mile down the river Nith from Friar's Carse, the home of Captain Robert Riddell of Glenriddell (1755–94). Despite the disparity in rank and income they had a lot in common: Riddell too was interested in song, collecting traditional tunes and composing his own, as well as enjoying wider antiquarian interests, and they collaborated in establishing a local library. Of more relevance to the present poem is their shared opposition politics: Glenriddell was an exponent of reform of the House of Commons franchise for both counties and burghs.

l. 4. *cap and rod*. The Phrygian cap, a cone of soft felt with the top pushed to one side: associated with liberty as the (reputed) marker of a freed slave in the Roman empire; slaves were freed by an official laying a rod on the individual's head while reciting a formula declaring him or her free. A goddess of liberty with a Phrygian cap was already appearing in the iconography of the French Revolution.

254 l. 17. *a Whig without a stain.* For this term, see note to p. 247, ll. 82–3. In reference to reformers like Glenriddell, the term signifies a veneration for an idealized version of the principles of government established by the 'Revolution' of 1688–9 which imposed limits on the powers of the monarch, and a desire to rid the present political system of the corruption that has allowed ministerial power, exercised on behalf of the King, to slide the constitutional balance back towards 'tyranny'.

l. 26. *his Country's cause.* Not just Scotland or Britain, but 'the Country' (represented by landed gentlemen like Glenriddell) as opposed to 'the Court' (the king's ministers).

l. 29. *The Rights of Men.* Thomas Paine's book *The Rights of Man* had probably not yet been published when this poem was written, but the rhetoric of 'natural rights' goes back at least to John Locke's *Two Treatises on Government* (1690), an important theorization of Whig political values.

l. 34. *tyrants, Jacobites, and tories.* 'Tyranny' was a bugbear of Whig rhetoric; for Jacobites, see headnote to 'There'll never be peace till Jamie comes hame' from *The Scots Musical Museum* on p. 168; for Tories, see note to p. 246, l. 41.

l. 37. *Nimrod.* 'And Cush begat Nimrod: he began to be a mighty one in the earth. And the beginning of his kingdom was Babel, and Erech, and Accad, and Calneh, in the land of Shinar' (Genesis 10: 8, 10): the first mention of kingship in the Bible.

l. 39. *Semiramis.* An Assyrian queen who appears in Greek and Roman stories as a type of feminine political power.

l. 43. *Xerxes.* The Persian king (d. 465 BC) who invaded Greece in 480 BC.

l. 45. *the stubborn Whigs of Sparta.* The absolute commitment of the Spartans to civic life, making the rise of tyrants impossible, was a touchstone for Whig ideology. Spartan forces played the leading role in the defeat of Xerxes's forces at Plataea and Mycale (479 BC).

l. 46. *Magna charta.* See note to p. 247, ll. 82–3.

255 ll. 53–5. *Billy Pit . . . Has gagg'd old Britain, drain'd her coffer.* William Pitt the younger (1759–1806), prime minister. Pitt's priority at this point was getting the public finances in order, which meant new taxes: see note to p. 19, l. 119.

Ode. K451. A draft fragment of this poem (corresponding to the last verse paragraph) was published in Currie's 1800 *Works of Robert Burns*, as part of a letter to Mrs Dunlop of 25 June 1794, where Burns refers to his projected 'irregular Ode for Gen¹ Washington's birth-day' (L628); this fragment was republished in many nineteenth-century editions. Yet, although two manuscripts existed, the complete poem was only published in 1874 (in *Notes and Queries*, 5 March, pp. 242–3); and first included in an edition of Burns's work by William Scott Douglas in his *Complete Poetical Works of Robert Burns* (1876), Vol. II, pp. 426–8, under the title given in the letter to Mrs Dunlop. This text follows the transcription of one of the manuscripts in *Autograph Poems and Letters of Robert Burns in the collection of R. B. Adam* (Buffalo, NY, 1922), 38–40. George Washington, leader of the Continental Army in the Revolutionary War and first President of the United States, was born on 22 February 1732.

255   l. 1. *tube . . . shell*. Figures for wind-instruments and thus for song. Sparta and Athens were rival city-states in classical Greece, often imagined as the originators of political liberty. This line recalls the opening of 'Ode to Liberty' by William Collins (1746): 'Who shall awake the Spartan fife . . .?'; the singer continues, 'Let not my shell's misguided power | E'er draw thy sad, thy mindful tears' (ll. 1, 15; Lonsdale 442, 444). Collins's ode is an example of the *translatio imperii* or *translatio studii*, a poem that traces the progress of liberty (or power or learning) from Greece through Rome to its modern home in Britain. Burns's poem is a variation on this theme, imagining Liberty abandoning Britain in turn, and finding a home yet further west.

l. 2. *lyre Eolian*. Aeolus was the Greek god of the winds, and an Aeolian harp was 'a stringed instrument producing musical sounds on exposure to a current of air' (*OED*); it is possible Burns was thinking of the Aeolian islands, another part of Greece.

l. 4. *Columbia*. That is, America: the continent discovered by Christopher Columbus.

l. 7. *And dash it in a tyrant's face!*. The 'tyrant' is of course George III.

256   l. 29. *Alfred*. King of the West Saxons (*c*.848–99) who united the English kingdoms in their struggle against Danish invaders. He had been re-imagined as the prototype patriot-prince in Thomson and Mallet's opposition masque *Alfred* (1740): 'If not to raise our drooping *English* name, | To . . . make this land | Renown'd for peaceful arts to bless mankind, | And generous war to humble proud oppressors: | If not to build on an eternal base, | On liberty and laws, the public weal: | If not for these great ends I am ordain'd, | May I ne'er idly fill the throne of *England!*' (1. 5, p. 19).

l. 31. *The Bards that erst have struck the patriot lyre*. Perhaps including the Bard who appears at the end of *Alfred* to sing 'Rule Britannia': 'The nations, not so blest as thee, | Must in their turns, to tyrants fall' etc. (2. 5, p. 42). 'Patriot' has a quite specific meaning in eighteenth-century political rhetoric, as when the Hermit foresees a time 'when guardian laws | Are by the patriot, in the glowing senate, | Won from corruption' (1. 5, p. 19).

l. 35. *To make detested tyrants bleed*. The French Republic had executed the erstwhile Louis XVI in January 1793.

l. 39. *'The Tyrant's cause is mine!'*. When Britain went to war with France in February, it was entering a military and political alliance with absolutist monarchies such as Prussia, Austria, and Spain. The US government was of course sympathetic to the Republic.

l. 42. *the generous English name.* Perhaps recalls the 'English name' and 'generous war' of Alfred's speech, quoted above.

l. 49. *WALLACE.* William Wallace (d. 1305), one of the Guardians of Scotland who led armies against the occupying forces of Edward I of England in the Wars of Independence.

257 ll. 58–9. *that arm which . . . Braved Usurpation's boldest daring!.* In *Alfred*, the Hermit prophesies to the king a time 'when th' impatient arm | Of liberty, invincible, shall scourge | The tyrants of mankind' (1. 5, p. 17).

A poet's welcome to his love-begotten daughter. K60. A version of this poem was first published in one of Stewart and Meikle's chapbooks in 1799, then reprinted in some of the earlier nineteenth-century editions, beginning with Stewart's own in 1801 and again in *The Works of Robert Burns*, ed. The Ettrick Shepherd [James Hogg] and William Motherwell, Vol. II (1834); more morally fastidious editors (Currie, Cromek, Cunningham, Chambers) ignored it. But this version of the poem was either mangled in transcription, or came from an already-corrupted manuscript, since lost; it also omitted two of the eight stanzas in the present text (the fifth and sixth). There are three surviving manuscripts, and each arranges the poem's stanzas in a different order. The version in the Glenriddell manuscript was the first to be used in a printed edition, William Scott Douglas's *Complete Poetical Works of Robert Burns* (1876); but *that* version omits the present stanza 7. So the present text follows *The Poetry of Robert Burns*, ed. William Ernest Henley and Thomas F. Henderson (1896), Vol. 2, 37–9, who seem to have been the first to examine all the surviving manuscripts to select the most complete. Henley and Henderson number their stanzas: I have omitted this.

For Burns's affair with Elizabeth Paton in 1784, see notes to p. 48, l. 63 and p. 113, ll. 37–72. A daughter, also Elizabeth, was born on 22 May 1785. She was brought up by Burns's mother until the poet's death, when she moved back in with her own mother, by then married with other children. Burns sent a copy of this poem to a friend in a letter of 2 July 1787 (L118); another was enclosed in the letter to John Moore included in Appendix 1 (see p. 265).

l. 7. *fornicator.* The Kirk's name for a sexual miscreant: see 'The Fornicater' in this volume for Burns's mocking appropriation of the term.

l. 16. *Baith kirk and queir.* That is, against the whole body of the church (the 'queir' or choir being the eastern part of an old cruciform church-building).

258 l. 31. *bonie Betty.* Elizabeth Paton.

l. 42. *stocket mailins.* That is, rented land ready-stocked with cattle.

Appendix 1. From the Letters

The texts of these letters are taken from *The Letters of Robert Burns*, ed. J. De Lancey Ferguson and G. Ross Roy (Oxford, 1985). They are slightly simplified from that source by the omission of deleted words and of square brackets around interpolated sections.

259 *L125. To Dr John Moore, 2 August 1787.* Addressee: John Moore (1729–1802), born in Stirling, had studied medicine at the University of Glasgow. A varied career included posts as surgeon in the army and to the British ambassador in Paris. He settled in London in 1778, where he wrote travel and medical books. He had recently published a well-received novel, *Zeluco* (1786). Frances Dunlop (see headnote to L524 below) had sent him a copy of the Kilmarnock *Poems* and Moore had got in touch with the poet.

some little business I have to settle. Burns refers to his northern tour of that summer: he had taken the opportunity to chase up subscription money due for the Edinburgh edition.

'Turned my eyes to behold Madness and Folly'. Ecclesiastes 2: 12. This book of the Old Testament is supposedly written by Solomon, proverbial for his wisdom; Burns resembles him because Solomon 'loved many strange women' (1 Kings 11: 1).

Miss Williams. Helen Maria Williams (1762–1827), a poet from the radical culture of English Presbyterianism. At this point Williams seems to have been acting as Moore's amanuensis. She would later move to Paris to experience the Revolution at first hand, as recorded in *Letters from France* (1790–6).

escutcheons. An escutcheon is the shield in a coat-of-arms: the badge of (supposedly) long-held gentility.

'My ancient but ignoble blood . . . since the flood'. Pope's 'Essay on Man', Epistle IV: 'Go! If your ancient, but ignoble blood | Has crept thro' scoundrels ever since the flood' (ll. 211–12; Pope 542).

Gules, Purpure, Argent. More heraldic jargon, for the colours used in a coat-of-arms: red, purple, silver.

Kieths of Marshal. George Keith, styled tenth Earl Marshall (1692/3–1778), forfeited the family estates, in the north-east of Scotland, for his deep involvement in the Jacobite rising of 1715.

'Brutus and Cassius are honorable men'. Mark Antony uses this phrase ironically of Caesar's assassins in Act 3, scene 2 of Shakespeare's *Julius Caesar*, ll. 75f.

260 *'Men, their manners and their ways'.* Pope again, in 'January and May': 'Sir, I have liv'd a Courtier all my Days, | And study'd Men, their Manners, and their Ways' (ll. 156–7; Pope 80).

a small farm. Mount Oliphant, to which the Burns family moved in 1766, was 70 acres (Leask 16).

brownies . . . spunkies. A brownie is, in this case, a goblin or evil spirit; a spunkie is a will-o'-the-wisp.

elf-candles. 'A spark or flash of light thought to be of supernatural origin' (*DSL*).

dead-lights. 'The name given by the peasantry to the luminous appearance which is sometimes observed over putrescent animal bodies' (*DSL*).

The vision of Mirza. An essay first published by Joseph Addison in *The Spectator*, 159 (1711), which takes the form of an ancient oriental account of a philosophical vision.

'For though in dreadful whirls . . . | High on the broken wave'. The lines quoted are from Joseph Addison's 'Hymn. On the Conclusion of his Travels'; *The Poetical Works of the Right Honourable Joseph Addison Esq.* (Glasgow, 1750), 203–4.

Mason's English Collection. Arthur Masson, *A Collection of Prose and Verse, from the Best English Authors. For the Use of Schools* (Edinburgh, 1764).

the life of Hannibal and the history of Sir William Wallace. The Life of Hannibal, translated from the French of M. Dacier (London, 1737); and *A New Edition of the Life and Heroick Actions of the renoun'd Sir William Wallace* (Glasgow, 1722), William Hamilton's modernization of Blind Harry's fifteenth-century epic poem *Wallace*.

261 *'without bounds or limits'.* Burns is remembering Thomas Watson's handbook to the theology of the Shorter Catechism, *A Body of Practical Divinity*, at the question 'What Kind of Spirit is God?': 'God's Omnipresency; the Greek Word for Infinite, signifies without Bounds or Limits' (the fourth edition, corrected and amended; Glasgow 1741, 34).

not even the MUNNY BEGUM'S scenes have tainted. A reference to the notorious political and economic corruption of British-controlled Bengal. Governor-General Warren Hastings appointed, as guardian of the heir of a Bengal noble family, Munny Begum, the boy's father's chief concubine. An Indian minister accused Hastings of taking a bribe in the case; Hastings had him charged with forging the evidence, found guilty, and hanged. This was one of several scandals that led to Hastings's trial in parliament, which began in 1788.

a Factor who sat for the picture I have drawn of one in my Tale of two dogs. See 'The Twa Dogs', ll. 93–100 (p. 7).

gin-horse Prudence. A gin-horse is one used to drive a mill. 'There is a species of the Human genus that I call, the Gin-horse Class: what enviable dogs they are!—Round, & round, & round they go . . . without an idea or wish beyond their circle; fat, sleek, stupid, patient, quiet & contented' (L600A to Maria Riddell, 1793).

262 *Eolian harp.* 'A stringed instrument producing musical sounds on exposure to a current of air' (*OED*).

a larger farm. Lochlie, near Tarbolton: 130 acres (Leask 16).

phthisical. Tubercular.

'To where the wicked cease from troubling, and where the weary be at rest'. Job 3: 17.

climacterick. 'A critical period or moment in . . . a person's life or career' (*OED*).

Solitaire. Recluse.

262 *Salmon's and Guthrie's geographical grammars.* William Guthrie, *A New Geographical, Historical, and Commercial Grammar; and Present State of the Several Kingdoms of the World* (London, 1770); Thomas Salmon, *A New Geographical and Historical Grammar* (London, 1749).

The Spectator. The essay-journal published daily in London by Joseph Addison and Richard Steele in 1711–13; much collected and anthologized.

Tull and Dickson on Agriculture. Jethro Tull, *The New Horse-Houghing Husbandry: or, An Essay on the Principles of Tillage and Vegetation* (London, 1731), a pioneering description of agricultural improvement; Alan Dickson, *A Treatise of Agriculture* (Edinburgh, 1762 and 1769).

The Pantheon. François Pomey, *The Pantheon: Representing the Fabulous Histories of the Pagan Gods and Most Illustrious Heroes, in a Short, Plain and Familiar Method by way of Dialogue*, trans. Andrew Tooke (London 1698, with many reprints through the following century).

Locke's Essay on the human understanding. John Locke, *An Essay Concerning Human Understanding* (London, 1690).

Stackhouse's history of the bible. Thomas Stackhouse, *A New History of the Holy Bible, from the Beginning of the World, to the Establishment of Christianity* (London, 1733).

Justice's British Gardiner's directory. Sir James Justice, *The British Gardener's New Director; Chiefly adapted to the Climate of the Northern Countries.* A fourth edition appeared in Dublin in 1765.

Boyle's lectures. Probably a collection of the work of Robert Boyle (1627–91) in either science or religion, although I can find no such collection with this title.

Allan Ramsay's works. Perhaps the two-volume set published in London in 1751 and 1761.

Taylor's scripture doctrine of original sin. John Taylor, *The Scripture-Doctrine of Original Sin proposed to free and candid Examination* (London, 1740). See note to p. 109, l. 112.

a select Collection of English songs. Joseph Ritson, *A Select Collection of English Songs* (London, 1783).

Hervey's meditations. James Hervey, *Meditations and Contemplations. In Two Volumes* (London, 1748 and reprinted many times).

vade mecum. 'A book or manual suitable for carrying about with one for ready reference' from the Latin 'go with me' (*OED*).

263 *the blind gropings of Homer's Cyclops.* Referring to the giant Polyphemos after Odysseus and his men blinded him in his single eye to secure their escape from his cave in Homer's *Odyssey* Book IX.

'where two or three were met together, there was I in the midst of them'. Jesus at Matthew 18: 20: 'For where two or three are gathered together in my name, there am I in the midst of them'.

un penchant á l'adorable moitiée du genre humain. A liking for the adorable half of the human kind.

a smuggling coast. The coast of Carrick, the southern district of Ayrshire, has plenty of hidden coves and caves suited to the landing of contraband. Burns studied at Kirkoswald in Carrick, about 15 miles from his home at Mount Oliphant.

Mensuration . . . Dialling. Mensuration is 'the branch of geometry that deals with the measurement of lengths, areas, and volumes'; to dial is 'to survey or lay out with the aid of a dial or miner's or surveyor's compass' (*OED*).

264 *the sun entered Virgo.* The sun enters this constellation in the last week of August.

'*Like Proserpine gathering flowers | Herself a fairer flower*'. Milton, *Paradise Lost*, Book IV, ll. 269–70 (with 'Like' for 'where'). In Greek myth Proserpina is kidnapped by the God of the Underworld, her absence throwing the world into winter.

phasis. 'Phase', in the sense associated with the changing appearance of the moon.

letters by the Wits of Queen Ann's reign. John Newbery, *Letters On the most common, as well as important, Occasions in Life, by Cicero, Pliny, Voltaire, Balzac, St. Evremont, Locke, Ld Lansdowne, Temple, Dryden, Garth, Pope, Gay, Swift, Rowe, and Other Writers of distinguish'd Merit; [with] A Dissertation on the Epistolary Style; With proper Directions for addressing Persons of Rank and Eminence. For the Use of young Gentlemen and Ladies* (London 1756).

Vive l'amour et vive la bagatelle. Long live love, and long live fun.

Tristram Shandy. Laurence Sterne, *The Life and Opinions of Tristram Shandy, Gentleman* (1760–7).

the Man of Feeling. Henry Mackenzie, *The Man of Feeling* (1771).

Winter, a dirge. See p. 85.

The death of Poor Mailie. See p. 33.

John Barleycorn. See p. 135.

songs first, second and third. Referring to the songs of the Kilmarnock *Poems*: 'It was upon a Lammas night', 'Now westlin winds, and slaught'ring guns', and 'From thee, Eliza, I must go' (pp. 114–117).

flax-dresser in a neighbouring town. The town was Irvine: see Map. Processing locally-grown flax into thread for linen was an important industry in Ayrshire. 'Dressing' flax meant combing out impurities to ready it for spinning.

burnt to ashes. Flax was notoriously flammable, and great care needed to be taken to avoid accidents like this.

265 *a belle-fille.* Burns clearly just means 'a pretty girl'.

265 *their mittimus, 'Depart from me, ye Cursed'.* 'Mittimus' originally referred to a type of legal document but came to mean 'a dismissal from an office or situation; a notice to quit' (*OED*). Burns quotes Matthew 25: 14.

the WELCOME *inclosed.* The poem included in this volume as 'A poet's welcome to his love-begotten daughter', p. 257; Burns refers to his affair with Elizabeth Paton, servant at Lochlie.

Pamela. Samuel Richardson, *Pamela; or, Virtue Rewarded* (1740).

Ferdinand count Fathom. Tobias Smollett, *Ferdinand Count Fathom* (1753).

Fergusson's Scotch Poems. Robert Fergusson, *Poems on Various Subjects*, published posthumously by Thomas Ruddiman, Edinburgh in 1779. Burns owned the third, 1785 edition of this two-volume set.

a neighbouring farm. Mossgiel, near Mauchline (118 acres).

'Come, go to, I will be wise!'. The editors of the *Letters* suggest that Burns is remembering Ecclesiastes 7: 23: 'I said, I will be wise; but it was far from me'.

'Like the dog to his vomit, and the sow that was washed to her wallowing in the mire'. The second Epistle of Peter 2: 22, describing backsliders: 'it is happened unto them according to the true proverb, The dog is turned to his own vomit again; and the sow that was washed to her wallowing in the mire'.

266 *rev^d Calvinists.* The orthodox Kilmarnock ministers Alexander Moodie and 'Black' John Russel (see notes to p. 25, l. 102 and p. 27, l. 184), whose feud is the target of Burns's 'burlesque lamentation' 'The Holy Tulzie' (K52: not included in the present volume).

Holy Willie's Prayer. See p. 230.

The Lament. See p. 77. The 'shocking affair' was his separation from Jean Armour by her parents.

pauvre Inconnu. Poor unknown.

I was about to indent myself. That is, commit himself in advance to work for a certain period on arrival in Jamaica until the cost of his passage was paid off.

'Hungry ruin had me in the wind'. Burns adapts a line from Thomas Otway's play, *The History and Fall of Caius Marius* (1680), where Marius describes Rome before he rescued it, 'When it lay trembling like a hunted Prey, | And hungry Ruine had it in the Wind' (Act 1, scene 1).

some ill-advised, ungrateful people. The Armours, again. In July 1786, as the *Poems* went to press, and Jean approached her time, 'James Armour realised that the Burns who had always seemed such a waster might have some money after all. . . . He set about getting a warrant requiring Burns to hand over a large sum of money or face jail with his assets confiscated' (Crawford, *The Bard*, 222).

267 *Greenock.* A major Atlantic port on the Firth of Clyde.

'*The gloomy night is gathering fast*'. Burns cites his song of this title, not included in the present volume, which he had published in the Edinburgh edition (K122).

a letter from Dr Blacklock to a friend of mine. Thomas Blacklock (1721–91), a celebrated Edinburgh poet and scholar. Blacklock's letter was to Ayrshire minister George Lawrie, who passed it on to Gavin Hamilton, who showed it to his friend Burns (Crawford, *The Bard*, 228).

Zenith . . . Nadir. The points in the heavens directly above the observer (from where astrology credits a star or planet with its greatest influence) and directly below (from where it has least).

Earl of Glencairn. For this important patron see headnote to 'Lament for James, Earl of Glencairn', p. 359.

'*Oublie moi, Grand Dieu, si jamais je l'oublie!*'. 'Forget me, Great God, if ever I forget it!'; that is, forget God's providential care in this instance.

'*to catch the manners living as they rise*'. In the first Epistle of the *Essay on Man*, Pope invites his friend Bolingbroke to 'Expatiate free o'er all this scene of Man . . . Eye Nature's walks, shoot Folly as it flies, | And catch the Manners living as they rise' (ll. 5, 13–14; Pope 504).

Wight. Fellow (a poetic archaism).

L515. To William Johnston, 13 November 1792. Addressee: For Captain William Johnston see headnote to 'Extempore on some late commemorations of the poet Thomson', p. 356.

268 '*Calm, thinking VILLAINS whom no faith can fix*'. From Alexander Pope, 'The Temple of Fame': 'Calm, thinking Villains, whom no Faith cou'd fix, | Of crooked Counsels and dark Politicks' (ll. 410–11; Pope 185).

L524. To Mrs Frances Dunlop, 6 December 1792. Addressee: Frances Anna Wallace (1730–1815), widow of John Dunlop of Dunlop (d. 1785). Mrs Dunlop had found consolation in the Kilmarnock *Poems* after the death of her husband, and after her spendthrift eldest son had sold off the Craigie estate which she had brought into the marriage and which had descended to her family from a cousin of William Wallace. Her friendship with the poet 'produced more letters than he addressed to any other single individual' (*Letters* 451).

Dunlop house. Dunlop is towards the northern end of Ayrshire: a long way from Burns in Dumfries.

'*Careless of the voice of the morning*'. This is not, as Burns claims, from the Book of Job, but from 'Carthon: A Poem' in Macpherson's 1765 *Works of Ossian* (Macpherson 134).

'*Staff and Shield*'. Perhaps recalling 1 Samuel 17: 7: 'And the staff of his spear was like a weaver's beam . . . and one bearing a shield went before him.'

a fine girl. Elizabeth Riddell Burns, born on 21 November. Her death three years later caused Burns desperate anguish.

268 *'The valiant in himself . . . like a coward'.* Prince Edward's lines in James Thomson's tragedy *Edward and Eleonora* (published 1739, though banned from the stage), Act 4, scene 7, ll. 44–51.

269 *'Who so unworthy . . . How cheap a thing were virtue'.* Gloster in the same play and the following scene, ll. 30–6.

'Attach thee firmly . . . sit loose'. The Hermit's advice to the king in Thomson's masque *Alfred* (1740), Act 1, scene 5.

' 'Tis this, my Friend . . . cloudless skies'. From a commendatory verse to the frequently reprinted James Hervey, *Meditations and Contemplations. In Two Volumes* (London, 1748), I, p. xvii.

our Theatre here. A theatre had opened in Dumfries in September 1792.

Ça ira. The anthem of the French revolutionaries ('So it will be').

a Placeman. That is, a government employee, dependent on the approval of his superiors.

The Rights of Woman. See p. 210.

270 *L528. To Robert Graham of Fintry, 31 December 1792.* Addressee: see note to title of 'Sketch of an Epistle to R. Graham, Esq. of Fintray', p. 393.

Collector. This was the excise post responsible for oversight of a county.

Revolution principles. That is, the principles of the division of powers between King, Lords, and Commons established in the Revolution of 1688–9.

Death's thousand doors stand open. From *The Grave* (1743), l. 394, a widely-read poem of the 'graveyard' school by Scottish minister Robert Blair, describing the prospects for 'the Wretch | That's weary of the World, and tir'd of Life' (ll. 389–90).

L530. To Robert Graham of Fintry, 5 January 1793.

271 *Borough-Reform.* This refers to the campaign to rid the town councils of their self-perpetuating, oligarchic power-structures. Burns acknowledges the local survival of a reform movement only where it was opposed to the most flagrant variety of corruption in the system.

Çà ira. The anthem of the French revolutionaries ('So it will be').

Edinʳ Gazetteer. See headnotes to 'Extempore on some late commemorations of the poet Thomson', p. 356, and L515 to William Johnston, above.

272 *The Rights of Woman.* See p. 210.

The Commemoration of Thomson. See p. 209.

Robt Riddel Esq: of Glenriddel. See note to the title of 'A Fragment—On Glenriddel's Fox breaking his chain', p. 404.

County Reform. The campaign to rid parliamentary elections for the counties of such abuses as the creation of votes by the great proprietors through the fictional distribution of their land among their allies.

Frank. The mark of postage paid, before the invention of adhesive stamps.

Savoy. Savoy was occupied and formally annexed to France in November 1792; it had previously belonged to the King of Sardinia.

invading the rights of Holland. The status of the Dutch Republic had been settled by treaty in 1788, with Britain and Prussia the guarantors: in November 1792 the government in Paris broke this treaty, set on a course that would lead to war with Britain.

A tippling ballad . . . on the Prince of Brunswick's breaking up his camp. This is a version of the song 'Poor bodies do naething but m–w' (see p. 237) which Burns had already sent to Robert Cleghorn, and which would eventually be published, with additions and subtractions, in *The Merry Muses of Caledonia* (1799).

273 *L531. To Mrs Graham of Fintry, 5 January 1793.* Addressee: Margaret Elizabeth Mylne of Mylnefield (1754–1816) had married Fintry in 1773: they had 14 children.

this little poem. Burns enclosed a copy of 'The Rights of Woman' (see p. 210).

L558. To John Francis Erskine, 13 April 1793. Addressee: John Francis Erskine (1741–1825) was the eldest son of an aristocratic family and later 27th Earl of Mar and 12th Lord Erskine. This exchange of letters was the only contact between Erskine and Burns.

This text is taken from the Glenriddell manuscript (see Introduction), into which Burns made a copy of this letter a year or two later, prefacing it with the explanation given here.

my friend Glenriddell. Robert Riddell of Glenriddell: see note to the title of 'A Fragment—On Glenriddel's Fox breaking his chain', p. 404.

to save from ruin an only brother. That is, Gilbert, still farming Mossgiel (their younger brothers John and William had died in 1785 and 1790).

274 *Executive Power & the Representative part.* That is, between the king's ministers and the House of Commons.

275 *my boys.* Burns is thinking of his three sons with Jean Armour; a fourth had been born to an Edinburgh servant girl, Jenny Clow, in 1788.

Appendix 2. Contemporary Reviews of the Kilmarnock Poems (1786)

276 *From The Edinburgh Magazine, or Literary Miscellany, for October 1786, pp. 284–5.* This was the first notice taken in print of Burns's work. The author is probably the magazine's publisher, James Sibbald (Crawford, *The Bard*, 234–5). Further poems by Burns appeared in the next two editions as well, and in January Burns wrote to Sibbald to thank him for his support: 'The warmth with which you have befriended an obscure man and young Author, in your last three Magazines—I can only say, Sir, I feel the weight of the obligation, and wish I could express my sense of it' (L71).

276 *Aristotle or Horace.* Here in their capacity as literary critics: Aristotle (384–322 BC) as author of the *Poetics*; Quintus Horatius Flaccus (65–8 BC) as author of the *Ars Poetica*.

Allan Ramsay and Ferguson. Allan Ramsay (1684–1758), influential post-Union revivalist of poetry in Scots; Robert Fergusson (1750–74), vivid chronicler of the Edinburgh scene: both important precedents for Burns's work in Scots.

Homer and Ossian. James Macpherson claimed Ossian, a bard in Gaelic myth, as the third-century author of the pieces 'translated' as *Fragments of Ancient Poetry* (1760) which had been preserved by oral tradition in the Highlands. These were in fact mostly prose-paraphrases of sixteenth-century heroic verse; Macpherson went on to attribute his two epic poems 'Fingal' and 'Temora' to the same source, completing 'Ossian''s claim to be the 'Northern Homer'.

doric simplicity. Theocritus wrote in the Doric version of Greek rather than the language of Athens. In his Preface to his 1721 *Poems*, Allan Ramsay appeals to this as a precedent for writing in Scots: 'The *Scotticisms*, which perhaps may offend some over-nice Ear, give new Life and Grace to the Poetry, and become their Place as well as the *Doric* Dialect of *Theocritus*, so much admired by the best Judges' (Ramsay Vol. I, p. xix).

277 *Rusticus abnormis sapiens, crassaque Minerva.* Horace again, in *Satire* 2.2: 'a peasant, an independent sage of homespun wisdom' (translation from Frank Stack, *Pope and Horace* (1985), 60). On pp. 285–8 the *Edinburgh Magazine* then reproduces 'Address to the Deil' complete; 'Epistle to J. Lapriak, an old Scotch Bard', ll. 43–78; 'The Holy Fair', stanzas IX–XI, XXI–XXII, and XXVI–XXVII; and 'Halloween', stanzas VII–VIII, XIII–XIV, and XVII–XXVII.

The Lounger No XCVII. Saturday, Dec. 9. 1786. The Lounger was a sin-gle-sheet essay-journal in the style of Addison and Steele's *Spectator*; most of its numbers are by Henry Mackenzie (1745–1831), including this one. A lawyer by training, the success of his sentimental novel *The Man of Feeling* (1771) and his other activities made him an important arbiter of taste in literary Edinburgh. Burns wrote to him in May 1787: 'I leave Edin^r tomorrow morning, and send you this to assure you that no little petulant self-conceit, no distance or absence shall ever make me forget how much I owe YOU' (L101).

'in the olden time' genius had some advantages which tended to its vigour and its growth. This recalls the theory of Hugh Blair, Professor of Rhetoric and Belles Lettres at Edinburgh University, which drew on the 'conjec-tural history' of his contemporaries to explain the origins of poetry: 'In the infancy of society, men live scattered and dispersed, in the midst of soli-tary rural scenes, where the beauties of nature are their chief entertain-ment. . . . Their passions have nothing to restrain them: their imagination has nothing to check it. They display themselves to one another without disguise: and converse and act in the uncovered simplicity of nature. As their feelings are strong, so their language, of itself, assumes a poetical

turn' ('A Critical Dissertation upon the Poems of Ossian'; Macpherson 345). As society develops, 'the understanding is more exercised; the imagine, less' and so poetry declines (346).

279 *faith in opposition to good works.* A point of Calvinist orthodoxy: see note to p. 95, l. 50.

a West-Indian clime. In 1786 Burns was planning to emigrate to Jamaica.

'wood-notes wild'. In Milton's 'L'Allegro' (*c*.1631), the happy man goes to the theatre to hear 'sweetest Shakespeare fancy's child, | Warble his native wood-notes wild' (ll. 133–4). In 1794 Burns wrote to his Edinburgh friend Alexander Cunningham (L620, 3 March):

> There is one commission that I must trouble you with.—I lately lost a valuable Seal, a present from a departed friend, which vexes me very much.—I have gotten one of your Highland pebbles, which I fancy would make a very decent one; & I want to cut my armorial bearings on it: will you be so obliging as enquire what will be the expence of such a business? . . . On a field, azure, a holly-bush, seeded, proper, in base; a Shepherd's pipe & crook, Saltier-wise, also proper, in chief.—On a wreath of the colors, a woodlark perching on a sprig of bay-tree, proper, for Crest.—Two Mottoes: Round the top of the Crest—'Wood-notes wild'—At the bottom of the Shield, in the usual place—
> 'Better a wee bush than nae bield.'—

FURTHER READING

IMPORTANT OR USEFUL EDITIONS OF BURNS'S WORK,
IN ORDER OF PUBLICATION

The Works of Robert Burns; with an account of his life, and a criticism on his writings, ed. James Currie, in four volumes (London: Cadell and Davies, 1800).

Poems Ascribed to Robert Burns, the Ayrshire Bard, not contained in any previous edition of his works hitherto published, ed. Thomas Stewart (Glasgow: Thomas Stewart, 1801).

Stewart's Edition of Burns's Poems, including a number of original pieces never before published, ed. Thomas Stewart (Glasgow: Thomas Stewart, 1802).

Reliques of Robert Burns; consisting chiefly of original letters, poems, and critical observations on Scottish songs, ed. R. H. Cromek (London: Cadell and Davies, 1808).

The Works of Robert Burns, with his life, ed. Allan Cunningham. In eight volumes (London: Cochrane, 1834).

The Works of Robert Burns, ed. The Ettrick Shepherd [James Hogg] and William Motherwell, in six volumes (Glasgow: Fullarton, 1834–6).

The Poetical Works of Robert Burns, ed. Robert Chambers (Edinburgh: Chambers, 1838).

The Life and Works of Robert Burns, ed. Robert Chambers, in four volumes (Edinburgh: Chambers, 1851; revised and expanded 1856–7).

The Poetical Works of Robert Burns, ed. Alexander Smith, in two volumes (London: Macmillan, 1865).

The Complete Poetical Works of Robert Burns, arranged in the order of their first publication, ed. William Scott Douglas, in two volumes (Kilmarnock: McKie, 1871; revised and expanded 1876).

The Life and Works of Robert Burns, ed. Robert Chambers, revised William Wallace, in four volumes (Edinburgh and London, 1896).

The Poetry of Robert Burns, ed. William Ernest Henley and Thomas F. Henderson, in four volumes (London: Jack, 1896).

The Songs of Robert Burns, now first printed with the melodies for which they were written, ed. James C. Dick (London: H. Froude, 1903).

The Merry Muses of Caledonia, ed. James Barke, Sydney Goodsir Smith, and J. De Lancey Ferguson (1959; reprinted with a new introduction by Valentina Bold, Edinburgh: Luath, 2009).

The Poems and Songs of Robert Burns, ed. James Kinsley (Oxford: Clarendon Press, 1968).

The Letters of Robert Burns, ed. J. De Lancey Ferguson, second edition ed. G. Ross Roy, in two volumes (Oxford: Clarendon Press, 1985).

The Kilmarnock Poems, ed. Donald A. Low (London: Dent, 1985).

The Songs of Robert Burns, ed. Donald A. Low (London: Routledge, 1993).

Robert Burns: Selected Poems, ed. Carol McGuirk (London: Penguin, 1993).

BIOGRAPHY

Crawford, Robert, *The Bard: Robert Burns, a Biography* (London: Jonathan Cape, 2009).

Mackay, James, *Burns: A Biography of Robert Burns* (Edinburgh: Mainstream, 1992).

Will, William, *Robert Burns as a Volunteer. Some fresh facts which further help to confound the poet's critics* (Glasgow, 1919).

BACKGROUND

Adam, Charles Elphinstone, ed., *A View of the Political State of Scotland in the Last Century. A confidential report on the political opinions, family connections, or personal circumstances of the 2662 county voters in 1788* (Edinburgh: David Douglas, 1887).

Brims, J., 'From Reformers to "Jacobins": The Scottish Association of the Friends of the People', in Tom Devine, ed., *Conflict and Stability in Scottish Society 1700–1830* (Edinburgh: John Donald, 1990), 31–50.

Brown, Callum G., *Religion and Society in Scotland since 1707* (Edinburgh: Edinburgh University Press, 1997).

Clark, Ian D. L., 'From Protest to Reaction: The Moderate Regime in the Church of Scotland, 1752–1805', in N. T. Phillipson and Rosalind Mitchison, eds., *Scotland in the Age of Improvement* (Edinburgh: Edinburgh University Press, 1970), 200–24.

Clive, John, 'The Social Background of the Scottish Renaissance', in N. T. Phillipson and Rosalind Mitchison, eds., *Scotland in the Age of Improvement* (Edinburgh: Edinburgh University Press, 1970), 225–44.

Crawford, Robert, *Devolving English Literature* (Oxford: Oxford University Press, 1992).

Daiches, David, *The Paradox of Scottish Culture: The Eighteenth-Century Experience* (Oxford: Oxford University Press, 1964).

Davis, Leith, 'At "sang about": Scottish Song and the Challenge to British Culture', in Leith Davis, Ian Duncan, and Janet Sorensen, eds., *Scotland and the Borders of Romanticism* (Cambridge: Cambridge University Press, 2004), 188–203.

Dwyer, John, *Virtuous Discourse: Sensibility and Community in Late Eighteenth-Century Scotland* (Edinburgh: John Donald, 1987).

—— 'Introduction—A "Peculiar Blessing": Social Converse in Scotland from Hutchison to Burns', in John Dwyer and Richard B. Sher, eds., *Sensibility and Society in Eighteenth-Century Scotland* (Edinburgh: Mercat Press, 1993), 1–22.

Fergusson, James, *Lowland Lairds* (London: Faber and Faber, 1949).

Gray, Malcolm, 'The Social Impact of Agrarian Change in the Rural Lowlands', in Tom Devine and Rosalind Mitchison, eds., *People and Society in Scotland, Volume I: 1760–1830* (Edinburgh: John Donald, 1988), 53–69.

Harris, Bob, 'Political Protests in the Year of Liberty, 1792', in Bob Harris, ed., *Scotland in the Age of the French Revolution* (Edinburgh: John Donald, 2005), 49–78.

Johnson, David, *Music and Society in Lowland Scotland in the Eighteenth Century* (1972; Edinburgh: Mercat Press, 2003).

Kidd, Colin, 'Scotland's Invisible Enlightenment: Subscription and Heterodoxy in the Eighteenth-Century Kirk', *Records of the Scottish Church History Society* 30 (2000), 28–59.

—— 'Burns and Politics', in Gerard Carruthers, ed., *The Edinburgh Companion to Robert Burns* (Edinburgh: Edinburgh University Press, 2009), 61–73.

Kinghorn, Alexander M., and Low, Alexander, eds., *Poems by Allan Ramsay and Robert Fergusson* (Edinburgh: Scottish Academic Press, 1985).

Mackenzie, Henry, *The Man of Feeling*, ed. Brian Vickers (1771; Oxford: Oxford University Press, 1987).

McLachlan, Christopher, ed., *Before Burns: Eighteenth-Century Scottish Poetry* (Edinburgh: Canongate, 2002).

Newman, Steve, 'The Scots Songs of Allan Ramsay: "Lyrick" Transformation, Popular Culture, and the Boundaries of the Scottish Enlightenment', *Modern Language Quarterly* 63.3 (Sept. 2002), 277–314.

Ozouf, Mona, *Festivals and the French Revolution*, trans. Alan Sheridan (Cambridge, MA: Harvard University Press, 1988).

Paine, Thomas, *The Works of Thomas Paine, Secretary for Foreign Affairs, to the Congress of the United States, in the late war*, ed. James Carey, in two volumes (Philadelphia: Carey, 1797).

—— *Rights of Man, Common Sense, and Other Political Writings*, ed. Mark Philp (Oxford: Oxford University Press, 1995).

Robertson, John, *The Scottish Enlightenment and the Militia Issue* (Edinburgh: John Donald, 1985).

Sher, Richard, *Church and University in the Scottish Enlightenment: The Moderate Literati of Edinburgh* (Edinburgh: Edinburgh University Press, 1985).

—— *The Enlightenment and the Book: Scottish Authors and their Publishers in Eighteenth-Century Britain, Ireland, and America* (Chicago: University of Chicago Press, 2006).

Smith, Adam, *The Theory of Moral Sentiments* (1759; Oxford: Oxford University Press, 1976).

Sterne, Laurence, *The Life and Opinions of Tristram Shandy, Gentleman*, ed. Ian Campbell Ross (1759–67; Oxford: Oxford University Press, 1983).

—— *A Sentimental Journey*, ed. Ian Jack (1768; Oxford: Oxford University Press, 1968).

Thompson, E. P., 'Patrician Society, Plebeian Culture', *Journal of Social History* 7.4 (Summer 1974), 382–405.

Watson, Steven, *The Reign of George III* (Oxford: Oxford University Press, 1960).

CRITICISM

Ashmead, John, and Davidson, John, 'Words, Music and Emotion in the Love Songs of Robert Burns', in John Dwyer and Richard B. Sher, eds., *Sensibility and Society in Eighteenth-Century Scotland* (Edinburgh: Mercat Press, 1993), 225–42.

Bentman, Raymond, 'Robert Burns's Use of Scottish Diction', in Frederick W. Hilles and Harold Bloom, eds., *From Sensibility to Romanticism: Essays Presented to Frederick A. Pottle* (Oxford: Oxford University Press, 1965), 239–58. Reprinted in Carol McGuirk, ed., *Critical Essays on Robert Burns* (New York: G. K. Hall, 1998), 79–94.

Burke, Tim, 'Robert Burns', in John Goodridge, ed., *Eighteenth-Century Labouring-Class Poets* (London: Pickering and Chatto, 2002), 103–15.

Butler, Marilyn, 'Burns and Politics', in Robert Crawford, ed., *Robert Burns and Cultural Authority* (Edinburgh: Edinburgh University Press, 1997), 86–112.

Butt, John, 'The Revival of Scottish Vernacular Poetry', in Frederick W. Hilles and Harold Bloom, eds., *From Sensibility to Romanticism: Essays Presented to Frederick A. Pottle* (Oxford: Oxford University Press, 1965), 219–37.

Carruthers, Gerard, *Robert Burns* (Tavistock: Northcote House, 2006).

—— ed., *The Edinburgh Companion to Robert Burns* (Edinburgh: Edinburgh University Press, 2009).

Crawford, Robert, ed., *Robert Burns and Cultural Authority* (Edinburgh: Edinburgh University Press, 1997).

Crawford, Thomas, *Burns: A Study of the Poems and Songs* (Edinburgh: Oliver and Boyd, 1960).

—— *Society and the Lyric: A Study of the Song Culture of Eighteenth-Century Scotland* (Edinburgh: Scottish Academic Press, 1979).

Daiches, David, *Robert Burns* (London: G. Bell and Sons, 1952).

Damrosch, Leo, 'Burns, Blake, and the Recovery of Lyric', *Studies in Romanticism* 21 (Winter 1982), 637–60.

Davie, Cedric Thorpe, 'Robert Burns, Writer of Songs', in Donald Low, ed., *Critical Essays on Robert Burns* (London: Routledge and Kegan Paul, 1975), 157–84.

Davis, Leith, 'The Poetry of Nature and the Nature of Poetry: Robert Burns and William Wordsworth', in *Acts of Union: Scotland and the Literary Negotiation of the British Nation, 1707–1830* (Stanford CA: Stanford University Press, 1998), 107–43.

—— 'Re-presenting Scotia: Robert Burns and the Imagined Community of Scotland', in Carol McGuirk, ed., *Critical Essays on Robert Burns* (New York: G. K. Hall, 1998), 63–76.

Fielding, Penny, 'Burns's Topographies', in Leith Davis, Ian Duncan, and Janet Sorensen, eds., *Scotland and the Borders of Romanticism* (Cambridge: Cambridge University Press, 2004), 170–87.

Jack, R. D. S., and Noble, Andrew, eds., *The Art of Robert Burns* (London: Vision, 1982).

Leask, Nigel, 'Burns, Wordsworth, and the Politics of Vernacular Poetry', in Peter de Bolla, Nigel Leask, and David Simpson, eds., *Land, Nation and Culture, 1740–1840: Thinking the Republic of Taste* (Basingstoke: Palgrave Macmillan, 2005), 202–22.

—— 'Robert Burns and Scottish Common Sense Philosophy', in Gavin Budge, ed., *Romantic Empiricism: Poetics and the Philosophy of Common Sense, 1780–1830* (Lewisburg, PA: Bucknell University Press, 2007), 64–87.

—— *Robert Burns and Pastoral: Poetry and Improvement in Late Eighteenth-Century Scotland* (Oxford: Oxford University Press, 2010).

Low, Donald A., ed., *Robert Burns: The Critical Heritage* (London: Routledge and Kegan Paul, 1974).

—— ed., *Critical Essays on Robert Burns* (London: Routledge and Kegan Paul, 1975).

—— *Robert Burns* (Edinburgh: Scottish Academic Press, 1986).

McGinty, Walter, *Robert Burns and Religion* (Aldershot: Ashgate, 2003).

McGuirk, Carol, *Robert Burns and the Sentimental Era* (Athens, GA: University of Georgia Press, 1985).

—— 'Scottish Hero, Scottish Victim: Myths of Robert Burns', in Andrew Hook, ed., *The History of Scottish Literature, Volume 2: 1660–1800* (Aberdeen: Aberdeen University Press, 1987), 219–38.

—— 'Poor Bodies: Robert Burns and the Melancholy of Anatomy', in Carol McGuirk, ed., *Critical Essays on Robert Burns* (New York: G. K. Hall, 1998), 32–48.

—— '"The Rhyming Trade": Fergusson, Burns, and the Marketplace', in Robert Crawford, ed., *'Heaven-Taught Fergusson': Robert Burns's Favourite Scottish Poet* (Phantassie: Tuckwell, 2003), 135–59.

McIlvanney, Liam, *Burns the Radical: Poetry and Politics in Late Eighteenth-Century Scotland* (Phantassie: Tuckwell, 2002).

Mathison, Hamish, 'Robert Burns and National Song', in David Duff and Catherine Jones, eds., *Scotland, Ireland, and the Romantic Aesthetic* (Lewisburg, PA: Bucknell University Press, 2007), 77–92.

Murphy, Peter, 'Robert Burns', in *Poetry as an Occupation and an Art in Britain, 1760–1830* (Cambridge: Cambridge University Press, 1993), 49–93.

Radcliffe, David Hill, 'Imitation, Popular Literacy and "The Cotter's Saturday Night"', in Carol McGuirk, ed., *Critical Essays on Robert Burns* (New York: G. K. Hall, 1998), 251–79.

Simpson, Kenneth, ed., *Love and Liberty. Robert Burns: A Bicentenary Celebration* (Phantassie: Tuckwell, 1997).

Skoblow, Jeffrey, *'Dooble tongue': Scots, Burns, Contradiction* (Newark: University of Delaware Press, 2001).

Weston, John C., 'Burns's Use of the Scots Verse-Epistle Form', *Philological Quarterly* 49.2 (April 1970), 188–210.

—— 'Robert Burns's Satire', in Andrew Noble and R. D. S. Jack, eds., *The Art of Robert Burns* (London: Vision, 1982; reprinted in Carol McGuirk, ed., *Critical Essays on Robert Burns*. New York: G. K. Hall, 1998), 117–33.

GLOSSARY

THIS glossary is based on the one included in the Edinburgh editions of *Poems, Chiefly in the Scottish Dialect*. Most definitions below are taken from this glossary: these are marked with (E) only where they are juxtaposed with definitions marked (K) from the much smaller glossary appended to the 1786 Kilmarnock edition; with definitions from *Dictionary of the Scots Language* (*DSL*) or from Kinsley's 1968 edition (Kinsley); or with expansions, definitions, or examples of my own, marked (ed.). Definitions in the Kilmarnock glossary were almost always taken over into the Edinburgh glossary, though sometimes in amended form. The meanings given of these words in Scots is generally in addition to, not instead of, any meanings they may have in English.

The Kilmarnock glossary is prefaced with the following explanation: 'Words that are universally known, and those that differ from the English only by the elision of letters by apostrophes, or by varying the termination of the verb, are not inserted. The terminations may be thus known; the participle present, instead of *ing*, ends, in the Scotch Dialect, in *an* or *in*; in *an*, particularly, when the verb is composed of the participle present, and any of the tenses of the auxiliary, *to be*. The past time and participle past are usually made by shortening the *ed* into *'t*.'

The Edinburgh glossary replaces this with advice on pronunciation: 'The *ch* and *gh* have always the guttural sound. The sound of the English diphthong *oo*, is commonly spelled *ou*. The French *u*, a sound which often occurs in the Scotch language, is marked *oo*, or *ui*. The *a* in genuine Scotch words, except when forming a diphthong, or followed by an *e* mute after a single consonant, sounds generally like the broad English *a* in *wall*. The Scotch diphthongs, *ae*, always, and *ea* very often, sound like the French *é* masculine. The Scotch diphthong *ey*, sounds like the Latin *ei*.'

a' all
aback behind, away (K); away, aloof (E)
abiegh at a distance (K); at a shy distance (E)
aboon above, up
abread, abreed abroad, in sight
ack to act (ed.)
ae one (K)
aff off
aff-loof unpremeditated
aft, aften oft
afore before
agley wide of the aim (K); off the right line, wrong (E)
aiblins perhaps
aik oak (ed.)

ain own
airn iron
airt point of the compass, quarter, direction (*DSL*)
aith an oath
aits oats
aiver an old horse (K)
aizle a red ember (K); a hot cinder (E)
a-jee to one side, aside, off the straight (*DSL*)
alake alas
alane alone
amaist almost
amang among
an' and, if (E)
ance once
ane one, an (K)

anither another

as as if, e.g. as they would never part: as if they would never part (ed.)

ase ashes (K)

asklent asquint, on the slant, on one side (*DSL*)

aspar apart, aspread, with legs apart (*DSL*)

aught eight

auld old

auldfarren sagacious, cunning, prudent

ava at all, of all (K)

awa away

awkart aukward

awn the beard of oats, etc. (K)

awnie bearded (E)

ay, aye yes; always (ed.)

ayont beyond

ba' ball

backlins-comin coming back, returning

bad did bid (E); bade (ed.)

baggie the belly

bairan baring (K)

bairn a child

bairn-time a family of children, a brood

baith both

bake a biscuit (*DSL*)

bane bone

banie, bainie bony (K); having large bones, stout (E)

bang attack, onslaught (*DSL*); bide a bang: endure an onslaught (ed.)

barefit bare-footed

barkin barking

barmie of or like barm (E); i.e. yeast (ed.)

batch a crew, a gang

bauk a crossbeam

bauk-en' the end of a beam

bauld bold

bauldly boldly

baws'nt having a white stripe down the face (K)

be't be it

bear barley (ed.)

bee to let be, to leave in quiet (K); to give over, to cease (E)

beese beasts; specifically body and head vermin (*DSL*)

beet to add fuel to fire

behint, behin' behind

beld bald (*DSL*)

bellys bellows (K)

belyve by and by

ben into the spence or parlour

benmaist furthest in, in the second inner room (*DSL*)

besom broom (ed.)

bestead, bestad situated, circumstanced (*DSL*)

beuk a book

bicker (1) a kind of wooden dish, a short race

bicker (2) to move quickly, to run, to rush (*DSL*)

bid desire (*DSL*); bid nae better than: want nothing more than to (ed.)

bide (1) stay; bade: did stay

bide (2) tolerate, stand (usually in the negative: canna, downa); bade: endured (*DSL*)

biel, bield shelter (K)

bien wealthy, plentiful

big (v) to build

biggin (n) a building (K); a building, a house (E)

biggit builded

bill bull

billie a brother, a young fellow

birk birch-tree (ed.)

birkie a clever fellow

birr force, energy, enthusiasm (*DSL*)

birsie bristle, hair (*DSL*)

birth berth (ed.)

bit crisis, nick of time (E); at the bit: at the critical point (*DSL*)

bizz a bustle, to buzz

blastet worthless (K)

blastie a shrivell'd dwarf; a term of contempt

blather the bladder (K)

blaud a flat piece of anything; to flap

blate bashful, sheepish

blaw to blow, to boast (E); boasting, e.g. muckle blaw (ed.)

blellum 'an idle talking fellow' (*DSL*)

blether to talk idly; nonsense (E); in latter sense esp. as blethers (ed.)

bleth'ran, bleth'rin talking idly

bleezan, bleezin blazing

bleeze blaze

blin' blind (ed.)

blink a glance, an amorous leer, a short space of time (K); a little while, a smiling look; to look kindly, to shine by fits (E)

blinker a term of contempt

blinkin smirking

blue-gown one of those beggars who get annually, on the King's birthday, a blue cloke or gown with a badge

bluid blood

bluidy bloody

blype a shred of cloth, etc. (K); a shred, a large piece (E)

bodies people, folk; a body: one, e.g. a body's sel: oneself (ed.)

bodle a small old coin

bogle a ghost, spectre, or phantom, causing fright (*DSL*)

bonie, bony handsome, beautiful

bonilie handsomely, beautifully

bonnock a kind of thin cake of bread

boord a board (E); i.e. table (ed.)

boortrie the shrub elder, planted much of old in the hedges of barn-yards, etc.

boost behoved (K); behoved, must needs (E), e.g. I shortly boost to pasture: I shortly must to pasture, i.e. I shortly must go to pasture (ed.)

boot o' boot: into the bargain (Kinsley)

botch an angry tumour

bow-kail cabbage

bow't bended, crooked

bowse to drink deeply, booze (ed.)

brachens fern (E); i.e. bracken

brae a declivity, a precipice, the slope of a hill

braid broad

braik a kind of harrow

braindge to run swiftly forward

braindge't reeled forward

braing to rush forward recklessly, to plunge (*DSL*)

brainge to draw unsteadily (K)

brak broke, made insolvent

branks a kind of halter, or bridle, for horses or cows (*DSL*)

brash a sudden illness (K)

brat a worn shred of cloth (K)

brats coarse clothes, rags

brattle a short race, hurry, fury

braw fine, handsome

brawlie, brawly very well, finely, heartily

braxie a morkin sheep (K); that is, a sheep that has died by disease or accident (*DSL*)

bread, breid breadth (ed.)

breastet sprung forward (K); did spring up or forward (E)

breef an invulnerable charm (K); an invulnerable or irresistible spell (E)

breeks breeches

brent (1) smooth, unwrinkled (*DSL*)

brent (2) bold, shameless (*DSL*)

brie juice, liquid (E); barley-brie: whisky (ed.)

brisket the breast, the bosom

brither a brother

brock a badger (*DSL*)

brogue an affront (K); a hum, a trick (E)

broo liquid or moisture of any kind (*DSL*)

broose a race at country weddings who shall first reach the bridegroom's house on returning from church

brugh a burgh

brulzie, bruilzie a broil, a combustion

brunstane brimstone

brunt did burn

brust to burst

buckskin an inhabitant of Virginia

buirdly stout-made, broad-built

bum-clock a humming beetle that flies in the summer evening

bumman, bummin humming as bees

bure did bear (E); bure the gree: held or won first supremacy; bure sic hands: fought so vigorously (Kinsley)

burn water, a rivulet

Burnewin *q.d.* burn the wind, a Blacksmith (K)

busk to adorn, to deck, to dress up (*DSL*)

busle, bussle a bustle; to bustle

but without (E); in this sense often in combination with or, e.g. but house or hald (ed.)

but and ben the country kitchen and parlour (K)

by himsel lunatic, distracted (E); i.e. beside himself (ed.)

byke a swarm or crowd of people (*DSL*)

byre cow-stable

ca' to call, to drive (K); i.e. to drive horses, livestock, etc.; ca' hame: drive home (ed.)

cadie, caddie a person, a young fellow

cadger a carrier

cairds tinkers (K)

cairn a loose heap of stones (K)

callan a boy

caller fresh, sound (E); esp of air, food etc. (ed.)

cannie gentle, mild, dextrous; cannily: dextrously, gently

cant a merry old story (*DSL*)

cantie, canty chearful, merry

cantraip a charm, a spell

cape stane cope stone (K)

careerin chearfully

carl a fellow; a man of the common folk, not a gentleman (*DSL*)

carlin a stout old woman

cartes cards

caudron cauldron, pot (ed.)

cauf calf

cauld cold

caup a small, wooden dish with two lugs, or handles (K); a wooden drinking vessel (E)

cavie hen-coop (*DSL*)

chamer parlour, best room or spare room in a house, often an upper room (*DSL*)

chanter a part of a bagpipe (E); i.e. that part which can be played separately of the bag and drones (ed.)

chap (1) a person, a fellow

chap (2) a blow (E), e.g. with a tool, or on a door etc. (ed.)

chap (3) a measure of drink (ed.)

chapman pedlar (ed.)

chiel, cheel a young fellow

chimla, chimlie a fire grate

chimla lug the fireside

chow to chew; cheek-for-chow: side by side

chuffie fat-faced (K)

claes, claise cloaths

claith cloth

claithing cloathing

clarket, clarkit wrote (E); to record in writing, to enter up in a book (*DSL*)

clash an idle tale, the story of the day

clatter to tell idle stories; an idle story

claught to grasp, seize forcibly, clutch (*DSL*)

claut to clean, to scrape

clavers clover (*DSL*)

claw to scratch

cleed clothe (*DSL*)

cleek (1) seize, snatch, steal, pilfer (*DSL*)

cleek (2) in dancing, to link arms and whirl round (*DSL*) clew (1) scratched (ed.)

clew, clue (2) ball (of thread or yarn) (ed.)

clink money, cash (*DSL*)

clinkan, clinkin jerking, clinking

clinkumbell who rings the church bell

clips shears

clish-ma-claver idle conversation

clock to hatch; a beetle

clockin hatching

cloot the hoof of a cow, sheep, etc.

clootie, cloots an old name for the Devil (E). From the Devil's cloven hoof: 'clootie' means 'cloven' (*DSL*)

clour a bump or swelling after a blow

clout a patch; to mend or patch, especially pots and shoes (*DSL*); cloths (ed.)

coble a fishing boat

coft bought (*DSL*)

cog, coggie a small wooden dish without handles (K)

colic-grips the pains or gripes of colic, a bowel condition (ed.)

collie a general and sometimes a particular name for country curs (K)

cood the cud

coof, cuif a blockhead, a ninny

cooket, cookit appeared and disappeared by fits

coor (1) cover or protect (*DSL*)

coor (2) crouch, cringe, cower (*DSL*)

coost did cast

cootie a pretty large wooden dish (K)

core corps, party, clan

corky-headed, -heidit feather-brained, empty-headed (*DSL*)

corn't fed with oats

cotter the inhabitant of a cot house or cottage

countra country

couthie kind, loving

cove cavern

cowe to terrify, to keep under; to lop; a fright, a branch of furze, broom, etc.

cowran, cowrin cowering

cowte colt

crabbet, crabbit crabbed, fretful

crack conversation, to converse (K); a story, an entertaining tale (*DSL*)

craft, croft a field near a house, in old husbandry

craig neck; throat, gullet (*DSL*)

crambo-clink, crambo-jingle rhymes, doggerel verses

crank a harsh, grating sound (K); the noise of an ungreased wheel (E)

crankous fretting, peevish (K); fretful, captious (E)

cranreuch the hoar frost

crap a crop, the top (E); craps o' heather: heather tips, heather shoots (ed.)

craw a crow

crazy frail or infirm; hence craz'd (ed.)

creel a basket; to have one's wits in a creel: to be crazed, to be fascinated

creeshie greasy, dirty (*DSL*)

crood, croud to coo as a dove

croon a hollow, continued moan (K); to make a noise like the continued roar of a bull, to hum a tune (E)

crooning humming (E)

croose, crouse chearful, courageous; crously: chearfully, courageously

crouch to bow low (*DSL*)

crouchie crook-backed (K)

crowdie-time breakfast time

crowl to creep (K)

crump hard and brittle, spoken of bread

crunt a blow on the head with a cudgel

cummock a short staff (K); a short staff with a crooked head (E)

curchie a courtesy (E); i.e. a curtsy (ed.)

curling a well-known game on ice; curler: a player at ice

curpan, curpin the crupper (K)

Cushat the dove or wood pigeon
custock the stem of kail or cabbage (*DSL*)
cutty short, diminutive
cutty sark a short chemise or undergarment (*DSL*)

daffin merriment, foolishness
daft merry, giddy, foolish
dails deals, i.e. planks to be used for tables or benches (ed.)
daimen now and then, seldom (K)
dainty pleasant, good humoured, agreeable
darg, daurk a day's labour (K); han'-daurk: manual labour (ed.)
darklins darkling (E); i.e. in the dark (ed.)
daud, dawd the noise of one falling flat, a large piece of bread, &c. (K)
daur dare
daur't dared
daut, dawt to caress, to fondle (K)
dead death (Kinsley)
dead-sweer very loath, averse (K)
dearthfu' dear (E), i.e. 'costly, expensive': *OED* suggests this is Burns's coinage (ed.)
deave to bother, to annoy; esp. to annoy or weary by constantly talking or asking questions (*DSL*)
Deil the Devil (ed.)
Deil-ma-care! no matter! for all that! (E); deil ane: not one (ed.)
deleeret delirious (K)
descrive to describe
dight to wipe, to clean corn from chaff; cleaned from chaff
ding to worst, to push (E); be shifted, be worn out (Kinsley), e.g. facts are cheels that winna ding (ed.)
dinna do not
dirl shake, cause to vibrate (*DSL*)
disrespeket disrespected
diz'n, dizzen a dozen
doit (v) to be enfeebled or confused in mind, absent-minded (*DSL*)

doited stupified, hebetated
donsie unlucky, dangerous (K)
dool sorrow; to sing dool, to lament, to mourn
dorty saucy, nice
douce, douse sober, wise, prudent
doup buttocks (*DSL*)
dow am *or* are able to, can; downa: am *or* are not able to, cannot
dowf, dowff pithless, wanting force
dowie crazy and dull (K); worn with grief, fatigue, etc. (E)
doylt, doylte stupified, hebetated (K)
doyte to go drunkenly or stupidly (K)
draigle soil, bespatter (*DSL*)
drap a drop; to drop
draw to pull out; draw a stroke: raise a hand for a blow (*DSL*)
dreep to ooze, to drop
dreigh tardy, long-delayed (*DSL*)
dribble drizzling, slaver
driddle to toddle, dawdle, saunter (*DSL*)
drift a drove
droddum the breech (E), i.e. the posterior, esp. as object of chastisement (ed.)
droll half-witted, slightly crazed (*DSL*)
droop-rumpl't that droops at the crupper (E), i.e. of a horse, at its rump (ed.)
droukit drenched, soaked (*DSL*)
drouth thirst, drought
druken drunken
drumlie muddy
drummock meal and water mixed raw (K)
drunt pet, pettish humor (K); pet, sour humour (E)
dub a small pond
duds rags of clothes (K)
duddie ragged
dung worsted, pushed, driven (E), i.e. past tense of ding (ed.)
durk dirk, dagger (ed.)
dush to push as a bull, ram, &c. (K)

dyke low dry-stone wall (ed.)
dyvor debtor, bankrupt (*DSL*)

e'e the eye; **een**: the eyes
e'en, e'enin evening
eerie frighted, particularly the dread of spirits (K); frightened, dreading spirits (E)
eild old age (K)
eldritch fearful, horrid, ghastly (K)
en' end (ed.)
eneugh enough
enow enough (ed.)
ettle aim, purpose, design, object (*DSL*)
eydent constant, busy (K); diligent (E)

fa' (1) fall, lot (K); to fall (E); befall, e.g. in phrases of imprecation (shame fa' thee) or good wishes (*DSL*)
fa' (2) to have something fall to one's share; hence, gen. with canna, mauna, etc., to venture to obtain, win, come by (*DSL*)
faddom't fathomed
fae a foe
faem foam (K)
fain fond (of); eager (to); amorous; gladly (*DSL*), e.g. wad fain: would dearly (ed.)
fairin fairing, a present (E); specifically one bought at a fair (*DSL*)
fallow fellow
fand did find (E), found (ed.)
fareweel farewell
farl a cake of bread
fash trouble, care; to trouble, to care for (E); bother, bother about (ed.)
fatt'rels ribband ends, &c. (K)
fauld fold; sheep-pen (*DSL*)
fause false (ed.)
fause-hoose a conical structure of wooden props built inside a corn-stack to facilitate drying (*DSL*)

faussont, fawsont decent, orderly (K); decent, seemly (E)
faut fault (E); harm, injury (*DSL*)
fear to frighten, to scare (*DSL*)
fear't frightened
fearfu' frightful
feat neat, spruce
fecht to fight (K)
feck (1) value, worth, return, result (*DSL*)
feck (2) (large) number or portion (*DSL*)
feckless ineffective, weak, paltry (*DSL*)
feg fig (E); as in expressions such as ne'er mind a feg (ed.)
fell keen, biting (E)
fen, fend an effort, attempt, shift, esp. to maintain oneself. Freq. in phr. to mak a fen (*DSL*)
fetch to stop suddenly in the draught, and then come on too hastily [of a draught-horse] (K); to pull by fits (E)
ferlie, ferly a wonder, to wonder; also a term of contempt (K)
fidge to fidget; **fidgin**: fidgeting (E); **fidgean-fain**: restlessly eager (ed.)
fiel comfortable, cosy; soft, smooth and pleasant to the touch (*DSL*)
fier sound, healthy (K); esp. in expression hale and fier (*DSL*); a brother, a friend (E)
fient, fiend, a petty oath (E); a strong negative (*DSL*); e.g. the fient a pride: not a bit of pride; fient haet: not one (ed.)
fissle to make a russling noise, to fidget; a bustle
fit, fitt a foot (ed.)
fittie-lan' the near horse of the hindmost pair in the plough (K); from 'fit-o-land', the horse 'treading the unploughed land while its neighbour walks in the furrow' (Kinsley)
fizz to make a hissing noise like fermentation

flaff flap, flutter (*DSL*)
flainen flannel
flair flatter; brag, boast (*DSL*)
flee fly (ed.)
fleech to supplicate in a flattering
  manner
fleesh fleece (K)
fleg a kick, a random blow
flether to decoy by fair words
fleth'ran flattering
fley to frighten (K)
flichter to flutter (K); to flutter as
  young nestlings when their dam
  approaches (E)
flinders shreds, broken pieces
flingin-tree a flail
flisk to fret at the yoke (K)
fliskit fretted (E)
flit transport from one place to
  another (*DSL*)
flunkies livery servants (K)
fodgel plump, buxom, well-built
  (*DSL*)
foggage grass which grows among
  crops, and is fed on by horses and cat-
  tle after the crop is removed (*DSL*)
forbad forbade (ed.)
forbears ancestors (K),
  forefathers (E)
forby, forbye besides (K)
forfairn distressed, worn out, jaded
forgat forgot (ed.)
forgather to meet, to encounter with
forgie forgive (ed.)
forjesket jaded (K)
foord ford
foughten troubled, harassed
fouth abundance, plenty (*DSL*)
fow, fou, fu' (1) full, drunk &c. (K)
fow (2) a bushel (K)
frae from (ed.)
freath froath (K); i.e. froth (ed.)
fud the human posteriors, the
  buttocks (*DSL*)
fuff to blow intermittedly (K)
funnie full of merriment
fur, furr a furrow

furm a form, a bench
fyke trifling cares; to piddle, to be in a
  fuss about trifles (E); (n) fuss (ed.)
fyle to dirty, to soil (K)

ga' gall, pustule, sore (Kinsley)
gab the mouth; to speak boldly (K); to
  speak boldly or pertly (E)
gae to go; gaed: went; gaen or gane:
  gone; gaun: going
gaet, gate way, manner, practice (K);
  way, manner, road (E)
gailies fairly well, pretty well (*DSL*)
gang to go, to walk
gangrel a tramp, vagrant, vagabond
  (*DSL*)
gar to make, to force to (E); e.g. gar
  you trow: make you believe (ed.)
garten a garter
gash wise, sagacious, talkative; to
  converse (K)
gat got (ed.)
gate, or gaet way, manner, road
gawsie, gaucy jolly, large (K)
gear riches, goods of any kind
geck to toss the head in pride or
  wantonness (K)
gentles great folks
geordie a guinea
get a child, a young one
gie to give; gied: gave; gi'en: given
gif if, whether (*DSL*)
gilpey a young girl (K)
gin (conj.) if, against
gin (prep.) by, before (*DSL*), e.g. gin
  night: by the time night comes (ed.)
girdle iron griddle for making scones,
  oatcakes, etc. (*DSL*)
girn to grin; to twist the features in
  rage, agony, etc.
gizz a wig (K); a periwig (E)
glaikit stupid, foolish; thoughtless,
  irresponsible, flighty, frivolous (gen.
  applied to women) (*DSL*)
glaizie smooth, glittering (K);
  glittering, smooth like glass (E)
gleg sharp, ready

glib-gabbet that speaks smoothly and readily

glint to peep (K)

gloamin the twilight

glowr to stare, to look; a stare, a look

glunch a frown; to frown (K)

goave, gove to stare stupidly or vacantly (*DSL*)

gowd gold

gowf (v) to hit or strike with the open hand (*DSL*)

gowk a fool or simpleton; the cuckoo (*DSL*)

graff grave (*DSL*)

graip a pronged instrument for cleaning stables

graith accoutrements, furniture, dress

grane, grain a groan; to groan

grape to grope

grapet groped

grat cried, wept (ed.)

graunie a grandmother

great intimate, familiar

gree to agree; to bear the gree: to be decidedly the victor

greet to shed tears, to weep

grippet catched, seized

grips gripes, colic pains (ed.)

grissle gristle

groat to get the whissle of one's groat: to play a losing game

grousome loathsomely grim (K)

grozet a gooseberry

grumphie a sow

grun' ground

grunstane a grindstone

gruntle the visage; a grunting noise (K)

grushie of thick, stout growth (K); thick, of thriving growth (E)

guid, gude good

guid-een good evening

Guidfather, Guidmither father-in-law and mother-in-law

Guidman, Guidwife the master and mistress of the house; Young Guidman, a man newly married

guid-mornin good morrow

guidwillie, guid-willie kindly, hearty, cordial, generous, open-handed (*DSL*)

gully large knife (*DSL*)

gumlie muddy

gusty tasteful (E); i.e. tasty (ed.)

ha' hall (E); ha'-Bible: the great bible that lies in the hall (E); ha' folk: servants (*DSL*)

haddin, haudin possessions, means of support, property, inheritance (*DSL*)

haerse horse (ed.)

haet fient haet: a petty oath of negation, nothing (E); e.g. fient haet o' them: not one of them; deil-haet ails them: damn-all ails them (ed.)

haffet the temple, the side of the head

hafflins nearly half, partly

haggis a kind of pudding boiled in the stomach of a cow or sheep

hail small shot (*DSL*)

hain to save, to spare (K)

hairst harvest

haith a petty oath

hal, or hald hold, hiding place (K); an abiding place (E)

hale whole, tight, healthy

hallan a particular partition wall in a cottage (E); specifically sheltering the living-space from the door, or between the human accommodation and that for animals (*DSL*)

hallions a person of slovenly dress or appearance, a good-for-nothing idler, a rascal (*DSL*)

hame home; hameward: homeward; hamely: homely

han', haun hand

hap to wrap, to cover

hap-step-an'-lowp hop, skip and leap

hash a term of contempt (K); a sot (E)

haud to hold

haughs low-lying rich lands, valleys

haurl to drag, to peel (K)
haverel a quarter-wit (K); a
  half-witted person; half-witted (E)
havins good manners, decorum,
  good sense
Hawkie a cow, properly one with a
  white face
healsome healthful, wholesome
hech! Oh! strange!
hecht to forebode (K); to foretell
  something that is to be got or given;
  foretold; the thing foretold (E)
heeze to elevate, to raise
hersel herself
herrin a herring
het hot
heugh a crag, a coal-pit (K)
hie high
hing to hang
hilch to hobble, to halt
himsel himself
hirpl to walk crazily, to creep
hirplan, hirplin creeping
hissel so many cattle as one person
  can attend
histie dry, chapt, barren (K)
hitch a loop, a knot
hizzie hussy, a young girl
hoast, host to cough
hoddan the motion of a sage country
  farmer on an old cart horse (K)
hogshouther to justle with the
  shoulder (K); a kind of horse play by
  justling with the shoulder (E)
hool outer skin or case
hoolie slowly, leisurely; Hoolie! take
  leisure! stop!
hoord a hoard; to hoard
Hornie one of the many names of the
  Devil
hotch to fidget, to hitch about with
  impatience or discomfort (DSL)
Houghmagandie a species of gender
  composed of the masculine and
  feminine united (K); fornication (E)
houlet owl (ed.)
howe hollow (K); a hollow or dell (E)

howe-backet sunk in the back,
  spoken of a horse etc.
howk to dig (K)
howket, howcket (adj) digged (E)
hoy to urge incessantly (K); to urge (E)
hoyte a motion between a trot and a
  gallop (K); to amble crazily (E)
huff to hector, bully; to scold, chide,
  storm at (OED)
hurchin an uncouth person;
  occasionally applied to a
  mischievous child (DSL)
hurdies the loins, the crupper

I' in
icker an ear of corn (K)
ier-oe a great grand child (K)
ilk, ilka each
ill-willie malicious, unkind (K);
  malicious, niggardly (E)
ingine genius (K); genius, ingenuity
  (E)
ingle fire, fire-place (E)
ingle-cheek the fireside,
  chimney-corner (DSL)
irie melancholy (DSL)
I'se I shall or will
ither other, one another

jad, jade also a familiar term among
  country folk for a giddy young girl
jauk to dally at work (K); to dally, to
  trifle (E)
jaup (n) a quantity of liquid suddenly
  spilt or thrown in the air (DSL)
jaup (v) (1) to splash or ripple in a
  container, spill over (DSL)
jaup (v) (2) to splash, bespatter, e.g.
  with mud or water (DSL)
jaw to pour out abruptly, splash, spill,
  throw (DSL)
jillet a jilt, a giddy girl
jimp to jump, slender in the waist,
  handsome
jingle to rhyme (OED)
jink to dodge, to turn a corner;
  a sudden turning a corner

jinker that turns quickly, a gay sprightly girl, a wag

jirt a jerk

jundie to justle (K)

jo sweetheart, lover (*DSL*)

jocteleg a kind of knife (K)

jouk to stoop (K); to stoop, to bow the head (E)

jow a verb, which includes both the swinging motion and pealing sound of a large bell

jowler a heavy-jawed dog of the hound type (*DSL*)

kae a daw (K); i.e. a jackdaw (ed.)

kail coleworts; a kind of broth

kain, kane fowls, etc. paid as rent by a farmer

kebar, caber beam, rafter (*DSL*)

kebbuck a cheese

keek a peep; to peep

kelpies a sort of mischievous spirits, said to haunt fords and ferries at night, especially in storms

ken to know; kend, kent, ken't: knew

kenning, kenning a very little of anything, a trifle (*DSL*)

ket a hairy, ragged fleece of wool (K)

kiaugh carking anxiety (K); 'carking' means harassing or vexing (ed.)

kilt to truss up the cloaths

kimmer a young girl, a gossip

kin' kind

kintra country (ed.)

kirk church (ed.)

kirn the harvest supper; a churn; to churn

kirsen to christen (K)

kist chest, shop-counter

kitchen any thing that eats with bread; to serve for soup, gravy, &c. (E); to give a relish or flavour to, to season (*DSL*)

kittle to tickle; ticklish, likely

kittlen a young cat

kiutle to cuddle, to caress, to fondle (K)

knaggie like knags or points of rock

knappin-hammer a hammer for breaking stones

knoit knock, beat, strike sharply (*DSL*)

knowe a small round hillock

kye cows

kyte stomach, belly (*DSL*)

kythe to discover, to show one's self

laggen the angle at the bottom of a wooden dish (K)

Lalland lowland (ed.)

lampet, laimpit a kind of shell-fish (E); i.e. a limpet (ed.)

laigh low

laik, lake lack, want, deficiency (*DSL*)

laith loath

laithfu' bashful (K)

laithron, laidron a term of abuse for a lazy, loutish person (*DSL*)

laird a landowner (ed.)

lallan lowland; Lallans, Scotch dialect

lan' land, estate

lane lone; my lane, thy lane, &c.: myself alone, thyself alone, &c.

lanely lonely

lang long; to think lang: to long, to weary (E); lang syne: long ago (ed.)

lap did leap

lave the rest, the remainder, the others

laverock, lav'rock the lark

lay, lea untilled ground left fallow, pasture (Kinsley)

lea'e leave

leal loyal, true (K)

lear, pronounced lare learning

lee-lang live-long

leeze me on a term of congratulatory endearment (K); from lief is me: dear is to me (*DSL*)

leuk a look; to look

lien lain, did lie (ed.)

lift (1) the sky

lift (2) a load, a consignment of goods (*DSL*)

lightly sneeringly; to sneer at

limmer a woman of easy virtue (K); a kept-mistress, a strumpet (E)

link to trip along (K)

linn a waterfall

lint flax; lint in the bell: flax in flower

lintwhite a linnet

loan the place of milking

lo'e love (ed.)

loof the palm of the hand, pl. looves

loot did let (K); let out, uttered (Kinsley)

lough loch, lake (ed.)

loun a fellow; a ragamuffin; a woman of easy virtue

loup jump (ed.)

lowe flame; to flame (K)

lowse to loose

lug the ear; a handle

luggie, lugget caup a small wooden dish with one handle (K)

lum the chimney

lunch a large piece of cheese, flesh, etc.

lunt smoke; to smoke (K); a column of smoke; to smoke (E)

lyart grey (K); of a mixed colour, grey (E); usually of hair (ed.)

mae more

mair more

maist, 'maist most; almost

mak to make

Mallie Molly

mang, 'mang among

manteele a mantle (K)

mashlum meslin, mixed corn

maskin-pat tea-pot (*DSL*)

maukin a hare

maun must

maut malt, specifically as the basis of ale or whisky (*DSL*)

meere a mare

meikle, mickle much (ed.)

mell to meddle with (K)

melvie to soil with meal (K); to coat with a film of meal or flour, as a miller's clothes (*DSL*)

men' mend

mense good breeding (K); good breeding, decorum (E)

menseless ill-bred, rude, impudent

messan, messin a small dog

midden a dunghill

midden-hole a gutter at the bottom of the dunghill

mim prim, affectedly meek

min', mind mind; remembrance (E); remember (ed.)

mind't mind it; resolved, intending

minnie mother, dam

mishanter mishap, unfortunate accident, disaster (*DSL*)

misteuk mistook

mither a mother

mixtie-maxtie confusedly mixed

mizzle muzzle (*DSL*)

modewurk a mole (K)

monie, mony many

moop to nibble as a sheep (K)

moorcock grouse (ed.)

moorlan of or belonging to moors

morn the next day, tomorrow

mottie full of motes

mou the mouth

muckle, meikle great, big; much

muslin-kail broth made up simply of water, barley, and greens (K)

mutchkin an English pint

mysel myself

na no, not, nor

nae no, not any

naething nothing

naig a horse

nane none

nappy strong ale (*DSL*)

near hand nearly, almost (*DSL*)

neebor a neighbour

negleket neglected

neuk, newk nook

niest next

nieve the fist (K)

niffer an exchange or barter (*DSL*)

nit a nut

noddle brain (ed.)

norland of or belonging to the North

noteless unnoticed, unknown

nowt, nowte black cattle (K)

o' of

o'erlay a neck-cloth worn by men, which hung down before, and was tied behind (DSL)

o't of it

onie, ony any

or is often used for ere, before (E), e.g. or lang: before long (ed.)

orra spare, extra, odd, superfluous (DSL)

oughtlins in any way, at all, in the least degree (DSL)

oursel, oursels ourselves

outler lying in the fields, not housed at night (K)

owre over (K); over, too (E)

owrehip a way of fetching a blow with a hammer over the arm

pack (1) intimate, familiar (K); twelve stones of wool (E)

pack (2) gar them pack: send them packing (ed.)

painch the paunch (K)

paitrick, pairtrick a partridge

pang to cram (K)

parratch, porritch pottage (K); oatmeal pudding, a well-known Scotch dish (E)

pat did put; a pot

pattle, pettle the plough-staff (K); an implement with a spatulate blade, usually carried on a plough for clearing the mould-board of soil (DSL)

paughty proud, saucy (K); proud, haughty (E)

paukie, pawkie cunning, fly

pay't paid; beat

peghan the crop of fowls, the stomach (K)

penny-wheep small beer (K)

phiz face (OED)

phraise fair speeches, flattery; to flatter

phraisin flattery

pickle a small quantity

pine pain, care (K); pain, uneasiness (E)

pintle penis (DSL)

pit to put (E); also make as in e.g. it pits me mad (ed.)

plack an old Scotch coin; plackless: pennyless

pleugh a plough; pleugh-pettle: a plough-staff

pliskie trick (K)

pliver plover (DSL)

pock bag (DSL)

poind to seize and sell the goods of a debtor in lieu of debt

poortith poverty

poosion to poison; to spoil, to render unpalatable or nauseating (DSL)

Poossie, pussie a hare or cat

pout, powt a chicken

pouther, powther powder

pow the head, the skull

pownies a little horse

pou, pow, pu to pull

pouch pocket (DSL)

preen a pin

prent print

prie to taste

prief proof (K)

prig to haggle over the price, to bargain (DSL)

primsie affectedly nice (K); demure, precise (E)

pund pound, pounds

pyke pick (out or off) (DSL)

quat quit, did quit (K)

quakin, quaikin quaking (K)

queer amusing, funny, entertaining (DSL)

quey a cow from one year to two years old

raep, rape rope (K)

ragweed the plant ragwort

raible to repeat by rote (K); to rattle nonsense (E)

rair to roar; rair't: roared (E); rairan: roaring (ed.)

raize to madden, to enflame

ramfeezl'd overspent (K); fatigued, overspent (E)

ram-stam thoughtless (K); forward, thoughtless (E)

randie rough and belligerent in manner, riotous, ruffianly, aggressive, esp. of a beggar who uses intimidation to extort alms (*DSL*)

rant a romp or boistrous frolic; to romp, roister, make merry (*DSL*)

rarely excellent, very well

rash a rush; rash-buss: a bush of rashes

ratton a rat

raucle stout, clever (K); rash, stout, fearless (E)

raught did reach (K)

raw a row (E); i.e. a line in order (ed.)

rax to stretch

ream (n) cream (E)

ream (v) to form a froth or foam, to mantle (*DSL*)

reave to rob

reck to take heed (K)

red-wud stark mad

rede counsel, to counsel (K)

reek smoke; to smoke

reeket smoked, smoky

reest to be restive (K); to stand restive (E)

reestet (1) stood restive

reestet (2) shrivelled (K); stunted, withered (E)

reft split, cleft (*OED*)

remead remedy

requit requital

restricked restricted

rief reaving (K)

rig a ridge (E); specifically, the unit of ploughed land, twenty or more feet

across, and raised about three feet high in the middle, sloping down on either side to aid drainage (Kinsley)

riggin the roof (*DSL*)

rin to run, to melt

ringwoodie, rigwiddie ill-favoured (a word used of a witch) (*DSL*)

ripp a handful of unthreshed corn, &c. (K)

risk to make a noise like the breaking of small roots with the plough

rive (1) to wrench from its place, uproot, dig up, force out (*DSL*)

rive (2) to tear, rend, rip, lacerate (*DSL*)

rockin a meeting on a winter evening (K)

roon a shred, a remnant

roose to praise, to commend

roun' round, in the circle of neighbourhood

roupet, rupet hoarse, as with a cold

row, rowe to roll, to wrap

row't rolled, wrapped

rowt, rowte to bellow (K); to low, to bellow (E)

rowth, routh plenty

rozet rosin

rung a cudgel

runkle a wrinkle (K)

runt the stem of the colewort or cabbage

ryke, reak reach, stretch (*DSL*)

's is

sae so

saft soft

sair (adj) sore (K); hence sairly (ed.)

sair (v) serve

sall shall (ed.)

sang a song

sark a shirt

sarkit provided in shirts

saugh the willow

saul soul

saumont salmon

saunt a saint (K)

saut salt; saut-backet: a small wooden box for holding salt, kept near the kitchen fireplace (*DSL*)

saw to sow (E); i.e. seed (ed.)

sax six

scaud to scald

scaur apt to be scared

scawl a scold (K)

scho she (*DSL*)

scone a kind of bread

sconner to loathe (K); a loathing; to loathe (E); to feel surfeited or nauseated (*DSL*)

scraich to scream as a hen, partridge, etc.

screed to tear (K); to tear; a rent (E)

screigh, scriegh to cry shrilly (K)

scriech a scream; to scream

scrieve to run smoothly and swiftly (K); to glide swiftly along (E)

scrievin gleesomely, swiftly (E)

scrimp scant; to stint (K)

'se shall, e.g. I'se: I shall (ed.)

see'd did see

sel self; a body's sel: one's self alone

sen' send

servan' servant

set set off, start out (*DSL*); ill-set: badly-disposed (*DSL*); it sets you ill: it puts you in a false position (ed.)

settlin to get a settlin: to be frighted into quietness

shaird a shred, a shard (E)

shaver a humorous mischievous wag (K)

shavie a trick, practical joke, imposition, swindle (*DSL*)

shaw a little wood; to show (K); to show; a small wood in a hollow place (E)

sheen bright (K); bright, shining (E)

sheep-shank to think one's self nae sheep-shank: to be conceited

sheugh a ditch, a trench

shiel temporary or roughly-made house or shed (*DSL*)

shift (1) the crop grown in any particular season in a system of crop rotation (*DSL*)

shift (2) to change places with (*DSL*)

shog shock

shool a shovel

shoon shoes

shore to offer, present as a mark of favour; threaten, bode unpleasant consequences (for) (*DSL*)

shouther, showther the shoulder

sic such

sidelins sidelong, slanting

siller silver; money

silly deserving pity or compassion; hapless, helpless; (of things) flimsy, unsubstantial (*DSL*)

simmer summer

sin son

sin', sin since (E)

skaith to damage, to injure; an injury (E)

skeigh, skiegh (of horses) mettlesome, fiery, proud (K); proud, nice, high-mettled (E)

skelp to strike, to slap; to walk with a smart tripping step; a smart stroke (E)

skelpie deserving to be smacked; skelpie-limmer: a mischievous girl, a little hussy (*DSL*)

skinking easily poured, thinly diluted; skinking ware: thin clear soups, potages, consommés, or the like (*DSL*)

skinkle to glitter, gleam, sparkle, scintillate, to have a bright showy appearance (*DSL*)

skirl a shrill cry (K); to shriek, to cry shrilly (E)

skyte a sudden, sharp, glancing blow, so as to make what strikes rebound in a slanting direction from that which is struck (*DSL*)

sklent (v) to slant, to fib (K); slant; to run aslant, to deviate from truth; sklented: ran or hit in an oblique direction; sklentin: slanting (E)

slae sloe

slap a gate, a breach in a fence

slee sly; sleest: slyest

sleeket sleek

sliddery, slidd'ry slippery

slype to fall over like a wet furrow (K); to fall over like a wet furrow from the plough (E)

sma' small (K); a small quantity or amount, little, not much (*DSL*)

smeddum powder of any kind (K); dust, powder (E)

smeek smoke (*DSL*)

smiddie smithy

smoor, smuir to be choked, stifled, suffocated; esp. to perish by being buried in a snowdrift (*DSL*)

smoutie smutty, obscene, ugly

smytrie a numerous collection of small individuals (K)

snash abusive language (K); abuse, Billingsgate (E)

snaw snow; to snow

sned to chop, to lop off; to cut off the tops and roots of turnips etc. (*DSL*)

sneeshin snuff; sneeshin-mill: snuff-box

snell bitter, biting

snick the latchet of a door

snick-drawing trick-contriving (K); literally 'latch-lifting' (ed.); to draw a sneck (fig.): to insinuate oneself into an affair surreptitiously; to act in a crafty stealthy manner (*DSL*)

snirtle snigger, make a noise through the nose when attempting to stifle laughter (*DSL*)

snool one whose spirit is broken with oppressive slavery; to submit tamely, to sneak

snoove to go smoothly and constantly; to sneak

snoov't went smoothly

snowk to scent or snuff as a dog, horse, &c.

sodger soldier (ed.)

sonsie having sweet, engaging looks; lucky, jolly

sooth truth; a petty oath

soupe, sowp a spoonful, a small quantity of any thing liquid (E); a drink, something to drink (ed.)

souple flexible, swift

souter shoemaker, cobbler (*DSL*)

sowens type of porridge made from fermented oat-husks and meal (ed.)

sowth to try over a tune with a low whistle

sowther to cement, to solder (K)

spae to prophesy, to divine

spail chip or sliver of wood, splinter (*DSL*)

spairge to spurt about like water or mire; to soil (K); to dash; to soil as with mire (E)

spak did speak

spavet having the spavin (E); i.e. in horses: an arthritic condition causing lameness (ed.); spavie: this condition, also jocularly applied to human beings (*DSL*)

speel to climb

speet spit (meat, fish, etc.) (ed.)

spence the country parlour

spier to ask, to enquire

splatter a splutter; to splutter

splore a ramble (K); a frolic, and riot, a noise (E)

sprachle, sprauchle to move or make one's way laboriously or in a hasty, clumsy manner, esp. in an upward direction (*DSL*)

sprattle to scramble

spreckl'd spotted, speckled

spring a quick reel in music, a Scotch reel

sprit a tough-rooted plant something like rushes

sprittie rushy (K); full of sprits (E)

spunk fire, mettle, wit (E); a spark of light; tinder-stick (ed.)

spunkie fiery; will o' wisp (K); mettlesome, fiery; will o' wisp or *ignis fatuus* (E)

squad a crew, a party

squatter to flutter in water (K); to flutter in water as a wild duck &c. (E)

squattle to sprawl

stacher to stagger

stack a rick of corn, hay, etc.

staggie diminutive of stag (K)

stan' to stand

stane a stone

stank a pool of standing water (K)

stark stout

startle to run as cattle stung by the gadfly

stauk stalk, stride (*DSL*)

staumrel awkward, blundering, stupid (*DSL*)

staw (1) did steal (E); i.e. moved stealthily (ed.)

staw (2) to surfeit, satiate, sicken, or disgust with excess of food (*DSL*)

steek to shut; a stitch

steer to molest, to stir

steeve firm (K); firm, compacted (E)

stegh to cram the belly (K)

stell a still

sten to rear as a horse (K)

stents tribute, dues of any kind

stey steep

stibble stubble

stibble-rig the reaper who takes the lead (K)

stick-an-stowe totally, altogether

stilt to halt, to limp

stimpart the eighth part of a Winchester bushel (E); i.e. a measure of grain (ed.)

stirk a cow or bullock a year old

stock a plant of colewort, cabbage, etc.

stoor sounding hollow, strong, and hoarse

stoup, stowp a kind of jug or dish with a handle

stoure dust, more particularly dust in motion

stownlins by stealth

straik to stroke

strappan tall and handsome

straught straight

streek to stretch (*DSL*)

striddle to straddle

stroan to pour out like a spout (K); to spout, to piss; stroan't: spouted, pissed (E)

strunt spiritous liquor of any kind; to walk sturdily

studdie an anvil

stuff corn or pulse of any kind

sturt trouble; to molest

sturtan frightened

sucker sugar

sud should

sugh the continued rushing noise of wind or water

suthron southern; an old name for the English nation

swaird sward (E); that is, grass-covered ground, turf (*OED* 'greensward')

swall swell (*DSL*)

swank stately, jolly

swankie a tight strapping young fellow or girl

swat did sweat

swatch a sample

swats newly-brewed weak beer (*DSL*)

sweer lazy, averse; dead-sweer: extremely averse

swinge to beat, whip, flog, belabour, drive with blows (*DSL*)

swirlie knaggy, full of knots (E); 'knaggy' means 'knotty, rough, rugged' (*OED*)

swith! get away (K); i.e. as an exclamation (ed.)

swoom swim (*DSL*)

swoor swore, did swear

syne since, ago, then (K); lang syne: long ago (ed.)

tack a lease or tenancy, esp. the leasehold tenure of a farm; an agreement or compact in general (*DSL*)

tae toe (ed.)

taen taken (ed.)

taet a small quantity (K)

tak to take (E); tak aff: to drink to the bottom, or at one draught (*OED*)

tald, tauld told

tane e.g. the tane and the tither: the one and the other (ed.)

tap the top (E)

tapetless unthinking (K); heedless, foolish (E)

tapsalteerie upside down, topsy-turvey, in(to) utter confusion or disorder (*DSL*)

tarrow to murmur at one's allowance (K)

tarry-breeks a sailor

tauted, tawted matted together (K); matted together, spoken of hair or wool (E)

tawie that handles quietly (K); that allows itself to peaceably be handled, spoken of a horse, cow, etc. (E)

ten hours bite a slight feed to the horses while in the yoke in the forenoon

tent (1) a field pulpit

tent (2) heed, caution; to take heed (E); in the latter sense a transitive verb: attend to, take care of; tak tent: take care (ed.)

tentie heedful, cautious

tentless heedless

teugh tough (ed.)

thack thatch; thack an' raep: all kinds of necessaries, particularly clothes (K)

thae these

thairm gut, intestine; as used for e.g. sausage-skin, or fiddle-strings (ed.)

theekit thatched (ed.)

thegither together

themsel, themsels themselves

thysel thyself

thick intimate, familiar

thig to beg, ask for charity (*DSL*)

thir these

thirl to thrill

thirl'd thrilled, vibrated

thole to suffer, to endure

thowe thaw (K)

thowless slack, pithless (K); slack, lazy (E)

thrang throng, a crowd

thrapple windpipe, gullet (*DSL*)

thrave a measure of cut grain, consisting of twenty-four sheaves (*DSL*)

thraw to sprain; to twist; to contradict (E); for thrawin: to prevent warping (Kinsley)

threap to maintain by dint of assertion

thrissle thistle

throw'ther pell-mell, confusedly

thud to make a loud, intermittent noise

tight competent, capable, alert, vigorous (*DSL*)

till to (ed.); till't: to it (E)

timmer timber

tinkler tinker

tip, toop a ram

tippeny weak ale sold at twopence the Scots pint (*DSL*)

tither other (ed.)

tine to lose

tint lost

tirl to knock gently, to uncover (K); to make a slight noise, to uncover (E)

tittle to whisper

tocher a marriage portion (E); i.e. a dowry (ed.)

tod a fox

toddle to totter like the walk of a child

toom empty

toun, town a hamlet; a farmhouse

tout the blast of a horn or trumpet; to blow a horn, &c.

tow a rope

towmond, towmont a twelvemonth

towze, touse to pull or knock about, treat or handle roughly (*DSL*)

towzie rough, shaggy

toy a very old fashion of female
head-dress

toyte to walk like old age (K); to totter
like old age (E)

tozie, tosie (1) cosy, snug, agreeably
warm; (2) merry and elevated in
drink (*DSL*)

trashtrie trash (K)

trig spruce, neat

trimly excellently

trode trodden (ed.)

trow to believe

trowth truth; a petty oath

tug raw hide, of which, in old
times, plough traces were frequently
made

tulzie a quarrel; to quarrel, to fight

twa two

'twad it would

twal twelve; twalpennie-worth: a
small quantity, a penny-worth

twathree a few

twin to part

tyke a dog

unco strange; uncouth; very; very
great; predigious

uncos news

under hidin in hiding (*DSL*)

unkenn'd unknown

upo' upon

usquabae whisky, from the Gaelic
uisge beatha: water of life (ed.)

vap'rin vapouring (E); i.e. acting in
a fantastic or ostentatious manner
(*OED*)

vauntie proud, boastful, vain (*DSL*)

vera very

wa' wall; wa's: walls

wabster a weaver

wad (1) would; wadna: would not (E);
can mean would *have*, e.g: wad been:
would have been; wad stan't: would
have stood (ed.)

wad (2) to bet; a bet, a pledge (E)

wae woe; sorrowful (E); wae worth:
may ill betide (*DSL*)

waesucks! waes me! alas! O the pity!

waft the woof (E); i.e. those threads at
right angles to the warp threads in a
textile (ed.)

wair to lay out, to spend (K)

wale choice; to choose (E);
in former usage also in sense of 'the
best' (ed.)

walie big and strong; plump, buxom,
thriving (*DSL*)

wallop to make violent struggling
movements (*DSL*)

wame the belly

wamefou' a bellyfull

wanchancie unlucky

wanrestfu' restless

wark (1) work, labour (*DSL*)

wark (2) a building, esp. of a public or
imposing kind (*DSL*)

warl', warld world (E); warl's gear:
earthly possessions (ed.)

warly worldy, eager on amassing
wealth

warran a warrant; to warrant

warsl'd wrestled

warst worst

wast waste (ed.)

wastrie prodigality

wat wet; I wat: I wot, I know (E);
red-wat-shod: up to the ankles in
blood (*DSL*)

water-brose brose made simply of
meal and water (K) [i.e.] without the
addition of milk, butter, &c. (E)

water-kelpies a sort of mischievous
spirits that are said to haunt
fords, &c. (K)

wattle a twig, a wand

wauble to swing (K); to swing, to
reel (E)

waught a long pull, swig, or gulp of
any drink; gude-willie-waught: such
a draught taken with good-will, a
hearty or cordial swig (*DSL*)

wauken to awake

wauket thickened as fullers do cloth (K)

waur worse; to worst (E); in latter sense e.g. waur't thee: give you the worst of it (ed.)

we'se we shall

wean, weanie child

wearie monie a wearie body: many a different person (E) (not a sense listed in *DSL*: ed.)

weary fa' the devil take—, confound— (to express exasperation) (*DSL*)

weason weasand (E); i.e. gullet (ed.)

wecht a wooden hoop with skin stretched over it, used in winnowing grain (*DSL*)

wee little; wee-things: little ones; wee-bit: a small matter (E); a wee: a short time (ed.)

weel well; weelfare: welfare

ween to surmise, guess, imagine (*DSL*): already an archaic/literary usage in eighteenth-century English, but seems to have retained more general currency in Scots (ed.)

weeper a broad white cuff worn by widows (*OED*)

weet rain; wetness (E); to wet, to moisten (ed.)

westlin westerly (*DSL*)

wha who

whaizle to wheeze (K)

whalpet whelped

whang a piece of cheese, bread, etc.

whare where

whare'er wherever

whase whose

wheep to fly nimbly; to jerk; penny wheep: small beer

whid the motion of a hare running but not frightened; a lie (E)

whiddan running as a hare or coney (E)

whigmeleerie a piece of ornamentation, used with depreciatory force, gew-gaw, bauble (*DSL*)

whisht! silence!; to hold one's whisht: to be silent

whisk to sweep (K); to sweep; to lash (E)

whissle a whistle; to whistle (E); to get the whissle of one's groat: to play a losing game (E); to be paid in one's own coin, to get one's just deserts (*DSL*)

whitter a hearty draught of liquor

whittle a knife (*DSL*)

whunstane a whin-stone

whyles whiles, sometimes

wi' with

wiel a small whirlpool (K)

wifie a diminutive or endearing term for wife

wight (1) person; (2) sturdy, vigorous, brisk, energetic (*DSL*)

willyart awkward, shy, bashful (*DSL*)

wimple to meander

win to wind, to winnow

win't winded, as a bottom of yarn (E); i.e. wound (ed.)

win' wind; win's: winds

winn to winnow

winna will not

winnock a window

wintle a wavering, swinging motion (K); a staggering motion; to stagger; to reel (E)

winze an oath (K)

wiss wish

wonner wonder, a term of contempt (K)

woo' wool

woodie, widdie a twig or wand of willow or other tough but flexible wood, or several of these twisted or interlaced to make a cord or rope and used for various purposes (*DSL*)

wooer-bab the garter knotted below the knee with a couple of loops and ends (K); i.e. on the *male* leg: a sign of the wearer's intention to propose marriage (*DSL*)

woor wore (ed.)

wordy worthy (ed.)

worset worsted

wrack to vex, to trouble (K); to tease, to vex (E)

wrang wrong; to wrong

wud mad, distracted

wumble a wimble (E); i.e. a gimlet, a tool for drilling small holes (ed.)

wylecoat a flannel vest

wyte blame; to blame

ye is frequently used for the singular (K); this pronoun is frequently used for Thou (E)

yell dry, spoken of a cow (K); barren, that gives no milk (E)

yerk to lash, to jerk

yestreen yesternight

yett gate (*DSL*)

yill ale

yird, yerd, yirth earth

yokin yoking; a bout

yon that, those (of distant objects) (ed.)

'yont beyond

young-guidman a new married man (K)

yoursel yourself

yowe a ewe

INDEX OF TITLES

Entries in italics link titles used by James Kinsley in his edition (see Further Reading) to their titles in this edition.

INDEX OF FIRST LINES

MORE ABOUT

OXFORD WORLD'S CLASSICS

American Literature

British and Irish Literature

Children's Literature

Classics and Ancient Literature

Colonial Literature

Eastern Literature

European Literature

Gothic Literature

History

Medieval Literature

Oxford English Drama

Philosophy

Poetry

Politics

Religion

The Oxford Shakespeare

A complete list of Oxford World's Classics, including Authors in Context, Oxford English Drama, and the Oxford Shakespeare, is available in the UK from the Marketing Services Department, Oxford University Press, Great Clarendon Street, Oxford OX2 6DP, or visit the website at www.oup.com/uk/worldsclassics.

In the USA, visit www.oup.com/us/owc for a complete title list.

Oxford World's Classics are available from all good bookshops. In case of difficulty, customers in the UK should contact Oxford University Press Bookshop, 116 High Street, Oxford OX1 4BR.

ALEXANDER POPE	**Selected Poetry**
ANN RADCLIFFE	**The Italian**
	The Mysteries of Udolpho
	The Romance of the Forest
	A Sicilian Romance
CLARA REEVE	**The Old English Baron**
SAMUEL RICHARDSON	**Pamela**
RICHARD BRINSLEY SHERIDAN	**The School for Scandal and Other Plays**
TOBIAS SMOLLETT	**The Adventures of Roderick Random**
	The Expedition of Humphry Clinker
LAURENCE STERNE	**The Life and Opinions of Tristram Shandy, Gentleman**
	A Sentimental Journey
JONATHAN SWIFT	**Gulliver's Travels**
	Major Works
	A Tale of a Tub and Other Works
JOHN VANBRUGH	**The Relapse and Other Plays**
HORACE WALPOLE	**The Castle of Otranto**
MARY WOLLSTONECRAFT	**Mary and The Wrongs of Woman**
	A Vindication of the Rights of Woman